*Cognitive Psychology*

# THE CENTURY PSYCHOLOGY SERIES AWARD

## 1966

Each year Appleton-Century-Crofts gives an award for a distinguished manuscript in psychology selected by the Editors of the Century Psychology Series. Considered will be works of two hundred typed pages or longer which provide a significant contribution to the field of psychology.

*Editors*
RICHARD M. ELLIOTT
GARDNER LINDZEY
KENNETH MacCORQUODALE

1962 BERNARD RIMLAND
*Infantile Autism: The Syndrome and Its Implications for a Neural Theory of Behavior*

1963 EDWARD E. JONES
*Ingratiation: A Social Psychological Analysis*

1964 JACK BLOCK
*The Challenge of Response Sets: Unconfounding Meaning, Acquiescence, and Social Desirability in the MMPI*

1965 MERLE B. TURNER
*Philosophy and the Science of Behavior*

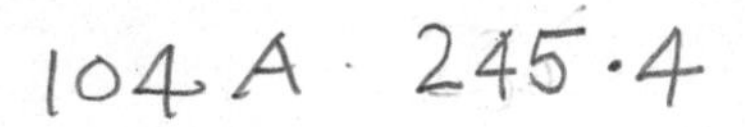


*ULRIC NEISSER*
*Cornell University*

# *COGNITIVE PSYCHOLOGY*

*NEW YORK*

*APPLETON-CENTURY-CROFTS*
DIVISION OF MEREDITH CORPORATION

628-2

Library of Congress Card Number: 67-27727

PRINTED IN THE UNITED STATES OF AMERICA
E 66509

*for* Arden

# Preface

Two years have passed since I settled down to write a dispassionate survey of cognitive psychology. The result is not quite what I had expected. It is still a survey of sorts—I have done my best to review the relevant material—but it is by no means as neutral or as eclectic as had been planned. More precisely, *I* am the one who is not so neutral, who discovered in writing this book that he has a definite commitment to a particular kind of psychology. Did I come to this commitment because the facts reviewed here allow of no other interpretation? Or did I find no other interpretation because this was the one I had unconsciously set out to make? The reader will draw his own conclusions on this point. My own view, as will appear in other contexts later, is that rationalization and discovery can never be entirely separated, even in the simplest cognitive act. In Chapter 5 I argue that even *reading* a book is a constructive process rather than a simple absorption of information from the pages; this must apply far more obviously to writing one.

The organization of this book follows a sequence which is logically implied by the definition of cognitive psychology given in the first chapter. It follows stimulus information "inward" from the organs of sense, through many transformations and reconstructions, through to eventual use in memory and thought. Whatever the merits of this organization may be, it surely has at least one disadvantage. Many readers will be interested in particular topics that cut across the sequence; topics which are classically treated as single units in textbooks. Such a reader may want to review the present status of attention, or reaction time, or eye movements, or "subliminal perception"; he may not want to read the book as a whole. To make the volume of some value to him, I have tried to see that such topics are adequately referenced in the index. The detailed table of contents and the brief chapter summaries may help too. In this way, I still hope to preserve some of the usefulness of the dispassionate survey that was originally planned.

A book like this cannot be written without a great deal of assistance. To begin with, financial help is necessary, and in my case this was generously provided by the Carnegie Corporation of New York. In addition, one must have a base of operations. Ideally, there should be an office where one can be undisturbed while disturbing others—demanding secretarial services, using library facilities, consuming office supplies, buttonholing people to talk to, kibitzing other people's work as a diversion from one's own. All this and more I found at the Unit for Experimental Psychiatry, affiliated with both the Pennsylvania Hospital and the University of Pennsylvania, where I wrote this book. Their support of my work was made possible in part by Contract No. Nonr-4731(00) from the Office of Naval Research.

The Unit is a group of people as well as an institution, and I have benefited from discussions with many of them. In particular, conversations with Martin Orne have had a considerable influence on my views, as will be apparent at various places in the text. Many other persons, of course, have played significant roles in my thinking—far too many to acknowledge here. I do want to mention Oliver Selfridge; the references to him in the pages ahead are a very inadequate expression of my intellectual debt. I also owe much to the Department of Psychology at Brandeis University, chaired earlier by A. H. Maslow and now by R. B. Morant, which for so long provided me with the right milieu for intellectual exploration.

I am indebted to various friends who read parts of this manuscript and commented on it: Harris Savin, Paul Kolers, Henry Gleitman, Lila R. Gleitman, Jacob Nachmias, Oliver Selfridge, Martin Orne, Saul Sternberg, Peter Sheehan, Frederick J. Evans, Richard Thackray, and Donald N. O'Connell. Their advice has been of great help to me, and their encouragement was much appreciated.

A number of persons at the Unit for Experimental Psychiatry deserve my special thanks for their help in preparing the manuscript: Jo Anne Withington for her organizational efforts; Janice Green, Mignon McCarthy, Carol Lebold, Santina Clauser, and Mae Weglarski for much typing and proof-reading; and especially William Orchard, for many kinds of valuable assistance.

I am also obliged to many publishers for permission to reproduce various figures. The specific acknowledgments will be found in a special section at the back of the book.

U. N.

# Contents

Preface vii

*PART I—INTRODUCTION*

Chapter 1

The Cognitive Approach 3

*PART II—VISUAL COGNITION*

Chapter 2

Iconic Storage and Verbal Coding 15

*Transient iconic memory—Backward masking—Effects of a masked stimulus—Verbal coding—Perceptual set as a coding variable—The span of apprehension—Ease of coding*

Chapter 3

Pattern Recognition 46

*The nature of the problem—Displacement and rotation—Ill-defined categories and expectancies—Template matching—Decision time and visual search—A simple feature-analyzing model—Features and parts*

Chapter 4

Focal Attention and Figural Synthesis 86

*Focal attention—Preattentive control—Figural synthesis—Familiarity—Search and reaction times again—Analysis-by-synthesis—Two theoretical summaries*

Chapter 5

Words as Visual Patterns 105

*The word-apprehension effect—Spelling patterns—Figural synthesis of words—The fragment theories—The distinc-*

*tion between perception and response—The effect of repeated exposures—Perceptual defense—Subception—Reading for meaning*

Chapter 6
Visual Memory 138

*Visual snapshots and their integration—Visual imagery and visual synthesis—Dreaming and related states—The functions of imagery—The experimental control of dreaming—Special kinds of imagery: drugs, schizophrenia, hypnosis—Electrically induced imagery, and other evidence for "hypermnesia"*

*PART III—AUDITORY COGNITION*

Chapter 7
Speech Perception 173

*Some very elementary acoustics—Auditory mechanisms—Phonemic description—Segmentation—Theories of speech perception—The analysis-by-synthesis of speech*

Chapter 8
Echoic Memory and Auditory Attention 199

*Echoic memory—The shadowing experiments—The filter theory—The filter-amplitude theory—Attention as auditory synthesis*

Chapter 9
Active Verbal Memory 219

*Recoding—Auditory characteristics of verbal memory—Slots or associations?—Rhythm and structure in auditory memory—Decay vs. interference—Two kinds of memory or one?*

Chapter 10
Sentences 243

*Linguistics and Gestalt psychology—Grammatical structure: general considerations—Phrase-structure grammars—Cues to phrase structure—Transformational grammar*

*PART IV—THE HIGHER MENTAL PROCESSES*

Chapter 11

A Cognitive Approach to Memory and Thought 279

*The Reappearance Hypothesis—The Utilization Hypothesis —Cognitive structures—The problem of the executive—The multiplicity of thought—Primary and secondary processes reconsidered—A summing up*

*REFERENCES* 307

Illustration Credits 335

Name Index 339

Subject Index 345

# *Part I*

# *Introduction*

*Chapter 1*

# The Cognitive Approach

It has been said that beauty is in the eye of the beholder. As a hypothesis about localization of function, the statement is not quite right—the brain and not the eye is surely the most important organ involved. Nevertheless it points clearly enough toward the central problem of cognition. Whether beautiful or ugly or just conveniently at hand, the world of experience is produced by the man who experiences it.

This is not the attitude of a skeptic, only of a psychologist. There certainly is a real world of trees and people and cars and even books, and it has a great deal to do with our experiences of these objects. However, we have no direct, *im*mediate access to the world, nor to any of its properties. The ancient theory of *eidola,* which supposed that faint copies of objects can enter the mind directly, must be rejected. Whatever we know about reality has been *mediated,* not only by the organs of sense but by complex systems which interpret and reinterpret sensory information. The activity of the cognitive systems results in—and is integrated with—the activity of muscles and glands that we call "behavior." It is also partially—very partially—reflected in those private experiences of seeing, hearing, imagining, and thinking to which verbal descriptions never do full justice.

Physically, this page is an array of small mounds of ink, lying in certain positions on the more highly reflective surface of the paper. It is this physical page which Koffka (1935) and others would have called the "distal stimulus," and from which the reader is hopefully acquiring some information. But the sensory input is not the page itself; it is a pattern of light rays, originating in the sun or in some artificial source, that are reflected from the page and happen to reach the eye. Suitably focused by the lens and other ocular apparatus, the rays fall on the sensitive retina, where they can initiate the neural processes that eventually lead to seeing and reading and remembering. These patterns of light at the retina are the so-called "proximal stimuli." They are not the least bit like *eidola.* One-sided in their perspective, shifting radically several times each second, unique and novel at every moment, the proximal stimuli bear little resemblance to either the real object that gave rise to them or to the object of experience that the perceiver will construct as a result.

Visual cognition, then, deals with the processes by which a perceived, remembered, and thought-about world is brought into being from as unpromising a beginning as the retinal patterns. Similarly, auditory cognition is concerned with transformation of the fluctuating pressure-pattern at the ear into the sounds and the speech and music that we hear. The problem of understanding these transformations may usefully be compared to a very different question, that arises in another psychological context. One of Freud's papers on human motivation is entitled "Instincts and their Vicissitudes" (1915). The title reflects a basic axiom of psychoanalysis: that man's fundamental motives suffer an intricate series of transformations, reformulations, and changes before they appear in either consciousness or action. Borrowing Freud's phrase—without intending any commitment to his theory of motivation—a book like this one might be called "Stimulus Information and its Vicissitudes." As used here, the term "cognition" refers to all the processes by which the sensory input is transformed, reduced, elaborated, stored, recovered, and used. It is concerned with these processes even when they operate in the absence of relevant stimulation, as in images and hallucinations. Such terms as *sensation, perception, imagery, retention, recall, problem-solving,* and *thinking,* among many others, refer to hypothetical stages or aspects of cognition.

Given such a sweeping definition, it is apparent that cognition is involved in everything a human being might possibly do; that every psychological phenomenon is a cognitive phenomenon. But although cognitive psychology is concerned with all human activity rather than some fraction of it, the concern is from a particular point of view. Other viewpoints are equally legitimate and necessary. Dynamic psychology, which begins with motives rather than with sensory input, is a case in point. Instead of asking how a man's actions and experiences result from what he saw, remembered, or believed, the dynamic psychologist asks how they follow from the subject's goals, needs, or instincts. Both questions can be asked about any activity, whether it be normal or abnormal, spontaneous or induced, overt or covert, waking or dreaming. Asked why I did a certain thing, I may answer in dynamic terms, "Because I wanted . . . ," or, from the cognitive point of view, "Because it seemed to me . . ."

In attempting to trace the fate of the input, our task is both easier and harder than that of dynamic psychology. It is easier because we have a tangible starting point. The pattern of stimulation that reaches the eye or the ear can be directly observed; the beginning of the cognitive transformations is open to inspection. The student of motivation does not have this advantage, except when he deals with the physical-deprivation motives like hunger and thirst. This forces him to rely rather more on speculation and less on observation than the cognitive theorist. But by the same token, the latter has an additional set of responsibilities. He cannot make assumptions casually, for they must conform to the results of 100 years of experimentation.

Recognition of the difference between cognitive and dynamic theory does not mean that we can afford to ignore motivation in a book like this one. Many cognitive phenomena are incomprehensible unless one takes some account of what the subject is trying to do. However, his purposes are treated here primarily as independent variables: we will note that they can affect one or another cognitive mechanism without inquiring closely into their origin. This strategy will break down in the final chapter; remembering and thinking are too "inner-directed" to be treated in such a fashion. As a consequence, the last chapter has a different format, and even a different purpose, from the others.

The cognitive and the dynamic viewpoints are by no means the only possible approaches to psychology. Behaviorism, for example, represents a very different tradition, which is essentially incompatible with both. From Watson (1913) to Skinner (1963), radical behaviorists have maintained that man's actions should be explained only in terms of observable variables, without any inner vicissitudes at all. The appeal to hypothetical mechanisms is said to be speculative at best, and deceptive at worst. For them, it is legitimate to speak of stimuli, responses, reinforcements, and hours of deprivation, but not of categories or images or ideas. A generation ago, a book like this one would have needed at least a chapter of self-defense against the behaviorist position. Today, happily, the climate of opinion has changed, and little or no defense is necessary. Indeed, stimulus-response theorists themselves are inventing hypothetical mechanisms with vigor and enthusiasm and only faint twinges of conscience. The basic reason for studying cognitive processes has become as clear as the reason for studying anything else: because they are there. Our knowledge of the world *must* be somehow developed from the stimulus input; the theory of *eidola* is false. Cognitive processes surely exist, so it can hardly be unscientific to study them.

Another approach to psychological questions, a world apart from behaviorism, is that of the physiologist. Cognition, like other psychological processes, can validly be studied in terms of the underlying neural events. For my part, I do not doubt that human behavior and consciousness depend entirely on the activity of the brain, in interaction with other physical systems. Most readers of this book will probably have the same prejudice. Nevertheless, there is very little of physiology or biochemistry in the chapters ahead. At a time when these fields are making impressive advances, such an omission may seem strange. An example may help to justify it. For this purpose, let us consider recent work on the physical basis of memory.

No one would dispute that human beings store a great deal of information about their past experiences, and it seems obvious that this information must be physically embodied somewhere in the brain. Recent discoveries in biochemistry have opened up a promising possibility. Some experimental findings have hinted that the complex molecules of DNA and RNA, known to be involved in the transmission of inherited traits, may be the substrate of memory as well. Although the supporting evidence so far is shaky, this hypothesis has already gained many adherents. But psychology is not just something "to do until the biochemist comes" (as I have recently heard psychiatry described); the truth or falsity of this new hypothesis is only marginally relevant to psychological questions. A pair of analogies will show why this is so.

First, let us consider the familiar parallel between man and computer. Although it is an inadequate analogy in many ways, it may suffice for this purpose. The task of a psychologist trying to understand human cognition is analogous to that of a man trying to discover how a computer has been programmed. In particular, if the program seems to store and reuse information, he would like to know by what "routines" or "procedures" this is done. Given this purpose, he will not care much whether his particular computer stores information in magnetic cores or in thin films; he wants to understand the program, not the "hardware." By the same token, it would not help the psychologist to know that memory is carried by RNA as opposed to some other medium. He wants to understand its utilization, not its incarnation.

Perhaps this overstates the case a little. The hardware of a computer may have some indirect effects on programming, and likewise the physical substrate may impose some limitations on the organization of mental events. This is particularly likely where peripheral (sensory and motor) processes are concerned, just as the input-output routines of a program will be most affected by the specific properties of the computer being used. Indeed, a few fragments of peripheral physiology will be considered in later chapters. Nevertheless they remain, in the familiar phrase, of only "peripheral interest."

The same point can be illustrated with quite a different analogy, that between psychology and economics. The economist wishes to understand, say, the flow of capital. The object of his study must have some tangible representation, in the form of checks, gold, paper money, and so on, but these objects are not what he really cares about. The physical properties of money, its location in banks, its movement in armored cars, are of little interest to him. To be sure, the remarkable permanence of gold has some economic importance. The flow of capital would be markedly different if every medium of exchange were subject to rapid corrosion. Nevertheless, such matters are not the main concern of the economist, and knowledge of them does not much simplify economic theory.

Psychology, like economics, is a science concerned with the interdependence among certain events rather than with their physical nature. Although there are many disciplines of this sort (classical genetics is another good example), the most prominent ones today are probably the so-called "information sciences," which include the mathematical theory of communication, computer programming, systems analysis, and related fields. It seems obvious that these must be relevant to cognitive psychology, which is itself much concerned with information. However, their importance for psychologists has often been misunderstood, and deserves careful consideration.

Information, in the sense first clearly defined by Shannon (1948), is essentially *choice,* the narrowing down of alternatives. He developed the mathematical theory of communication in order to deal quantitatively with the transmission of messages over "channels." A channel, like a telephone line, transmits information to the extent that the choices made at one end determine those made at the other. The words of the speaker are regarded as successive selections from among all the possible words of English. Ideally, the transmitted message will enable the listener to choose the same ones; that is, to identify each correctly. For practical purposes, it is important to measure the *amount* of information that a system can transmit, and early applications of information theory were much concerned with measurement. As is now well known, amounts of information are measured in units called "bits," or binary digits, where one "bit" is represented by a choice between two equally probable alternatives.

Early attempts to apply information theory to psychology were very much in this spirit (e.g., Miller, 1953; Quastler, 1955), and even today many psychologists continue to theorize and to report data in terms of "bits" (e.g., Garner, 1962; Posner, 1964a, 1966). I do not believe, however, that this approach was or is a fruitful one. Attempts to quantify psychological processes in informational terms have usually led, after much effort, to the conclusion that the "bit rate" is not a relevant variable after all. Such promising topics as reaction time, memory span, and language have all failed to sustain early estimates of the usefulness of information measurement. With the advantage of hindsight, we can see why this might have been expected. The "bit" was developed to describe the performance of rather unselective systems: a telephone cannot decide which portions of the incoming message are important. We shall see throughout this book that human beings behave very differently, and are by no means neutral or passive toward the incoming information. Instead, they select some parts for attention at the expense of others, recoding and reformulating them in complex ways.

Although information measurement may be of little value to the cognitive psychologist, another branch of the information sciences, computer *programming*, has much more to offer. A program is not a device for measuring information, but a recipe for selecting, storing, recovering, combining, outputting, and generally manipulating it. As pointed out by Newell, Shaw, and Simon (1958), this means that programs have much in common with theories of cognition. Both are descriptions of the vicissitudes of input information.

We must be careful not to confuse the program with the computer that it controls. Any single general-purpose computer can be "loaded" with an essentially infinite number of different programs. On the other hand, most programs can be run, with minor modifications, on many physically different kinds of computers. A program is not a machine; it is a series of instructions for dealing with symbols: "If the input has certain characteristics . . . then carry out certain procedures . . . otherwise other procedures . . . combine their results in various ways . . . store or retrieve various items . . . depending on prior results . . . use them in further specified ways . . . etc." The cognitive psychologist would like to give a similar account of the way information is processed by men.

This way of defining the cognitive problem is not really a new one. We are still asking "how the mind works." However, the "program analogy" (which may be a better term than "computer analogy") has several advantages over earlier conceptions. Most important is the philosophical reassurance which it provides. Although a program is nothing but a flow of symbols, it has reality enough to control the operation of very tangible machinery that executes very physical operations. A man who seeks to discover the program of a computer is surely not doing anything self-contradictory!

There were cognitive theorists long before the advent of the computer. Bartlett, whose influence on my own thinking will become obvious in later chapters, is a case in point. But, in the eyes of many psychologists, a theory which dealt with cognitive transformations, memory schemata, and the like was not *about* anything. One could understand theories that dealt with overt movements, or with physiology; one could even understand (and deplore) theories which dealt with the content of consciousness; but what kind of a thing is a schema? If memory consists of transformations, what is tranformed? So long as cognitive psychology literally did not know what it was talking about, there was always a danger that it was talking about nothing at all. This is no longer a serious risk. *Information* is what is transformed, and the structured pattern of its transformations is what we want to understand.

A second advantage of the "program analogy" is that, like other analogies, it is a fruitful source of hypotheses. A field which is directly concerned with information processing should be at least as rich in ideas for psychology as other fields of science have been before. Just as we have borrowed atomic units, energy distributions, hydraulic pressures, and mechanical linkages from physics and engineering, so may we choose to adopt certain concepts from programming today. This will be done rather freely in some of the following chapters. Such notions as "parallel processing," "feature extraction," "analysis-by-synthesis," and "executive routine" have been borrowed from programmers, in the hope that they will prove theoretically useful. The test of their value, of course, is strictly psychological. We will have to see how well they fit the data.

The occasional and analogic use of programming concepts does not imply a commitment to computer "simulation" of psychological processes. It is true that a number of researchers, not content with noting that computer programs are *like* cognitive theories, have tried to write programs which *are* cognitive theories. The "Logic Theorist," a program developed by Newell, Shaw, and Simon (1958), does more than find proofs for logical theorems: it is intended as a theory of how human beings find such proofs. There has been a great deal of work in this vein recently. It has been lucidly reviewed, and sympathetically criticized, by Reitman (1965). However, such models will not be discussed here except in passing. In my opinion, none of them does even remote justice to the complexity of human mental processes. Unlike men, "artificially intelligent" programs tend to be single-minded, undistractable, and unemotional. Moreover, they are generally equipped from the beginning of each problem with all the cognitive resources necessary to solve it. These criticisms have already been presented elsewhere (Neisser, 1963c), and there is no need to elaborate them now. In a sense, the rest of this book can be construed as an extensive argument against models of this kind, and also against other simplistic theories of the cognitive processes. If the account of cognition given here is even roughly accurate, it will not be "simulated" for a long time to come.

The present volume is meant to serve a double purpose. On the one hand, I hope to provide a useful and current account of the existing "state of the art." In discussing any particular phenomenon—immediate memory, or understanding sentences, or subception, or selective listening—an attempt is made to cover the significant experiments, and to discuss the major theories. On the other hand, it must be admitted that few of these discussions are neutral. When the weight of the evidence points overwhelmingly in one direction rather than another, I prefer to say so frankly. This is especially because in most cases the indicated direction seems (to me) to be consistent with a particular view of the cognitive processes. Some of the chapters only hint at this theory, while in others it emerges explicitly. When it does, the first person singular is used rather freely, to help the reader distinguish between the facts and my interpretation of them. In the end, I hope to have presented not only a survey of cognitive psychology but the beginnings of an integration.

The title of this book involves a certain deliberate ambiguity. In one sense, "cognitive psychology" refers generally to the study of the cognitive mechanisms, quite apart from the interpretations put forward here. In another sense, "cognitive psychology" is a particular theory to which I have a specific personal commitment. By Chapter 11, it will have become so specific that Rock and Ceraso's (1964) "Cognitive Theory of Associative Learning" will be rejected as not cognitive enough! If the reader finds this dual usage confusing, I can only say that it seems unavoidable. Such double meanings are very common in psychology. Surely "Behavior Theory" is only one of many approaches to the study of behavior, just as "Gestalt Psychology" is not the only possible theory of visual figures (Gestalten), and "Psychoanalysis" is only one of many hypothetical analyses of psychological structure.

The present approach is more closely related to that of Bartlett (1932, 1958) than to any other contemporary psychologist, while its roots are at least as old as the "act psychology" of the nineteenth century. The central assertion is that seeing, hearing, and remembering are all acts of *construction,* which may make more or less use of stimulus information depending on circumstances. The constructive processes are assumed to have two stages, of which the first is fast, crude, wholistic, and parallel while the second is deliberate, attentive, detailed, and sequential.

The model is first elaborated here in five chapters on visual processes. These chapters include an account of the very temporary, "iconic" memory which stores the output of the first stage of construction; a review of various theories of pattern recognition together with relevant data; a specific presentation of the constructive theory as applied to visual recognition; a survey of reading and tachistoscopic word-perception insofar as they are understood; and a discussion of visual memory, imagery, and hallucination. Four subsequent chapters on hearing [1] cover the perception of words, considered in terms of both acoustics and linguistics; various theories of auditory attention, including one which interprets it as a constructive process; the classical "immediate memory" for strings of words; and an account of linguistic structure together with its implications for psychology.

The final chapter on memory and thought is essentially an epilogue, different in structure from the rest of the book. Because of the tremendous scope of these higher mental processes, no attempt is made to cover the relevant data, or to refute competing theories, and the views put forward are quite tentative. Nevertheless, the reader of a book called

[1] Sense modalities other than vision and hearing are largely ignored in this book, because so little is known about the cognitive processing involved.

*Cognitive Psychology* has a right to expect some discussion of thinking, concept-formation, remembering, problem-solving, and the like; they have traditionally been part of the field. If they take up only a tenth of these pages, it is because I believe there is still relatively little to say about them, even after 100 years of psychological research.

There is another respect in which this book may seem incomplete. The cognitive processes under discussion are primarily those of the American adult, or at least of the college student who is so frequently the subject of psychological experiments. Although there will be occasional references to the developmental psychology of cognition, it will not be reviewed systematically. In part, this is because the course of cognitive growth is so little understood. However, even in areas where development is being actively studied, such as concept formation and psycholinguistics, I have not felt qualified to review it.

One last word of explanation is necessary, before concluding an introduction that is already overlong. Many topics that the reader may have expected to find have now been set aside. We will consider neither physiological mechanisms nor information measurement nor computer simulation nor developmental psychology; even remembering and thought are to receive short shrift. Despite these omissions, it must not be thought that the field which remains to be explored is a narrow one. Although the core of the material presented here is taken from within experimental psychology itself, there is extensive use of data and concepts from other fields, including psychiatry and clinical psychology (especially in connection with hallucinations); hypnosis; the social psychology of the psychological experiment; the physiology and psychology of sleep; the study of reading, which too often has been relegated to educational psychology; computer programming; linguistics and psycholinguistics. The reader may hesitate to follow along a path that seems so full of side alleys, and perhaps blind ones at that. I can only hope he will not be altogether discouraged. No shorter route seems to do justice to the vicissitudes of the input, and to the continuously creative processes by which the world of experience is constructed.

# *Part II*

# *Visual Cognition*

# *Chapter 2*

# *Iconic Storage and Verbal Coding*

The "persistence" of visual impressions makes them briefly available for processing even after the stimulus has terminated. This stage of cognition is here called "iconic memory." Its properties provide a frame of reference for the discussion of backward masking, of certain effects of set and order in tachistoscopic presentations, of some paradoxes of reaction time, and of the so-called "span of apprehension." In addition, explanations are proposed for certain findings that seem to challenge this frame of reference, including the reputedly "subliminal" perception of masked stimuli.

Among the instruments of psychological research, none has a more illustrious history than the tachistoscope. For more than 80 years, subjects have been trying to identify briefly-exposed stimuli, and psychologists have been elaborating their reports into theories of visual perception. Some of these theories have had serious repercussions in the world outside the laboratory. Tachistoscopic experiments have led educators to embrace the "whole-word" method of reading instruction, consumers to fear the dangers of "subliminal advertising," and psychoanalysts to believe that "repression" and "primary-process mentation" are demonstrable visual phenomena. Yet some of the consequences of brief exposures are only now becoming clear, and recent developments have shed a new light on the older interpretations.

In the most common kind of tachistoscopic experiment, the subject is presented with many successive exposures of the same material, each a little longer than the one before. After each exposure, he describes the material as best he can. Eventually, given a long enough exposure, his report becomes a correct description of the stimulus, and we say that his "threshold" has been reached. These "thresholds" are easily shown to depend on the nature of the material shown, the subject's familiarity with it, his emotional attitudes, and the like.

If we are to understand how these variables and others affect performance, we must begin by abandoning a set of assumptions on which much of the research has implicitly been based. Taken together, these assumptions add up to the position that is sometimes called *naive realism.* Even psychologists who ought to know better have acted as if they believed (1) that the subject's visual experience directly mirrors the stimulus pattern; (2) that his visual experience begins when the pattern is first exposed and terminates when it is turned off; (3) that his experience, itself a passive—if fractional—copy of the stimulus, is in turn mirrored by his verbal report. All three of these assumptions are wrong. The information reaching the eye is subjected to complex processes of analysis, extended in time. Visual experience results from some of these processes. As for verbal report, it depends partly on visual experience—i.e., on further transformations of the information given there—and partly on other factors.

In an introductory paragraph these statements sound rather blunt, but the next few chapters may justify them. The burden of the argument will be that perception is not a passive taking-in of stimuli, but an active process of synthesizing or constructing a visual figure. Such a complex constructive act must take a certain amount of time. Yet it cannot be denied that, under some conditions, one can easily see a figure exposed for a single millisecond, or even less. This creates a dilemma for theory. The problem would be resolved, however, if the visual input were somehow preserved (for further processing) for some time even after the stimulus itself was over. Happily, this turns out to be the case.

Our knowledge about this brief but crucial form of visual persistence owes much to the recent and seminal experiments of Sperling (1960a) and Averbach and Coriell (1961). Their work leaves no doubt that the subject can continue to "read" information in visual form even after a tachistoscopic exposure is over. This kind of transient memory is, in a sense, the first visual cognitive process, and most of this chapter is devoted to it. After reviewing the evidence for its existence in the next section, I will go on to argue that it underlies a number of phenomena in visual cognition, including backward masking, perceptual set, and the span of apprehension.

## *TRANSIENT ICONIC MEMORY*

Sperling was by no means the first to suggest that the visual sensation may outlast the stimulus, and his monograph (1960a) contains many references to earlier observations. The streak of light which appears when a lighted cigarette is moved in a dark room, the positive (and perhaps the negative) afterimages described in every psychology textbook, and especially the insistence of many subjects that they see more in a tachistoscopic flash than they can remember—all of these are cases in point. Woodworth (1938) long ago presented a sophisticated discussion of the issues involved. What was new in Sperling's work was an ingenious demonstration of the role this process actually plays in tachistoscopic perception, and a new method of measuring its decay.

Sperling used tachistoscopic exposures of 50 msec. (milliseconds), which is surely brief enough to prevent directed eye movements. (The reaction time of the eye is about 200 msec., or $\frac{1}{5}$ of a second). He exposed rectangular arrays of letters, for example,

TDR
SRN
FZR

which the subject was to read. Typically, only four or five letters would be correctly reported, no matter how many had been presented. Earlier experimenters would have been content with the conclusion that the "span of apprehension" was limited under these conditions. Sperling went further, using what he called "partial reports." By means of a prearranged signal, he instructed the subject to read only a *single* row of the display. The signal was a tone sounded immediately *after* the display was turned off. A high-pitched tone indicated that the top row should be reported, while tones of low or intermediate pitch indicated the bottom or the middle row. The result was almost 100 percent accuracy in the reports of the critical row! However, accuracy decreased if the tone was delayed for even a fraction of a second, and with delays of a second or more, it dropped to the level characteristic of ordinary full reports. Some of the data appear in Figure 1.

The method of Averbach and Coriell (1961) was similar, except that the subjects were asked to report only a single letter instead of a whole row, and it was signaled by a visual pointer instead of a tone. The pointer was usually a black bar aimed at the position where one of the letters had been. (In some trials, a circle surrounding this position was used to produce "erasure"—a phenomenon to be considered later.) The display, and the experimental procedure, are shown in Figure 2. The results of the experiment were closely analogous to those of Sperling, as Averbach and Sperling noted in a joint paper (1961). In both studies, subjects were able to "look at" selected portions of a display that had already been turned off.

Sperling's results are apparently easy to replicate (Glucksberg, 1965). On the other hand, the complications created by the visual cue and the simplified task (a single letter to be identified) apparently make Averbach's method relatively tricky. Attempted replications by Mayzner *et al.* (1964) and by Eriksen and Steffy (1964) failed to find any decay in

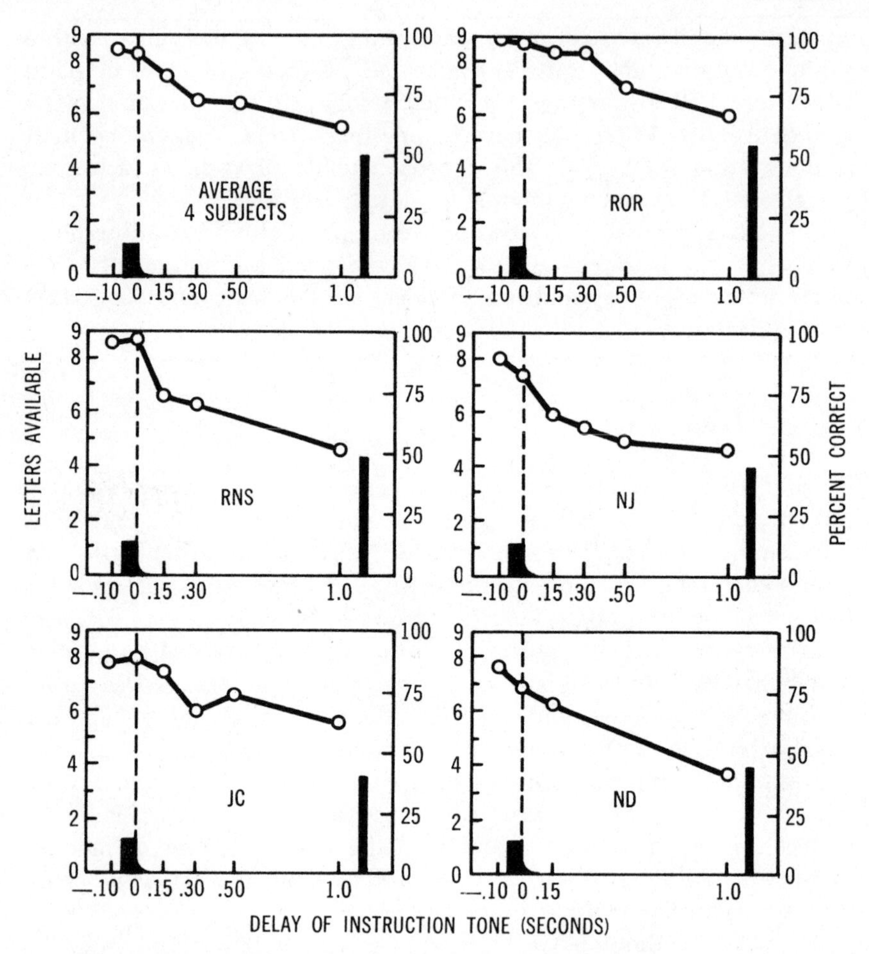


Figure 1. Decay of transient iconic memory in Sperling's (1960a) experiment. The stimulus, a $3 \times 3$ letter-square, was flashed for the period indicated by the bar at left. The ordinate at right shows the percent of the critical 3-letter row reported correctly (method of partial report), at the signal delay shown on the abscissa. The bar at right shows the accuracy of full reports with the same material.

accuracy with time over the first 700 msec. In both cases differences in procedure may account for the difficulty, but there is no doubt that the use of a later visual stimulus to control the readout of an earlier one creates problems. The discussion of backward masking (below) will make this point even more emphatic.

It seems certain, then, that the visual input can be briefly stored in some medium which is subject to very rapid decay. Before it has decayed, information can be read from this medium just as if the stimulus were still active. We can be equally certain that this storage is in

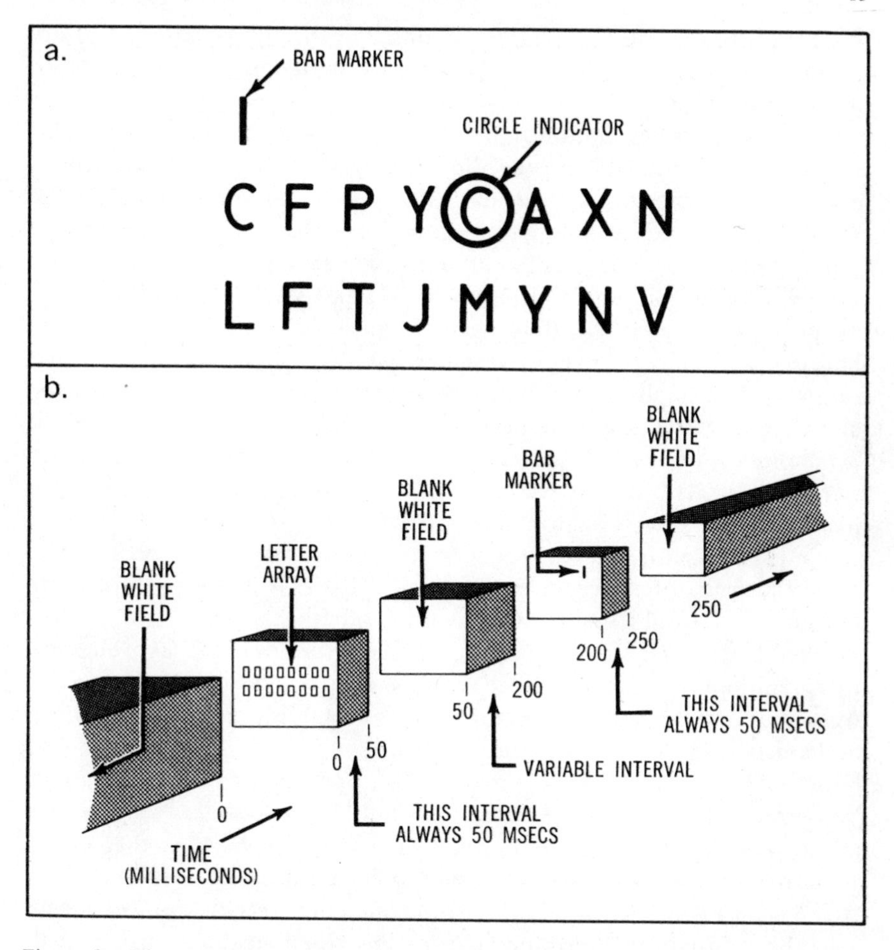


Figure 2. The experiment of Averbach and Coriell (1961). Figure 2a shows a typical stimulus pattern; Figure 2b outlines the procedure.

some sense a "visual image." Sperling's subjects reported that the letters appeared to be visually present and legible at the time of the signal tone, even when the stimulus had actually been off for 150 msec. That is, although performance was based on "memory" from the experimenter's point of view, it was "perceptual" as far as the experience of the observers was concerned.

What should such a process be called? The subjects say they are looking at something, and it needs a name. Sperling and others have used the term "image," but I would prefer to avoid a word with so many other meanings. The relation between this kind of "visual persistence" on the one hand and afterimages, memory images, eidetic images (and even retinal images!) on the other are extremely complex, as will appear in Chapter 6. Certain important questions can hardly be phrased at all if this form of storage has a name already shared by too many other phenomena.

There seems no alternative but to introduce a new term for the transient visual memory in question. I will call it "the icon" or "iconic memory." The choice is not ideal; Bruner (1964, 1966) has already used "iconic" with quite a different meaning. He distinguishes "enactive," "iconic," and "symbolic" representations of experience, based on motor activity, images, and words respectively. My excuses for absconding with one of his words are, first, that even two meanings for "icon" are better than half-a-dozen for "image"; second, that Bruner's category-names are confusing and might better be avoided. They violate ordinary psychological practice in many respects. We commonly speak of images as "symbolic," while verbal activity has a substantial motor or "enactive" component of its own. We shall see later that such a component is even involved in the most visual of representations.

The icon is defined behaviorally and introspectively. Some readers will also be interested in its anatomical basis: is it, for example, "in the retina"? I would suspect that it isn't, but the question will not be pursued here. There is an important place for eventual neurological interpretations of cognitive processes, especially where peripheral mechanisms are at issue, but we should strive to establish the existence of a mechanism and discover its properties first.

How long does iconic memory last? Sperling's data suggest about one second as a rough approximation, since after a second's delay the partial reports were no more accurate than whole reports. At that point the icon apparently became too unclear to be of any use. The subject then had to base his report on another, fundamentally verbal, form of memory. The translation ("recoding") from the visual medium to a verbal one can continue only so long as the icon is still legible.

If iconic storage is a process in the visual system, its duration should depend on visual variables like intensity, exposure time, and post-exposure illumination. Indeed, all of these do affect performance in the tachistoscopic task; it may be that they do so in large part by controlling the duration of the icon. The post-exposure field is especially important in this respect. The icon remains legible for as long as five seconds if the post-exposure field is dark, but less than a second if it is relatively bright (Sperling, 1960a, 1963; also see the section on backward masking below).

The duration of the stimulus itself (i.e., the exposure time) had little effect in Sperling's experiment. However, Mackworth (1963a) showed that it can be critical, as users of the tachistoscope have long known. She found that the number of digits correctly reported from a $2 \times 5$ array increased sharply with exposure time up to the first 50 msec.

(Figure 3). Under her conditions the icon must have been fully established by that point, since further increases in stimulus duration had little effect. Mackworth's (1962, 1963a) approach to the problem was originally very similar to that advanced by Sperling. The additional assumptions made in some of her other papers (1963b, 1964) will not be considered here.

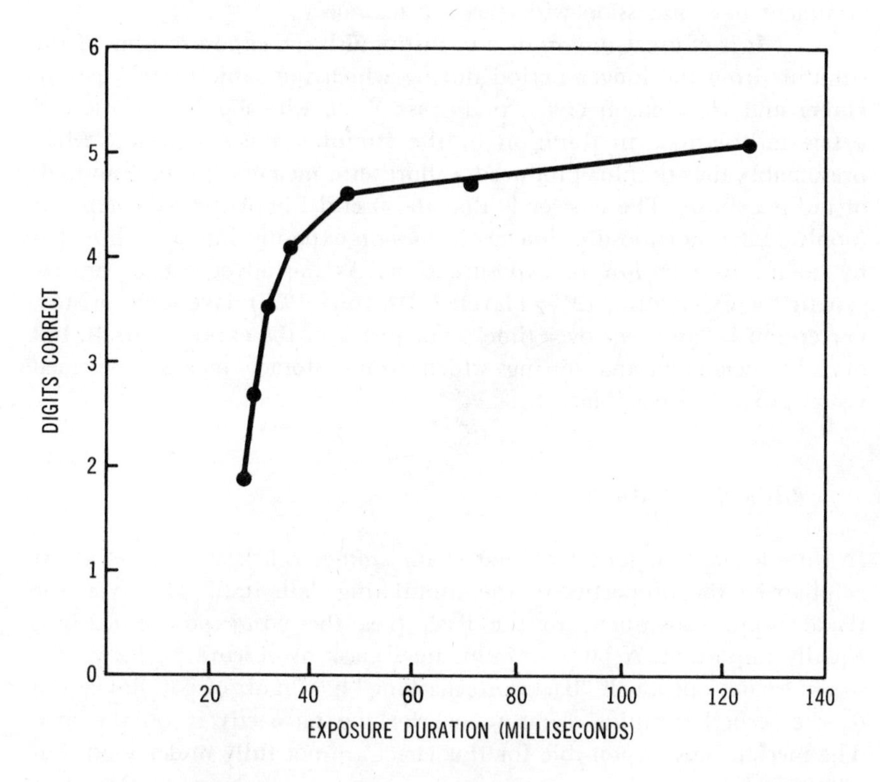


Figure 3. The effect of exposure duration, in Mackworth's (1963a) experiment.

The form of Mackworth's curves depended partly on the intensity of the flash, and this is as it should be. Both the length and the strength of the stimulus must affect the duration of the subsequent icon, at least until some critical duration is reached. Even a flash lasting a fraction of a millisecond permits the subject to read several letters, if only it is bright enough. Ideally, one might expect the icon resulting from a 2-msec. flash, at a given level, to last just as long as if it had been produced by a flash twice as intense but only lasting 1 msec. Such "perfect summation" of visual energy is known to occur for the subjective brightness of brief flashes; why not for the duration of the iconic memory which they produce? Indeed, some recent results do suggest that summation may occur over rather long intervals where the duration of the icon is concerned. This is at least a possible interpretation of the finding (Kahneman & Norman, 1964; Kahneman, 1965a) that, when visual acuity is being measured, intensity and time summate over much longer periods than in brightness judgments. Acuity judgments take time, and would be facilitated by prolonging the useful life of iconic storage. (I owe this argument to a discussion with Jacob Nachmias.)

It is of great importance to distinguish the exposure time of the stimulus from the longer period during which the subject can "see" it. Haber and Hershenson (1965, p. 46) ask ". . . why should variation of a few milliseconds in duration of the stimulus affect accuracy, when presumably the stimulus produced a short-term memory lasting hundreds of milliseconds?" The answer is that the useful life of the icon *depends* (nonlinearly) on exposure time, as it does on exposure intensity, but it is by no means *identical to* exposure time. As the advocates of "microgenetic theory" (Smith, 1957; Flavell & Draguns, 1957) have long insisted, perception is "an event over time"—not just over the exposure itself, but over the whole period during which iconic storage makes continued visual processing possible.

### *BACKWARD MASKING*

In considering how long transient iconic storage can last, we have so far emphasized the properties of the stimulating flash itself. However, the visual input subsequent to the flash (i.e., the post-exposure field) is equally important. A later stimulus may mask or obscure an iconically-stored earlier one. Such "backward masking" has an air of paradox about it: the second stimulus seems to be working retroactively on the first. The mechanisms responsible for this effect are not fully understood, but it cannot be ignored.

The visual system is physical and finite, and so it must be limited in its temporal resolving power. It cannot be expected to switch instantaneously from one activity to the next when the stimulus is altered. Hence there must be at least a short aftereffect of visual stimulation, and the transient icon may be nothing more. This interpretation immediately suggests that a second stimulus will have some effect on how a first brief one is perceived, because in any finite system they will overlap at least a little. The existence of backward masking is therefore not surprising, and we must expect that the masking effect will depend on the nature of the second stimulus and its relation to the first.

In the simplest case, the second stimulus is a homogeneous field. This is the usual practice in tachistoscopic experiments. Even under this apparently simple condition, paradoxical effects can occur, including color reversals in the icon (Sperling, 1960b). The most general finding, however, is simply that bright post-exposure fields lead to poorer visibility than dark ones. One principal reason for this has been set out clearly by Eriksen (Eriksen & Hoffman, 1963; Eriksen & Steffy, 1964). Because the visual system has limited resolving power in time, the brightnesses in successive fields will necessarily add together to some extent. This summation will effectively reduce the brightness-contrast of the figure first shown, and thereby make it less legible. An example from Eriksen and Steffy will help to make this argument clear. Let us suppose that a black figure has a brightness of only 10 foot-lamberts in a certain exposure apparatus, while its white background is at 90 foot-lamberts (a contrast ratio of 9:1). Suppose further that the figure is just barely recognizable in a 10-msec. exposure when it is followed by a dark field. When a homogeneous field of 90 foot-lamberts follows it instead, more light energy is added to both the figure and the ground. If the successive fields were perfectly integrated, this would mean that the figure was actually at 100 foot-lamberts (90 + 10) and the ground at 180 (90 + 90). As a result, the contrast ratio would have become less than 2:1. Actual backward masking may not be quite so drastic since summation is generally incomplete. On the other hand, other processes besides summation may be involved, as Kahneman (1965b) has pointed out.

A bright post-exposure field is necessarily superimposed on, and combined with iconically-stored information, making it less legible. In a sense, the post-exposure field may be said to reduce the duration of the icon, or more accurately to reduce its *useful* duration. Presumably the stored information decays gradually, and there is no precise moment when the icon "ends." However, a time comes when it is no longer clear or detailed enough to be legible, and this time must come sooner if it is unclear from the start. This is the reason why the post-exposure field affected the duration of iconic storage in Sperling's experiments: a low-contrast icon becomes illegible much sooner than one of high contrast.

This kind of "masking" should be produced, not only by a continuously lit second field, but even by a brief flash of light if it is not too long delayed. Such masking by flashes should be symmetrical in time: a flash 50 msec. *before* a figure should mask it as effectively as a flash 50 msec. *after*. Eriksen and Lappin (1964) seem to have confirmed these predictions.

The "temporal summation" or "integration" of successive visual stimuli is of interest for its own sake. According to one tradition in psychology, successive stimuli will be integrated only if they fall within the same discrete "psychological moment," or "quantum of psychological time" (Stroud, 1955). The complexities of this theory cannot be reviewed here, though I hope to do so in a later publication. For the present, I can only say that it seems extremely implausible, and that temporal integration is almost certainly continuous. Within a sensory modality, the processing of every momentary input is interwoven with and influenced by the processing of all other input adjacent to it in time.

Backward masking becomes more complex if the stimulus is followed by a patterned figure rather than by a homogeneous field. The general finding is that the subsequent figure will make the earlier one much more difficult to see, especially if their contours lie close together. This phenomenon is often called "metacontrast" (Alpern, 1952, 1953; Raab, 1963, and others), sometimes "erasure" (Averbach & Coriell, 1961), and occasionally just "backward masking" (Eriksen & Collins, 1964). It has been given varying theoretical interpretations.

The most obvious explanation is the one proposed by Eriksen, following the same line of reasoning proposed for homogeneous post-exposure fields. To some extent the two patterns—the original stimulus and the "masking" stimulus—coexist even though one follows the other, and so they are processed together. Because the resulting total figure is more complex than the original stimulus alone, it is harder to identify. This interpretation predicts that "backward masking" should be most pronounced when the two stimuli are simultaneous, and drop off gradually as they are separated further in time. Such functions (called "type-A curves" by Kolers, 1962) were indeed obtained by Eriksen and Collins (1964). Their stimulus field always contained one of the three letters *A, T,* or *U;* the subject had only to decide which one. A ring surrounding the letter was presented, either concurrently with it or shortly thereafter. Masking was greatest for concurrent presentation, and decreased gradually with greater delays until none could be demonstrated at 100 msecs. In a subsequent experiment, Eriksen and Collins (1965) showed that this type of masking, like that with simple flashes, is symmetrical in time.

However, the situation is not as simple as this analysis would suggest. Many other experimenters, including the early workers in metacontrast (Werner, 1935; Alpern, 1953), have found that masking is not always greatest at zero or short delays. Instead, perception of the first stimulus may be much more affected by a masking pattern delayed by 20 to 100 msecs. than by one which comes simultaneously! Such findings, which seem paradoxical because the maximum effect of the second stimulus does not occur when it is closest to the first, were called "type-B curves" by Kolers (1962), and are often referred to as "U-shaped functions." Figure 4, taken from Weisstein and Haber (1965), shows the effect clearly, although the page must be turned upside down to realize why the function might be called "U-shaped." These data were obtained from subjects who had to decide whether an encircled letter was *O* or *D,* with the circle delayed by varying amounts after the letter itself.

Kolers (1962) gives a detailed description of the conditions under which the paradoxical type-B time-course can be expected in place

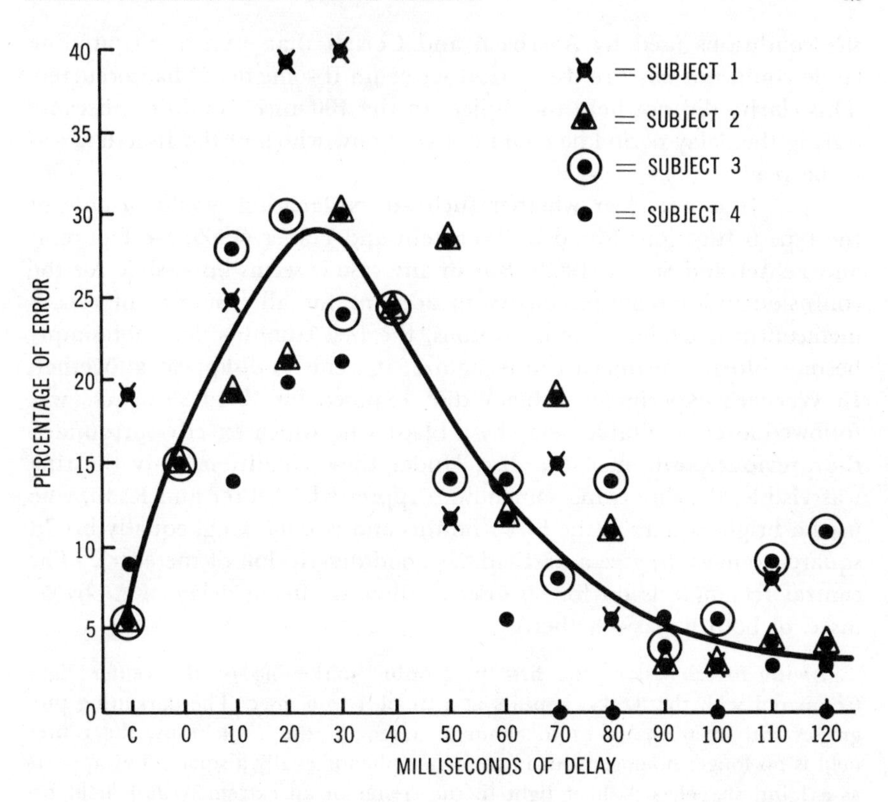


Figure 4. A "U-shaped" backward masking function, obtained by Weisstein and Haber (1965).

of the simpler type-A, and others have corroborated and extended his findings. The situation is complex, depending on such variables as the direction of contrast (light stimuli on dark ground, or dark on light), the amount of contrast, the durations of the masked and masking stimuli, the task of the subject (to detect a flash or to identify a letter), and the difficulty of the discrimination required (especially the separation of the relevant contours).

Averbach and Coriell (1961) report a type-B masking function, which they call "erasure," when the letter to be reported is indicated by a surrounding circle instead of a bar marker (See Figure 2a). The two indicators give equivalent results if they appear just as the stimulus goes off, but at a delay of 100 msec. performance is much worse with the circle than the bar. This suggested to Averbach and Coriell that the circle literally "erased" the enclosed letter. However, Eriksen and Collins (1965) have proposed an explanation of this effect in terms of simple summation and type-A masking. They argue that iconic storage was so clear under the conditions used by Averbach and Coriell that even a surrounding circle could not obscure the critical letter until some decay had occurred. This clarity did not help the subject in the 100-msec. condition, because during the delay period he could not yet know which of the 16 letters was to be read.

It is not clear whether such an explanation would dispose of the type-B functions found by Weisstein and Haber (1965; see Figure 4) and Fehrer and Smith (1962). But in any case it seems impossible for the confusion-and-summation theory to account for all instances of type-B metacontrast. Under some conditions, the first stimulus does not simply become blurred or difficult to recognize: it seems to disappear altogether. In Werner's experiment, a black disc, exposed for 12 to 25 msecs., was followed after a suitable delay by a black ring which exactly surrounded the previous position of the disc. Under these conditions only the ring was visible, the disc being somehow "suppressed." Fehrer and Raab, who used a bright square as the first stimulus and two flanking, equally bright squares to mask it, give a particularly good description of the effect. (The central rectangle is on for 50 msec., followed after a delay of $\Delta t$ by 50 msec. of both flanks together.)

> . . . with foveal vision, the first perceptible darkening of the center light (compared with the flanks) appears at a $\Delta t$ of 4 to 6 msec. The darkening progresses with increases in $\Delta t$ to about 35 msec. At this asynchrony, the center field is no longer homogeneous in color nor phenomenally a square, but appears as a faint, shapeless flash of light in the center of an extremely dark field between the flanks. Maximum suppression occurs with a $\Delta t$ of approximately 75 msec. With increases in $\Delta t$ beyond about 90 to 100 msec., depending on *S*, the center flash brightens again. At approximately 120 msec., it appears as a square preceding the flanks, and of the same brightness as the flanks. Its apparent duration, however, is less than that of the flanks. With a $\Delta t$ of about 150 msec., both brightness and duration of the center seem the same as those of the flanks . . . In peripheral vision, . . . the apparent darkening of the center light was more pronounced than with foveal vision. With $\Delta t$s from 50 to 100 msec., the entire center square area appeared completely dark (Fehrer & Raab, 1962, pp. 144–145).

This phenomenon seems mysterious indeed. The flanks do not impair the perception of the central square if they are simultaneous with it, but if they come somewhat later they can make it disappear entirely. What can be happening in the icon during this period?

Perhaps the most plausible answer is still that given by Werner in 1935: contours are not simply "registered," but must be actively constructed, which takes time. If the masking stimuli arrive when the contour of the original shape has been just partially formed, they initiate a new contour-process which somehow absorbs the original one. Werner wrote, "The process of forming the contour of the disk has been identified with the inception of the whole process of constructing the ring . . . a specific, separate perception of the contour of the disk, in consequence of this fact, is lacking" (1935, pp. 42–43). The reasons why this theory attracts me will become clear in Chapter 4. However, there are arguments against it (see Kolers & Rosner, 1960). Schiller and Smith (1966) hint at a different interpretation, relating metacontrast to apparent movement. Kahneman (1964) has also contributed a sophisticated discussion of metacontrast, backward masking, and summation. It is fair to say that the phenomenon is still not well understood, but for the present we can keep Werner's interpretation as a working hypothesis. Complete figure formation can take 100 msec. or more and is especially vulnerable in some of its later phases.

Why are the effects of backward masking not more apparent in ordinary visual experience? Primarily because normal eye movements are not frequent enough. In reading, the eyes make only three to five fixations per second, remaining still for at least 200 msec. at a time. In most other visual activities, even longer pauses are common. (The eyes are not really "still" during each fixation, of course, but the effect of the small nystagmoid fluctuations is irrelevant here.) Whatever the reason for this limit on the rate of fixation, it is certainly useful in avoiding metacontrast. Probably we could never see anything well at ten fixations per second. Gilbert (1959) has made this argument explicitly.

Although we cannot expect to find metacontrast effects in observing a stationary scene, they might be detectable when moving contours are inspected. Frohlich's (1925, 1929) illusion has often been interpreted from this point of view (e.g., Alpern, 1953). An illuminated stripe which appears suddenly and then moves to the left (say) is not correctly localized at first: the subject reports its onset at a point too far to the left. Is it possible that the stripe in a later position exerts a backward-masking effect on its initial image? This interpretation would be promising, except for the implication that all positions of the stripe should mask each other, leading to invisibility!

Apart from the case of moving figures, the eye normally has at least 200 msecs. to process a stimulus pattern, and the type-B masking curves show that much of this time may be needed. At least under some conditions, the perceptual experience of "seeing" a specific form apparently does not take place until many milliseconds after the stimulus arrives at the retina. It is important to realize, however, that this sense of the word "see" does not include all the effects of visual stimuli. Processing begins as soon as the stimulus arrives and continues for an appreciable time. Before a stimulus is masked by another that arrives 75 msec. later, it has already initiated some activity, which may not have been altogether in vain. The early processes may have measurable consequences even if they do not result in "seen" figures with definite contours.

### *EFFECTS OF A MASKED STIMULUS*

The visual effects of a stimulus which has suffered masking are still not well understood. There is every reason to believe that they will depend on variables such as the duration and intensity of the stimuli involved, and the interval between them. Under some circumstances, for example, the masked stimulus may result in a perception of visual movement, even when it is not seen directly. This was reported by Fehrer and Raab (1962), whose description of type-B masking has been reported above, while with different stimulus conditions Fehrer and Biederman (1962) succeeded in eliminating movement.

There are other ways in which the first stimulus may affect the appearance of the subsequent pattern. Smith and Henriksson (1955) report such a case with the modified Zöllner illusion in Figure 5. The lines were presented briefly, followed by the square; subjects who reported seeing the lines were eliminated from the experiment. Nevertheless there was a slight tendency to report the usual distortion of the square into a trapezoid. (This experiment would bear repeating since its outcome may have been influenced by nonperceptual factors, of the kind to be discussed below in connection with the work of Smith, Spence, and Klein, 1959.)

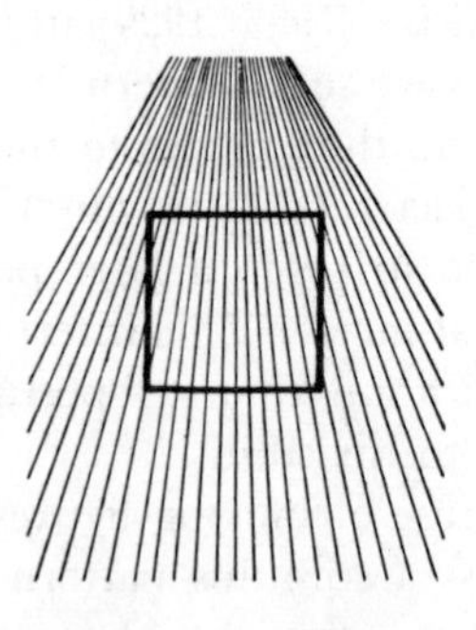

Figure 5. Zöllner illusion used by Smith and Henriksson (1955).

Another demonstration of such an effect was provided in an experiment by Guthrie and Wiener (1966). Their stimuli are shown in Figure 6. One of the *A* stimuli was exposed very briefly, immediately followed by the *B* stimulus for 450 msecs. The subjects made mood and character judgments of the *B* figure. It was judged more *hostile* and *aggressive* when preceded by the relatively angular $A_2$ and $A_4$ than by the more curvilinear $A_1$ and $A_3$. This fits with the fact (also demonstrated by Guthrie and Wiener) that angular forms, even in otherwise meaningless nonsense figures, are judged to have more negative characters than curved figures do. It is particularly important that $A_3$ and $A_4$ (with a gun) did *not* have effects greater than $A_1$ and $A_2$ (without). Guthrie and Wiener conclude that it is not the meaning but the figural properties of the masked stimulus which can affect the overall course of processing.

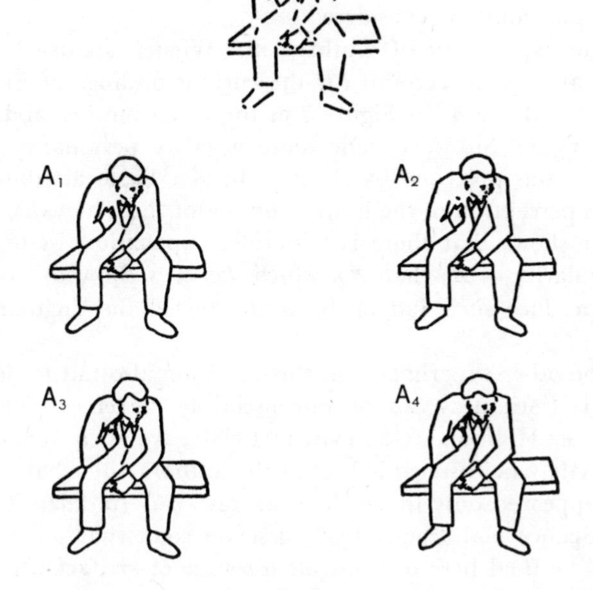


Figure 6. Stimuli used by Guthrie and Wiener (1966).

This seems a sensible conclusion, if either Werner's contour-absorption or Eriksen's summation-confusion interpretation of backward masking is accepted. The meaning of a masked stimulus can hardly influence later processing if no identifiable shape has yet been produced! Nevertheless, some theorists (e.g., Spence, 1961) seem to feel that the meaning of a stimulus *is* available under these conditions, albeit not consciously. They have presented experimental data in support of their view. If they are right, the preceding account of masking, together with all other research on the phenomenon, is irrelevant to the real sensory capacities and processes of the organism.

The claim that masked stimuli can be unconsciously perceived is often based on Freud's "primary process" model of thinking. This is a model which I have found quite valuable (see Chapter 11), but its direct extensions to perception seem unjustified. Can we really suppose that a stimulus which has suffered complete backward masking, so far as careful laboratory observation is concerned, has in fact been fully identified by the subject on an unconscious level? In view of the very specialized nature of backward masking, which is almost impossible to produce without tachistoscopic control of the stimuli, it seems unlikely that evolution would have equipped us with sophisticated unconscious mechanisms for dealing with it. If we did have such mechanisms, it seems equally unlikely that they would be wasted at a level where they could hardly be an aid to survival! Nevertheless, the experiments of this group exist and must be considered.

The experiment of Guthrie and Wiener discussed above was actually an attempt to account for the curious findings of Eagle (1959). He used either $A_1$ or $A_2$ of Figure 7 as the first stimulus, and masked it with the *B* figure. Subjects made more negative personality judgments of *B* when it was preceded by $A_1$ than by $A_2$; Eagle attributed this to unconscious perception of the hostile content of $A_1$. The work of Guthrie and Wiener shows that there is a simpler expanation in terms of the greater angularity of $A_1$ than $A_2$, which (as they showed) could be expected to produce such judgments if it affected the angularity of the *B* figure.

The other experiments in this tradition also fail to demonstrate that a masked stimulus can be unconsciously perceived. The first, by Klein, Spence, Holt and Gourevitch (1958) gave such tenuous results that it can safely be disregarded; even the authors note that "the principal effects appeared only in subtle measures . . ." (p. 262). The second, by Smith, Spence and Klein (1959) deserves somewhat more consideration. It will be used here to illustrate a source of artifact which is often poorly controlled in studies of subliminal stimulation. The subjects were asked to give character-and-mood descriptions of an outline face, which was repeatedly interrupted by very brief presentations of the word *ANGRY*, or alternatively by *HAPPY*. Early flashes of the words were at durations below 10 msecs., where they were invisible even under optimum conditions of attention; later presentations approached the range where they might conceivably have been noticed, although most subjects did not report them. There was a significant tendency for the descriptions given just after a flash of *ANGRY* to be less favorable than those after *HAPPY*, and this tendency was at least as marked on the very early trials (e.g., at 4 msecs.) as on the later ones. The authors conclude that at these very short durations the words must have been read unconsciously.

However, a more plausible explanation is available. It is well known that subjects are quick to discern the aims of an experiment, and able to pick up subtle cues from the experimenter's behavior to guide their responses. Orne (1959, 1962a) has pointed out that all experiments have "demand characteristics" from the subject's point of view. A good,

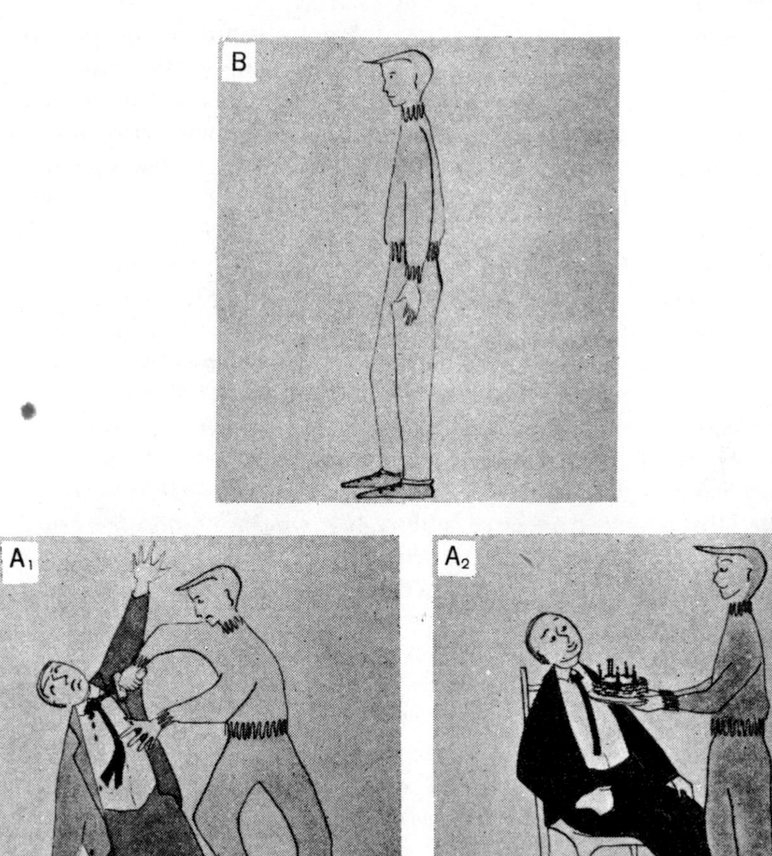

Figure 7. Stimuli used by Eagle (1959).

cooperative subject will naturally use every available cue to discover what is expected of him, because he wants the experiment to succeed. There are many such cues in every study, even a totally automated one, but a particularly obvious source is the experimenter's behavior. Rosenthal (1963, 1965) has shown that the expectations of the experimenter can mediate these demand characteristics quite unintentionally. The famous case of "Clever Hans" (Pfungst, 1911) showed that even a horse can produce spectacular "mental" effects by picking up subtle cues from a human who knows the right answers. We can expect no less from college students, especially in experiments where the subjects' ostensible task makes little sense to them.

Smith *et al.* (1959) were aware of this possibility, and used two experimenters, one of whom interrogated the subject while the other manipulated the words. If the interrogator had really been "blind" about the word being flashed, this precaution would have been adequate. But the experimental design always called for four initial presentations of *HAPPY* followed by four of *ANGRY* before any irregularity was introduced into the sequence, and the interrogator seems to have known this. Hence there is a real possibility that the subjects were unintentionally and subtly encouraged to give "happy" reports on some early trials and "angry" reports on the others, in exactly that range of durations where the most mysterious and "unconscious" effects were observed.

This interpretation may strike the reader as farfetched, but in fact the manipulation of verbal report by personal interaction is by no means unusual. It occurs daily whenever we say what we believe someone else wants to hear. Many alert experimenters can cite instances of this effect in their own research, although it was rarely documented before Rosenthal's (1963) systematic studies. The alternative explanation, in terms of accurate unconscious perception under metacontrast conditions, is in fact the farfetched one.

These comments are not meant in criticism of Smith *et al.* In fact, they must be given credit for at least attempting to control for this possibility, at a time (1959) when there had been little public discussion of it. Other experimenters, both earlier and later, have been less sensitive. For example, the method of word-association seems particularly vulnerable to experimenter effects as it is usually used. In one common procedure, after being exposed to a very brief or a masked stimulus, the subject is read a list of words to which he must associate. Stimulus-words that are somehow related to the subliminal flash often turn out to produce different responses and latencies than do control words. This is not surprising, if the experimenter who reads them aloud is aware which ones are critical.

Kolers (1957) used an interesting variant of the metacontrast method in a study of "subliminal stimulation in problem-solving." His subjects had to find similarities between the top and bottom rows of complex displays which were repeatedly and briefly presented. Their scores were better if, before each presentation, the correct answer appeared briefly under conditions of backward masking. The design of the experiment makes it unlikely that an experimenter-bias effect could have been at work. However, the task was one which encouraged vigorous and frequent exploratory motions of the eyes, and it is clear that a single well-timed eye movement between flashes could have eliminated masking. Kolers reports no interrogations of his subjects, so we cannot be sure that none of them ever saw the masked cue on any of the repeated trials. In a somewhat similar study, Gerard (1960) failed to find a positive effect.

Working from a very different theoretical interpretation indeed, Averbach and Coriell (1961) and Sperling himself (1963, 1967) have also assumed that complex stimuli can be identified and stored in the brief period before a masking pattern appears. Of course, they do not claim that this process is unconscious. Sperling (1963) displayed an array of letters for a few milliseconds and then substituted a pattern of dots to "erase" the display. A typical result appears in Figure 8. The subject could report one letter (on the average) if the masking pattern came after 10 msec. of display, two letters if it came only after 20 msec., and so on. Sperling concluded that letters were read from the display at the rate of one every 10 msec., or 100 per second, until the moment when it was erased by the masking pattern.

We shall see below that such a rate would be over ten times faster than the maximum estimated by other methods. This discrepancy has led Sperling (1967) to a model which interpolates a third memory, a "recognition buffer" between the icon and its verbal recoding. But a readout rate of 100 letters per second seems extremely unlikely on other grounds. Under normal conditions it would be quite useless. The eye tends to remain stationary for 200 msec. at a time. If Sperling were right, an observer could read 20 letters during this period, although only five or six would find room in verbal memory and be used further. All things considered, a simpler explanation of the data in Figure 8 seems preferable.

In my opinion, this and other "erasure" experiments demonstrate only the familiar effect of exposure time on legibility (e.g., Mackworth, 1963a, and Figure 3 above). The subject reads letters not only from the stimulus while it is on but from the icon afterwards, despite the presence of the mask. Performance does improve with increasing exposure time, but not because he then can read more letters *during* the exposure; only because longer exposures lead to longer-lasting icons. In the "erasure" paradigm, the icon becomes illegible sooner than usual because it is degraded by the masking stimulus. Only for this reason does performance depend more sharply on exposure time. (Sperling—1963, p. 26—considers this interpretation and rejects it on phenomenal grounds. The display *appears* to be terminated by the onset of the mask, rather than to continue as in ordinary tachistoscopic presentations. However, another interpretation of this subjective experience is possible, and will be presented below.)

In short, it seems very unlikely that figures or letters can be identified in the first few milliseconds of an exposure. When a masking flash follows 75 msec. after a display which the subject does not report, we cannot assume that it was nevertheless identified and registered unconsciously. Furthermore, if part of the display is reported despite the mask, we must not suppose that the processing which led to the report

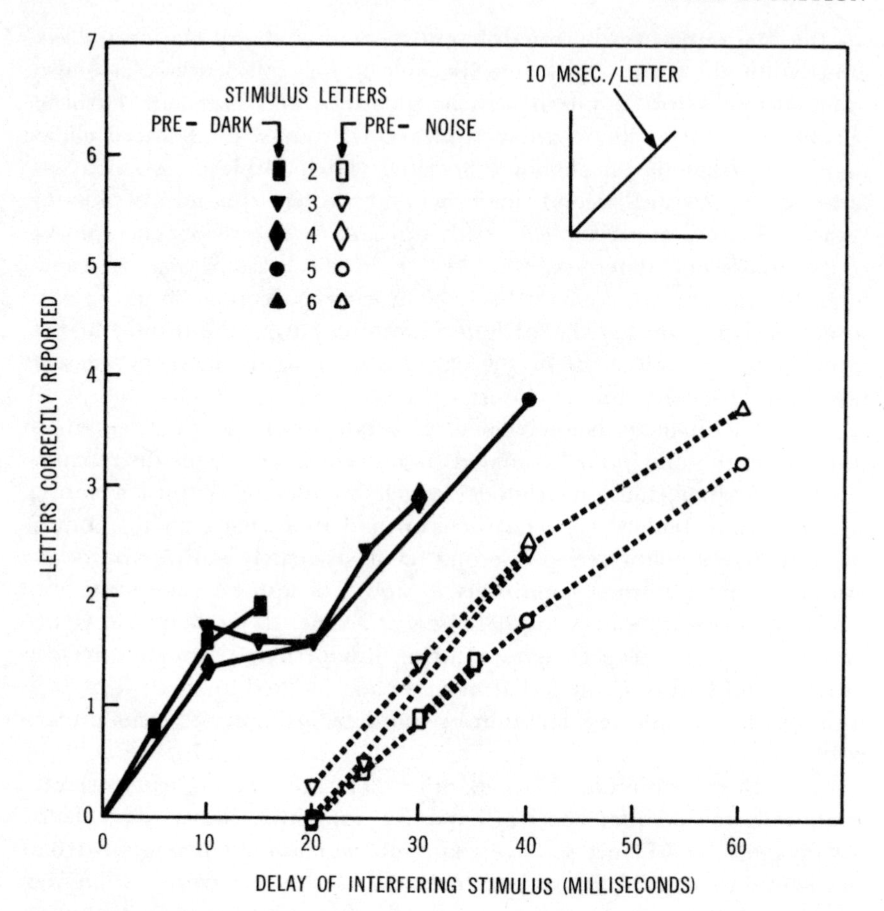


Figure 8. Number of letters read correctly as a function of the delay of a masking stimulus, in Sperling's (1963) "erasure" experiment. The preexposure field was either light or dark, and the number of stimulus letters was also varied.

occupied only those 75 msec. However, it would be a mistake to assume that such a display can have *no* effect in its early moments. What is dubious is only the formation of contours and the identification of shape. In particular, the ingenious work of Elizabeth Fehrer and her associates shows that a masked stimulus is quite capable of eliciting a response, though not one which depends on details of pattern.

Fehrer and Raab's (1962) account of the metacontrast phenomenon has already been quoted. The principal task of their subjects, however, was not phenomenological description but rapid response. Although the first stimulus disappeared under metacontrast conditions, leaving only an impression of movement, careful measurement showed that reaction time to the stimulus-followed-by-mask was *no longer* than to the first stimulus alone. This result has been replicated by Schiller and Smith (1966). In another study, Fehrer and Biederman (1962) used a metacontrast situation so carefully contrived that subjects had no cues at all to distinguish between trials on which a first stimulus preceded the mask and trials on which it was omitted. Nevertheless in this situation also, reaction times were no longer than to the first stimulus alone. ". . . RT can be initiated and determined by an event which is so successfully masked that it is often not detected by careful phenomenal observation" (Fehrer & Biederman, 1962, p. 130).

This rather dramatic result shows that visual information is processed in several different ways at once, "in parallel." While the construction of contours has only begun at one level, a message that "something has happened" is already on its way to determine a response. In this situation, the subject's response is not dependent on his having "seen" the stimulus figure clearly. It is only necessary that some sort of visual activity be initiated. This saves many milliseconds of response time, with clear biological advantages. It is reminiscent of the difference between "sensory" and "motor" reaction times which has long been established (e.g., Woodworth, 1938, pp. 306–308). The magnitude of this difference—up to 100 msec.—is comparable to the maximum interstimulus interval for metacontrast. We may speculate that a "sensory" reaction is one which waits for full figure-formation, while a "motor" reaction does not.

This possibility that gross information about the visual stimulus may be used before pattern analysis is complete also resolves the paradox in Sperling's masking experiments. In an attempt to find out whether iconic memory could survive a masking flash, he measured the *subjective duration* of a masked display. To this end, observers had to match its duration by adjusting the length of a simultaneous tone. The brief tones they chose seemed to show that the perceived display ended just at the instant when the stimulus was actually replaced by the mask. Sperling (1967) took this to mean that iconic memory played no role in this case, and that "erasure" was instantaneous. This, in turn, led him to infer the implausible reading rates mentioned above. I prefer to believe that the onset of the masking stimulus can be signalled to a higher level *while the letters are still being read.* The mechanisms which register this onset are different, simpler, and faster than those which identify the letters, just as in Fehrer's experiments the mechanisms which trigger a "motor" reaction are faster than those of figure-formation. This is a further reason for preferring the term "icon" to Sperling's "image." It is hard to argue with a subject who says his "image" terminated at a certain moment, but it seems apparent that the processing of iconic information can continue past this point. Visual cognition is not a single and simple interiorization of the stimulus, but a complex of processes.

### *VERBAL CODING*

If iconic storage lasts for a second or two at best, how can performance in tachistoscopic experiments be explained? The icon will certainly have disappeared long before the subject can finish naming four or five letters. We must assume that information is quickly "read" into another, somewhat more permanent, form of memory. On logical, phenomenological, and empirical grounds, the new storage medium must be words. The subject formulates and remembers a verbal description of what he has seen. His introspections reveal an active process of inner speech in the period between exposure and report. That is why auditory confusions are commonly encountered in such experiments (Sperling, 1963). The subject may err by reporting a letter which *sounds* like the correct one though it does not look like it. These errors will be considered further in Chapter 9, in connection with verbal memory.

Sperling gives a simple account of this stage of cognition. "(1) The observer sees the stimulus material for a short time. (2) He scans it, selecting certain information to rehearse (verbally). (3) He later reports what he remembers of his rehearsal" (1963, p. 20). The existence of such a verbal coding process explains a number of classical findings of cognitive psychology, as we shall see. Nevertheless, it would be rash to conclude that this is the *only* way visual information can be preserved. After all, children and animals also learn from visual experience, obviously without verbalizing it. There are certainly other, more directly visual ways to store information after the decay of the icon; they will be discussed in Chapter 6.

To the extent that tachistoscopic performance depends on verbal coding—and this is a very substantial extent—an accurate report of the whole pattern is possible only if the subject can complete a verbal description of it before the icon has faded. It is easy to see why *visual variables* affect performance if this is true: exposure time, intensity, and the post-exposure field all help to determine how long the icon is available. However, performance must also depend on certain *coding variables*. What part of the pattern does the subject begin to encode first? How efficient is his code, and how appropriate to the pattern presented? The remainder of this chapter will deal with these variables and their effects.

If the stimulus patterns consist of discrete, easily-named elements like letters, the potential importance of coding variables is particularly obvious. When the number of letters presented is so large that they cannot all be coded before the icon fades, some must inevitably be lost. Those which are encoded first have the best chance of survival. What Sperling (1960a) showed is that an appropriately-timed signal can preserve *any* given letter (or small set of letters), by controlling the order of encoding. However, similar effects should appear even without a specific signal if, for any reason, the subject tends to read the display in one order rather than another. In particular, the well-established habit of reading from left to right should result in a gradient of accuracy across the tachistoscopic field. Such a result has been repeatedly obtained, and while it was initially misunderstood, recent workers have not hesitated to interpret it in terms of the fading "image" or "trace" which here is called the "icon."

In 1952, Mishkin and Forgays studied the tachistoscopic perception of single words presented to the right or to the left of the fixation point. They found that English words are more easily recognized on the right, while Yiddish ones (which are normally read in the opposite direction) are more easily recognized if they appear on the left. Working within the framework of Hebb's (1949) theory, they assumed that experience had somehow sensitized that portion of the visual system which can play an anticipatory role in the reading process. In English, words to the right of the fixation point will fall on the fovea after the next eye movement; Mishkin and Forgays thought that this constant confirmatory stimulation might result in better articulation of the "cell-assemblies" on that side.

Five years later, Heron (1957) showed that their interpretation had been wrong. When a string of letters is presented *across* the fixation point, those at the left side, not those on the right, are more accurately reported. This gradient of accuracy corresponds exactly to the order in which the subject reports "reading" the letters. So clear is the scanning process that Heron's subjects believed they were fixating each letter in turn, although this could not have been the case with 100-msec. exposures. When the letters were arranged in some other pattern, for example as a square, the gradient of accuracy again corresponded to the introspectively-given order of encoding.

Bryden (1960) clarified this question further, and provided additional support for the interpretation in terms of coding priority. If a row of familiar forms (squares, circles, etc.) is used instead of a row of letters, the left-hand end is still the best reported. However, this bias can be entirely reversed if the subjects are asked to report the forms from right to left instead! (Such reversal instructions do not work well for rows of letters, because one cannot easily alter the habit of reading from left to right. Under reversal instructions, subjects often begin by encoding the letters in their normal order, then reverse it before making their overt report. Not surprisingly, this leads to a poorer overall level of performance.) Bryden's interpretation, in terms of verbal recoding of a rapidly fading icon, is exactly like Sperling's.

The original results of Mishkin and Forgays (1952) can also be explained in terms of the Sperling-Heron-Bryden hypothesis. When a word appears to the right of the fixation point, the scan is poised to begin at the proper place: the left end of the word. Words appearing to the left of fixation require an extra step if they are to be read in the normal direction. This extra step may use up time which would be better employed in examining the icon.

A series of studies by Harcum and his collaborators (for references see Camp & Harcum, 1964) also support the view that nearly all position-effects with isolated letters are created by priorities in verbal encoding. However, there is an apparent exception to this rule. Although the left end of a row of letters is more accurately reported than the rest (by a wide margin: see Crovitz & Schiffman, 1965), the right end is still better than the middle. This may mean that there is some genuine "interference" among adjacent visual letters, as Woodworth and Schlosberg (1954, p. 104) suppose, which makes the middle letters harder to see. On the other hand, it may result only from decay in *verbal* memory. So far, we have argued as if a letter that had once been rescued from the icon and verbally coded was certain to reach the actual report. However, a recency effect in purely verbal memory is also to be expected (see Chapters 8 and 9), and would account neatly for the improved accuracy of the right-hand end of the display.

The process of "scanning" cannot be a matter of successive ocular fixation; tachistoscopic presentation is too quick for that. Nevertheless, two recent studies of coding suggest that it is connected with eye movements in an intimate way. Bryden (1961) and Crovitz and Davies (1962) both recorded the direction of the first eye movements *after* the stimulus presentation. They found a clear trial-by-trial correlation between the part of the display most accurately reported and the post-exposure movements of the eyes, which seemed to jump to the position that would have been appropriate if the letters had still been on the screen. The latency of these "appropriate" eye movements was between 150 and 200 msecs. in the Crovitz-Davies study; 85 percent of the post-exposure movements in that latency range were in the right direction. During this period the subject was probably still reading from the icon.

Although these eye movements have no obvious adaptive purpose, they are evidently related to those of ordinary vision. Under normal conditions, a region of the visual field which attracts our attention, perhaps because we wish to read what is written there, becomes the next point of fixation. Eye movements like those observed in these experiments are thus the normal accompaniment of a flow of attention from one object to the next. This observation invites consideration of a whole series of traditional problems. What is attention? How is it controlled? What can we perceive without it? These questions belong in Chapter 4, where it will be argued that attention is basically a *special allocation of cognitive resources,* and also that some processes (including the reaction times studied by Fehrer and Raab) can occur preattentively. In Chapter 6, we will see that dreams and eidetic images involve similar "life-like" eye movements. First, however, we must consider some other phenomena that can be dealt with in terms of iconic memory and verbal encoding. One of the most important is just as traditional as attention itself: the question of preparatory set.

### *PERCEPTUAL SET AS A CODING VARIABLE*

Sperling's (1960a) experiment, with which this chapter began, showed that partial report of a briefly-presented stimulus is more accurate than full report. This finding was surprising only because the signal, indicating the part to be reported, was not given until *after* the stimulus had terminated. Because of this feature of the design, Sperling concluded that the signal controlled the order in which the icon was verbally coded. If he had told the subject *in advance* to report only a given row, the improvement in performance would not have been astonishing. We would simply have said that the subject was "set" to "see" the row in question. This raises a major theoretical question. Does a "set" operate primarily by controlling the order in which different parts or aspects of the stimulus are coded?

Bryden's (1960) experiment, discussed above, already asumes an affirmative answer to this question, at least for some kinds of stimuli. A subject can be "set" for one or the other end of an array of separate figures, simply by instructing him in advance about the direction in which he is to scan them. Most experiments on perceptual set have used a somewhat different procedure. The subject has been "set" for *attributes* of the stimulus pattern, rather than for discrete parts of it. In Külpe's work at the turn of the century, the focus of set was sometimes the color of a group of elements, sometimes their number, sometimes their positions or the overall figure they formed. As in many similar experiments, the effect of set was to improve the accuracy with which the critical attribute was reported. Very recently, the experiments of Harris and Haber (1963), subsequently extended by Haber (1964a, 1964b, 1966), have clarified this familiar phenomenon. They succeeded in showing that the improved performance on "set" attributes is indeed achieved by encoding them first.

The stimuli used by Harris and Haber could be coded in two different ways. Each stimulus, flashed for 100 msec., consisted of a pair of cards shown side by side; every card had an array of small figures on it, which varied in shape, number, and color. To describe such a figure, either to himself or to the experimenter, a subject could use one of two basic formats. He could speak in terms of *objects,* as in reporting "two red circles, four blue stars." On the other hand, he could also arrange his report by *dimensions:* "red, blue; two, four; star, circle." Each subject received an appreciable amount of training in the use of one or the other of these codes. (A questionnaire given after the experiment helped to check on whether the training had taken effect.) Tachistoscopic recognition trials then began. Sometimes a "set" was established by telling the subject that a correct report of one of the dimensions, perhaps color, was ten times as important as any other; on other trials he might be told that all dimensions were equally important.

Under these conditions, the traditional superiority of the emphasized attribute appeared only in the subjects using the "dimensions code"; there was no effect of set among those who used the "objects code." The reason is evident. In the dimensions code, it is easy to rearrange the priority of encoding to put the emphasized dimension first. This is what the "dimensions coders" actually did (see especially Haber, 1964b, for evidence on this point), and it ensured that the critical attribute was verbalized before the icon had faded to illegibility. The "objects coders," on the other hand, could not do this. English syntax did not permit them to change from "two red circles, four blue stars" to any format beginning "red, blue . . ." even when color was the emphasized dimension on a given trial; to do so would have meant giving up the objects code altogether. But, although the "object coders" could not take advantage of the differential emphasis, their coding system was faster and easier to use. As a result, they obtained higher results on the average, despite their poorer results on emphasized dimensions.

It is important to see that the main effect of set is on the order of encoding, not just on the order of overt report. In most cases these coincide; subjects tend to report the emphasized, first-encoded dimensions before the less important ones if they are allowed to. However, this coincidence is not a necessary one. In some conditions, Harris and Haber forced the subjects to report dimensions in an order which did not reflect the original set. For example, the prescribed order—not established until a short time after the exposure—might be "numbers, shapes, colors." Even in this condition, scores on color were higher if it had been emphasized originally. Like all the set effects, this superiority appeared only in subjects using the "dimensions code," who were able to encode color first even if forced to hold back their report of it. This finding is not unique. Although the difference between priority of coding and priority of report has not always been remarked (Lawrence & LaBerge, 1956), we have already noted it in Bryden's (1960) study of tachistoscopic read-out.

The upshot of these experiments is simple enough. A "perceptual set" operates by affecting what the subject does during the brief period of iconic storage. This does not mean, however, that the set affects only "response" and not "perception." To decide *when* a set operates is not to decide *how* it operates. A number of experimenters have tried to determine whether the effects of set are "perceptual" or not by seeing if a set given before the stimulus is more effective than one given immediately after (Lawrence & Coles, 1954; Long, Reid, & Henneman, 1960; Long, Henneman, & Garvey, 1960; Reid, Henneman, & Long, 1960). Such a method assumes that information which follows the end of an exposure cannot have a "perceptual" consequence. The argument is faulty, because it fails to consider the duration of the icon. There are no instantaneous perceptions, no unmediated glances into reality. The only way to use the term "perception" sensibly is in relation to the extended processes that can go on as long as the icon continues. Thus, while it is true that sets can be imposed after the stimulus has terminated, they may nevertheless be exerting genuinely visual, as opposed to simply verbal, effects. This distinction will be clarified further in Chapter 5. For the present, we must turn to still another phenomenon that results from verbal encoding of iconically-stored information.

### *THE SPAN OF APPREHENSION*

One of the oldest "constants" in psychology is the number of objects which can be "seen" in a single glance; it is variously estimated as four, five, six, or seven. In some versions of the experiment, the subject is simply asked *how many* objects (dots, letters, figures, etc.) are present in a briefly exposed field. In other procedures, he must *identify* as many as possible. The two procedures give similar results, with perhaps somewhat higher scores if only counting is necessary. Whipple's comment is typical for the early students of the problem:

> . . . if we give but a single glance at a heterogeneous collection of objects, such as the goods displayed in a store-window, or a jumble of odds and ends in an old tool-chest, we are able to grasp and enumerate only a very few, perhaps four or five, of these objects (1914, p. 263).

Although Sperling's (1960a) study is most important for its use of partial reports, it also provided further confirmation of the classical findings. When the tachistoscopic flash contained only a few letters, the subjects could report all of them. When too many letters were presented, errors appeared and the number of correct identifications remained at a limiting value. This value, which ranged from 3.8 to 5.2 in his experiment, is the "span of apprehension." Sperling interpreted the span as a limitation on verbal memory. If that memory is full to capacity, no more letters can be rescued from the icon no matter how long it may last. The classical discontinuity between presentations below and above the "span" is easily explained in these terms. If the icon lasts long enough to permit the full verbal storage capacity to be used, any smaller number of items will present an easy task, while larger numbers will "overflow" and produce errors.

On this interpretation, the "span of apprehension" depends fundamentally on the "span of immediate memory." Miller (1956a) raised this possibility in his famous paper on "The Magical Number Seven," without committing himself definitely, but ten years later it seems to be an inescapable conclusion. The fact that the span of apprehension averages only four or five (rather than the seven characteristic of immediate memory) probably results from the high rate of encoding. In a tachistoscopic experiment the subject must read the fading icon as rapidly as possible; we will see later (Chapter 9) that the verbal memory span is markedly reduced at high speeds.

What about the simpler "apprehension" task in which the subject need only report the *number* of items, without identifying them? Here too, a discontinuity appears in the data, usually at about six. Reports of smaller numbers are so rapid and accurate that Kaufman, Lord, Reese, and Volkmann (1949) ascribed them to a special process, "subitizing," which can determine the number of dots in a field without counting. It is not too difficult to imagine such a process, if it is based on the overall *shape* of the dot-pattern. Three dots nearly always make a triangle, for example, and four may often make a recognizable quadrilateral. However, while subjects may indeed use shapes as number-cues on occasion, it seems likely that they frequently engage in real counting as well. This might also produce a discontinuity at about six items, if the icon fades before they can count any higher! To the extent that counting is important, we would expect the span of apprehension to vary with exposure time and intensity, since these affect the duration of the icon. Precisely this result was obtained by Hunter and Sigler (1940). The same reasoning suggests that the span should be reduced by the backward-masking procedure which Sperling and Averbach call "erasure." This prediction was confirmed by Averbach (1963); up to about 100 msec., the span increases with longer presentation of the display prior to a masking stimulus.

The processes of counting and naming assumed here are covert rather than explicit. It is obviously important to determine how long they take. At what rate can material be entered into verbal memory? This speed cannot be calculated from the exposure time itself, because the icon outlasts the stimulus. Unlike Sperling and Averbach, I believe it cannot be calculated from exposure time in a backward-masking situation either; the mask degrades the icon but probably does not terminate it immediately. However, a first approximation to the rate can be obtained from *reaction times* in a span-of-apprehension experiment. Whenever the subject must count "one, two, three . . ." to determine how many items there are, his total processing time should increase with the number presented. Such an increase has been reported by Saltzman and Garner (1948) and other investigators (see Woodworth & Schlosberg, 1954). Reaction times average about $1/10$ of a second longer for every additional item to be enumerated. However, if we assume that "subitizing" (reaction to overall shape) occurs on some of the trials which enter into these averages, then this figure must slightly underestimate the time being used on the occasions when real counting takes place.

On this interpretation, the reaction-time figures agree fairly well with other estimates of the rate of counting. Landauer (1962) found that silent counting was no faster than its overt counterpart; the subject whose data he presents took about 1.7 seconds to count from "one" to "ten," or 170 msec. per digit. Pierce and Karlin (1957) had found earlier that subjects could repeat familiar phrases ("This is the time for all good men . . .") at eight or nine words per second. It is safe, then, to estimate the counting time in such experiments at over 100 msec. for each digit. Taking in new information is much slower, of course; Pierce and Karlin found that familiar monosyllables could not be read in much less than 300 msec. each. We will return to this question, with more data, in Chapter 5.

The notion that counting is often involved in the span of apprehension, even with small numbers, is a controversial one. After all, introspection rarely reveals a clear *experience* of counting in such short exposures. However, this hardly proves that none has taken place. Introspection does not reveal the separate and successive impacts of my fingers on the typewriter keyboard either, unless I adopt a very special attitude and a special mode of typing as well. An attempt to describe the counting process in these experiments would only change it and slow it down. Introspection is necessarily a poor guide to very rapid cognitive processes.

### *EASE OF CODING*

The accuracy with which a briefly exposed stimulus is reported must depend on the code that the subject has available. If the verbal representation is long and clumsy, he may well forget some of it before making his overt report. This factor should be especially important under conditions where other limitations on the coding process are removed—e.g., with long, clear presentations. Even several seconds of exposure to *149162536496481* will not permit the subject to report it accurately as long as he tries to remember "one four nine one six . . ." On the other hand, "the first nine squares" encodes it succinctly and will generally lead to a perfect reproduction. A binary string like *00000000,* which the subject can call "eight zeroes," is more easily reproduced than *10010110,* which he will probably call "one oh oh one oh one one oh." The importance of such factors in long-term memory is well known (Katona, 1940), but they should be effective in the short run also.

Glanzer and Clark (1963a, 1963b) have substantiated this point in several experiments. Using patterns of zeroes and ones like those above, they first established the "describability" of each pattern by asking a group of subjects to give a full verbal description of it during a 30-second exposure. A different group of subjects was then used to determine how accurately the patterns could be reported after exposures of ½ second. Correlations ranging around −0.80 were obtained between the average length of a pattern's description and the proportion of subjects who got it right in the brief exposure. For various reasons, the authors believe that the critical attribute of the accurately-reported patterns was indeed the brevity of their description, as opposed to their symmetry, simplicity, or redundancy.

What determines the ease with which a pattern lends itself to verbal description? Its visual properties must be relevant; some patterns are intrinsically more easily described than others. However, the subject's training is also an important variable, since it determines the verbal descriptions he has available. In principle, one should be able to teach new "languages" which would improve performance in the Glanzer-Clark paradigm. A code that suggests itself immediately is the so-called "octal number system," in which any triad of zeroes and ones is represented by a single digit: *000* is *zero, 001* is *one, 010* is *two . . . 111* is *seven.* Recoding from binary to octal produces dramatic improvements in the ordinary immediate-memory experiment, where the exposure time is so long as not to be an important variable (see Chapter 9). However, two recent experiments have shown that octal coding does *not* improve performance at tachistoscopic exposure speeds.

The first of these was conducted by Klemmer (1964). Instead of zeroes and ones, he used 21 bulbs which were (or were not) lighted up in a 100-msec. flash. The bulbs were arranged in groups of three. Half a second after a flash like *001 101 000 110 010 101 011,* the subjects were asked to reproduce some one particular triad. After eleven days of initial practice with this task, they were taught the octal number system. This would permit them—at least in principle—to represent the entire display with seven words (the example above becomes "one five zero six two five three"). As it turned out, however, performance was *not* improved by this training. Even with 40 more days of practice, the subjects were no more accurate than they had been before the octal code was introduced. A similar experiment by Pollack and Johnson (1965) has produced equally negative results.

These studies do not seem to support the view that coding variables are crucially important in visual identification. However, it is important to note that the exposures used by Klemmer (100 msec.) and Pollack and Johnson (40 msec.) were much shorter than those of Glanzer and Clark. In such brief flashes, unless the experimental procedures happened to produce a long-lasting icon, performance must have been limited by visual factors as well as verbal ones. No matter how efficient a verbal code may be, the subject must recognize a visual pattern (e.g., *011*) before he can name it ("three"). Recognition itself is a complex process, as the next chapter will show.

*Chapter 3*

# *Pattern Recognition*

The problem of pattern recognition, or stimulus equivalence, is ubiquitous in psychology. This chapter considers the solutions that have been proposed from the time of Gestalt psychology to the present, including recent techniques developed for computer programs. The two main theoretical approaches are "template-matching," in which each new input is compared with a standard, and "feature-analysis," in which the presence of particular parts or particular properties is decisive. The various theories are examined in the light of relevant observations, including recognition tests with displaced, rotated, or ill-defined figures, studies of decision time and visual search, stopped-image experiments, single-cell physiological recording, and certain developmental studies of visual discrimination. It is concluded that recognition is mediated, in part, by a hierarchy of "feature analyzers."

The arguments of the last chapter do not so much explain letter-recognition as assume it. By some process that operates on iconically-stored information, the subject "reads out" a letter—he recodes a visual pattern into an essentially auditory one. What can we say about this process? How does the subject know an *A* when he sees one?

The obvious answer, that he knows because it looks like an *A*, is not very helpful and may even be wrong. One could argue with equal force that it looks like an *A* only because he knows what it is. Neither statement exhausts the issue, because not all *A*s look alike. There are capital *A*s and small *A*s and elite *A*s and pica *A*s and script *A*s and block *A*s; large *A*s and small *A*s; slanted *A*s and straight *A*s. There are configurations, like the one in Figure 9, which look like an *A* in certain contexts and like an *H* in others. Finally, there are hand-printed and handwritten *A*s, whose variety is truly astonishing. A few genuine hand-printed specimens are shown enlarged in Figure 10. They are all recognizable; no subject misidentified any of them in an actual experiment (see Neisser & Weene, 1960, where the method of collecting such specimens is described). Nevertheless, they are quite diverse. If all of these are *A*s "because they look alike," we must consider what process creates their similarity. And if they look alike only because they are classified as *A*s, we must consider what mechanism might do the classifying.

Figure 9. The effect of context on letter-recognition (after Selfridge, 1955).

This problem has many names. In the language of behaviorism, it is a matter of stimulus generalization or of stimulus equivalence. In the terminology of Gestalt psychology, it is the problem of contact between perceptual process and memory trace: the so-called "Höffding step." Among philosophers, the question is usually formulated in terms of "universals" and of "abstraction from particulars." For Bruner and his associates, it is the problem of categorization. In computer technology, it is called "character recognition" when only letters and numbers are to be identified, or more generally "pattern recognition." It does not arise only in tachistoscopic perception but in all perception, and not only with *A*s but with all sets of stimuli that elicit a consistent response.

The present chapter surveys some of the available data on human pattern recognition, in an effort to relate them to the theories that have been proposed. The first section below considers the nature of the problem, rather briefly. Then, two further sections deal with some of the empirical observations that are too frequently ignored in current speculation. After a brief theoretical excursion to consider the simplest possible models, those involving "template-matching," empirical findings appear again in a section on decision-time and search experiments. After the reader has been introduced to some widely used ideas by way of a model of visual search, the main theoretical review deals with Hebb's "part" theory and the "feature" theories of Bruner, Selfridge, and Sutherland. Since even these approaches leave many problems unsolved, the next chapter will take up some further notions, especially focal attention and figural synthesis.

### *THE NATURE OF THE PROBLEM*

The problem of pattern recognition has been formulated here in connection with tachistoscopic experiments, but it must be dealt with in general terms. Whenever a stimulus evokes a single response consist-

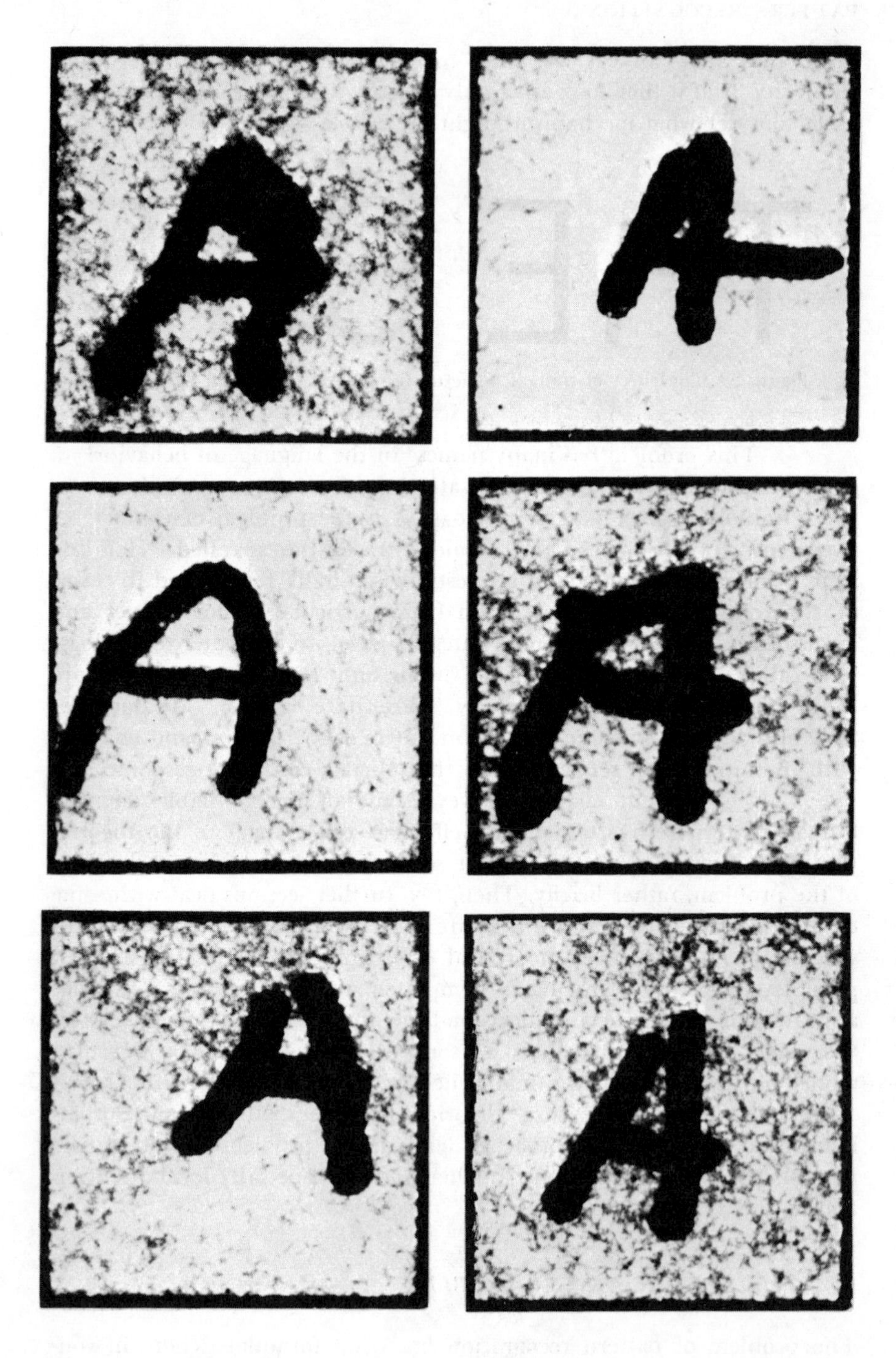

Figure 10. Recognizable specimens of hand-printed *A*s.

ently, we can say that it is being "recognized." The problem for theory is to describe the processes of recognition. It is a difficult problem because many different stimuli may be equivalent in producing the same reaction. Following Bruner, Goodnow, and Austin (1956), I will treat the consistent response as a category and use "categorization" as a synonym for "pattern recognition."

This does not mean that either of these words is a synonym for "perception." Bruner's claim that "all perception is necessarily the end-product of a categorization process" (1957b, p. 124) must be rejected. Many cognitive processes, such as iconic storage itself, do not involve categorizing to any serious extent. Of course, the nervous system has only a finite capacity to discriminate, so very similar inputs must often give rise to the same iconic pattern. In a sense, one might say that these are "categorized together." This use of the term makes it uninteresting, however, since even a photographic plate is categorial in the same way. There is little value in speaking of "pattern recognition" or "categories" unless genuinely diverse inputs lead to a single output. A stage of cognition which preserves the shape, size, position, and other formal characteristics of the stimulus should be called "literal," or perhaps "analog," but not "categorial." The transient icon is probably "analog" in this sense, and some of the more permanent forms of visual memory may also be (see Chapter 6).

It is true that categorization is involved whenever a subject *names* what he sees. But not all responding is naming, and Bruner's claim that "neither language, nor the tuning that one could give an organism to direct any other form of overt response, could provide an account (of perceptual experience) save in generic or categorial terms" (1957b, p. 125) should not go unquestioned. Visual tracking, drawing, and beating a rhythm are examples of overt responses that may sometimes be analog instead of categorial. This is not a mere matter of definition. The act of drawing often *is* categorial, reflecting only stereotypes and expectations instead of the real form of the stimulus. Yet it hardly follows that all drawing is of this sort, or that the interplay between categorial and literal processes cannot be studied. Even where tachistoscopic recognition of letters is concerned, some reservations are appropriate. The task obviously does demand rapid categorization: the subject must assign one of 26 names to each figure before the icon has faded. Nevertheless, we should bear in mind that this may not be typical of all, or even most, cognitive activity. Not all situations demand classification so explicitly as does a choice among 26 well-defined alternatives; not all classification, even when it occurs, is made under time pressure.

Within the letter-recognition situation, the main theoretical problem is that of "stimulus equivalence." How does it happen that so many different visual configurations are all called "A"? If this were not the case, theorizing would be relatively simple. Even then, however—even if every *A* were an exact foveal replica of a centrally stored prototype—we would still find that one critical step demanded a theoretical explanation. A new *A* presented to the eye would still be only a peripheral event; recognition requires that it make contact with appropriate centrally stored information.

It was this step which the Gestalt psychologists called the "Höffding function" (Köhler, 1940; Rock, 1962), after the nineteenth-century Danish psychologist who saw it as a necessary refinement of simple association theory (Höffding, 1891). To say that the sight of bread gives rise to the idea of butter "by virtue of previous association," as was (and is) so commonly assumed, is to miss a crucial step. The present sight of bread, as a stimulus or a perceptual process, is not generally associated with butter; only stored memories of bread are associated in this way. Hence we must assume that the present event is somehow identified as bread first, i.e., that it makes contact with "memory traces" of earlier experiences with bread. Only then can the preexisting association be used. Association cannot be effective without prior pattern recognition.

According to the Gestalt psychologists, a very simple mechanism would suffice for the Höffding step if only all glimpses of bread (or all *A*s) were alike, even to their position on the retina. In that case the "memory trace" or central representation could be an exact copy of the perceptual event that had occurred previously. It would be "aroused" or "contacted" by overlap; perhaps all of its neurons would be simultaneously fired by their mates in the perceptual system. Such an arrangement is depicted in Figure 11a.

This solution (which the Gestalt psychologists rejected in its simple form) is one example of an approach to pattern recognition in terms of "prototypes," or "canonical forms," that is most often called *template-matching* (Selfridge & Neisser, 1960; Uhr, 1963; Gibson, 1963). A new figure is identified by noting its coincidence, or congruence, with a basic model. Template-matching is not uncommon in daily life. To determine if a particular fingerprint was made by one of his suspects, a detective may superimpose it, successively, on the prerecorded prints of each one until he obtains a match. Even then, the new print and the standard will probably not be quite identical: the sample will be smudged or distorted or partially incomplete. Nevertheless, the detective will be satisfied as long as the match is reasonably good, and better than any other. In a sense, he computes a correlation coefficient between the two patterns and asks if it is near 1.00.

Höffding observed that simple template-matching has some obvious inadequacies as a theory of pattern recognition. Ordinary experi-

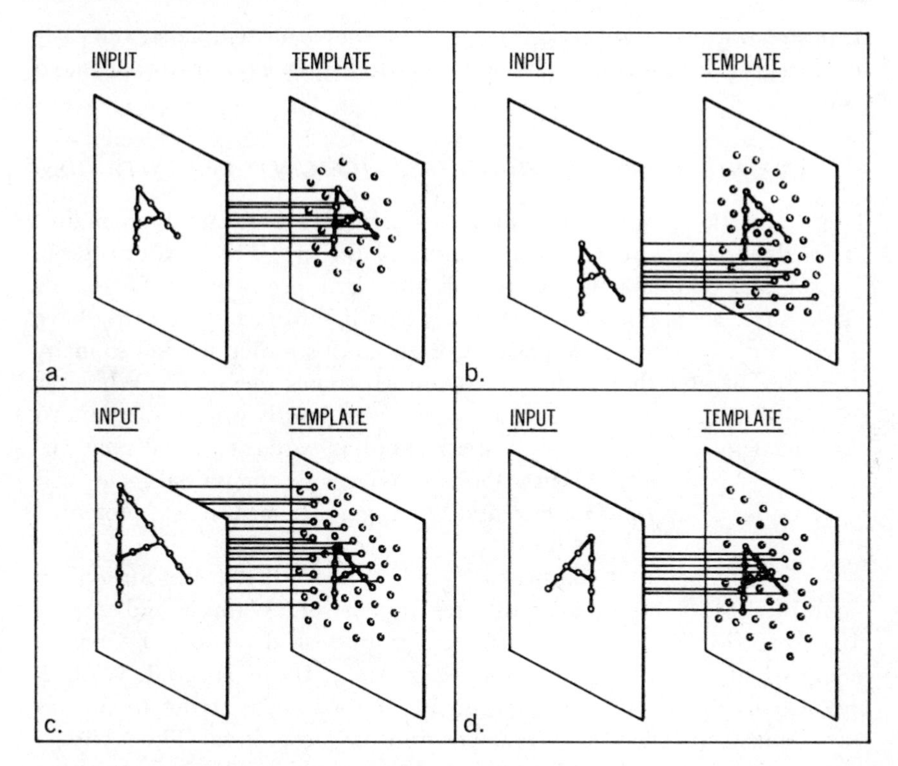


Figure 11. Problems of template-matching. Figure 11a shows an input which matches the template; 11b, a mismatch due to change of position; 11c, a change of size; 11d, of orientation.

ence suggests that we can recognize a form even in a new retinal position (Figure 11b) and despite size changes (Figure 11c) or rotations (Figure 11d), although any of these operations must destroy the congruence necessary for recognition. Thus one must choose between elaborating the template model considerably and abandoning it altogether. As Hebb has pointed out, "it is hard to reconcile an unlocalized afferent process with a structural (and hence localized) mnemonic trace" (1949, p. 15).

Unlike the Gestalt psychologists, who never gave up the notion of templates altogether, Hebb himself chose the second alternative. To him, and no doubt to most of those concerned with the problem today, it seems likely that patterns are identified in terms of their "attributes." These attributes may just be the lines and angles which make up the figure—this is Hebb's interpretation—or they may be more complex. In the "feature" theories of Selfridge (1959) and Sutherland (1959), figures are identified in terms of attributes like "concavity" and "horizontality," which are characteristics of the whole rather than simple parts. Such theories have many advantages over those based on templates, but they too will need considerable elaboration before they explain the observed facts.

### *EMPIRICAL OBSERVATIONS: DISPLACEMENT AND ROTATION*

There is little doubt that familiar patterns are recognized no matter where they happen to fall on the retina of the eye. This creates a problem for any template theory: how is the right prototype to be found? To be sure, we might assume that any familiar form must *already* have fallen on every conceivable position of an adult's retina, leaving so many templates behind that contact with one becomes inevitable. Whatever the plausibility of this approach may be, it will hardly work if the pattern to be recognized is unique. But are unfamiliar patterns indeed recognizable in new positions? If a new form is exposed in one retinal locus, will it subsequently appear familiar, and be properly named, if it is presented to another?

In general, the answer is "yes." Köhler (1940) cites an experiment by Becher which demonstrates this point; Wallach and Austin (1954) mention four others which went unpublished because the experimenters had been trying to prove the contrary. Undiscouraged, Wallach and Austin carried out an experiment of their own, trying to find at least some small effect of retinal position on recognition. Their critical stimulus was Figure 12, which tends to be seen as a "dog" when presented horizontally and as a "chef" when presented vertically. Given at 45°, it becomes an ambiguous figure. In general, a subject who has seen a

Figure 12. Ambiguous figure used by Wallach and Austin (1954) and Rock (1956).

"biased"—i.e., unambiguous—version of such a figure tends afterwards to see the ambiguous one with the same bias. (This fact itself is considered below, in Chapter 6.) Wallach and Austin tried to use this "aftereffect" as a sensitive index of pattern recognition. How will the ambiguous pattern be seen if both unambiguous versions have already been presented to the subject, each at a different retinal position? Will it be "controlled" by the previous exposure which happened to share the same retinal locus? They found this to be the case and concluded that "traces" are somehow "localized" in the nervous system.

Although this result does seem to show some effect of input position, it should not be given too much weight. There are many reasons why a test stimulus might have been more readily interpreted in terms of the pattern that had appeared on the same side of the visual field than of the contralateral one. They share the same relations with the visually given framework, and may even share specific feelings of eyestrain. If such explanations seem *ad hoc,* we must remember that the persistence of recognition despite changes in the locus of the input is a far-ranging and biologically useful principle, which we should not abandon lightly. Its wide generality can be illustrated by a familiar psychological demonstration Take off your shirt and ask someone to trace a letter of the alphabet on your back with his finger. You will have little difficulty in identifying the letter he marks out, although it is quite unlikely that such a pattern ever appeared on your back before! This indifference to locus, and even to modality, is a remarkable phenomenon. In many ways, it seems closely akin to the transferability of motor skills. Having learned to make letters with a pencil in your hand, you can also make them, perhaps a little awkwardly, with one held in your teeth or your toes or even the crook of your elbow. We will consider later (Chapter 4) whether these motor equivalences may have the same basis as the perceptual ones.

While the process of pattern recognition may indeed be indifferent to the *locus* of the input, its *orientation* seems to be more critical. Everyday experience testifies to the perceptual changes which can be produced by rotation. Turn a square by 45° and you get a diamond instead; rotate a page of this book by 90° and you will find it difficult to read. The phenomenal effects of visual rotations have often been discussed (e.g., Arnheim, 1954, pp. 65–70). However, there was little serious experimentation in this area before the intricate series of studies by Rock (1956, also Rock & Heimer, 1957). Using the "chef-dog" figure (Figure 12) in the manner of Wallach and Austin, he found that rotation of the retinal image does not prevent recognition of relatively simple figures. They can be easily identified despite any change of orientation. However, the results suggest that this is only true as long as the subject knows which side of the figure is supposed to be "the top." Phenomenal orientation is all-important. An ambiguous figure tilted at 45° is *not* identified in terms of a previously exposed upright version *unless* the subject knows (through instructions) or perceives (with the aid of a tilted framework) that such a rotation has occurred. On the other hand, recognition encounters no difficulty if the head, and thus the retina, is itself turned 90°. This is apparently because the subject, aware of his own head movement, still knows which part of the stimulus pattern is really "up." Interestingly enough, a concurrent rotation of the stimulus, which together with the head movement actually leaves retinal orientation unchanged, *does* impair recognition—again unless the subject knows about it.

In short, while it is true that patterns can be recognized despite rotation, this accomplishment depends on a rather complex mechanism. The perceiver must isolate from the figure, or construct within the figure, a directed axis of orientation which defines some part as the top and another as the bottom. Only then is he able to identify it as pertaining to an earlier pattern which was also specifically oriented. Without this intervening stage of processing, recognition may not occur. These findings deserve careful consideration by pattern-recognition theorists, especially those who have been tempted by simple accounts based on peripheral neurology.

Rock's principle of phenomenal orientation holds only for what he called "simple" figures; it breaks down for reading, and for the identification of partial and ill-defined patterns. In the Höffding tradition, Rock and Heimer regard this as proof that "traces preserve their original orientation" after all (1957, p. 510). To me, it seems more likely that these tasks are affected because they involve eye movements. To read a page turned by 90°, the eyes would have to move up-and-down rather than left-to-right—not an easy change to make in such an overlearned motor skill. This explanation makes it easy to understand why a rotation of 180° (turning the page upside down) is less troublesome than one of 90°. The residual difficulty at 180° may appear because the necessary saccadic movements are then in the opposite direction.

Kolers, Eden, and Boyer (1964) have studied the effect of various rotations and transformations on reading speed. Rotation of the whole line or page through 180° (Figure 13b) is surprisingly easy to cope with. Kolers has pointed out that the Greeks once used a style of writing called *Boustrephedon* in which every other line was rotated in this way! Other transformations, such as arraying the letters from right-to-left (Figure 13c) or inverting each one individually (Figure 13a), produce much greater difficulties. On first consideration, these results seem paradoxical. Figure 13b involves *both* inversion (from top-to-bottom) *and* reversion (from left-to-right), yet it is easier than the lines which contain only a "single" transformation! However, such a finding makes perfect sense from Rock's viewpoint. Figure 13b is the only transform in which all the letters have the same relationship to each other, and to a phenomenally given "top" of the line, as in normal text. This relationship, and not retinal orientation itself, is what distinguishes *6* from *9* or *u* from *n*. When it is disrupted, reading becomes much more difficult.

However, it would be misleading to break off the discussion at this point. Other observations with rotated figures seem to carry a different implication or at least confuse matters considerably. For the most part, these are observations on children. It has been remarked (for exam-

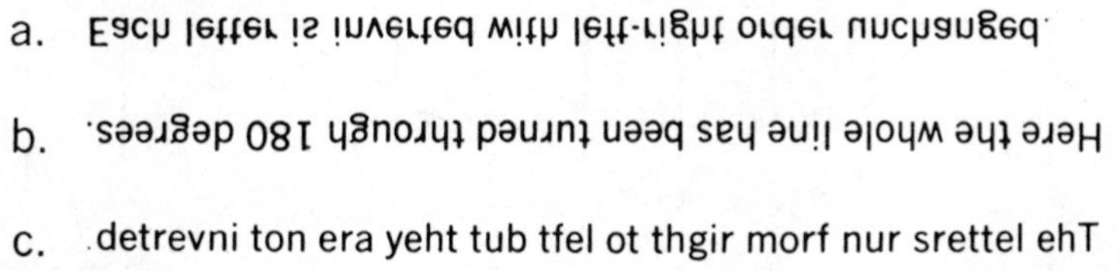

a. Each letter is inverted with left-right order unchanged.

b. Here the whole line has been turned through 180 degrees.

c. .detrevni ton era yeht tub tfel ot thgir morf nur srettel ehT

Figure 13. Transformations of text like those used by Kolers, Eden, and Boyer (1964). Figure 13a shows inversion of individual letters; 13b, the inversion of the line as a whole; 13c, a left-right reversal.

ple by Arnheim, 1954) that preschoolers often look at pictures without bothering to turn them right-side-up, and draw letters in reversed or inverted form. This suggests that their perceptual processes are relatively more "indifferent to orientation" than those of adults. Yet it would certainly be hard to believe that the complex reorienting mechanisms used by Rock's subjects would be still more effective in children! Moreover, Ghent and her collaborators (Ghent, 1960; Ghent & Bernstein, 1961) have shown clearly that children are *not* good at identifying rotated figures. Even though this book is not primarily concerned with developmental psychology, a short digression to deal with these apparent paradoxes cannot be avoided.

The important distinction to be made here is between active compensation for rotation, which Rock demonstrated in adults, and the simple failure to distinguish between two orientations of a figure. Both can lead to the same overt result. After all, many properties of figures remain invariant no matter how they have been turned. A rotated *A* still has a sharp point, a rotated *P* still has a closed loop, a *Y* still has a central acute angle, a *C* remains rounded. If recognition is based on the presence of critical features such as these, rather than on templates, it can also display "indifference to rotation." A subject who identified all rounded letters as *C*s would recognize a *C* in any orientation whatever, though of course he could not distinguish it from an *O*. If such simple and "orientation-proof" features are particularly important for pattern recognition in children, a number of superficially conflicting observations can be understood.

One paradigmatic experiment in this area is that of Gibson, Gibson, Pick, and Osser (1962). The children in their study were given a standard form like those at the left of Figure 14 and were to pick out any other forms that were "exactly like" it from a row that included at least one standard as well as the numerous transformations shown in the figure. The focus of Gibson *et al.*'s interest was on errors of commission: what kinds of incorrect stimuli would the children select? It turned out that some transforms, like the "perspective" shifts in columns 10 and 11 of Figure 14, were erroneously chosen by many children of all ages. Others,

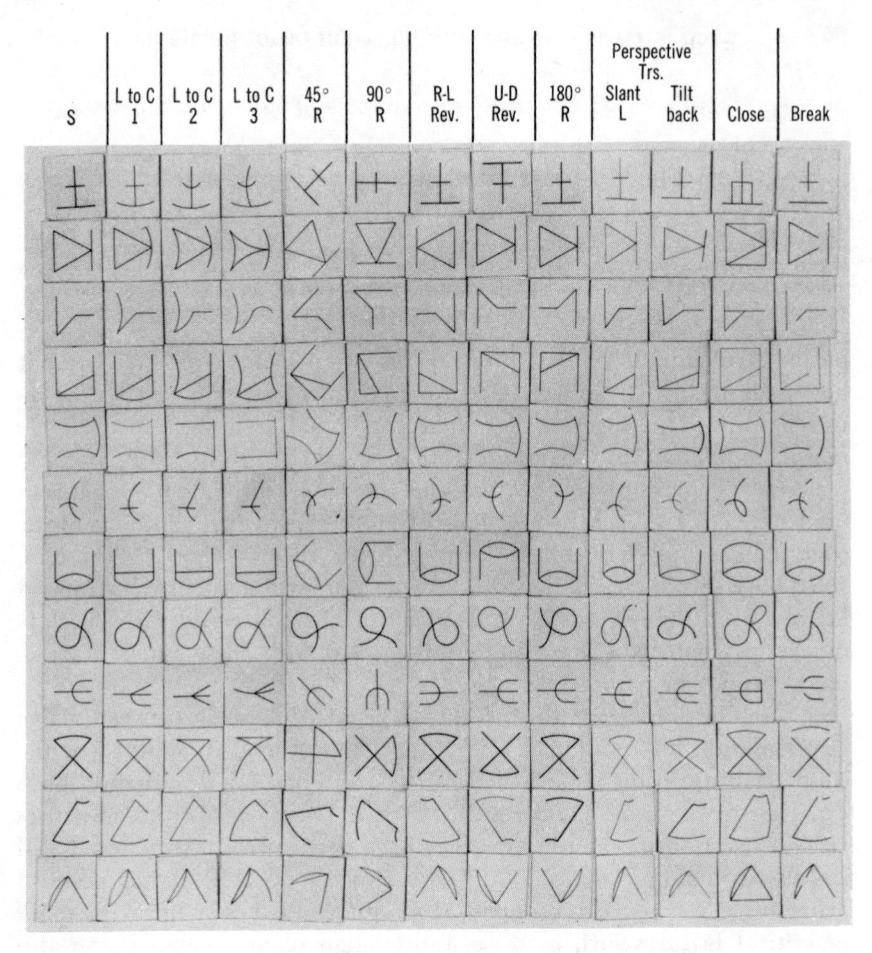


Figure 14. Stimuli used by Gibson, Gibson, Pick, and Osser (1962).

like the breaks and closures illustrated in columns 12 and 13, were rarely mistaken for the standards by any subject. However, the rotations (in columns 5–9) showed a clear developmental trend. Preschool children found them difficult to distinguish from the standards, while older children had much less trouble.

This result fits well with the general observations about preschool indifference to rotation and makes it clear that a confusion, a lack of discrimination, is involved. We need only suppose that the younger chillren are liable to notice just those features and properties that fail to distinguish between a pattern and some rotational transform of it. Even when these children make a correct match, they do so on the basis of simpler processes than an adult would use.

On such an interpretation, Ghent's findings are no longer paradoxical. She briefly displayed a single figure, having warned the children that it might be upside down in some cases. Afterwards, they were asked to pick it out of an array of figures that were all right-side-up. With both meaningful (Ghent, 1960) and meaningless (Ghent & Bernstein, 1961) stimuli, the children made more errors when the first figure was inverted than when its orientation matched that of the subsequent display. And, especially, in the first study, younger children made more errors than their older schoolmates. We may assume that here too, perception was fragmentary, and that the partial cues obtained in the brief exposure often led the children astray. The "bottom" of a rotated figure may have looked like the bottom of some other figure in the set of alternatives, for example. Adults in such an experiment might have noticed more during the brief flash, might have reconstructed the figure as a whole, and might have "rotated it mentally" before comparing it with the standard, as they did in Rock's experiment. Such complex processing was apparently beyond the capacity of most of the children. In this situation, then, fragmentary perception often prevented the children from matching a stimulus to its rotated twin correctly; in the experiment of Gibson *et al.*, fragmentary perception led to frequent confusions between them.

In a tachistoscopic study with adults, Mandes and Ghent (1963) showed that single figures are harder to recognize if the critical feature is at the bottom or at the right than if it is near the top or left. Their subjects did not know what orientation any particular figure would have. This finding is reminiscent of Bryden's (1960) work, discussed in Chapter 2. He showed that the left end of a string of figures is better reported than the right. Bryden went further, however, and showed that his tendency can be reversed if the subjects are told to scan from right-to-left. Mandes and Ghent might have made the same finding if they had used similar instructions. Such results, like those of Rock and Heimer (1957), show again that what matters for adults is how the subject "takes" the figure. Only where eye movements are involved, or at least highly overlearned scanning directions (Bryden's subjects could not reverse their letter scanning), are adults unable to compensate for rotations that they know about.

So much for displacement and rotation; what about size? It would seem to be just as important a variable as orientation, but there are very few relevant experiments. Ordinary experience does suggest that retinal size, at least, is of little importance for recognition. Hebb (1949, p. 91) assumes that this is true, buttressing his argument with animal experiments. Unquestionably, a person who stood 3 feet away when he was introduced to you will be recognizable in a fresh glance when he is across the room, his retinal image much diminished. But in such a situation there are many other cues, and you would probably "recognize" him even with his back turned. A study of this problem with the reversible-figure method of Rock (1956) and Wallach and Austin (1954) would be extremely useful. My hunch is that the results would bear out the principles established by Rock and Heimer (1957) for orientation. If the subject *knows* that a present figure has been somehow enlarged with respect to a past one, recognition should be easy; without this knowledge it may not occur.

What is the relation of all this to the familiar constancies of shape and size? The letters on this page keep their phenomenal shapes even when you tilt the book backward and skew the retinal image; they stay the same apparent size despite great changes in the retinal projection when the book is moved back and forth. Is this because they have already been recognized? Although we cannot go into the intricacies of perceptual constancy here, it is clear that the best answer is "no." Even unfamiliar objects would keep their shapes and sizes through such transformations. Instead, it seems that the constancies operate *before* recognition, to make recognition possible. This is not an invariable principle, however: there have been occasional demonstrations that size or shape judgments are affected by an identification already made.

### *EMPIRICAL OBSERVATIONS: ILL-DEFINED CATEGORIES AND EXPECTANCIES*

In theoretical accounts of pattern recognition, easily specified transformations like displacement and rotation have played the most prominent part. Any such transform leads to what may be called a "well-defined category." The analogy here is to Minsky's definition of a "well-defined problem" as one which provides "some systematic way to decide when a proposed solution is acceptable" (1961, p. 9). By this definition, the group of all patterns produced by rotating a given figure through any number of degrees is a well-defined category: there are fixed criteria for deciding whether any new figure belongs to it. But, just as many interesting problems turn out to be "ill-defined" (see Reitman, 1964, 1965, for discussion of this point), so also do most categories lack clear-cut boundaries and formulations. The *A*s in Figure 10 are unmistakable, but none of them is a simple transformation of any other, or of a standard. A little reflection shows that an *A* is actually a difficult thing to define.

Ill-defined categories are the rule, not the exception, in daily life. The visual distinctions between dogs and cats, or between beauty and ugliness, are ill-defined, just like the conceptual differences between creative science and hack work, or health and neurosis. So are the EEG patterns which indicate a particular stage of sleep, the X-ray shadows which suggest a tumor, the style of painting which identifies a Picasso, or the features which continue to characterize the face of a friend through the years.

In all such cases, there are two possibilities. The simple alternative is that an apparently "ill-defined" category is actually definable by some feature of the situation that has escaped the investigator's attention. The much-publicized work of the ethologists (e.g., Tinbergen, 1951) has shown that this is often true in animals. The situation which elicits fighting in the stickleback fish is no vaguely defined "hostile act," but a red spot of a certain kind. Similar discoveries are sometimes made about human perception, as when Hess (1965) recently discovered that the attractiveness of a face depends in part on whether its pupils are dilated.

However, much as these simple solutions might appeal to the cognitive theorist, it is clear that they will not work for many important categories. Attempts at mechanical pattern recognition have made this obvious. There is real need for a mechanical or computable way to distinguish among EEG patterns, for example, and a great deal of sophisticated effort has been expended to develop systems with this capacity, but no satisfactory ones have been built. Their failure is eloquent testimony that the criteria involved are anything but simple. Much effort has also gone into the recognition of handwritten or hand-printed letters. Some of these programs have achieved considerable success, but only with the aid of considerable complexity. The mechanisms by which they succeed will be discussed later. The point to be noted here is that genuinely ill-defined categories do exist and are regularly used by people in their daily activities. Any serious account of human pattern recognition will have to deal with them.

Assignment to a category is not always the endpoint of a cognitive process; it can be the beginning. Theories of pattern recognition do not only have to explain what mechanisms might lead to identification, but also how prior identification might affect these mechanisms. The stimulus which is identified as "13" when the subject is expecting numbers becomes "B" when he expects letters (Bruner & Minturn, 1955); the pattern which is readily described as an "S" on one occasion may be called a "5" or a "snake" or even a "meaningless blur" on others, or go unnoticed altogether. These are the familiar effects of "set" or "expectancy." In Chapter 2 some "set" effects were ascribed to priority of encoding, following the argument of Harris and Haber (1963). The same factor may be at work more generally. In terms of a template theory, one might suppose that the subject who expects numbers tries out "13" before he gets around to "B" and becomes somehow committed to it. The same principle could be used in an attribute model: the subject may look for different features when he is set for numbers than when he expects letters.

Detailed consideration of this issue is best left for Chapter 5, in connection with the identification of words. Nevertheless, it seems wise to stress the relationship between sets and ill-defined categories here. We have seen how many forms the letter *A* can take; does a subject who expects "a letter" have all of them in readiness, along with every version of *B, C, D, . . . Z?* Evidently, what he has in readiness is an ill-defined category. The same conclusion follows from an experiment by Leeper (1935), who asked subjects to identify figures such as those of Figure 15.

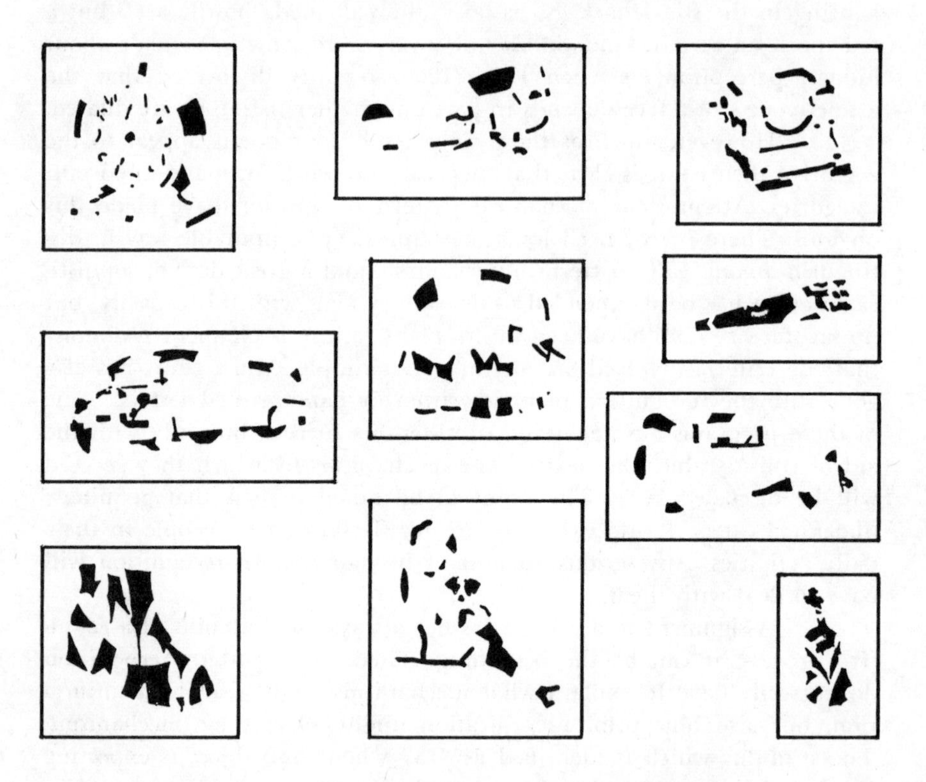

Figure 15. Figures used by Leeper (1935).

He found that verbal cues like "it is a musical instrument" were powerful aids to pattern recognition. Note that the figure at the lower right, which remains difficult even with this hint, becomes easy to organize if you are specifically told that it represents a violin. Yet "violin" itself is an ill-defined category, so far as its visual properties are concerned: what exactly do violins look like?

A more recent experiment by Bugelski and Alampay (1961) shows how such effects can be induced even without explicit verbal instructions. After showing several pictures of animals, they presented subjects with the ambiguous "rat-man" for identification (Figure 16). Most saw it as a rat, while subjects without special pretraining generally see the man instead. It is evident that the experimental group had

Figure 16. Rat-man figure used by Bugelski and Alampay (1961).

formed a "set" for animals, ill-defined though such a category may be.

Categorial sets do not always succeed in affecting visual organization. When he used a more complex figure that could be given two alternative interpretations, both relatively compelling (Figure 29 of Chapter 6), Leeper (1935) found verbal cues to be ineffective, while another procedure—the use of appropriately similar *visual* presentations—had a marked effect. This represents not merely a "set" but a species of visual memory, and will be discussed in Chapter 6. It is evident that we do not fully understand the powers and limitations of perceptual sets. It is equally evident that any theory of pattern recognition must reckon with them, and especially with their ill-defined characteristics.

## *THEORIES OF PATTERN RECOGNITION: TEMPLATE-MATCHING*

In the face of all these data, is a template theory possible? How could an input which was displaced, enlarged, or rotated find its template? How could a single template correlate well with every member of an ill-defined category?

The Gestalt psychologists had a simple answer to all these apparently difficult questions: "similarity." The present *A*, however it may be shaped and wherever it may be located, is similar to past *A*s; the present perceived loaf of bread is similar to previously perceived loaves, and thus to their "traces." Somehow the two similar mental or neural processes make contact, and we read "A" or go on to think of butter. Unfortunately, this answer offers little comfort to the theorist. Without some definition or criterion of similarity no empirical prediction is possible; we are left to guess whether any particular stimulus will be recognized or not. Without any explicit model or mechanism, the notion of "similarity" is only a restatement of the observed fact that some inputs are recognized while others are not. Yet psychologists have rarely suggested any supplementary mechanisms in connection with a template theory. Lashley's (1942) theory of "interference patterns," vague as it is, was perhaps the only serious attempt of this sort.

Far more specific solutions to Höffding's problem have been offered, however, in the attempt to program computers so they might recognize alphabetic characters or other patterns. Although many programmers have turned away from template-matching altogether, as we shall see, others have made it workable for a limited range of patterns. This is usually done by inserting a level of analysis *between* the input and the template. In this procedure, called "preprocessing," certain operations are routinely applied to the input at an early level. In general, preprocessing operations are of two kinds. One, only slightly interesting for our purposes, produces more accurate matches simply by "cleaning up" the input. This is almost essential for artificial systems, because they usually start with photographs or printed material which contains numerous small imperfections. A hand-printed *A,* converted to a crude mosaic for input to a computer, will generally include many isolated dots and blanks which are of no significance (Figure 17a). Indeed, even machine-printed material is surprisingly liable to such flaws. A simple clean-up program which fills small holes (Figure 17b) and eliminates isolated points (Figure 17c) can simplify the task of identification considerably. These are extremely *local* processes, and the transformations they produce are quite independent of the gross form or actual identity of the letter. Local processes which are functionally similar to these certainly operate in human vision to overcome the disturbances created by nystagmus, scattered light, intraocular irregularities, and so on.

Local preprocessing is, perhaps, of minor theoretical interest. But, in computers, a more powerful possibility is available: the input figure can be *normalized.* Regardless of where it first appears, it can be effectively moved so that its center (defined in some geometrical sense) coincides with the center of the input area. It can then be symmetrically expanded or contracted until its height and width reach some standard value, and rotated until its longest axis reaches a fixed orientation. If the actual identifying processes operate only on this normalized "image," they will be indifferent to changes in the position, size, and orientation of the original input. There are many preprocessing schemes which will

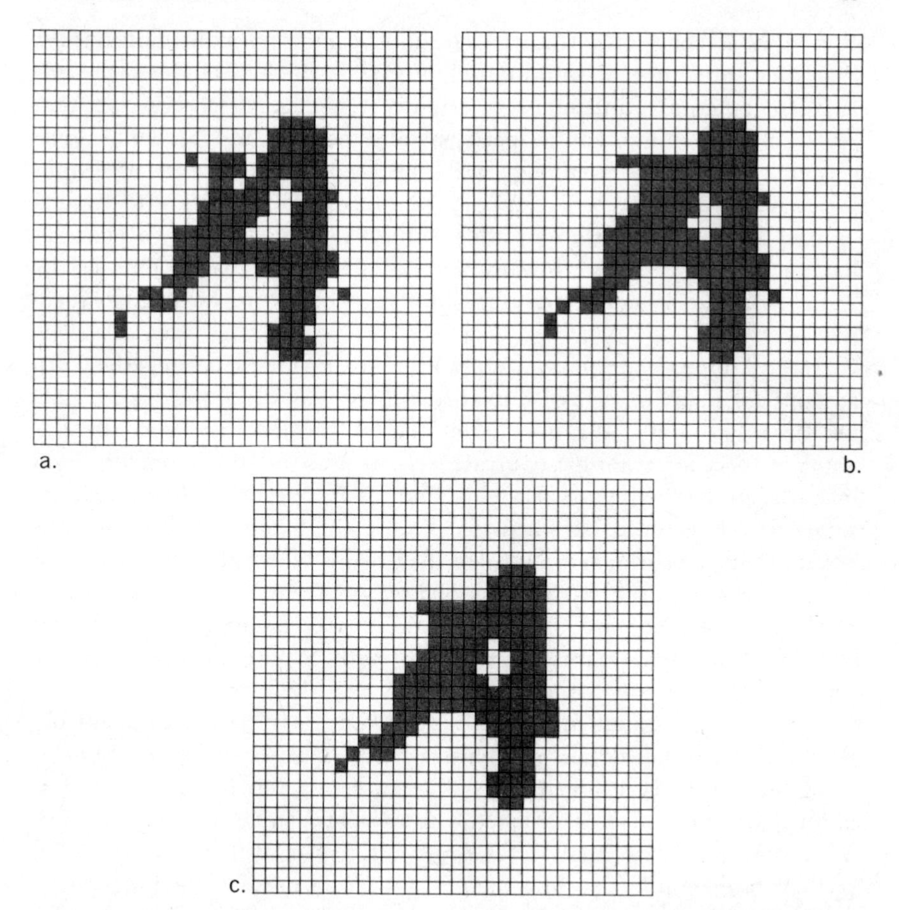


Figure 17. Local preprocessing of a hand-printed *A* by a computer, after Selfridge and Neisser (1960). In Figure 17a, all grid squares touched by the lines are filled in; in Figure 17b, "outliers" are eliminated; in 17c, "holes" are filled.

accomplish this. The model put forward by Pitts and McCulloch (1947, recently reviewed by Arbib, 1964), was perhaps the first to be suggested, and is often cited in this context. They proposed a specific—and rather complex—transformation which would give the same output for every member of certain well-defined categories. Today their procedure seems particularly vulnerable to the criticisms which follow.

The hypothesis that an additional level of processing intervenes between the input and the template is not entirely farfetched. Something very like "normalization" occurs when we move our eyes to fixate an object of interest, manipulate the retinal size of letters by holding a book at a preferred distance, or turn a picture right-side-up to look at it.

Viewed as a theory of pattern recognition in man, normalization implies that there are internal information processes which play the same role as these external adjustments. Certainly the general observation that recognition *is* indifferent to position, and perhaps to size, lends some support to this theory, though we shall see that other interpretations are available. More specific support comes from the studies with rotated figures, which showed that an adult subject is able to "take" a figure as having its "top" turned toward the bottom of the page. That is, he seems to rotate it subjectively, to normalize it, before he tries to identify it.

Although normalization and template-matching together can account for many aspects of human pattern recognition, they can hardly be the whole story. We have seen that in children, at least, there is another basis for stimulus equivalence. An even more convincing argument stems from the existence of ill-defined categories, for which no single template could be adequate. The *A*s in Figure 10 illustrate this point. Every one was actually identified as an *A* by all the subjects of our letter-recognition experiment (Neisser & Weene, 1960), without any use of context. Yet some of them are rather like *R*s, and others like *H*s or *4*s, if only their quantitative overlap with hypothetical templates is considered.

A final argument against a template theory is the frequent observation that small details can have a great influence on the category to which a pattern is assigned. The difference between a *Q* and an *O* is minute compared with the shape differences between *O*s, but it is decisive. The curvature of a small line segment can alter the expression of a cartoon face completely. The theoretical significance of this observation is not that the category is ill-defined (though it may be, in the case of facial expressions) but that such a critical feature would be quite insignificant in an overall comparison between a specimen *Q* and a template. It is evident, then, that figures are not always categorized on the basis of their overall, global properties.

Before turning to the attribute theories which these observations suggest, one more aspect of template-matching must be considered. The process of identification is not quite complete even after an input, from a well-defined category, has been normalized. There still remains the task of determining *which* template overlaps or correlates with the new pattern most strongly. The matching process must be carried out with each of the relevant alternatives, or at least with many of them. Here there are two theoretical alternatives which have given rise to a good deal of discussion: are the necessary comparisons conducted one at a time or all at once?

The successive alternative is sometimes designated by the misleading term "scanning" (e.g., Wiener, 1948). The intended analogy is with genuinely spatial searches, as when the sky is scanned with a radar beam in search of aircraft. But the search for a fitting template is not carried out through a real space, unless, as seems unlikely, the several templates are neatly laid out in different parts of the brain. Used in this way, the metaphor leads to confusion between a possibly sequential consideration of alternatives, on the one hand, and several genuinely spatial scans on the other. One kind of real "scanning" occurs when we examine a scene, or a list, by moving our eyes across it. In fact, we noted in Chapter 2 that a successive "scanning" readout can occur even without eye movements. These genuine progressions through different spatial positions must be clearly distinguished from the sequential conduct of a series of different *operations,* like a number of template comparisons. [To add to the confusion, some authors have proposed a kind of "scan" as a solution to one aspect of Höffding's problem: the input which occurs at a new retinal (and cortical) *position* may be somehow swept across the visual cortex until it finds a match at the old locus. I find it hard to take this notion seriously, though others do. It is logically equivalent to normalization for position only.]

A sequential search through alternative templates is not the only way to locate a match. We may also imagine that all of them are examined simultaneously, "in parallel." Such systems are not difficult to visualize. An array of tuning forks operates as a parallel recognition system for frequency, for example. If a fork of unknown pitch is struck near such an array, it is "compared with" the whole array at once and "arouses" only the fork which has a similar resonant frequency. (The Gestalt psychologists had a system of this sort in mind when they spoke of contact "by similarity" between perceptual process and trace.) Given the resources of electronic or neural circuitry, highly complex parallel systems can be constructed. The curiously shaped magnetic numerals which appear on many bank checks are "read" by a computer with 14 parallel recognition circuits, one for each character of the American Bankers Association "alphabet." The machine is so constructed that all circuits examine a representation of the input letter simultaneously, and the circuits are matched to the shapes of the letters so that not more than one of them is ever tempted to respond (Evey, 1959).

The distinction between sequential and parallel processing, which has arisen here in the context of template-matching, is just as relevant if recognition is based on properties or features. In such models, we can also ask whether the critical operations are carried out one at a time or all at once. Before elaborating on the theoretical consequences of these two alternatives, we must look at some observations on the temporal characteristics of human performance. Since extra cognitive operations must take more time in sequential systems, but not necessarily in parallel ones, such data are very relevant.

## *EMPIRICAL OBSERVATIONS: DECISION-TIME AND VISUAL SEARCH*

In a disjunctive reaction experiment, the subject must make one of *n* different responses, depending on which of *n* stimuli has appeared. Such reaction times can be used to study the speed of categorization. On the sequential theory, one would expect longer decision times with more alternatives; this is indeed the classical result, usually attributed to Merkel. Hick reopened the question in 1952 with an experiment in which the dependence of reaction time on *n* took a particularly neat form. Every time he doubled the number of alternatives, the reaction time was increased by a fixed amount. This meant that the time was a linear function of the logarithm of *n;* i.e., of the amount of "stimulus information." This was precisely what might be expected from some sequential feature-testing models; ideally, doubling the number of alternatives would mean that one more binary feature was needed to distinguish them. For a template theory, Hick's results were less comforting. If each of *n* templates were successively correlated with an input, the total time might be expected to grow linearly with *n,* not with log *n.*

Very much more linear functions do actually appear in a slightly different kind of experiment which, following Sternberg (1967), may be called "character-classification." Here the subject has only two responses, which we may call "yes" and "no" even if they are actually switch-closures. Sternberg (1963, 1966) used the digits from *0* through *9* as stimuli, assigning one, two, or four of them to the "yes" category and the remainder to "no." The average decision time increased by about 35 to 40 msecs. for every additional digit assigned to the smaller ("yes") set. He concluded that there is "an internal serial-comparison process whose average rate is between 25 and 30 symbols per second" (1966, p. 652).

The sequential-testing model also provides a good fit to the data of other experimenters, including Nickerson and Feehrer (1964), Shepherd (1964), Kaplan and Carvellas (1965), and Kaplan, Carvellas, and Metlay (1966). Kaplan and his collaborators do not measure classification-time directly. Instead, they estimate it from search rates, following a suggestion I had made earlier (Neisser, 1963b). If a subject successively examines the items on a list, looking for a particular target, his search rate can easily be converted into a measure of the average time spent with any single item. On a template model, this is the time needed to compare the item with a template of the target. If there are several targets, any of which can terminate the search, the subject must make several template comparisons for every item he examines. If he makes the comparisons sequentially, one after the other, the time-per-item must depend on the number of potential targets. The search procedure corresponds rather closely to Sternberg's character-classification experiments, despite superficial differences between the two paradigms. The termination of a search with "I've found it!" (or some key-pressing equivalent) is like a "yes" response, and the act of continuing the search corresponds to "no."

Kaplan's group has used several different variants of the search technique and found evidence for sequential processing in all of them. In the first experiment of Kaplan, Carvellas, and Metlay (1966), the subject glanced at a small group of letters which were the targets for a given trial, and then looked through a line of ten letters in an effort to find them all. Search time was recorded by eye-movement photography. In a second experiment described in the same paper, subjects had to search for and cancel certain letters in a block of newspaper copy; their search rate (between cancellations) was measured by hand-movement photography. A third method was used by Kaplan and Carvellas (1965). They asked subjects to scan an array flashed on a screen, in search of any member of a predefined set of letters. In this study the search rate was not measured directly; it was inferred, as in my own experiments, from the variation of total time with the position of the target in the display. (The method is illustrated with some of my own data in Figure 18. A straight line has been fitted to the observed search times by the method of least squares; its slope shows how much additional time is needed for each additional item examined.) Each of the Kaplan experiments found that time-per-item increased linearly with the number of different targets for which the subject was searching.

Results like these seem to give strong support to a sequential theory. However, another set of findings makes quite a different impression. Some of this work has been reviewed by Leonard (1961); more recent references are cited by Morin, Konick, Troxell, and McPherson (1965). In essence, it appears that Merkel's principle simply fails to apply when letters, numbers, or words are the stimuli, and their names are the responses. The time needed to respond then does *not* depend on how many numerals are used in the experiment, nor on the range of vocabulary from which a word is chosen (Pierce & Karlin, 1957). The number of alternatives is also unimportant if the stimuli and responses are highly "compatible," as when Leonard (1959) required his subjects to press down with the finger that had just been stimulated. Even with other material, the number of alternative possible stimuli may cease to affect reaction time after a great many trials (Mowbray & Rhoades, 1959). However, not all familiar or well-practiced materials display this freedom from Merkel's principle. Morin *et al.* (1965) showed that the time needed to name colors, symbols, animals, and the faces of friends *does* grow with the number of alternatives; only for letters did they find no increase.

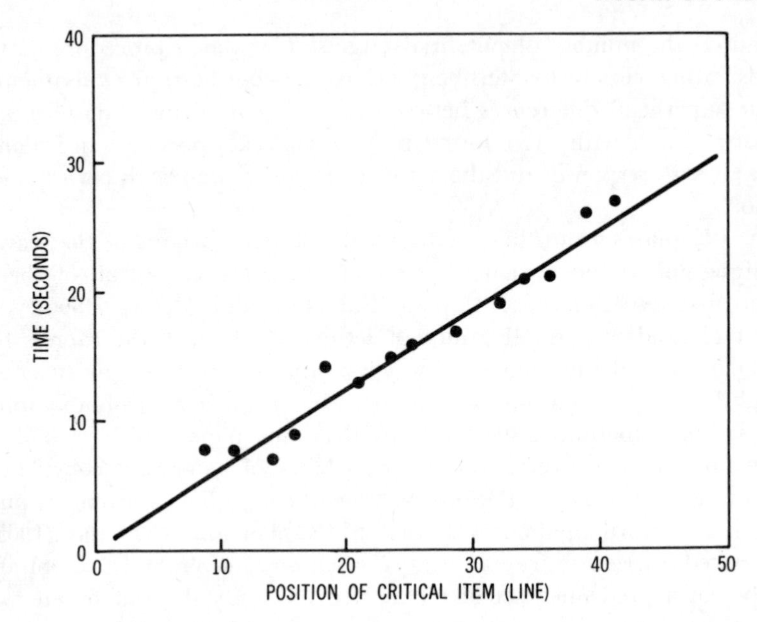


Figure 18. A line fitted to a set of observed search times. Its slope estimates the scanning rate (Neisser, 1964a).

There is evidently something special about the patterns used in reading, and about overlearned responses. We will consider later what it might be.

One might be tempted to account for these findings with a modified template theory, perhaps by assuming that naive subjects examine templates sequentially while practiced ones can do it in parallel. However, I do not believe that even this view is tenable. Instead, some form of feature or attribute theory seems to be necessary in cases where the number of alternatives does not matter. To clarify this point, I must briefly discuss some experiments carried out by my associates and myself at Brandeis University (Neisser, 1963b; Neisser, Novick, & Lazar, 1963; Neisser & Lazar, 1964; Neisser & Beller, 1965; Neisser & Stoper, 1965). Our experimental materials were 50-line lists, like the one in Figure 19a. Each contained a single "target letter" at an unpredictable position. As soon as the list appeared, the subject began scanning down from the top, looking for the target (*K* in Figure 19a). When he found it, he turned a switch which stopped a clock, and the total search time was recorded. From a dozen such times, the scanning time-per-item can be reconstructed by the method discussed earlier and illustrated in Figure 18. With practice in simple scans of this sort, subjects readily reach speeds of ten lines per second or more. The final speed depends, among other things, on the difficulty of the discrimination required. It takes much longer to find the *Z* in Figure 20b than in Figure 20a.

| a. | b. |
|---|---|
| EHYP | ZVMLBQ |
| SWIQ | HSQJMF |
| UFCJ | ZTJVQR |
| WBYH | RDQTFM |
| OGTX | TQVRSX |
| GWVX | MSVRQX |
| TWLN | ZHQBTL |
| XJBU | ZJTQXL |
| UDXI | LHQVXM |
| HSFP | FVQHMS |
| XSCQ | MTSDQL |
| SDJU | TZDFQB |
| PODC | QLHBMZ |
| ZVBP | QMXBJD |
| PEVZ | RVZHSQ |
| SLRA | STFMQZ |
| JCEN | RVXSQM |
| ZLRD | MQBJFT |
| XBOD | MVZXLQ |
| PHMU | RTBXQH |
| ZHFK | BLQSZX |
| PNJW | QSVFDJ |
| CQXT | FLDVZT |
| GHNR | BQHMDX |
| IXYD | BMFDQH |
| QSVB | QHLJZT |
| GUCH | TQSHRL |
| OWBN | BMQHZJ |
| BVQN | RTBJZQ |
| FOAS | FQDLXH |
| ITZN | XJHSVQ |
| VYLD | MZRJDQ |
| LRYZ | XVQRMB |
| IJXE | QMXLSD |
| RBOE | DSZHQR |
| DVUS | FJQSMV |
| BIAJ | RSBMDQ |
| ESGF | LBMQFX |
| QGZI | FDMVQJ |
| ZWNE | HQZTXB |
| QBVC | VBQSRF |
| VARP | QHSVDZ |
| LRPA | HVQBFL |
| SGHL | HSRQZV |
| MVRJ | DQVXFB |
| GADB | RXJQSM |
| PCME | MQZFVD |
| ZODW | ZJLRTQ |
| HDBR | SHMVTQ |
| BVDZ | QXFBRJ |

**Figure 19.** Lists for visual searching (Neisser, 1964a). In Figure 19a, the target is *K;* in 19b, the target is a line that does not contain the letter *Q*.

| a. | b. |
|---|---|
| ODUGQR | IVMXEW |
| QCDUGO | EWVMIX |
| CQOGRD | EXWMVI |
| QUGCDR | IXEMWV |
| URDGQO | VXWEMI |
| GRUQDO | MXVEWI |
| DUZGRO | XVWMEI |
| UCGROD | MWXVIE |
| DQRCGU | VIMEXW |
| QDOCGU | EXVWIM |
| CGUROQ | VWMIEX |
| OCDURQ | VMWIEX |
| UOCGQD | XVWMEI |
| RGQCOU | WXVEMI |
| GRUDQO | XMEWIV |
| GODUCQ | MXIVEW |
| QCURDO | VEWMIX |
| DUCOQG | EMVXWI |
| CGRDQU | IVWMEX |
| UDRCOQ | IEVMWX |
| GQCORU | WVZMXE |
| GOQUCD | XEMIWV |
| GDQUOC | WXIMEV |
| URDCGO | EMWIVX |
| GODRQC | IVEMXW |

Figure 20. Lists for visual searching (Neisser, 1964a). The target is *Z* in both lists.

A template theory would suggest that the subject compares each letter on the list with a template of the target and stops only if it fits. This seems extremely unlikely. Subjects insist that they do not "see" individual letters at all, that everything is a blur from which the target "stands out." The times involved suggest that practiced subjects take in several lines at a glance. Indeed, tasks which require line-by-line examination (e.g., "which line of Fig. 19b does not contain a *Q?*") produce much slower search rates. Nor do search times increase linearly with the width of the column, as a letter-template view might suggest. (They do increase slightly, however, for reasons which we are still exploring.)

One of our most interesting findings was that multiple searches take no longer than simple ones, provided that the subjects are sufficiently practiced. It is possible to look for "*Z* or *K*" as rapidly as for one of these targets alone. In fact, a subject can look for any of *ten* targets just as rapidly as for a single one (Neisser, Novick, & Lazar, 1963). This finding is theoretically important, since it seems to rule out sequential comparison as the mechanism involved. However, ten targets is not a remarkable number in terms of human cognitive capacity. The experienced readers in a "newsclip" agency are a case in point. Such a reader can search through the daily paper at over 1000 words a minute, looking for any reference to the agency's clients, of whom there are usually hundreds. The feasibility of multiple search in such a practical context suggests that our own results are not due to artifacts or to demand characteristics.

### *THEORIES OF PATTERN RECOGNITION: A SIMPLE FEATURE-ANALYZING MODEL*

The general tenor of these results suggested an interpretation in terms of parallel processing and separate features, based on the more general "Pandemonium" model proposed by Selfridge (1959). A brief account of this interpretation may be helpful, even though I now believe that it should be substantially modified. Such an account will at least show an attribute model in explicit form and prepare the reader for the more general theories which follow.

The fundamental assumption was that the cognitive system used in searching is hierarchically organized. At its first level are "analyzers" which test the input for the presence of various specific features. The details of these features are not known: they might be parts of letters, certain kinds of gaps between them, even global properties like roundness, angularity, or the occurrence of parallel lines. There must be very many such analyzers, all operating simultaneously on every relevant portion of the input. Behind them, the model postulated a level of "letter-analyzers." These are not at all like templates; they do not resemble the input patterns. Instead, each one responds to a particular weighted, probabilistic combination of tests at the earlier level. No single attribute is uniquely necessary to arouse the Z-analyzer, for example; various combinations can do so. Moreover, in tasks where isolated letters are to be identified (e.g., tachistoscopic recognition), a given set of features will generally arouse more than one letter-analyzer. Identification then depends on which is most strongly aroused. Dominant activity by a single one was thought of as the equivalent of "seeing" the letter, and thus as the prerequisite for an identifying response.

In the search situation, letter-analyzers other than those for the target can be effectively "turned off," while all the feature-analyzers continue to test the input. This means that activity is confined to the feature level until the target actually appears. As a result, the irrelevant letters themselves are not seen. Practice is effective because it brings different and faster first-level analyzers into play. In many cases, these are sensitive to features that characterize whole blocks of letters, rather than to properties of letters individually. In more difficult discriminations, no really fast analyzers ever suffice, and so practice does not have much effect on the search rate.

When the subject is asked to look for any of several targets, in a multiple search task, more first-level operations are needed than before. Again, however, no letter-analyzers become active until a target has been found. Because the operations at the feature level are in parallel, the extra ones do not increase the search time. The subject should not be thought of as waiting until all the feature-analyzers have finished with a given stimulus-item or group, before proceeding to the next one. Instead, he settles on a fixed scan rate; one that allows most of the necessary feature-processing to occur on most glances. Occasionally some of it remains unfinished; this is one source of the frequent errors of omission in these experiments.

The principle of "parallel processing," which distinguished this model from certain other theories of pattern recognition, actually appeared in it in two distinguishably different forms. First, the feature-analyzers of the model were thought to be *spatially parallel;* the same operations can be carried out simultaneously all over the effective portion of the retina. A *Z* anywhere in the field immediately arouses the analyzers for acute angles, parallels, etc., and thus eventually activates the *Z*-analyzer. It is this postulate which no longer seems plausible to me, and which will be rejected in Chapter 4. In addition, the feature-analyzers are *operationally parallel.* That is, they work independently of one another; the test for acute angles is in no way contingent on any other test outcome. Indeed, in the model the analyzers were supposed to operate *simultaneously* as well as independently, and it is this simultaneity which appears in the experiments with multiple targets. Nevertheless, an operationally parallel system could be "simulated" even on a computer that carries out only one operation at a time. Its defining property is not simultaneity, but the fact that no analyzer depends on the course or the outcome of processing by the others.

These two concepts of parallel processing can be further clarified by considering their opposites, which may be called *serial* and *sequential* processing respectively. A spatially serial activity is one which analyzes only a part of the input field at any given moment. The reading of letters from a tachistoscopic display, discussed in Chapter 2, is a good example of serial processing. On the other hand, the term *sequential* refers to the manner in which a process is organized; it is appropriate when the analysis consists of successive, interrelated steps. A model involving feature-analyzers is sequential if the output of earlier analyzers determines which ones are to be applied later.

Any particular scheme for sequential analysis can be specified in terms of the familiar type of diagram called a "decision tree" because it has so many alternative "branches." For an example of such a tree, it will be helpful to consider Feigenbaum's (1963) EPAM program, the "Elementary Perceiver and Memorizer" (see also Feigenbaum & Simon, 1962, 1963). EPAM actually develops its decision tree—which Feigenbaum

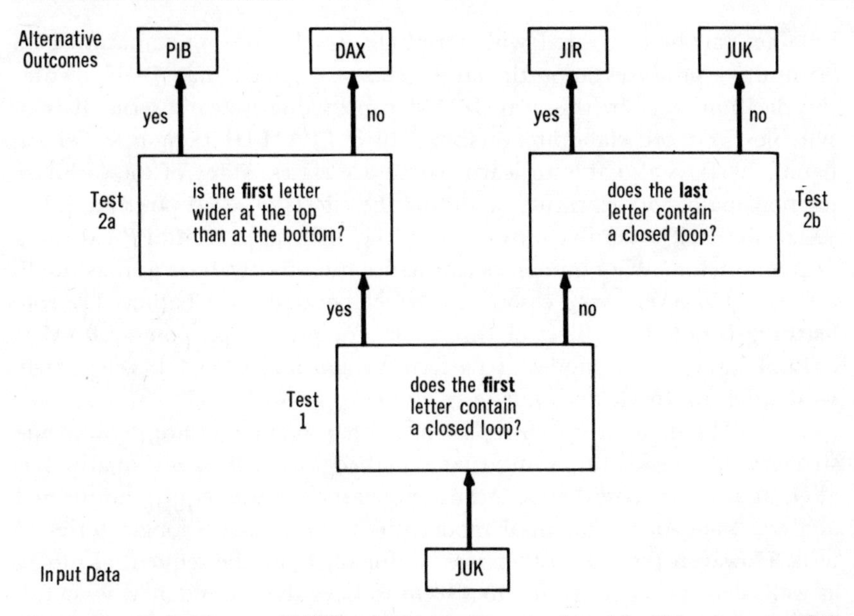


Figure 21. A decision tree which might have been developed by Feigenbaum's (1963) EPAM program.

calls a "discrimination net"—as a result of encounters with stimuli. A very simple and partially developed EPAM tree is illustrated in Figure 21.

Given a nonsense syllable, this tree would apply two tests, and thereby identify it as one of four possible alternatives. Tests *2a* and *2b* are never *both* applied, whatever the input may be; instead the outcome of test *1* assigns the input to one "branch" or the other, and the second test is contingent on the branch chosen. This system is extremely efficient, since it reduces the number of necessary tests to a minimum. On the other hand, it is quite vulnerable to error, since even a single misstep will put the program irrevocably on the wrong branch. By contrast, a single malfunctioning test will generally have little effect in an operationally parallel program.

This use of EPAM as an illustrative example is very far from doing it justice. Two of its other accomplishments should not go unmentioned. First, if EPAM misclassifies a syllable—as must happen when no test in the system happens to distinguish it from another syllable already incorporated—a new test will be invented, and new branches grown accordingly. For example, the tree in Figure 21 would sort *DEF* to the same terminal as *DAX,* but if it found that they differed in some respect—perhaps in whether or not the *last* letter was wider at the top than the bottom—a test based on this difference would replace the present *DAX* terminal and lead to two distinct branches. Second, "response" syllables can be associated with terminals, so that the presentation of a "stimulus" produces a particular "response," which may itself reenter the decision tree. In this way EPAM can gradually learn serial lists of syllables. A more elaborate version, called EPAM-III (Simon & Feigenbaum, 1964), is also able to learn paired associates. Many of the ordinary phenomena of rote learning, including the effects of serial position, intraserial similarity, familiarization, and the like, appear in EPAM to a degree which matches human performance quantitatively as well as qualitatively. However, for reasons to be elaborated in Chapter 11, rote learning is not the subject of this book. For present purposes, EPAM is only of interest as a model of pattern recognition, where its relentlessly sequential approach does not seem quite appropriate.

The data on searching for more than one target are perhaps the strongest reason for supposing that visual cognition is operationally parallel, at least at some levels. Additional targets must require additional analyzers, and in a sequential model this would mean a longer series of tests. However, there are other reasons for rejecting the sequential model as well. Perception generally does seem to have the redundancy, wastefulness, and freedom from gross misrepresentation that characterize a parallel process. This point has been noted by Brunswik (1956, pp. 91–92), and by others also. Moreover, one might expect a parallel process to resist introspection, since so much unrelated activity is going on simultaneously. The early stages of perception do have precisely this quality. So do some kinds of thinking, as we shall see later on.

## *THEORIES OF PATTERN RECOGNITION: FEATURES AND PARTS*

We must turn now from this particular model of the way letters are identified to more general conceptions of pattern recognition, especially those based on some kind of feature analysis. It is appropriate to begin with the work of Oliver Selfridge, on which the visual search model was based. Selfridge (1955, 1956) was one of the first workers in the computer field to recognize the complexity of the problem. My Figure 9, for example, is taken from his discussion of context effects, in a paper (1955) which introduced the notions of preprocessing and feature extraction as well. In 1959, he proposed a more systematic model for pattern recognition, called "Pandemonium," which is represented in Figure 22. In a Pandemonium, each possible pattern (perhaps each letter of the alphabet) is represented by a demon (the "cognitive demons," in the upper row of Figure 22). Being egotistic, such a demon incessantly looks for evidence (suitable results offered by inferior "computational demons") that he is being depicted in the "image," or input. To the extent that he

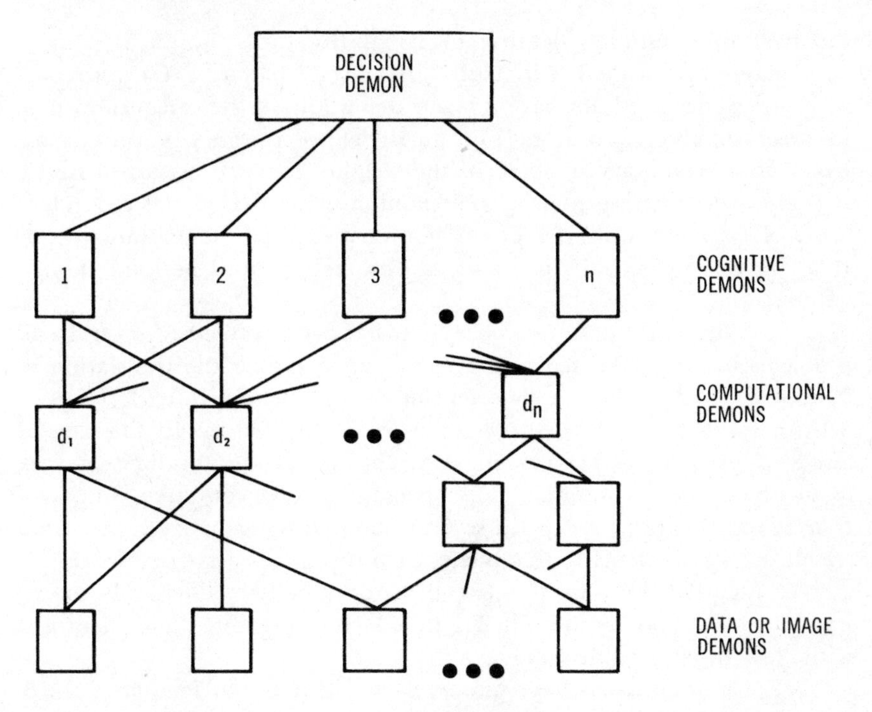


Figure 22. Parallel processing in Selfridge's (1959) "Pandemonium" program.

finds such evidence, he shouts loudly, and the loudest shout in his Pandemonium is taken by the "decision demon" as identifying the stimulus. The computational demons perform operations of varying complexity on the input, all simultaneously. They are the feature-analyzers of the search model, while the cognitive demons correspond to the letter-analyzers.

Such a theory is far removed from template-matching, and also from sequential testing, as a comparison among Figures 11, 21, and 22 will illustrate. In principle, a Pandemonium can recognize *any* pattern, as long as some weighted combination of the features being tested serves to distinguish category-members from nonmembers. The features to be analyzed (by the computational demons) may be of any desired sort. Whole-qualities ("Does it have a closed perimeter?" "Is it concave downward?") are as eligible as partial ones ("Does it have a little *Q*-defining stroke at the bottom?"). Moreover, a Pandemonium can easily improve its performance through learning. It need only be told, trial by trial, whether its identification of the preceding pattern was correct, so it can increase or decrease certain "weights" associated with the cognitive demon that was selected. (These weights govern the cognitive demon's dependence on the particular computational demons which shouted on the trial in question.) Because of its ability for self-improvement, a Pandemonium can deal with truly "ill-defined" patterns. The programmer or designer need not have *a priori* definitions of the categories which it is to recognize. Even a "set" for an ill-defined category is conceivable, based on a temporary increase in the weights given to certain features. It is also worth noting that a Pandemonium with a large and redundant array of computational demons is not very sensitive to malfunction or error. If one demon fails to shout, the others may well be loud enough without him.

The Pandemonium conception has been applied to several real problems in automatic pattern recognition, including the translation of hand-sent Morse code and the identification of hand-printed letters (see Selfridge & Neisser, 1960, for a summary of this work). In the case of hand-printed letters (Doyle, 1960), a system with about 30 rather complex feature-analyzers was simulated on a general-purpose computer. In operation, it was first presented with several hundred letters as examples from which to "learn." During this phase, each input was accompanied by its correct identification. In the test phase, unfamiliar letters—all drawn from the same pool as those in Figure 10—were presented and identified with close to 90 percent accuracy.

Other theorists have also preferred features to templates. N. S. Sutherland (1957, 1959), starting from the discriminative capacities of animals rather than from the design of automata, arrived at a theory very similar to Selfridge's, and has continued to develop it (1963a, 1963b). The term "analyzer" was introduced by him. He argued that, if an animal can discriminate between two stimuli, it must possess some mechanism which reacts differentially to the two; discrimination learning consists of attaching suitable responses to the outputs of the right analyzers. The experimenter can infer a good deal about the analyzers by noting (*a*) what patterns can and cannot be discriminated by the animal, and (*b*) what new patterns can elicit the same response in a transfer test.

Sutherland's original work was done with octopuses (Sutherland, 1957). These animals easily discriminate between vertical strokes and horizontal ones, but apparently cannot distinguish a line sloping 45° to the right from one which slopes 45° to the left. This led Sutherland to assume that they possess analyzers for verticality (specifically, for the ratio of maximum vertical extent to square root of area) and horizontality, but not for other inclinations. The theory was subsequently elaborated to deal with differences in discriminative capacity between octopuses and rats, and to include other hypothetical analyzers as well.

Bruner, too, has emphasized that pattern recognition depends on the identification of specific features or *attributes* of the stimulus. "That thing is round and nubbly in texture and orange in color and of such-and-such size—therefore an orange" (1957b, p. 124). Less interested in specific mechanisms than Selfridge or Sutherland, he has devoted more attention to other aspects of the pattern-recognition process. These include the various effects of set and expectancy on recognition, and the processes which serve to verify tentative identifications by "match-mismatch signals" or "confirmation checks."

All of these theories share a willingness to postulate rather complex processes at the level of feature-analysis. Selfridge's computational demons extract properties like "concave downward"; Sutherland assumes the existence of analyzers for "horizontality"; Bruner speaks of such attributes as "round" or "nubbly in texture." How does the organism come to have such useful and highly specific systems? Bruner is not specific on this point, but Sutherland (1959) argues explicitly that they must be innate. For Selfridge, too, they are effectively "inborn" and unmodifiable. A Pandemonium can modify the weights assigned to various feature-tests, but it cannot construct any new ones. Those originally provided by the programmer must suffice.

Many psychologists find it unlikely that the organism could start out with such highly differentiated and well-adapted structures. They would prefer to think that the feature-analyzers themselves are developed by experience. One such alternative has been explored by Uhr (1963; see also Uhr, Vossler, & Uleman, 1962) in a computer program. His program incorporates a level of feature-analyzers, whose combined outputs lead to recognition just as in a Pandemonium. But Uhr's feature-analyzers are simply $5 \times 5$ matrices of black and white (much smaller than the figures being categorized). They can contain *any* arbitrary local pattern, and function like templates for the portion of the input they happen to cover. At the start, the operating set of analyzers is chosen at random from among the $(2)^{25}$ possible matrices of this sort, but it is subject to change as the result of experience. Old "features" (i.e., specific matrices) are discarded if they do not contribute to correct recognition, and new ones are then tried. He has achieved considerable success with this program, not only in recognizing letters but with other ill-defined patterns as well.

Uhr's program, while it is more susceptible to modification by experience than the other theories we have considered, still has a good deal of initial structure. Some theorists, however, have assumed that the organism starts out with very little structure and must acquire virtually *everything* from experience. Ideally, one might think of the newborn nervous system as only a randomly connected network of neurons, which develops complexity gradually through commerce with the environment. This assumption leads to what are called "neural net" theories. If such a network could actually develop the functional equivalent of analyzers within a plausible number of trials—which is doubted by Minsky and

Selfridge (1961)—the analyzers to appear first might be relatively simple and local. The attributes they could detect might well be elementary *parts* of figures, rather than wholistic features like roundness. Such, at least, was the argument made by Hebb (1949) in his influential book, which is still the most thoughtful and wide-ranging discussion of visual cognition that we have.

Hebb's account of pattern recognition in the mature individual resembles the other feature-oriented theories in many respects. The first level of processing is assumed to consist of "cell-assemblies" which act much like feature-analyzers or demons. However, the only features extracted at this level are lines, angles, and contours. In effect, this model (like Uhr's) is a cross between a feature and a template theory: the "features" are really simple templates for parts. To solve Höffding's problem—that response does not seem to depend on retinal locus—Hebb uses spatially parallel processing. The cell-assemblies, or part-templates, are reduplicated all over the input region, and corresponding ones are connected together. In this way, a line of a particular orientation (say) excites what is effectively the same assembly wherever it happens to appear. The cell-assemblies themselves are supposedly combined by selective experience into what Hebb calls "phase sequences," whose role is similar to that of cognitive demons.

Hebb's reason for restricting himself to parts, instead of the more general class of features later envisaged by other theorists, is his fundamental assumption that the entire system develops from an undifferentiated neural net on the basis of experience. However, we may well ask whether cell-assemblies would actually be formed, and maintain their integrity, under the conditions he describes. This question has been frequently raised, and modifications of the theory have been suggested to make the cell-assembly a more plausible product of visual experience (e.g., Milner, 1957). Other neural net theories, like Rosenblatt's (1958) "Perceptron," have been challenged on similar grounds: could such a net ever learn any nontrivial categorization? Minsky thinks not (1961; also Minsky & Selfridge, 1961), and indeed the achievements of the "Perceptron" have not substantiated the early claims of its proponents. There is no doubt that any attempt to develop a powerful cognitive system out of randomness, whether as psychologically sophisticated as Hebb's or as naive as Rosenblatt's, faces grave difficulties. (Further discussion of the "Perceptron" may be found in the review of pattern recognition by Uhr, 1963, and in Arbib, 1964.)

Problems of perceptual development are, strictly speaking, outside the scope of this book. However, we cannot ignore another difficulty faced by such theories. Even if part-templates do exist, it is hard to see how they could account for pattern recognition in adults. One obvious source of difficulty is the identification of ill-defined patterns. The *A*s of

Figure 10 do seem to have properties in common, but congruent angles and lines are hardly the whole story. Moreover, there seems to be a complex, nonlocal, and innate feature-analyzer at the very heart of Hebb's theory, in the form of what he calls "primitive unity" (1949, p. 19). Even persons opening their eyes for the first time, after a cataract operation, see visual objects as separate and individual wholes. As far as Hebb is concerned, this elementary figure-ground segregation is simply a fact outside his explanatory system. To me, it indicates the presence of at least some feature-analyzers that do not look at parts, but at properties of whole figures. If analyzers of this sort are present from the beginning, why not assign them some serious role in later pattern recognition? In Chapter 4, we will see that this means at least a partial retreat from the notion of parallel processing, and we will examine the arguments for making such a retreat. First, however, an empirical detour is necessary. A review of pattern recognition would hardly be complete without consideration of some recent experiments that bear specifically on the differences among parts, features, and templates.

## *EMPIRICAL OBSERVATIONS: FEATURES AND PARTS*

One important line of research in recent years has been the study of perceptual fragmentation. Under certain stimulus conditions, perceived figures break into segments, some or all of which may disappear. The effect can be observed in a particularly striking way with the optical technique known as the "stopped image" (Pritchard, Heron, & Hebb, 1960; Pritchard, 1961). In this procedure, eye movements are compensated for and cannot produce any shift of the optical image on the retina; that is, they do not change the proximal stimulus. Perceived figures soon disappear in whole or in part when this is done, presumably because of "fatigue" at the retina or elsewhere in the visual system. Similar effects occur even with ordinary ocular fixation on figures which are faint or defocused (McKinney, 1963, 1966).

The disappearance of parts in these experiments is not haphazard. Lines come and go as wholes, for example, so that triangles generally lose one side at a time, while the letter *T* loses either its entire upright or its entire crosspiece. Parallel lines tend to appear and disappear together, even at considerable separations. Curvilinear figures often undergo simplification and gap-completion. Whenever possible, the fragmentation tends to produce meaningful patterns rather than nonsensical ones. Figure 23 illustrates this phenomenon. A monogram breaks into recognizable letters more often than into unnamable fragments; a word characteristically loses exactly those letters which will leave another definable word behind; the eye in a profile disappears and reappears as a unit.

Figure 23. Perceptual fragmentation in "stopped images." The figures at the left are stimulus patterns; the others are typical products of fragmentation (from Pritchard, 1961).

As Hebb points out in his stimulating review (1963), the occurrence of fragmentation tends to support the notion that there are functional subsystems in perception, even if the nature of the fragments is not always what would have been predicted from his theory. Certainly, it gives little comfort to a template hypothesis.

A particularly interesting result is that of McKinney (1966). He used the figures illustrated in Figure 24 as fragmentation targets. One group of subjects was shown the patterns labelled *1, 2, 3, 4, 5,* and *6,* with the indication that each was a letter. Another group was given patterns *7, 2, 8, 4, 9,* and *6.* They were *not* told to expect. letters, and thought of all the patterns as meaningless. In the upshot, patterns *2, 4,* and *6* (shown to both groups) underwent far less fragmentation for subjects who saw them as letters than for those who took them to be meaningless designs! McKinney interprets his data in terms of the verbal labels ("L," "T," and "V") used by the first group of subjects, and thus as resulting from "neural firing in the language centre" (1966, p. 241). However, another possible interpretation should not be overlooked.

We have already referred to Orne's (1959, 1962a) observation that every experiment has "demand characteristics"—that all subjects try to figure out what is expected of them, and most subjects try to behave

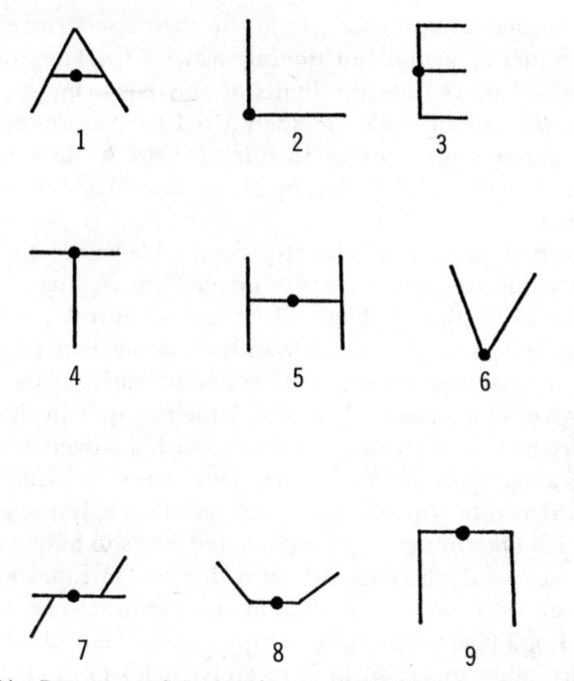


Figure 24. Patterns used in McKinney's (1966) study of fragmentation.

accordingly. Sometimes it is difficult to make sense of an experiment, and under those conditions subtle cues from the experimenter's behavior may be particularly important; such a case was considered in Chapter 2. In other instances, demand characteristics may arise simply from the nature of the task. This is a very real possibility in fragmentation studies. A subject who is shown letters under conditions where they soon become indistinct and asked to "report if any portion of the letter seems to break up and disappear" may interpret his task as one of holding it together as long as possible. On the other hand, a subject shown meaningless patterns may interpret similar instructions in the opposite way to see if he can break them up.

It should be carefully noted that the demand-characteristic interpretation does not suggest that the subject is deceiving the experimenter, or reporting phenomena which he has not actually seen. Common experience shows that the effect of intention on the perception of ambiguous figures is very great. Merely by "trying," we can affect the way Figures 12, 16, 26, or 29a appear to us. It seems more than likely that a similar kind of "trying" could affect the appearance of the stimuli in a fragmentation experiment. This possibility is particularly plausible in terms of the "constructive" theory of visual cognition to be presented in the next chapter.

A second kind of data relevant to these issues comes from microelectrode studies of neural functioning. Strictly speaking, neuroanatomy and physiology are outside the limits of this book, but an exception is justified in the case of work so widely cited by pattern-recognition theorists. The major contributions in this field are by Lettvin, Maturana, McCulloch, and Pitts (1959), and by Hubel and Wiesel (1959, 1962; also Hubel, 1963).

Lettvin and his collaborators were able to record the activities of single fibers in the optic nerves of unanesthetized frogs, while presenting various visual stimuli. These fibers are not direct extensions of the first layer of receptors; they come from the intermediate ganglion cells of the eye. Hence, if any feature-analyzers occur early in the frog's visual system, Lettvin *et al.* expected to record their *out*put in the optic nerve. They had come to suspect the existence of such analyzers from Selfridge's arguments about pattern recognition and hoped to demonstrate their physiological reality. In this, they were astonishingly successful.

Each fiber in the frog's optic nerve seems to have its own "receptive field"—a useful physiological term due to Hartline, which denotes the region of retina where stimulation can produce some activity in the fiber. The frog's fibers turn out to be quite selective in the *kind* of stimulation which must appear in their receptive fields to produce a response. One type of fiber, termed a "net convexity detector" (or, less formally, as a "bug perceiver") responds if a small dark object enters the receptive field or moves about in it, and continues to respond if the object becomes stationary in the field. Such fibers do not respond to large moving edges, nor to changes in the overall illumination. Other fiber types found included "sustained contrast detectors," "moving edge detectors," and "net dimming detectors." All of them have rather obvious significance in the life of the frog, as he catches flies, escapes from the looming shadows of predators, and the like. The results seem to show clearly that complex *features* of the input, not simply its parts, are abstracted very early in the visual system. (For a more detailed introduction to this work, see Arbib, 1964.)

Hubel and Wiesel used a similar method, but their experimental animal was the cat, and their most interesting recordings were from cells in the visual cortex rather than those in the optic nerve. They found cells that were much concerned with the *orientation* of stimuli on the retina. Many of these had what Hubel and Wiesel called "simple fields." These fields were divided into excitatory and inhibitory areas in such a way that a particularly oriented edge, at just the right position, gave a much stronger response than any other stimulus. In other "complex" fields, the exact position of the edge seemed irrelevant as long as it was somewhere in a relatively large area, but its orientation remained critical. Hubel and Wiesel surmised that these latter cells could be fired by any of a cluster of the former, more specific ones. As in the case of Lettvin *et al.*'s fiber types, these elements were all reduplicated throughout the input area; that is, they were spatially parallel. Unlike the optic-nerve fibers of the frog, however, related cells in the cat's cortex were generally close to one another.

These data pose particular problems for neural net theories, at both of the levels discussed earlier. The notion that "cell-assemblies" are developed by experience alone becomes especially suspect. Experience is not likely to modify the retina of the frog, nor to produce neat anatomical arrangements in the feline cerebrum. Moreover, the Lettvin *et al.* data also pose a challenge of the second kind. Even at early levels of the visual system, there seem to be analyzers for complex attributes of the input, not just for parts. While this finding is compatible with a model like that of Selfridge (1959), it cannot easily be reconciled with Hebb's views.

The observations of Hubel and Wiesel are not as troublesome in this respect. They suggest an analysis in terms of oriented line-segments, which could fit a part-template interpretation of pattern recognition if one is willing to assume that the templates are innately given. Such an interpretation has been particularly attractive to Sutherland, whose "analyzers" for horizontality and verticality were very much like oriented and generalized line-segments to start with. In recent papers (1963a, 1963b) he has explicitly incorporated the Hubel-Wiesel discoveries into his theorizing. On the assumption that the octopus has more cells sensitive to horizontal orientation than to vertical, and more of either than of the obliquely-oriented kind, Sutherland has been able to explain a wide range of results.

It seems clear that this theoretical approach is a fruitful one. Parallel analyzers for specifically oriented line-segments may well be a part of man's visual equipment, as they are of the cat's. Nevertheless, we must face the fact that most of the data about human pattern recognition cannot be accounted for by analyzers of this sort. They hardly even explain our ability to recognize rotated figures under the right circumstances, as discussed above, let alone our recognition of ill-defined figures. Other arguments against taking such mechanisms as the cornerstones of theory have been presented by Gyr, Brown, Willey, and Zivian (1966).

A third set of experiments that deserve mention here are certain studies of pattern recognition in young children, carried out by Eleanor Gibson and her associates at Cornell University (see Gibson, 1965, for a general review). Their study of rotational and perspective transformations (Gibson, Gibson, Pick, & Osser, 1962) has already been mentioned. Using the same techniques, Pick (1965) has attempted a very direct test of the template theory (she prefers the term "prototype"), as opposed to

| Features | A | B | C | E | K | L | N | U | X | Z |
|---|---|---|---|---|---|---|---|---|---|---|
| Straight segment | | | | | | | | | | |
| Horizontal | + | | | + | | + | | | | + |
| Vertical | | + | | + | + | + | + | | | |
| Oblique / | + | | | | + | | | | + | + |
| Oblique \ | + | | | | + | | + | | + | |
| Curve | | | | | | | | | | |
| Closed | | + | | | | | | | | |
| Open vertically | | | | | | | | + | | |
| Open horizontally | | | + | | | | | | | |
| Intersection | + | + | | + | + | | | | + | |
| Redundancy | | | | | | | | | | |
| Cyclic change | | + | | + | | | | | | |
| Symmetry | + | + | + | + | + | | | + | + | |
| Discontinuity | | | | | | | | | | |
| Vertical | + | | | | + | | | | + | |
| Horizontal | | | | + | | + | + | | | + |

Figure 25. One possible set of distinctive features for letters (from Gibson, 1965). Each letter is characterized by those features marked "+" in its column.

feature-analysis. She first taught 60 kindergarten children to distinguish each of three standard shapes (like those in Figure 14) from several of its transforms. The "confusion items" presented to each child all involved the *same* three transforms of every standard. For a particular child, these might include changing one line to a curve, rotating by 45°, and right-left reversal. When the child could successfully distinguish each standard from all of the corresponding confusion items, he was transferred to a new task. One group now had to distinguish the *same standards* from new confusion items, involving novel transformations; this should have been easy if templates of the standards had been developed during training. A second group of subjects was transferred to new standards, but the new confusion items were generated by applying the *same transforms;* this should have been easy if analyzers for the relevant dimensions had been developed during training. In fact, it was this second group which transferred more readily, thereby supporting the analyzer rather than the template theory. Even the template group, however, outperformed a third set of subjects who received *both* new standards and new templates.

The Gibson group assumes that letters are recognized by a feature-analytic process, very like Selfridge's Pandemonium. Pick's data support this view, although her stimuli were not actual letters but only letter-like forms. In addition, Gibson, Osser, Schiff, and Smith (1963), strongly influenced by the Jakobson-Halle notion of "distinctive features" in spoken language (see Figure 34 of Chapter 7), made an explicit attempt to discover the critical features by which letters are identified. They began with several alternative sets of features based chiefly on speculation; one such set appears in Figure 25. (Notice that some are rather global, like the "cyclic change" which is characteristic of *B* and *E*.) If this set were the correct one, one might expect to find more visual confusions between letters that differ by only a few features, like *B* and *E*, than between letters different in many, like *B* and *C*. To some extent, this expectation was confirmed in empirical results obtained from four-year-old children in a matching task. However, the findings were not clear-cut.

All of these data tend to support the view that pattern recognition involves some kind of hierarchy of feature-analyzers. Nevertheless, there is reason to doubt that any theory which involves only parallel processing, whether of features or parts, can be adequate. The next chapter will clarify this point, and introduce some additional theoretical concepts.

*Chapter 4*

# *Focal Attention and Figural Synthesis*

None of the theories considered in the preceding chapter can do justice to human or even mechanical pattern recognition, unless they are supplemented by some notion of "attention." There must be a way to concentrate the processes of analysis on a selected portion of the field. This implies that there are also "preattentive processes": wholistic operations which form the units to which attention may then be directed, and which can directly control simple motor behavior. The act of attention itself is better thought of as "constructive" than as "analytic," primarily because—as Chapter 6 will show in detail —the mechanisms of imagination are continuous with those of perception. Here the notion of construction is applied only to various incidental aspects of perception and learning, and is exemplified by the "analysis-by-synthesis" method for the automatic recognition of handwriting.

The notion of focal attention can be conveniently approached by way of a fundamental dilemma, faced by all theories based on spatially parallel processing. In parallel theories, such as Hebb's, a figure can be recognized anywhere on the retina because the critical analyzers or cell-assemblies are reduplicated everywhere and connected together. It is in these terms that Hebb (1949, pp. 84–94) gives his well-known account of the mechanism by which a triangle is perceived. However, he does not explain the perception of a pair of triangles presented together, and indeed it is difficult to do so without an additional assumption. If the many assemblies sensitive to angles or to triangles all lead to the same central result, two triangles should produce the same result as one (except, perhaps, for a certain increase in intensity). For that matter, a field of parallel lines should produce the same response as a single line; a set of concentric circles must be equivalent to a single circle. To explain spatial stimulus equivalence by reduplication is to explain too much. Even a newly visual person can distinguish between one triangle and two, or between a single line and a field of parallels. The ability to do so is based on what Hebb called "primitive unity," and these examples are intended to show that its role in pattern recognition is much greater than has been supposed.

This problem is not solved by Pandemonium either. Schemes for mechanical letter-recognition, including Selfridge's (1959), have generally presented letters to the machine *one at a time*. "Primitive unity" is thus established by fiat, so the program can get on with the task of categorization. If this is not done, if instead several letters appear in the input field of such a machine, they must be somehow isolated before they can be identified. Technically, this stage of processing is called "segmentation." Without it, parallel processing of an input which includes several different letters or objects would lead to chaos. Most computer programs have avoided the segmentation problem, because it is either trivial (when the letters are separated by wide blank spaces) or extremely difficult (as in cursive handwriting). We will return later to the difficult case, and to one particular program which has tried to deal with handwriting. Some more general considerations are necessary first.

## *FOCAL ATTENTION*

Even if we did not have to account for the phenomenal difference between "one" and "two" figures, spatially parallel processing would still fail as a theory on strictly quantitative grounds. To deal with the whole visual input at once, and make discriminations based on any combination of features in the field, would require too large a brain, or too much "previous experience," to be plausible. Minsky makes this point very clearly in the following quotation, which deals entirely with pattern recognition in computers. He also indicates the direction which a solution must take, whether in machines or men.

> Because of its fixed size, the property-list scheme [i.e., an array of feature-analyzers—U. N.] is limited (for any given set of properties) in the detail of the distinctions it can make. Its ability to deal with a compound scene containing several objects is critically weak, and its direct extensions are unwieldy and unnatural. If a machine can recognize a chair and a table, it surely should be able to tell us that "there is a chair and a table." To an extent, we can invent properties which allow some capacity for superimposition of object characters. But there is no way to escape the information limit. What is required is clearly (1) *a list (of whatever is necessary)* of the primitive objects in the scene and (2) a statement about the relations among them . . . Such a description entails an ability to separate or "articulate" the scene into parts . . . The important thing about such "articular" descriptions is that they can be obtained by *repeated application of a fixed set of pattern-recognition techniques.* Thus we can

obtain *arbitrarily complex* descriptions from a fixed complexity classification-mechanism. The new element required in the mechanism . . . is the ability to articulate—to "attend fully" to a selected part of the picture and bring all one's resources to bear on that part . . . It seems likely that as machines are turned toward more difficult problem areas, *passive* classification systems will become less adequate, and we may have to turn toward schemes which are based more on internally-generated hypotheses . . . (Minsky, 1961, pp. 16–17; the italics are his).

Visual objects are identified only after they have been segmented, one from the other. This permits the perceiver to allot most of his cognitive resources to a suitably chosen part of the field. The analyzers are *not* normally "in parallel" all over the visual input, but operate chiefly on the field of *focal attention*. The qualifying adjective "focal" is necessary here, because "attention" is often discussed in quite a different sense. Hebb, for example, despite his interest in "attention," never discusses selectivity within the visual field at all. Instead, he equates "attention" with "perceptual set" or "expectancy" (1949, p. 102). In this sense of the word, a person may be "attending" to *B* rather than *13* in the Bruner-Minturn (1955) experiment, and his categorization may be determined accordingly. This phenomenon is real enough, but very different from selecting one visual figure rather than another for examination *before* knowing what it may represent.

The term "focal attention" is taken from Schachtel, a psychoanalyst who has tried to account for the growing child's increasing interest in and understanding of the real world without giving up the traditional analytic concern with affects and drives. A chief tool for this cognitive development is focal attention, ". . . man's capacity to center his attention on an object fully, so that he can perceive or understand it from many sides, as clearly as possible" (1959, p. 251). Of course, selective attention was not discovered by Schachtel; psychologists have discussed it for a century. Solley and Murphy (1960, Ch. 9) provide a historical review of the subject. Like most writers, they regard all attention as the manifestation of a single process, and as an allocation of "energy." However, the metaphor of energy has never been very enlightening where cognition is concerned. If even mechanical recognizers will need some such capacity to deal with complex problems, we had better abandon the energetic model and treat attention as an aspect of information-processing. (It is worth mentioning that, so far as I know, no existing computer program has this capacity. This is one reason why, except in highly specific applications, pattern recognition by machine is still greatly inferior to its human counterpart.)

It seems to me, therefore, that attention is not a mysterious concentration of psychic energy; it is simply an allotment of analyzing mechanisms to a limited region of the field. To pay attention to a figure is to make certain analyses of, or certain constructions in, the corresponding part of the icon. The theoretical need for cognitive processing is by no means eliminated when attention comes into play. Our knowledge of the object of attention is not more "direct" than knowledge of other objects. In a sense it is less so, since more sophisticated and restricted modes of processing are being applied.

Since the processes of focal attention cannot operate on the whole visual field simultaneously, they can come into play only after preliminary operations have already segregated the figural units involved. These preliminary operations are of great interest in their own right. They correspond in part to what the Gestalt psychologists called "autochthonous forces," and they produce what Hebb called "primitive unity." I will call them the *preattentive processes* to emphasize that they produce the objects which later mechanisms are to flesh out and interpret.

The requirements of this task mean that the preattentive processes must be genuinely "global" and "wholistic." Each figure or object must be separated from the others in its entirety, as a potential framework for the subsequent and more detailed analyses of attention. However, processes can be "global" without being mysterious, or even very subtle. Very simple operations can separate units, provided they have continuous contours or empty spaces between them. Computer programs which follow lines or detect gaps, for example, are as easily written as those which fill holes and wipe out local irregularities. (Those who prefer analog to digital models, for physiological reasons, may note that similar forms of organization can be achieved by chemical and electrical field processes. These were the models preferred by the Gestalt psychologists; e.g., Köhler, 1924.)

For the most part, I will treat the preattentive processes as if they were a single level of operations, themselves parallel, serving to form the objects of focal attention. But this is an oversimplification; even these early processes can apparently have hierarchical depth. On request, you can focus your attention onto a single letter of the page (for example, the *q* which occurred earlier in this sentence). Having found it, you can note whether it is well formed, or how it differs from such letters as *p* and *b*. The preattentive processes keep the *q* a separate and integral unit while you do so. This is an acquired skill, very difficult for young children and illiterates. They must get along with much more crude objects of attention, such as the entire block of print on the page, or the whole word in which the *q* is embedded. Thus it would be a mistake to assume that the preattentive mechanisms of figural unity are all innate, although some of them must be.

Following the preattentive mechanisms comes the second level of pattern analysis, which operates on the "objects" segregated by the first. Here it is determined that an object is "round and nubbly in texture," or a triangle, or a long-lost friend. These operations necessarily come after the preattentive ones and depend on them. This means that the processes of pattern recognition are, after all, partly sequential. In giving up the hypothesis that all visual processing is *spatially* parallel, we necessarily introduce successive stages into our model of cognition, i.e., mechanisms which are not *operationally* parallel either. Attentive acts are carried out in the context of the more global properties already established at the preattentive level. In this way—and I think only in this way—can we understand the phenomena stressed by the Gestalt psychologists, many of which seem so out of place in modern theories based on parallel processing of features and parts.

The insistence that "the whole is more than the sum of its parts" meant that the appearance of a part depends on the whole in which it is embedded. A few examples will suffice to recall the power (and the obviousness) of those effects. The contour which divides figure from ground "belongs" to the figure only and changes its shape radically if a figure-ground reversal occurs (Figure 26). The color of an area can

Figure 26. Rubin's ambiguous figure, the "Peter-Paul Goblet."

depend on the figure to which it seems to belong, as in the Benussi ring (Figure 27). A parallelogram made up *of* crosses is very different from a parallelogram *and* crosses (Figure 28); the two constellations will be described and remembered differently (Asch, Ceraso, & Heimer, 1960). Observations like these, which cannot be explained by a single level of

Figure 27. The Benussi ring (in a version taken from Osgood, 1953). The ring appears to be a uniform shade of grey until a thread is laid across it extending the black-white contour; then its two halves seem differently colored.

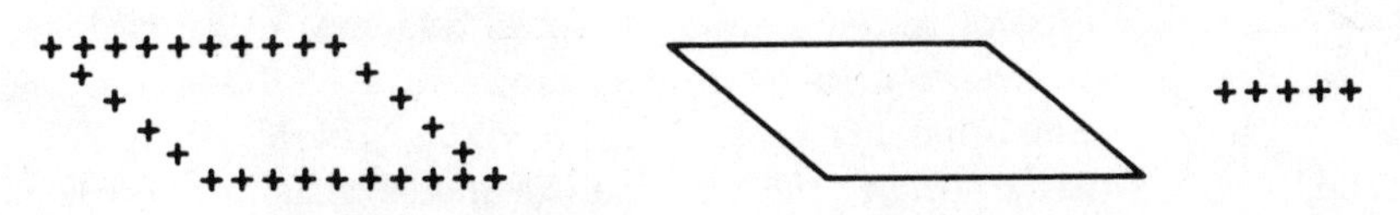

Figure 28. A parallelogram made up *of* crosses is not the same as a parallelogram *and* crosses (after Asch, 1962).

feature analysis, pose no particular problem if a predominantly global level of analyzers *precedes* the extraction or construction of details, and can influence its outcome. Moreover, the logical necessity, and the observed fact, of focal attention means that such a preliminary level must exist. In terms of information processing, the whole is *prior* to its parts.

## *PREATTENTIVE CONTROL*

My emphasis on focal attention does not mean that it is a prerequisite for all responses. When particular figures are identified or categorized, focal attention is usually involved, but it is not impossible for the preattentive processes to elicit responses directly under some circumstances also. There seem to be two classes of movements which are most often under preattentive control. One of these, which includes head and eye movements, consists of redirections of attention itself. Attention is not directed at random; it is frequently guided by cues already extracted from the visual input. *Motion* is an effective cue of this sort. When something moves in a portion of the field to which we are not attending, it usually captures our attention almost at once.

Much cognitive activity in daily life is preattentive. That is one reason why tachistoscopic research often seems so inappropriate to psychologists concerned with everyday cognition. A subject paying sharp attention to a fading iconic blur, in an effort to decide which of the 26 letters it represents, is functioning very differently from a man who "recognizes" the familiar sights of his office as he enters in the morning, or notes out of the corner of his eye that his secretary has already come in. Such a man can easily be deceived—the picture on the wall may have been changed, the secretary may be a substitute—and he will be in for a surprise when he notices the deception. His response will then be the redirection of attention, together with appropriate orienting responses, as he focuses on the newly interesting object.

Such a man will probably have a succession of secretaries who rightly complain that he never pays any attention to them. But they will have to admit that at least he rarely collides with them or the office furniture which he takes equally for granted. This suggests that there is another type of response under preattentive control, in addition to the direction of attention itself: guided movements. Walking, driving, visual tracking, and other responses that are more "literal" than "categorial," more "analog" than "digital," can be made without the use of focal attention. Most drivers have occasionally been startled to realize that they have not been paying attention to the road for the last half-hour. In walking, the same experience is so common as to arouse no interest. In these cases, the behavior has been steered entirely by the preattentive analyzers. These mechanisms are crude and global, and will not suffice for fine decisions; hence the driver must quickly become alert if a difficult situation arises.

There are other examples of the preattentive control of attention and movement. In many conjuring tricks, for example, the attention of the audience must be directed away from some critical maneuver. This is accomplished subtly, often just by a movement made elsewhere in the field. The dancer who reacts to his partner's lead, the audience that moves in "empathy" with a prizefighter, and the sleepwalker who skillfully avoids obstacles are other cases in point. It is evident that not only the flow of attention, but also many kinds of bodily movement, can be controlled by preattentive pattern analysis. Perhaps this is not surprising if approach is regarded as the prototype of attention itself.

A third effect of the preattentive processes is often spoken of by psychoanalytically-oriented theorists, but deserves very cautious treatment. Information analyzed without focal attention is said to be transformed, stored, and later used in the complex ways characteristic of Freudian "primary-process thinking." Can we accept this conclusion? Unfortunately, most of the supposedly relevant evidence is based on studies using *subliminal* rather than nonattended stimuli, typically in tachistoscopic situations where the subject is actually paying keen attention to the critical portion of the visual field. The theory put forward here would not predict positive results from such experiments. The preattentive processes are necessarily cruder and less accurate than the focal ones and could not be expected to reach below the threshold of an attentive subject. To be sure, positive results are often obtained in experiments with "subliminal" cues, but they can generally be explained in terms of some unintended aspect of the experimental procedure. The studies involving backward masking have already been dealt with in these terms in Chapter 2, and others will be considered as they become relevant in the next two chapters.

The surprising (to me) fact is that virtually no published studies in this tradition have used visual stimuli outside the focally attended portion of the visual field. Genuinely supraliminal but presumably nonattended stimuli were indeed used in two studies by Pine (1960, 1961), but the stimuli were auditory, and we must postpone a detailed discussion of them until Chapter 8. However, it is fair to say here that they are not conclusive. Hence we need not suppose that the preattentive processes control anything other than immediate bodily motion, or attention itself.

At a more general level, the accumulating evidence surveyed in Eriksen's recent book (1962) has led him to suggest that "learning without awareness" hardly ever takes place. In experiments where subjects are "conditioned" by supposedly irrelevant stimuli—the experimenter's "umm-hmm," the color of a line whose length is to be judged—learning seems to occur only in those who consciously realize the significance of the cue (Spielberger & DeNike, 1966). While "awareness" in these studies is not identical with "focal attention" as used here, they are evidently related. Thus we have some reason to believe that the effects of preattentive processes are limited to the immediate present, and that more permanent storage of information requires an act of attention. Still, it is best to leave the issue open for the present; there may be more to it than has yet appeared.

### *FIGURAL SYNTHESIS*

Since some readers may be dismayed by the stress I have put on so animistic a concept as "attention," it may be well to review its basis once more. If we allow several figures to appear at once, the number of possible input configurations is so very large that a wholly parallel mechanism, giving a different output for each of them, is inconceivable. To cope with this difficulty, even a mechanical recognition system must have some way to select *portions* of the incoming information for detailed analysis. This immediately implies the existence of two levels of analysis: the preattentive mechanisms, which form segregated objects and help to direct further processing, and the act of focal attention, which makes more sophisticated analyses of the chosen object. The observation that even a competent automaton would require processes of figure-formation and attention lets us understand why they have appeared, explicitly or implicitly, in so many psychological theories.

This means that the detailed properties and features we ordinarily see in an attended figure are, in a sense, "optional." They do not arise automatically just because the relevant information is available in the icon, but only because part of the input was selected for attention and certain operations then performed on it. Neither the object of analysis nor the nature of the analysis is inevitable, and both may vary in different observers and at different times. The very word "analysis" may not be apt. It suggests an analogy with chemistry: a chemist "analyzes" unknown substances to find out what they "really" are. A different metaphor would lead us to a different term: we do not ordinarily say that a sculptor "analyzes" a block of marble until he finds the statue that it "really" contains. But an analogy with the sculptor would be even further from the mark than that with the chemist. The visual input usually constrains the perceiver far more closely than most sculptors would tolerate. More appropriate than either of these is Hebb's (1949, p. 47) comparison of the perceiver with a paleontologist, who carefully extracts a few fragments of what might be bones from a mass of irrelevant rubble and "reconstructs" the dinosaur that will eventually stand in the Museum of Natural History. In this sense it is important to think of focal attention as a constructive, synthetic activity rather than as purely analytic. One does not simply examine the input and make a decision; one *builds* an appropriate visual object.

The notion that perception is basically a constructive act rather than a receptive or simply analytic one is quite old. It goes back at least to Brentano's "Act Psychology" and Bergson's "Creative Synthesis," and was eloquently advanced by William James (1890). However it is not put forward here on the basis of its historical credentials. Are there any empirical observations which it helps us to explain?

So far as the problems of pattern recognition are concerned, synthesis is little more than a metaphor. Instead of asking how the input is assigned to a proper category, we ask how it happens that the right kind of perceptual object is formed, and this seems to be only a semantic difference. We still need the specific concepts developed earlier: preattentive processes, priority of encoding, focal attention, stimulus analyzing mechanisms, and the like. However, the notion of synthesis becomes useful in dealing with certain further questions. Many of these center on hallucinations and illusions: a man who sees things that are not present must be constructing them for himself. The next two chapters will deal in part with such phenomena. In Chapter 5, it will appear that readers often see words or letters that are not before them, and Chapter 6 will treat extensively of visual imagery, both normal and abnormal. In both chapters we shall see that *the mechanisms of visual imagination are continuous with those of visual perception*—a fact which strongly implies that all perceiving is a constructive process.

The notion of constructiveness, or activity, being put forward here does not refer primarily to physical movements or to muscular action. The intimate relation between real motor activity and perceptual development has received much emphasis lately (see, for example, a lucid review by Gyr, Brown, Willey, & Zivian, 1966). Although I am sympathetic to this position, it will not be considered here. The present volume deals with cognitive processes in the adult, not with their development in the child. It is obvious that motor activity, "reafferent stimulation," and the like cannot be of much assistance to the subject of a tachistoscopic experiment. The relationship between cognitive "activity," as here conceived, and motor action is that much the same sort of integrated construction is necessary in both cases. Both are "schematic," in Bartlett's (1932) sense; both synthesize novel and temporary objects—percepts or movements—under more or less specific constraints.

In the present chapter, we will introduce the constructive approach by applying it to several minor issues which lie on the fringes of the pattern-recognition problem. These issues do not concern the process of categorization itself—where analytic metaphors may be just as good as synthetic ones—but some of its subjective accompaniments and aftereffects. They include (*a*) the difference between "perceptual" and "conceptual" categorization; (*b*) physiognomic perception; (*c*) recognition memory; (*d*) visual search. In addition, we must consider a particularly interesting computer program, which uses figural synthesis to carry out pattern recognition.

There is an unmistakable difference between "seeing" that two things look similar and "judging" that they belong in the same category.

The argument of Bruner, Goodnow, and Austin (1956) that both processes involve categorization is correct and yet leaves something out (as these authors themselves were aware). In a study of "concept attainment," one may learn that every card with two blue borders is "positive" and all other cards are "negative," but two positive cards do not look any more alike after one has discovered this. Visual synthesis proceeds as it did before, constructing perceived cards, borders, etc. What has changed are certain *non*visual cognitive operations which take place after visual synthesis is complete and make use of its products. For this reason, concept learning does not belong in a discussion of visual cognition. On the other hand, the various versions of the letter *A* in Figure 10 actually *look* somewhat alike, so their syntheses must be related. When the appearance of things is changed by perceptual learning (Gibson, 1953; see also the verbal examples in the next chapter), visual synthesis itself must be affected. The distinction is not easily made in theories which lack a notion of synthesis. Analytic models like Selfridge's Pandemonium and Hebb's phase sequences seem well adapted for perceptual classification and concept formation alike. Both tasks involve the detection of certain features, and assignment to a category based on those that have been detected. If visual objects are constructed and not merely analyzed, however, it is evident where the difference lies.

What is synthesized need not be clear or distinct. Earlier, when focal attention was defined as the allocation of cognitive resources to a part of the visual field, emphasis was placed on the greater *accuracy* which such an arrangement would permit. But to emphasize only this increased sharpness would be misleading. Paying attention is not just analyzing carefully; rather, it is a constructive act. In this synthesis we may aim for accuracy, but we need not. What we build has only the dimensions we have given it.

Interpreted in this way, the concept of figural synthesis may help to clarify the phenomenon often called "physiognomic" perception (Werner, 1948, p. 69; Koffka, 1935, p. 359). Everyone has perceived such traits as suppressed anger in a face, gaiety in a movement, or peaceful harmony in a picture. Often these perceptions seem very direct. We do not first notice the tightness of the jaw and then infer the anger; more often it is the other way around. Such reactions are not so rare that cognitive psychology can afford to ignore them. According to many developmental psychologists, they are the rule rather than the exception in children. There is no doubt that they can become excruciatingly powerful in particular psychoses, and under the influence of certain drugs. Under some conditions every visible object may take on a menacing or a horrifying or a lewd appearance; it may also happen that everything seems beautiful and graceful beyond all description. Such emotion-flooded experiences can be thought of as the result of particular kinds of construction. The same fragments of bone that lead one paleontologist to make an accurate model of an unspectacular creature might lead another, perhaps more anxious or more dramatic, to "reconstruct" a nightmarish monster. In themselves, the preattentive processes are neither "physiognomic" nor "geometric," neither emotional nor cool. They are constructive, but they make only chunks of raw material, out of which focal attention may synthesize many different products.

Incidentally, the notion of synthesis can be applied to perception in other modalities than vision, and it is possible that nonvisual stimuli may contribute information to help guide the construction of a visual "object," wholly or partly imaginary. Once we know how to construct a particular figure, we can make it "out of" practically any sensory material, or even without any at all, as in imagery. This is particularly relevant to the problem of the letter traced on the skin. As noted earlier, the versatility of pattern recognition resembles our equally impressive ability to transfer a once-learned movement to any limb of the body. The comparison is no longer remote. Perceiving a letter and writing one are synthetic activities of the same kind.

## *FAMILIARITY*

The notion of synthesis can also be applied to a different sort of "recognition." So far, this overworked word has been treated here as a synonym for "categorization." It has another common meaning as well, which appears in remarks like "I recognize that man." The two kinds of recognition often coincide, but they need not do so. You may classify a man correctly, perhaps by the nameplate on his desk, without personally recognizing him; you may recognize someone without knowing where you have seen him before or who he is. In this sense, "recognition" refers to a particular subjective experience, the experience of familiarity. Such experiences may occasionally be misleading (you may fail to recognize a man you know, or misrecognize a stranger), but they certainly occur. What is their relation to the processes of "pattern recognition"?

Before turning to this question directly, we must consider a common kind of psychological experiment which at first seems to bear on it. In the so-called "recognition method" of testing memory, a subject who has learned a list of items, perhaps numbers or words, must later pick them out of a longer list which contains confusion items as well. As long as commonplace materials like numbers are used, this method has little to do with *either* pattern recognition *or* the subjective experience of familiarity. It is only a sort of introverted association experiment. Since the subject has seen *all* the items on the second list before, he cannot simply say which ones seem familiar; he must try to recall which ones were associated with the first phase of the procedure. It is not surprising that performance on such a task is no better than ordinary recall, when the number of possible answers in the two procedures has been equated (Davis, Sutherland, & Judd, 1961).

Studies of familiarity have to use *novel* stimulus materials, so that the subject can later be asked "Have you *ever* seen this before?" Our everyday ability to recognize people we have not seen for years suggests that such studies should produce a high proportion of accurate responses, and indeed they do. Almost none of the subjects of Rock and Englestein's (1959) experiment who saw a single visual form for 20 seconds (under conditions which did not encourage them to memorize it) had any difficulty in picking it out of an array of ten similar figures after three weeks. It is true that their performance might possibly have depended upon covert verbalizations as well as purely visual processes, but this can be ruled out in Mooney's (1958, 1959) work. His subjects, given only very brief exposures of complex, amorphous, virtually indescribable black-and-white patterns, were able to pick them out of a series of similar patterns later. (In fact, recognition was as good following a tachistoscopic exposure as after a 10-second presentation.)

The most impressive, as well as the most sophisticated, study of familiarity-recognition is that of Shepard (1967). He asked his subjects to look through a series of 612 different pictures, mostly magazine illustrations. Going at their own pace, they took an average of about six seconds with each one. Afterwards, they were tested with 68 pairs, each consisting of a picture from the previous series together with a new one. When tested immediately after the original series, the subjects were able to pick out the familiar picture with a median accuracy no less than 98.5 percent! Many made no errors at all. Even in a test delayed by seven days, accuracy remained above 90 percent, although it dropped to near the chance level after four months. (For an extension of Shepard's method, see Fozard & Yntema, 1966.)

It would be a mistake to suppose that this sort of recognition depends on matching with a template. We often recognize persons who have been considerably changed by the passage of years. On the other hand, we may fail to recognize an unchanged face in a novel context. These considerations suggest a process which depends on features and focal attention, as in the model already developed for pattern recognition. However, it was noted earlier that familiarity is not the same thing as correct categorization. How can it be interpreted?

The notion of figural synthesis suggests one speculative possibility. What seems familiar is not the stimulus object, after all, but the perceived object. Perhaps we experience familiarity *to the extent that the present act of visual synthesis is identical to an earlier one.* Admittedly this is not an easily testable hypothesis, but it does have important consequences for the general interpretation of memory, to which we will turn in Chapter 11. It also suggests ways of understanding a number of phenomena: how familiarity-recognition can occur with an actually incorrect identification, or identification without recognition; why recognition depends on context, and yet may also transcend it; why we generally recognize our own images and hallucinations as familiar, but need not.

It is well known that tests of recognition do not always yield perfect scores. Their difficulty depends on the alternatives which are presented to the subject: when these are very similar to the item shown earlier, errors often result. On the present interpretation, it is not the absolute similarity among the items which is critical, but their similarity along dimensions used by the subject in the two acts of synthesis involved. A storekeeper will be taken in by a counterfeit bill if his *present* perception does not bring out those details which distinguish it from the real thing. But, no matter how carefully he looks now, it will still deceive him if these details were never elaborated in his *earlier* perceptions of genuine bills.

### *SEARCH AND REACTION TIMES AGAIN*

The notions developed in this chapter can be applied specifically to the empirical observations discussed in Chapter 3. We saw there that some experimental paradigms seem to yield evidence for operationally parallel processing, while others do not. Extra targets to look for do not add to the decision-time in search experiments, nor in certain highly compatible disjunctive reactions, but they definitely do increase latency in most character-classification studies. Perhaps the principle involved is simply this: conditions which encourage the subject to *synthesize* each pattern *individually* generally produce "sequential" results, while "parallel" data tend to appear where these conditions are absent. Presenting one stimulus at a time, penalizing the subject for errors, and allowing him relatively little practice are all conditions which might lead to separate figural syntheses and thus to sequential processing.

Where one stimulus is presented at a time, as in most reaction-time and character-classification experiments, the subject's natural response is probably to identify each one as it occurs, to make a "sensory" rather than a "motor" reaction. He waits until he has "really seen"—i.e., constructed—something, and then searches through his memory to find what response it demands. The results obtained by Sternberg (1963), Kaplan, Carvellas, and Metlay (1966), and others suggest that this search matches the input (or rather, the construction which the input stimulates) against each possible target in turn.

Sternberg (1967) has concerned himself directly with this question and has carried out an ingenious test of the full-identification hypothesis. It was again a character-classification experiment; the subject was to pull one lever if a briefly flashed numeral was one of those previously designated as targets, and to pull another lever if it was not. Again, the reaction time increased by about 35 msec. for each additional numeral originally assigned to the set of targets, i.e., for each comparison required. In a further condition, however, Sternberg partially obscured the stimulus with overlapping "visual noise," thereby slowing the reaction time by about 60 msecs. Now, if the subjects were systematically identifying (or "constructing") the visual object before comparing it with the potential targets, as I have argued here, the increase in latency should have been *independent of the number of possible targets.* It should be a constant amount, resulting from the greater difficulty of synthesis with a "noisy" stimulus.

Unfortunately, the outcome of the experiment was ambiguous. Subjects were run for two days; the change in reaction time produced by the "visual noise" did seem to be independent of the number of targets on the second day, but on the first day a positive relationship was observed. On the basis of the first-day findings, Sternberg (1967) doubts that his subjects typically identify each stimulus before deciding how to respond to it. To me, this possibility seems very much alive; it has too much theoretical utility to be casually discarded.

In our own studies of visual search (Neisser *et al.,* 1963, etc.), time-per-item does not depend on the number of targets being searched for, and practiced subjects report that they hardly "see" the irrelevant letters. This suggests that their responses do not depend on visual synthesis at all, but are directly under preattentive control. Through prolonged practice, the subjects develop preattentive recognition systems, sensitive to features of the display as a whole, which can signal the presence of a target letter. They are "watching" for *Z*-features only in the same sense that one is always "watching" for a movement or a flash of light at the periphery of the field: if it occurs, it catches one's attention. When a *Z*-feature appears, the subject presses the button and focuses on the *Z* itself in the same breath. This explains why the participants in a multiple-target experiment occasionally report that they stopped without knowing *which* of the several targets was actually present. Until they recheck, they only know that something of interest has appeared in the visual field.

The subjects of search experiments make many errors, generally by overlooking targets. This is not surprising. The preattentive mechanisms are not built for accuracy—that is a matter for focal attention. We can expect a certain crudeness whenever responses occur without attentive construction. We can also expect a dependence on global, nonspecific features rather than on details. These are the features which must be analyzed if the preattentive mechanisms are to fulfil their major function: to form objects on which the more selective processes of figural synthesis can be focused. Finally, we must expect preattentively controlled responses to be as phenomenally "immediate," as spontaneous, as figure-formation itself.

These are indeed the characteristics of detection in visual search, of "motor" as opposed to "sensory" reactions, and of responses to masked stimuli in the paradigm of Fehrer and Raab (1962). Moreover, many other responses can also become preattentive with sufficient practice. When they do, we often call them "automatisms." This is probably what happened to the heroic subject of Mowbray and Rhoades' (1959) experiment after some 40,000 trials, when his reaction time with four alternatives was no longer different from that with two alternatives. It is surely what happens in ordinary driving and walking, when these activities are carried out preattentively. There too, reaction time is probably independent of the number of different stimulus configurations that might demand a response. The number of such "alerting" situations must increase with one's driving experience; it would be hard to suppose that one's responses become correspondingly more delayed.

One other common situation, which also discourages focal attention to individual details, is worth special mention: the ordinary act of reading. Only novices read by identifying each letter; advanced readers make use of more partial cues. Further discussion of this point belongs in Chapter 5, but it is worth noting here that reading, more than most other real-life situations, encourages reliance on fragmentary features as opposed to full identification. Hence it is not surprising that Morin *et al.* (1965) found evidence for parallel processing only with letters. For other material, even as familiar as faces and colors, Merkel's principle seems to hold until extensive, specific practice is given.

### *ANALYSIS-BY-SYNTHESIS*

However speculative or vague the notion of figural synthesis may seem in dealing with such questions, it has also been applied to a very tangible problem, with a success that vouches for its usefulness. This application is to the recognition of handwritten letters, and words, by a computer. The handwriting problem, which a number of programmers have attempted, is especially difficult because successive letters are not separate in cursive script. The most successful attack on it is that by Eden (1962; see also Eden & Halle, 1961; Mermelstein & Eden, 1964; Lindgren, 1965c), based on a principle which he calls *analysis-by-synthesis.* We shall see in Chapter 7 that this principle also appears in a plausible theory of the perception of *speech,* which—like handwriting—is a continuous stream of idiosyncratic communicative activity.

Before turning explicitly to the identification of written material, Eden devoted his attention to some preliminary problems: the analysis of cursive motions into "strokes," the anatomy of the motions which produce the strokes, and the mechanical synthesis of "forgeries." Only after achieving some degree of success with synthesis did he turn to recognition. The recognition procedure generates tentative letters, trying out only those which would combine into admissible words, and checking each one stroke-by-stroke against the input. This approach may be said to avoid the problem of segmentation altogether, or more precisely to treat whole words as segments, within which synthesis takes place. After all, no need for letter-segmentation arises in the course of writing. One simply writes each letter when one has finished the last, i.e., when its synthesis is complete. In analysis-by-synthesis, only strokes have to be isolated before construction of the letters is undertaken. When a particular letter has been successfully matched, the attempt to match the next begins.

Another important aspect of the program is the way it uses contextual information. A knowledge of possible or probable words can be used to control the order in which various tentative syntheses will be explored. Having already constructed *coi-,* the program would try *n* rather than *m,* or *l* rather than *k.* This provides a tempting model for the roles that expectancy and context play in figural synthesis as it occurs in man. A similar approach can evidently be applied to the perception of speech as well.

At present, Eden's program uses information derived from the temporal succession of strokes, and thus can only read words written on a special input device. Whether it will eventually overcome this restriction and achieve the ordinary human capability to read handwritten documents is not certain, but its contribution to theory is already great.

## *TWO THEORETICAL SUMMARIES*

It may be useful to summarize these arguments from two points of view. First, let us consider how attention and figural synthesis apply to the tachistoscopic readout discussed in Chapter 2. Information reaching the eye from a briefly exposed stimulus is preserved for a short time in iconic memory. At this stage, the pattern has already been resolved into one or more segregated figures by the global wholistic processes I have called "preattentive." If the subject has been trained to give a quick, undiscriminating motor reaction, a response can be initiated even here, before he sees any figure in detail. However, the early parallel processes are limited in their function. They can control shifts of attention, including eye motions and gross bodily movements, but they provide neither fine structure nor emotional content.

The attentive synthesis of any particular letter or figure takes an appreciable time, of the order of 100 msec., and may be disturbed by new input arriving at critical points during this period. If a whole row of letters is to be identified, they must be synthesized one at a time. This is true even though the preattentive processes, which are parallel, have already formed all the letters into separate units, so the subject has the vague impression that he is "seeing them" all at once. To "identify" generally means to name, and hence to synthesize not only a visual object but a linguistic-auditory one.

Whatever figures—or whatever attributes of a single figure—are fully synthesized and named *first* have the best chance of being correctly reported. Later on, the icon will have decayed and accurate figural synthesis will have become impossible. Hence the span of apprehension is limited to what can be synthesized, and then verbally stored, while iconic memory lasts. Perceptual set is effective by controlling either the order in which various figures receive focal attention, or the synthesis which is then carried out. That is why set can affect the emotional, physiognomic appearance of things as well as the category to which we assign them and can cause us to see things which are not really present at all.

A second summary might be organized around the question asked at the beginning of Chapter 3. How does the subject know an *A* when he sees one? The suggestions made here are as follows: (1) The *A* is segregated from other simultaneously presented figures by preattentive processes. These mechanisms emphasize the global rather than the particular, the whole rather than the part, in the figures they construct. They are reduplicated in parallel all over the input field. (2) Focal attention is then devoted to the *A,* either as it is reached by an internally directed scan, or because of some attention-compelling feature detected by the preliminary mechanisms. To "direct attention" to a figure is to attempt a more extensive synthesis of it. Of course, synthesis presupposes some prior analysis, as the paleontologist must have some fragments of bone before he can build his dinosaur, and Eden's program must have strokes before it can synthesize letters. A Hebbian dissection into lines and angles may play a role here, although our ability to deal with ill-defined categories suggests that more complex analyzers like those of Selfridge and Sutherland also play a part. (3) The processes of attentive synthesis often lead to an internal verbalization (an auditory synthesis) that can be stored in active verbal memory (Chapter 9). They may also lead to a sequence of comparisons with stored records of earlier syntheses to determine the proper classification for the present stimulus.

Being very much under the control of developmental and dynamic factors, the processes of focal attention take varying forms in different persons and situations. In particular, their course can be quite different if the subject suspects that the letters of a tachistoscopic presentation form a *word* rather than a random array. The next chapter deals with this case.

# Chapter 5

## Words as Visual Patterns

Much evidence suggests that words can be recognized without identifying all the letters of which they are composed. Since a template theory of recognition is not tenable for words, some kind of analysis into features or fragments must be involved; possible features include letters, "spelling patterns," and overall shapes. The effect of familiarity on recognition thresholds may result either from the facilitation of visual synthesis itself or from changes in subsequent verbal inference, depending on what level of visual construction the subject has been set to undertake. Similar arguments apply to the effect of repeated tachistoscopic exposures, to so-called "perceptual defense," and to "subception." However, it is not clear how ordinary rapid reading is to be explained.

Few topics in psychology have generated so much heat as the recognition of words. Reading, whether of books or of briefly exposed words with emotional connotations, has been a source of continuous controversy since the nineteenth century. Yet despite its liveliness, an author who approaches this subject has some reason to fear that his readers may find it tiresome or even painful. In the last 20 years, psychologists have made tall mountains out of several molehills in this area, with discouraging results. The topics of perceptual defense and subception, in particular, have been studied at such great length that even those who continue to publish about them seem tired of the issues. Nevertheless, there has been no "closure"—no generally acceptable statement of the facts has appeared. Meanwhile, interest has been shifting back to a problem that is both more important practically and more difficult to solve: normal reading.

This chapter will attempt to assess the present status of some of these overworked problems. Moreover, they will be related as closely as possible to the unsolved questions about reading which are now moving back into scientific fashion. (In retrospect, it is remarkable that word-recognition was ever studied *without* regard to the nature of reading!) The sections on "Perception vs. Response," "Perceptual Defense," and "Subception" will deliberately be set among other material which deals with the reading process. Even so, those who were too wise or too young to have been concerned with these issues may wish to skip these sections entirely. Others, of course, will find them wrong rather than dull. In a field as battle-scarred as this one, one man's common sense is bound to be another's heresy.

It is frequently supposed that brief tachistoscopic presentation of a stimulus restricts the subject to primitive and rapid cognitive processes. This is not the case. Although the exposure may last only a few milliseconds, the relevant information is usually available much longer in the form of iconic storage (see Chapter 2). Under most conditions, the icon remains clear long enough for several separate acts of focal attention, as when a series of separate letters is to be read. Even afterwards, an immediate response is not usually required. Most experimental procedures leave ample time for reflection before any public guess about the word must be made. Given all this time, the subject will use every possible cue and inference to identify the stimulus.

In terms of the conceptual scheme of the preceding chapter, it seems that tachistoscopic presentation of a single word could lead to either of two alternative strategies, or to a mixture between them. On the one hand, the subject may focus his attention successively on the individual letters, constructing as many of them as he can in the time available. Having done this, he then tries to *infer* the identity of the word from the letters he has seen. On the other hand, instead of proceeding letter-by-letter, he may deploy focal attention over the entire word as a unit. This second process is the more interesting of the two, because it raises a new theoretical problem. What is the mechanism of recognition under these circumstances? The alternative answers are very like those discussed in the preceding chapter, but they must be reexamined in this new context. Before doing this, we must make sure that such a mechanism is needed. How do we know that wholistic strategies are ever used?

## *THE WORD-APPREHENSION EFFECT*

Even in the context of a letter-by-letter strategy, there are two possibilities. One may suppose either (*a*) that *all* the letters must be identified before a word can be named, or (*b*) that only a *few* letters are necessary. The first of these, at least, seems to be refuted by one of the best established facts in psychology. The "span of apprehension," which can encompass only four or five letters when they are unrelated, is far greater if they form a word. Since this phenomenon seems to have no classical name, it will be referred to here as the "word-apprehension effect." The early (and unchallenged) work on the effect was reviewed by Woodworth (1938), who noted that "familiar words, even as long as 12–20 letters, [can be] correctly read from a single exposure of 100 msecs." (p. 739).

Does this really prove that recognition of all the individual letters is unnecessary? It has sometimes been suggested, for example by Schumann (Woodworth, 1938, p. 742), that the subject *does* identify all the individual letters, with the word-apprehension effect arising only from a later economy in coding. Twelve letters like *RPEENHIPNSAO* may not exceed the "true" span of apprehension at all; perhaps they simply overload verbal memory. On this hypothesis, we could assume that the 12 letters are read in the same manner when rearranged to spell *APPREHENSION*, the burden on verbal memory being lightened subsequently because they can be encoded as a single spoken word.

Although this kind of recoding is a factor to be reckoned with in all tachistoscopic experiments, it does not provide a full explanation of the word-apprehension effect. Even four-letter words are more accurately reported than random strings of the same length, although the latter would fit comfortably into the memory span. Moreover, subjects often "recognize" words that were not actually present. They report *FOYEVER* as "FOREVER," or *DANXE* as "DANGER" (Pillsbury, 1897). There can be no doubt, then, that words can be recognized—prior to auditory storage—on the basis of something less than full identification of all their letters.

The second, and subtler, letter-by-letter strategy must still be considered. Perhaps subjects typically see only *some* of the letters of a word, and infer its identity directly from these. Just as one can g_ess the m_ssing le_ters in thi_ sente_ce, so also can one guess at letters which were not seen in a tachistoscopic exposure. Cannot the identification of long words and the occurrence of plausible errors both be explained on this interpretation? The subject sees a *T* and an *E*, and says to himself "T, E, therefore THE." "THE" is likely to occur to him because it is a common word, but in a context where parts of the body are expected he might infer "TOE" instead.

Such deliberate inference from separately perceived letters is surely one of the means by which words are identified. However, it cannot be the basis for identification in every instance, for a number of reasons. First, word-recognition is too fast; second, introspective accounts argue against any letter-by-letter analysis in many cases; third, there is explicit evidence for the effectiveness of cues other than letters.

How long does it take to recognize a word? The time cannot be safely inferred from tachistoscopic exposure durations because, as we have seen, a transient iconic storage outlasts the stimulus. On the other hand, ordinary "reading speeds" are also untrustworthy; a person who reads at 2,000 or 20,000 words a minute is surely not identifying every word on the page. The best estimates of the necessary time can be derived from certain procedures which force the subject to deal separately with every word in a list. One such experiment is that of Pierce and Karlin (1957). When their subjects were asked to read (aloud) a list of familiar three-syllable words, they attained rates of about three per second, or 350 msec. per word. With shorter words, somewhat higher speeds were achieved.

Even quicker recognition appeared in some of our own scanning experiments which involved meaningful words (Neisser & Beller, 1965; Neisser & Stoper, 1965). The subjects had to look down through a list of words, three to six letters in length, in search of one which denoted an animal, or (in another condition) a proper first name. This task evidently required them to examine each word and establish its meaning, or at least enough of its meaning to determine whether it belonged to the target class. Yet, with practice, scanning rates came to exceed five words per second; i.e., less than 200 msec. per word.

These times are incompatible with the hypothesis that the subject establishes several letters, one after the other, and then infers the identity of the word from them alone. The data considered in Chapter 2 indicate that even naming a single letter must take over 100 msec. This means that Pierce and Karlin's subjects would only have had time to identify at most three letters in each word, and the scanning subjects less than two. While such scanty information might permit an occasional lucky guess, it could not possibly be enough on the average. Hence we can be sure that words are not *always* read by the identification of component letters.

Introspective accounts of tachistoscopic perception confirm this conclusion. Although letter-by-letter identification is sometimes reported, on other occasions (depending in part on the attitude of the subject) the whole word seems to leap into awareness at once. Such immediate and wholistic perceptions are by no means always accurate. It is relatively easy to trick the perceiver into a false response by using suitable material, as Pillsbury (1897) showed. His alert subjects—several of whom were professional psychologists, including Titchener himself—often noticed that something was wrong; in reporting *FOYEVER* as "FOREVER" they would comment on what seemed to be a "hair" across the *R*. But on other occasions, they saw nothing amiss, even when the word they reported differed by several letters from the one presented in the tachistoscope.

The subject distinguishes between reading the entire word and seeing certain letters of the word. Usually the word as a whole is given as read definitely and distinctly as a whole, and then several letters are given as most definite, or as most clearly seen, while the others are not so clear, or the subject may be in doubt whether they were seen at all. In many cases it was noticed that the letters which were most certain and of whose presence the subject is most confident were not on the slide, but were added subjectively . . . for the individual, the centrally excited sensations are just as truly real parts of the word perceived as the peripherally excited (Pillsbury, 1897, p. 362).

If the identity of a word were always inferred from a few clearly identified letters, this result would be incomprehensible. Why should the subject be "most certain" of letters which were not actually there? Consequently Pillsbury rejected the letter-by-letter hypothesis and appealed instead to "general word-shape." This is a frequently invoked notion, to which Woodworth (1938, pp. 739–744) gives detailed consideration. (Words like *lint* and *list* have the same shape, while *line* and *lift* do not.) There is evidence that word-shape does indeed play a part in tachistoscopic identification. One relevant fact—known since the dawn of the tachistoscopic age—is that a word printed all in capital letters is harder to identify than one printed in normal lower-case type. (All capitalized words have the same rectangular shape; e.g., *LINE* and *LIFT*.) Moreover, an experiment by Havens and Foote (1963, also 1964; and Foote & Havens, 1965) has recently illustrated the extent to which subjects can use this cue. They showed that words like *lint,* whose distinctive shape is shared by other common words in the language, have higher thresholds than words (e.g., *drab*) without such shapemates. They concluded that subjects first identify the shape of a tachistoscopic word, and then tend to produce the most common word which is compatible with that shape.

We can be sure that word-*length* would also be a useful cue under some conditions. Long words are, of course, harder to identify than short ones (McGinnies, Comer, & Lacy, 1952; Postman & Addis-Castro, 1957; Rosenzweig & Postman, 1958). But with a restricted set of alternatives, length alone may be a useful cue. Given that an American city is represented by *P**********A,* a subject is much more likely to respond with "PHILADELPHIA" than with "PEORIA."

Shape and length can provide valuable information, especially in the tachistoscopic situation where the subject has time to weigh every cue. Of course, they cannot be the major factors in word-recognition. Words can be identified even when typed entirely in capitals, and words of the same length and shape can be distinguished from one another. But the fact that these cues are even slightly useful shows again that the explicit naming of parts is not prerequisite for recognition. We saw earlier that letter-naming was impossible in many cases for lack of time; shapes and lengths are even less likely to be verbally coded, since often they do not even have common names.

The reader may be quite dissatisfied with the argument to this point. Perhaps word-recognition does not always depend on the *explicit naming* of component letters, but may not the letters play a subtler role? Perhaps they are recognized below the level of awareness, faster than they can be named. If this is not the case, how can the process of recognition be understood at all? To deal with this question, we will have to make use of the analysis of pattern recognition developed in Chapter 3.

### *MECHANISMS OF RECOGNITION: SPELLING PATTERNS*

Perhaps the most frequently heard explanation of the word-apprehension effect is the statement that words are, after all, "perceived as single units," or "grasped as wholes." In its naive form, this explanation is entirely circular, because it uses the phenomenon to explain itself. Words can indeed be perceived as units, but why? Not just because they *are* units; whatever unity they have must be conferred on them by the perceiver. On what basis does he confer unity on *UNITY* but not on *NTUIY?*

The statement that words are "grasped as wholes" is not necessarily empty, however. It may be given either of two more useful interpretations. First, it may mean that words are recognized by template-matching, with the whole word as template. Second, it may mean that the whole word is treated in a single act of focal attention, rather than as a series of such acts corresponding to individual letters. While the second interpretation is often appropriate, as we shall see, the first is surely mistaken. Chapter 3 showed that template-matching was inadequate even as a theory of how letters are identified. It is still worse as an account of word-recognition. Words, like letters, can be recognized in new positions and orientations, in different type faces and styles, and over an enormous range of variation in hand-printing. Moreover, the spaces between the letters, which would play a crucial role in comparison with a wholistic template, are in fact unimportant. If one of your templates were *BAT,* the new stimulus *PAT* would match it far more closely than *B A T* does.

There is another, very different reason for rejecting the template approach. It lies in the curious fact that the "word-apprehension effect," as I have called it, is not limited to words! Certain kinds of meaningless strings of letters are far easier to see than others, even though no overall template for them can possibly exist. The classical demonstration of this phenomenon was provided by Miller, Bruner, and Postman (1954). Their stimuli were letter-by-letter "approximations to English," of the kind used so successfully by Miller in a number of experiments. A zero-order approximation is a string of letters drawn entirely at random, without regard to the frequency with which the various letters of the alphabet occur naturally in English, e.g., *OZHGPMJJ*. A first-order approximation, while still random, takes account of first-order frequencies: *E* is the most common letter, *T* the next, and so on. One of the first-order strings used by Miller *et al.* was *VTYEHULO*. A second-order approximation is one in which the probability that any *pair* of letters will occur together corresponds to the frequency with which that pair occurs naturally: *TH* is more common than *TE,* for example, and one of the experimental second-order approximations was *THERARES*. Higher orders of approximation are defined in a similar way. Those of the fourth order, like *VERNALIT,* are based on the natural frequencies of such tetrads as *VERN, ERNA, RNAL,* etc.

The reader will have noted from the examples in the last paragraph that higher orders of approximation are more "wordlike" than lower ones. The basic experimental finding was that they are also far more easily identified in the tachistoscope. If the subject is to report all the letters of *OZHGPMJJ* correctly, he must be given a much longer exposure than for *VERNALIT*. This result is of great importance since it rules out *both* a template theory *and* reliance on isolated individual letters. There must be critical features of these strings—and, by implication, of words as well—which are "larger" than individual letters but "smaller" than the word as a whole. Moreover, W. Hull (cited in Bruner, 1957a) has repeated this experiment with schoolchildren and has shown that the increase in perceptibility with high orders of approximation is especially marked in children who are good in spelling. This shows that the critical features involved are related to regularities in English spelling and supports the Gibson hypothesis to which we will shortly turn.

To be fair, I must add that my interpretation is not the one proposed by Miller, Bruner, and Postman themselves. They were relatively uninterested in the *process* of recognition, contenting themselves with a brief allusion to the activity of "trace aggregates." Instead, they wanted to show that the amount of information, as a quantity measured in "bits," was the same at threshold for all orders of approximation. *VERNALIT* represents less information than *OZHGPMJJ* because it is "redundant;" one has a better chance of guessing the successive letters correctly without having seen them. Using appropriate estimates of the redundancies involved, Miller *et al.* succeeded in showing that the "amount of information transmitted through the subject" at any given exposure duration was roughly constant. Although more letters were reported at higher orders of approximation, each letter represented correspondingly fewer "bits." Impressed by findings like these, some psychologists have continued to interpret such data in informational terms.

My own inclination is otherwise. As argued in Chapter 1, the upshot of more than a decade of research is that information measures have little or no direct relevance to performance in most cases.

The point demonstrated by Miller, Bruner, and Postman has been developed further by Eleanor Gibson and her associates at Cornell. The paper by Gibson, Pick, Osser, and Hammond (1962) advances an explicit hypothesis about what they call "the critical unit of language for the reading process" (p. 554). Their candidate for unit status is the *spelling pattern,* a "letter-group which has an invariant relationship with a phonemic pattern," i.e., a cluster of letters that corresponds to a sound. This concept requires some elaboration.

As linguists such as Charles Hockett and C. C. Fries have pointed out (e.g., Fries, 1963), English spelling is by no means so irregular as is frequently claimed. It is true that individual letters do not have consistent acoustic interpretations, but certain constellations of letters definitely do, especially when their positions in words are considered. To search for "the sound of *i*" in *win, wine,* and *action* is to search in vain, but each of these represents a familiar spelling pattern; we can pronounce *zin, zine,* and *uction* although we have never seen them before. The fragment *tion* at the end of a word, the patterns CVC and CVC*e* (C = consonant cluster, V = vowel cluster), and many other configurations give us very specific information about how words are to be pronounced. Most spelling patterns occur only in certain positions. Many words end with *CK,* for example, while none begin with it; many begin with *GL,* but none end with it. A string of letters like *CKURGL,* which violates these rules, is essentially unpronounceable as an English word.

Not every string of letters that occurs in English is a spelling pattern. The *cti* of *action* is not a functional unit: there is a similarly placed *cti* in *hectic,* with quite a different vocal representation. An arrangement of letters is a spelling pattern only if it stands for a specific pronunciation. Even then, the spelling pattern is not just the string of letters, but the string at a certain position in a word.

To illustrate the critical role played by spelling patterns in reading, Gibson, Pick, Osser, and Hammond studied the tachistoscopic perception of "pseudo-words." In many ways their experiment resembles that of Miller, Bruner, and Postman, but the pseudo-words were not designed to be "approximations to English." Instead, some preserved the spelling patterns of English while others did not. An unpronounceable pseudo-word was formed from each pronounceable one simply by interchanging the first and last consonant clusters. Thus the stimuli included *GLURCK* and *CKURGL, BESKS* and *SKSEB, GLOX* and *XOGL,* and so on. In general, the pronounceable items were correctly reported (in writing) at much shorter tachistoscopic durations than the unpronounceable ones.

Similar conclusions can be drawn from another experiment carried out by the same group, that of Gibson, Bishop, Schiff, and Smith (1964). These authors showed that pronounceable trigrams like *MIB* have lower thresholds than unpronounceable ones like *BMI*. This study also purported to show that "meaningfulness," as exemplified by familiar sets of initials like *IBM*, does not facilitate recognition. Perhaps we should suspend judgment on this point, since the subjects were not expecting meaningful initials. But the difference between *MIB* and *BMI* is clear enough and leaves no hope for theories based either on templates or on individual letters. Letter groups, in characteristic positions, are evidently important features in word-recognition.

The emphasis which the Gibson group puts on the pronunciability of the letter groups deserves careful analysis. At one level of theory (which unfortunately predominates in the 1964 paper), reliance on pronunciability is simply circular. It makes little sense to say that "pronunciability confers unity" (p. 182); a cluster of letters cannot be pronounced until *after* it has been identified. At the more sophisticated level of the 1962 paper, this circularity was avoided: the effect of pronunciation was clearly referred to past experience. As to the classical question whether it is the past frequency of the word as *stimulus* or as *response* which makes it easy to identify, Gibson, Pick, Osser, and Hammond (1962) conclude that neither is enough by itself. The critical variable is the "frequency of experiencing a grapheme-phoneme coincidence." The initial *GL-* becomes a perceptual unit because it is regularly pronounced in the course of reading. The medial *CTI* has no regular pronunciation, and hence does not become a distinctive feature. It is perhaps for this reason that Postman and Conger (1954) found no consistent relation between the frequency of English trigrams and their tachistoscopic thresholds: many common trigrams are not units of pronunciation.

The Gibson hypothesis asserts that, as each spelling pattern in the word is recognized, the subject produces the corresponding verbal unit. The string of (subvocally) spoken units which arises in this way fits together comfortably, at least if real words or pronounceable pseudowords are the stimuli, and thus what is actually a series of cognitive acts seems like the pronunciation of a single word. Indeed, "pronunciation of a single word" *means* precisely the production of such a phonemic series. Thus this theory provides a particularly attractive integration of perception and the verbal processes that result from it. The relation between the two becomes one of "isomorphism," in the sense in which that term was used by the Gestalt psychologists. The sequence of perceptual acts corresponds structurally to the articulatory sequence. If we also grant that the subject may fall back on letter-by-letter inference when spelling patterns fail (as in *CKURGL*), we have a theory of word-perception that covers a wide range of data.

However, at least one phenomenon does not fit comfortably into the spelling-pattern theory. Where do errors come from? In particular, how are we to explain those "letters . . . of whose presence the subject is most confident" that were not in the stimulus at all? These intrusions generally occur in cases where the subject has seen the word "as a whole"—a whole which happens to be inappropriate. If wholistic perception and errors of synthesis are to be explained, a deeper theoretical account of the processes involved will be necessary. And we need such an account anyway, for the spelling-pattern theory has only shifted the pattern-recognition problem to a new level without disposing of it. How does the subject know a *GL-* when he sees one?

## *MECHANISMS OF RECOGNITION: FIGURAL SYNTHESIS*

There would be little point to assuming the existence of templates for spelling patterns when we have rejected them for words and letters. Recognition, whether of spelling patterns or words as wholes, must be mediated by relevant *features,* as meaningless in themselves as the bone chips of the paleontologist. Some will argue that these features are the letters themselves, functioning below the level of awareness to define the spelling patterns which are formed from them. There are two reasons for rejecting this view. First, the experiment of Gibson, Pick, Osser, and Hammond (1962) proves that spelling patterns must be defined with reference to their positions in words. But this position cannot be mediated by the letters themselves; other visual units are necessarily involved. The difference between an initial *GL-* and a terminal *-GL* lies in their spatial relation to a white space on one side and to a further string of letters on the other. Some feature-analyzer sensitive to this relatively global stimulus-property must play a role in the process which identifies *GLOX* more easily than *XOGL.*

The second reason for rejecting the letters as the components which mediate recognition of spelling patterns (or of words, for that matter) is logical rather than empirical. Unless we accept a template theory for letters—and there are weighty arguments against it—it is not clear what such an assumption would mean. To recognize the letter *G* is to synthesize a figural unit on the basis of fragmentary (or global) features, and similarly for *L.* Some of the same features are doubtless involved when the product of synthesis is *GL-* rather than either letter alone, but if the *G* is not constructed as a separate unit, in what sense does it have an explicit part in recognizing *GL-?* In other words, spelling patterns seem to be constructions of the same order as individual letters: they are synthesized by the subject on the basis of simple features. The only definable units of perception are those which can be given a meaningful interpretation in a cognitive theory. I can only think of two indispensable levels of organization at which "units" could be said to exist: (*a*) the *products of figural synthesis,* introspectively available and usually given a verbal label in these experiments; (*b*) the *properties of stimulation* which help to determine that synthesis. The fact that letters are themselves the products of construction in some situations gives us no license to posit them as stages on the way to "larger" units on other occasions.

On this theory, there is no reason to exclude the whole word itself as a possible product of figural synthesis on occasion. To perceive words as wholes is no more mysterious than to perceive spelling patterns or letters as wholes; in every case we have to assume a synthesis based on a concatenation of features. While this assumption is compatible with the Gibson group's emphasis on spelling patterns, it goes appreciably further. Gibson's theory mentions only one kind of constructive act—that of producing the phonemic equivalent of the spelling patterns which appear visually. For the visual processes themselves, Gibson and Gibson (1955a, 1955b) prefer metaphors of analysis to those of synthesis. I am proposing, on the contrary, that the subject engages in two related constructive acts: he synthesizes a visual figure (which may be the word as a whole, *or* a spelling pattern) as well as a verbal sequence.

It is difficult to follow the Cornell group all the way with their emphasis on phonemic correspondence. The advantage of *GLURCK* over *CKURGL* in the tachistoscope can hardly be just that we have learned to pronounce initial *GL-* but not initial *CK-*. After all, perceptual learning occurs in many situations where no verbal responses are ever required. Gibson herself (1953) has written the definitive review of such phenomena. It seems certain that figural synthesis can be developed and improved in its own right, whether a verbal response regularly accompanies it or not.

The notion of figural synthesis helps us to understand—or at least to talk about—the constructive errors which were noticed by Pillsbury and many other experimenters. The subject constructs what he sees, either letter-by-letter, cluster-by-cluster, or in a single act of attention. When the whole word is the unit, an erroneous construction may lead him to report that he has "seen" letters that were not really present. Which strategy of synthesis he follows depends on many factors, including what he expects to see and also what he thinks he ought to do—i.e., the demand characteristics of the experiment. That is why wholistic reports are so common from some laboratories and fragmentary reports from others.

## *MECHANISMS OF RECOGNITION: THE FRAGMENT THEORIES*

The process of figural synthesis does not depend only on the features extracted from the input, just as the dinosaur constructed by a paleontologist is not based only on the bone chips he has found. Equally important is the kind of perceptual object the perceiver is prepared to construct. The importance of set and context on the perception of words has been demonstrated in a great many experiments. A typical finding is that of Tulving and Gold (1963). Given sentences like *Far too many people today confuse Communism with ------*, subjects naturally recognize *Socialism* more easily than *raspberry*. The advantage which the preferred word enjoys tachistoscopically is quite predictable from the ease with which subjects can guess it from context alone.

It is important to see that context can affect cognition in two different ways. On the one hand, it may predispose the subject to construct one visual figure rather than another; in this sense people tend to *see* what they expect to *see*. On the other hand, if what he constructs visually is not itself an acceptable response, context may help him to make a suitable interpretation; in this sense people tend to *say* what they think they ought to *say*. The distinction between visual construction and the inner speech which follows it is important for understanding both the processes involved and the phenomenal report which the subject gives of them. However, it is not necessarily equivalent to the difference between "perception" and "response," as often formulated in tachistoscopic research; we will return to this issue below.

The same two alternative explanations apply to the well-known effect of familiarity on recognition thresholds. In its original form (Howes & Solomon, 1951; Solomon & Howes, 1951), this phenomenon appeared as an effect of *language-frequency*. Words which occur often in ordinary use, as measured by the Thorndike-Lorge (1944) word counts, have lower thresholds than relatively rare words: *accept* is easier than *accede, yet* than *yam*. By now, this finding has been replicated and extended in literally hundreds of experiments.

Why should language-frequency have such an effect? One explanation that is sometimes proposed—though rarely taken seriously—is as follows: (*a*) the common words are more likely as *guesses,* even when the subject sees nothing at all; (*b*) these guesses are likely to coincide with the stimulus when it also is common; (*c*) this leads to an excess of correct responses for such stimuli. Various authors beginning with Solomon and Postman (1952) have seen the fallacy in this explanation, but it has been most clearly set forth by Savin (1963). His paper concerns the effect of word-frequency on auditory thresholds rather than on visual ones, but the same logic applies to both cases. The essence of the argument is that the English language has far too many words for pure guessing to be of much use. The *a priori* probabilities of most words in a vocabulary of 30,000 or more must be far less than, say, $1/100$; there is just not enough probability to go around for even 101 of them to reach even that level. Hence differences *between* the probabilities of any two words, except perhaps the very few most common ones, must be small indeed—far too small to show up in a few dozen experimental trials.

A much more plausible account of the word-frequency effect, first proposed by Solomon and Postman (1952) and recently elaborated by Savin (1963), Kempler and Wiener (1963), Newbigging (1961a), is what may be called "fragment theory." Newbigging states it concisely:

> . . . when a word is presented at a short duration, only a few letters or a fragment of the word is seen by the subject. This fragment may be common to a number of words, and if the subject is instructed to guess the word presented he will respond with the word of greatest frequency of occurrence (that is, response strength) which incorporates the seen fragment. If the stimulus is a low-frequency word, however, guesses to small seen fragments will be high-frequency words and therefore wrong . . . the subject redintegrates the stimulus word from a seen fragment, the size of the fragment required varying as a function of the frequency of the stimulus word (1961a, p. 124).

Fragment theory circumvents the difficulties of the pure guessing hypothesis by restricting the set of words from which the "guesses" are assumed to be drawn. Instead of coming from the subject's whole vocabulary in accordance with fixed probabilities, responses are limited to the presumably small number of words compatible with some fragment already seen. With this restriction, it becomes statistically possible to create a significant bias toward common alternatives.

Fragment theory leads to a number of specific predictions which have been experimentally confirmed. The incorrect guesses which the subject makes before recognition are generally more common than the misperceived stimulus itself (Newbigging, 1961a; Savin, 1963). If the misperceived stimulus is actually a common word, erroneous guesses about it include relatively fewer of the correct letters than when the stimulus is actually rare (Newbigging, 1961a). Even rare words have low thresholds if no similar words exist in the language (Savin, 1963). If two words have the same general shape, the rarer will have a high threshold because the common one will often appear as an erroneous response, while an equally rare word without a more common "shapemate" will not have so high a threshold (Havens & Foote, 1963).

The evidence is impressive, and it seems certain that subjects use partial cues in the way suggested by fragment theory. We must note, however, that the theory is noncommittal about the nature of the "fragments." They are usually discussed as if they were letters, although Havens and Foote emphasize global shapes. Perhaps both play a role, but the letter-features discussed in Chapter 3, and the spelling patterns emphasized by the Gibson group, cannot be ignored in many cases. Moreover, fragment theory is equally ambiguous about the locus of the integrative process. Most theorists treat this evidence as proving that the word-frequency effect is not "perceptual," as if only "responses" could be synthesized from fragments. But perception is a constructive process, and visual figures, as well as verbal hypotheses, are determined by fragments and plausible alternatives. Even when perception is wholistic, in that attention is devoted to the word as a whole, we have seen that it must depend on certain distinctive features. Thus there is no one "fragment theory" but a number of them, all sharing the notion that cognition often begins with incomplete stimulus information.

Effects like those due to word-frequency can also be obtained by direct manipulation of experimental variables. For example, the subject may initially be given a list or set of words, from which the tachistoscopic stimuli are supposedly to be chosen. Naturally, thresholds for words in the set are then lower than for other words (Neisser, 1954). Moreover, the shift in threshold is greater if the set is small (and the alternatives correspondingly few) than if it is relatively large (Reid, Henneman, & Long, 1960). A subject who knows that the word will be drawn from a single category, say "food words," will have a lower threshold than one whose expectation is less specific, e.g., "food or color words" (Postman & Bruner, 1949). The effect of word-frequency cannot appear if expectations are restricted by such a list (Pierce, 1963a; Foote & Havens, 1965). Specificity of an expectation, on the other hand, makes more difference with rare words than with common ones (Freeman & Engler, 1955). All these results are fully compatible with the fragment theories, on the assumption that expected words, like familiar ones, are the first to be constructed or inferred.

It is also possible to control "word-frequency" by giving varying amounts of experience with nonsense words. This method was first used by Solomon and Postman (1952) and has been frequently employed since. As the number of training trials with such stimuli is increased, their tachistoscopic thresholds go down steadily. (A related result in hearing, using monosyllables masked by noise, was obtained by Bruner, Miller, and Zimmerman, 1955.) This finding, too, is compatible with any interpretation of fragment theory. Experience with a nonsense word may serve to make its visual synthesis more likely, or may control the interpretation of a few labelled fragments at a later stage.

## *THE DISTINCTION BETWEEN PERCEPTION AND RESPONSE*

Do variables such as expectancy and experience actually affect "perception," or do they just create response biases? Can these factors determine what people *see* or only what they *say?* Most of those who have concerned themselves with this issue—including me (Neisser, 1954)—have formulated it in ways that cannot lead to a satisfactory result. The most common problem has been one of definition. Without some notion of what "perception" and "response" refer to, it is impossible (and unimportant) to assign an effect to one or the other. Nevertheless, psychologists working in this area have tended to rely on implicit definitions which do not withstand serious analysis.

My own study (Neisser, 1954) can serve as an example. I took the term "response" literally, to mean *verbal report*. On this interpretation, "response bias" could be defined as a tendency to make certain articulatory movements. The experiment showed, however, that when a subject expects a particular word to appear in the tachistoscope (e.g., *SEEN)*, the lowered threshold for that word is not shared by others that happen to be pronounced the same way *(SCENE)*. If the effect of set had been only to create a response bias, it should have been equally effective with these homonyms, which *are* the same response. Hence I rejected the response interpretation.

The trouble with my experiment was that no one who speaks of "response bias" really has such a restricted definition in mind. They usually wish to include *inner* speech as well as spoken report in the category of "responses." From this point of view, a subject who thinks to himself "It looked as if the first letter was S and the last was N. The only word on my list like that is SEEN, so that's what I'll report" has been subjected to a response bias. As Pierce (1963b) has pointed out, such a subject would not display a lowered threshold for homonyms: seeing *SCE* will *not* lead him to report *SEEN*.

A somewhat different example of rash definition underlies the notorious experiment of Goldiamond and Hawkins (1958). Having given their subjects varying numbers of trials to learn an array of nonsense words, they created an expectation that these words were to be shown tachistoscopically. However, only meaningless smudges were actually shown! The subjects, who were required to make some response on each trial, showed a marked word-frequency effect nevertheless. The number of times that a nonsense word was reported depended, in the usual way, on the number of previous training trials it had received. Goldiamond and Hawkins concluded that since the word-frequency effect appears in full strength even without a stimulus, it must act by altering response biases alone.

This experiment has been frequently and justly criticized because the authors seem to imply that stimuli make no difference at all, that there is "a stable response hierarchy that remains constant despite changes in available cues" (Kempler & Wiener, 1964, p. 59). Although Goldiamond and Hawkins may not have meant this, they certainly do not offer any model of the recognition process that could be applied when words *are* shown. However, another and more radical critique of their experiment can also be made. They assumed, without discussion, that no subject could have "perceived" the unpresented nonsense words. Implicitly, this accepts a definition of "perception" as something that *cannot occur in the absence of appropriate stimulation*. Such a restriction on what can be called "perception" seems extremely unwise. While we do not know whether their subjects did perceive any of the words (in a sense to be defined below), we should not reject the possibility out of hand just because no words were actually shown. It is certainly possible that some of the Goldiamond-Hawkins subjects may have hallucinated some of the words, "seen them with their own eyes," just as Pillsbury's (1897) subjects often saw letters which had not been presented. Even without any stimuli at all, dreams and hallucinations result in experiences which are phenomenally just like other perceptions.

The reader may wish to escape this possibility by defining a "hallucination" as something different from a "perception." But how do they differ? It will not suffice to define hallucinations as experiences which use no stimulus information, because many do: an automobile horn outside may make me dream of Gabriel's trumpet. Nor is it satisfactory to define perceptions as experiences which are faithful to the stimulus input: in general they are not. Besides, to limit perception in that way would be to exclude *a priori* the possibility that past experience or expectation could affect it, and thus make the experiment unnecessary. The Goldiamond-Hawkins assumption actually destroys the problem which their experiment was intended to solve. The concept of "perception" is useful only if we think of it as a process *in the subject*. To define it with reference to the presence or absence of an external stimulus is to stop treating it as a process and use it only as a category in a poor taxonomy of behavior. (For further discussion of this point, see Chapter 6.)

It is not only Goldiamond and Hawkins who have adopted this self-defeating assumption about perception; some of their critics have done so as well. Thus Mathews and Wertheimer (1958) and Minard (1965) also try to separate perceptual effects from response bias by using behavior in the absence of stimuli as a base line. Their argument, too, seems inappropriate. Behavior when a smudged blank slide is flashed may well be different from behavior with respect to a real word, but there is no justification for assuming that only the second case involves "perception."

The argument so far suggests that neither an oversimplified definition of "response" nor an equally oversimplified definition of "perception" can be useful. If these were the only concepts we had, it would be better to abandon the distinction altogether. Indeed, many psychologists are inclined to do just this. But there are two compelling reasons why such a course would be unwise. First, subjects constantly make the distinction in their own reports, at least if permitted to do so. They can often tell you whether they "really saw" the word or merely figured out what it might have been. Not everyone can do this articulately, and nearly all subjects are sometimes unsure whether they saw a word or not, but it is easy to collect any number of clear-cut instances. (The fact that a distinction is sometimes vague does not make it invalid, as long as it *is* clear much of the time. S. S. Stevens has often remarked that we do not deny the difference between day and night just because they are hard to distinguish at twilight.) In some way, cognitive theory must account for the difference between these two kinds of experiences.

This is an old argument, and most of my readers may long since have decided whether or not they are going to take phenomenal reports seriously. But quite apart from introspection, it is obvious that the processes which intervene between stimulus and response are complex. Even an automaton, which merely simulated some aspects of human cognition, and never reported any introspections, would still require a hierarchy of processes like those discussed in Chapters 3 and 4. If a variable like expectancy or familiarity affects the output of such a system, we can reasonably ask at what stage of processing its influence was first felt. To be sure, in some systems, there might be no stages separate and successive enough to warrant terms like "perception," "inference," and "response." However, we saw in Chapter 4 that pattern recognition in man is not an undifferentiated process of this sort. The concepts developed there will be useful here as well.

It seems best to reformulate the difference between "perception" and "response" as a difference between *visual processes* and *verbal processes*. This proposal involves both a definition and a theory. The definition of the difference between seeing and saying must rest ultimately on phenomenal report. If a carefully interrogated and cooperative subject says that he really saw the word in question, he is to be believed. In terms of the theory advanced in Chapter 4, reports of what was *seen* should be taken as describing the results of figural synthesis. Reports of what was merely inferred, or said in inner speech, depend more explicitly on subsequent verbal processes; i.e., they involve auditory synthesis. But since both vision and speech are constructive acts, it is not appropriate to think of this distinction as one between "perception" and "response." In some sense figural synthesis is surely a "response," while inner speech is "perceived" (by synthesis) just as other speech is.

We saw in Chapter 2 that visual processes may be available for as long as several seconds after the stimulus terminates. Since in the subject's own experience he is still "perceiving" during this time, *no introspective distinction between perception and iconic memory is possible.* This is an important difference between the view put forward here and that advanced by Haber (1966) in his recent review. Like most of those who have insisted (as I do) on a concept of perception distinct from mere verbal report, Haber has also tried (as I do not) to distinguish an apparently instantaneous perceptual act from every form of visual memory. This is surely an error of logic as well as a contradiction of experience. As soon as naive realism has been rejected, there is no longer any sensible way to define "perception" without including the persisting icon in the definition as well.

Having distinguished between visual processes and verbal processes, we can return to the problem of the word-frequency effect. Are common words more easily seen, or only more readily inferred? One particularly relevant experiment is that of Haber (1965). He told his subjects *in advance* what word would be presented, and then gave a sequence of tachistoscopic exposures. The subject was required to report the letters that he "was certain he perceived" on each trial, and no others. The threshold was not defined by the trial on which the subject could identify the word (he knew what it was all along) but by the point when he reported seeing all of the letters. Actually Haber's trials were not of increasing duration, as is usual in such experiments; all the exposures were equally long. The fact that letters become increasingly perceptible with repeated equal exposures is important in its own right, and we will consider it shortly. More relevant for the present is Haber's finding that the difference in threshold between rare and common words disappears completely with this procedure! At first sight, this seems to show that the word-frequency effect is purely verbal; it vanishes when there is no need to guess.

A similar conclusion was drawn by Foote and Havens (1965), who noticed that the word-frequency effect also disappears when the subject is given a list of alternatives from which to choose (see also Pierce, 1963a). Here too, its disappearance seems easy to understand in terms of the verbal, inferential version of the fragment theory. With free report, a subject who has seen *T–E* will say "THE" because it is the first word that comes to his mind which meets the constraints of what he has seen. Given only a set of alternatives like *TOE, TAP, LIE,* and *SHE* to consider, he can weigh all of them without regard to their familiarity.

Such arguments assume that the change from free report to multiple choice changes only the subject's verbal inferences, leaving the same process of visual synthesis as before. If this presupposition were valid, the disappearance of the frequency-effect would indeed mean that its locus had been verbal and not visual. However, the assumption may easily be doubted. A subject who already knows what the word is, or who expects to make a choice among a few alternatives which will shortly appear, may adopt a different visual strategy from one who must identify the word without help. A list, whether it has one word on it or four, must encourage part-perception as opposed to wholistic synthesis. Haber's subjects were essentially told to construct individual letters rather than whole words, and in the Foote and Havens experiment it may also have been the wisest thing to do. The fact that familiarity does not affect the visual processes with these letter-focused procedures does not mean it cannot do so under ordinary conditions.

The argument being made here is somewhat unorthodox and perhaps should be restated more succinctly. (1) Attention may be flexibly redistributed to parts of the visual field. To focus attention on a figure is to devote the lion's share of processing capacity to it, bringing relatively sophisticated analyzers to bear, and thus to construct an appropriate perceptual object. (2) There are therefore several possible ways to recognize a word. One may treat the whole word as a unitary object or may focus on some of the letters so that the identity of the word may be subsequently inferred. (3) In procedures which encourage letter-by-letter construction, the familiarity of the word matters only at the later stage of verbal inference. This is natural enough, since in such procedures the word does not *exist* as a whole until that stage is reached. (4) It is still quite possible that familiarity makes *visual* synthesis easier under conditions which encourage wholistic perception. Indeed, it is hard to imagine otherwise.

In other words, such variables as familiarity and "set" can indeed influence what people see (synthesize visually) as well as how they interpret what they have seen. But genuinely visual effects will appear only if the cognitive unit with which the subject is familiar, or for which he has been set, is the unit actually employed in his visual synthesis! (In the case of set, there is also a second condition. The set must be in operation during the brief life of the icon. Of course, this is not synonymous with the life of the stimulus. See Chapter 2.)

This hypothesis suggests that word-frequency will affect the perceptual experience of a subject who is trying to see whole words, but not of one who is trying to make out individual letters. Similarly, prolonged experience with the spelling patterns of English will affect the visual processes of a subject who is actually trying to see spelling patterns (whether in free report or in multiple choice; see Gibson, Pick, Osser, & Hammond, 1962), but it would not help someone who was expecting unrelated letters.[1] A readiness for letters rather than numbers may deter-

[1] The physical spacing of the letters may also help to determine the subject's strategy of synthesis. Mewhort (1966) has recently reported a tachistoscopic experiment using zero-order and fourth-order approximations to English, like those of Miller, Bruner, and Postman (1954); he has also varied the amount of space between the letters. The advantage of *VERNALIT* over *YRULPZOC* was much reduced by spaced presentation, i.e., *V E R N A L I T* and *Y R U L P Z O C*. This result could have been predicted from the hypothesis being advanced here; it must be relatively difficult to carry out the visual synthesis of a spaced-out spelling pattern. On the other hand, the result does not follow easily from considerations of "information transmitted" or of "redundancy."

mine whether a subject actually sees *B* rather than *13* in a situation (like that of Bruner & Minturn, 1955) which encourages identification of the whole figure. Such an expectancy would probably make no difference if the subject were asked to decide whether the pattern was continuous or broken at the bottom, since the field of focal attention would then be restricted to the critical area.

If the argument is embarrassingly obvious, I can only plead that it has been widely overlooked. So far as I know, it is compatible with all the experiments that have tried to decide whether certain variables affect "perception" or "response." It does not make these questions untestable, but suggests that critical experiments will have to include some provision for phenomenal report. If one wishes to affect the process of seeing, one must consider what and how the subject is trying to see, and one must ask him afterward what he has seen.

### *THE EFFECT OF REPEATED EXPOSURES*

One kind of "past experience" that clearly affects visual synthesis is a preceding exposure of the same word. The powerful cumulative effect of successive exposures was demonstrated by Haber and Hershenson (1965). They used various exposure times, but the repeated (up to 25) exposures of any given word were all of the same duration. As in the Haber (1965) experiment mentioned earlier, subjects were carefully instructed to report all and only the letters they had actually *seen,* whether or not they had already guessed what the word was. A word was scored as *"perceived"* only if all its letters were correctly reported.

The results were clear-cut and dramatic. At an exposure duration where less than 10 percent of the words were right on the first flash, successive flashes produced increasingly many correct reports; by the fifteenth presentation more than half of the words had been fully perceived. With slightly longer flashes, accuracy rose from 40 percent on the first trial until it was close to 100 percent after 10 to 25 exposures.

The subject's introspective reports leave no doubt that the repeated presentations had a genuinely visual effect.

> If the duration of a word was low, *S* was usually unaware of letters or parts of letters on the first flash—the flash was blank. On the second or third flash, with no change in duration, beginnings of letters and sometimes whole letters would appear. After several more flashes, a number of letters would be present—often the whole word. The percept of the word that developed after repetition was in no sense fuzzy, hazy, or the product of a guess. It assumed very clear status, so that *S* was never uncertain about his report, even though he was unable to see anything a few exposures earlier (Haber & Hershenson, 1965, p. 41).

A clearer account of figural synthesis is hard to imagine.

It is important that the subjects of this experiment were instructed to focus their attention on individual letters, rather than on the word as a whole. Apparently a fragment or letter synthesized visually on one trial can easily be reconstructed on the next one, freeing most of the subject's capacity for figural synthesis to work on a different fragment. In this way, more and more fragments are constructed until every letter has appeared. Since the critical processes operate letter-by-letter, it is not surprising that Hershenson and Haber (1965) found the same kind of "growth" even with seven-letter nonsense ("Turkish") words. The initial thresholds for nonsense words are higher, but in the manner in which they become perceptible with repetition, they do not differ from English words of the same length. In both cases, the improvement in performance is something other than the result of repeated equivalent opportunities to guess letters. If the subject were simply making guesses with a fixed probability of being right, the proportions correct on successive trials should follow a simple binomial expansion. They do not. Growth is too fast on early trials and too slow on later ones for a guessing model.

So far as I know, Haber and Hershenson were the first to study the consequences of repeated equal exposures on word-identification. However, the use of repeated *un*equal exposures is by no means unusual. In fact, the ordinary method of ascertaining tachistoscopic thresholds, the so-called "ascending method of limits," consists simply of exposing the word a number of times, each flash being a little longer than the flash before. One might suppose that this method would produce artificially low thresholds because of a cumulative effect, but experiments comparing it with a random order of presentation have generally found no differences (Postman & Addis-Castro, 1957; Pierce, 1963a). However, Harcum (1964) has pointed out that these studies made use of rather insensitive techniques. He has succeeded in showing that prerecognition exposures do facilitate recognition, even when they are shorter than the flash on which it finally occurs. The effect is very much smaller than the growth observed by Haber and Hershenson, presumably because even a small decrease in exposure time produces a large change in the duration of iconic memory, and, therefore, in the amount of visual synthesis that is possible.

Successive exposures, which seem to have no effect in some of these studies and a positive effect in others, may also be inhibitory. Using pictorial material, Wyatt and Campbell (1951) showed that a single exposure of moderate length produced *better* recognition than a series of exposures, culminating in the very same duration! The prerecognition exposures seemed to exert a definite negative effect on later perception. This phenomenon has been studied extensively by Bruner and Potter (1964). Apparently subjects make inappropriate visual syntheses during the early, unclear exposures, and these then interfere with the construction of the correct figure. If often happens that a picture which is brought into focus only gradually (which was the technique used by Bruner and Potter) goes on being misinterpreted even after a remarkably sharp level of focus is reached. Once the proper construction is attained, however, it can be "held" down through great losses of stimulus clarity.

On the basis of limited experimentation so far, then, it appears that preexposure of pictures tends to be inhibitory, while preexposure of letters is often helpful. This is not difficult to understand. A string of letters consists of relatively independent and well-defined units. Focal attention can work to identify each of them individually, in the limited time which the fading iconic memory leaves available. Once it has been identified, a letter is easy to reconstruct. What persists between trials is not a pictorial or iconic image, but a conviction that certain letters are present at certain positions in the display, leading the subject to construct them there again on subsequent exposures. For this reason, the time interval between trials is not a critical factor, as Haselrud (1964) has shown.

In other words, the beneficial effect of previous exposures appears with words because they consist of independent parts, each of known size and position, drawn from a known repertoire. The pictures used by Bruner and Potter (1964) or Wyatt and Campbell (1951) do not have these properties. A fragment perceived on the first trial will not be so easily reconstructed; on subsequent trials the subject may synthesize it inaccurately and at the wrong place. Moreover, the fragment may lead to unjustified hypotheses and expectancies about the remainder of the picture which can prevent a more adequate synthesis from appearing. Thus, the effects of successive and cumulative exposures depend on the nature of the material and on the subject's expectations concerning it.

## *PERCEPTUAL DEFENSE*

One particularly interesting application of fragment theory is to the perception of words with emotional connotations. Under ordinary laboratory conditions, thresholds for "dirty words" are markedly higher than for neutral, unemotional words (McGinnies, 1949). This effect has been called "perceptual defense." The same name has more recently been used for *any* threshold shift related to emotional connotations of the stimuli, regardless of direction (Brown, 1961). The emotional connotations are not always those of social taboo. Words which vary in "value," either for the population as a whole or on an individual basis, have also been used (Johnson, Thomson, & Frincke, 1960), and sometimes the "emotionality" of the words for each subject has been determined by a word-association test as by Minard (1965). In the case of these less vividly emotional stimuli, effects on threshold are harder to observe than with taboo words, but many experimenters have found them nevertheless.

As has been generally recognized, higher thresholds for (say) taboo words do not mean that subjects shut such words out of consciousness after having first perceived them unconsciously, any more than high thresholds for infrequent or unexpected words imply that *they* are unconsciously perceived. The threshold differences may reflect the operation of any—or several—of four different mechanisms: familiarity, expectation, preference, or suppression.

(1) Familiarity—taboo words may be less common than neutral ones (although this has been disputed), and words judged "unpleasant" tend to have lower language-frequencies than words judged "pleasant" (Johnson, Thomson, & Frincke, 1960). Moreover, words that seem pleasant to any particular individual may occur more often in his own speech, or in what he reads, than words which elicit negative attitudes.

(2) Expectation—whether or not they suffer from general unfamiliarity, dirty words are not often encountered in the official business of a university laboratory, and subjects may be unready for them. On this interpretation, high thresholds for taboo words are like those observed when the experimenter, after giving his subjects a list "of the words to be shown," presents one which was not on the list at all.

(3) The first two alternatives do not represent any extension of the principles involved in nonmotivational effects. The third possibility —preference—represents an additional assumption, but one which is very much in the spirit of the others. If both familiarity and expectation can help to determine the word which the subject synthesizes or infers from cues, perhaps his personal preferences can play a similar role. We take it for granted that such preferences (based on histories of reward, reinforcement, favorable experiences, and so on) can raise the probabilities of other responses; why not those involved here? However, such an effect would necessarily be hard to demonstrate, even if it exists. Our actions are rarely governed by generalized tendencies: we usually react in terms of specific situations and their demands instead. Just as the word-frequency effect disappears when the subject knows that all stimuli will be drawn from a limited set of alternatives, so a preference effect might disappear if he believes that his own feelings are irrelevant to the task. Nevertheless, a weak general tendency to construct pleasant rather than unpleasant words may very well exist, as maintained by Johnson *et al.* (1960) and other authors. Their results must be interpreted cautiously, however, in the light of the possibility to be considered next.

(4) The remaining source of high thresholds for emotional words, while still compatible with the fragment theory, introduces a new

factor. The subject may, more or less deliberately, refrain from reporting taboo words because he thinks he shouldn't. Given the fragment *-hore,* the subject may correctly infer *whore* and yet hesitate to present it as a hypothesis lest the psychologist present (or the attractive female assistant) conclude he is oversexed. As a result he remains silent, or reports *shore* instead, until he is so certain of *whore* that he feels unable to avoid it any longer. This interpretation suggests that thresholds for taboo words should drop sharply if suitable instructions lead the subjects to believe that such responses are acceptable, or even desirable, in the experimental situation. Precisely this result was obtained by Postman, Bronson, and Gropper (1953), and related findings have been reported by Lacey, Levinger, and Adamson (1953), and Freeman (1954, 1955).

Such an interpretation may also be relevant in a rather different experimental paradigm of "perceptual defense." Often the subject is first given a word-association test, and words which elicit particularly slow reactions are then selected for further use on the assumption that they have some personal emotional significance. Together with control words, they serve as stimuli in a subsequent tachistoscopic experiment. A number of such studies have been carried out (e.g., Brown, 1961; Minard, 1965), and they frequently show that the "emotional" words have higher or lower threshold than the others. But many college students understand the purpose of word-association tests, all too well; some of the subjects in these experiments must surely have concluded that the experimenter was especially interested in their thresholds for the "emotional" words! Whether this would result in an increased or a decreased readiness to construct or report such words is hard to say, but it may well have contributed to the outcome. Such a possibility cannot be discounted even in experiments where the "goodness" and "badness" of words is culturally rather than individually defined (e.g., Johnson, Thomson, & Frincke, 1960; Newbigging, 1961b), although it is less compelling in these cases.

Is perceptual defense a visual or a verbal process? To the extent that it results from the unfamiliarity or unexpectedness of emotionally loaded words, we must ascribe it to the same mechanisms that produce set and word-frequency effects in general. As argued earlier, these are probably visual under some conditions and verbal under others, depending on the way in which the subject distributes his attention. If there is an effect of *preference* on tachistoscopic thresholds that is independent of set and familiarity—which is far from proven—it too might operate at either the visual or the verbal level. No experiment reported so far has been adequate to answer this question, whose theoretical importance has been greatly exaggerated. Finally, in those cases where the demand charactristics of the situation lead subjects to suppress taboo or dangerous responses, it has usually been assumed that the suppression was entirely verbal. This assumption is plausible enough, but perhaps it should not go entirely unchallenged. The fact that subjects see and report taboo words easily when they feel safe does not prove that they see them just as easily, changing only their report, in more threatening situations. The question remains open. While we can surely account for the results of McGinnies (1949) without positing a perceptual effect, it is still possible that one took place. Careful retrospective interrogation of subjects in such experiments might help to clarify this question.

### *SUBCEPTION*

The term "subception" (Lazarus & McCleary, 1951) refers to the subject's use of information obtained from a subthreshold tachistoscopic exposure. It is a phenomenon independent of "perceptual defense," which refers primarily to changes in the threshold itself. As we have seen, such threshold changes tend to affect certain classes of words—unexpected, unpleasant, dangerous to report—more than others, and they may take peculiar forms if the subject's attitudes and expectancies are not well understood. Some kinds of subception, however, arise quite generally, if only because subjects generally see fragments of words at durations too short for correct identification.

By definition, subception must be measured by some index other than correct report of the word presented. The most obvious index of this kind is a partial report; a subject who correctly remarks that the stimulus is "a long word ending in -TION" has certainly perceived something at a subthreshold exposure. Such partial reports occur very frequently when the subject is asked for them, and the underlying visual experiences must occur often even when he is not. Hence we can easily understand the finding of Bricker and Chapanis (1953): when the first guess at a word is wrong, the second (made without an additional exposure) will often be right. We need only assume that both guesses are based on an accurately perceived fragment. However, results obtained with two other indices of subception have aroused considerably greater interest. These are (*a*) autonomic responses made to emotion-arousing stimuli, in the absence of correct report; (*b*) prerecognition hypotheses related to the as-yet-unidentified stimulus in a meaningful way.

The subception experiment of Lazarus and McCleary (1951) employed an autonomic index, the galvanic skin response or GSR. It has long been known that this change of conductivity can be conditioned to a stimulus which originally does not affect it, simply by pairing the stimulus repeatedly with electric shock. Using this procedure, Lazarus and McCleary conditioned the GSR to five nonsense words, as discriminated from five others that were not accompanied by shock. In a subsequent tachistoscopic test, the GSR naturally tended to appear when the subject thought he saw a "shock word." More important, however, is that it also appeared on some trials when a shock word was presented *but a nonshock word was reported.* Were the subjects registering the words, and being alarmed by those which signified shock, without consciously perceiving them?

In trying to answer this question, we must not forget that responses are never directly activated by stimuli, but only as the result of some kind of cognitive processing. This point requires repeated emphasis. Many psychologists, who readily agree that some notion of cognitive analysis is necessary if we are to understand what the subject thinks or says, become naive realists again when conditioning experiments are discussed. Nevertheless, the visual pattern *GAHIW* cannot "directly" arouse a GSR any more than it can lead "directly" to verbal identification. The arguments of Chapter 3 apply to *any* system which recognizes patterns, whether it is animate or mechanical, and regardless of the form of its output. If there is some stimulus equivalence for the GSR—if versions of *GAHIW* which are displaced, distorted, fragmented, etc. also arouse it—then pattern-recognition mechanisms like those discussed earlier must intervene between input and output.

With this in mind, we can examine several alternative interpretations of the Lazarus-McCleary data. The most dramatic of these is what Eriksen (1958) has called the "superdiscriminating unconscious." Perhaps there is an entirely separate cognitive system which feeds into emotional and unconscious mental processes and which is much more sensitive than the mechanisms we have considered so far. This kind of unconscious perceptual mechanism might be responsible for the observed GSRs. If such a system existed, it could serve another function as well—the emotions it aroused might interfere with the activity of the more prosaic cognitive system which is involved in verbal report. This would explain the higher thresholds for emotional words obtained in the perceptual defense experiments.

We have already seen that no such explanation for perceptual defense is actually necessary. The observed changes in threshold can be easily accounted for along more mundane lines. Since there are other ways to account for the subception data as well, the theory of the superdiscriminating unconscious has little in its favor. Nevertheless, because it has been frequently put forward and heavily publicized (as in the furor over "subliminal advertising" some years ago) a few more words may be appropriate. The trouble with this theory is not only its lack of unambiguous experimental support; many theories command our allegiance even while the evidence that supports them remains weak. In general, these are theories which seem plausible for other reasons. Superdiscrimination does not have such an advantage. As pointed out in Chapter 2, it is a poor bet on evolutionary grounds alone. Why should two such different cognitive systems develop? Why should not the control of adaptive behavior be vested in the organism's most sensitive cognitive system? Why should we assume that all ordinary measurements of psychophysical capacity are at least an order of magnitude wide of the mark? (In addition, Dulany and Eriksen, 1959, have directly compared the sensitivities of the conditioned GSR and of verbal report in a brightness discrimination, finding that the former is usually less accurate than the latter and never more so.)

As an account of the Lazarus and McCleary data, the fragment theories are far more attractive than a superdiscriminative unconscious. Indeed, this has often been proposed (e.g., Bricker & Chapanis, 1953). The fragment which the subject sees on a given trial, say *GA*– – –, may not be enough to trigger a correct report. Unsure of what he has seen, the subject may conclude his deliberations (Lazarus and McCleary made him wait five seconds before speaking, so a clear GSR reading could be obtained) by ignoring the tentative fragment and guessing at random. Nevertheless the *GA*– – – may already have triggered an autonomic response, just as a footstep heard late at night may alarm us even though we insist half-heartedly that there is nothing to be afraid of. There is no question of superdiscrimination here. The footstep is essentially a "fragment" of the whole burglar, and recognition of the fragment is enough to set off a fear reaction though it is not enough to affect a verbally held opinion.

Up to this point, my interpretation seems compatible with that of Eriksen (1956, 1958, 1960). He argues that both the autonomic response and the verbal response are "correlated" with the stimulus and that they "are not perfectly correlated with each other." This is indisputable. Such correlations *must* be obtained if the GSR depends on any stage of cognition except the verbal report itself. There is no magic about the GSR in this respect. Eriksen (1958) has shown that results analogous to "subception" can be obtained with other indicators, including some as non-autonomic as lever-positioning. It is only necessary that the indicator be partially independent of verbal report.

However, a very different interpretation becomes necessary if subception can reveal the meaning of ordinary words, chosen from a full vocabulary. We can plausibly assume that the fragment *GA*– – – became conditioned to the GSR in the Lazarus and McCleary study, but we cannot assume that it has independent connotative meaning to begin with. The whole point of alphabetic writing is that such fragments do *not* have meaning and can appear freely in words as diverse as *GAILY, GAWKY,* and *GAUGE.* Nevertheless, there often seems to be evidence of subception in the verbal responses which the subject makes before he finally comes up with a correct identification. On occasion, these "prerecognition hypotheses" are strikingly congruent to the as-yet-unreported word in their meaning (e.g., Postman, Bruner, & McGinnies, 1948). If the stimulus words come from distinct classes with clearly different connotations (e.g., pleasant and unpleasant), and the subject is asked to guess which class an as-yet-unidentified word comes from, he may be right more often than the laws of chance would suggest (Eriksen, Azuma, & Hicks, 1959). Moreover, his incorrect guesses at the word itself often come from the same class as the true stimulus (Johnson, Thomson, & Frincke, 1960), as would be expected if he sometimes suspects its class membership in advance.

This kind of subception, involving advance knowledge of the meaning of stimulus words, presents particular problems; apparent demonstrations of it must be scrutinized carefully. The experiment of Eriksen, Azuma, and Hicks (1959), for example, contains an internal paradox. The authors report a significant number of trials on which the subjects were right about class membership but wrong about the word's identity—which seems to be a clear case of subception. However, they failed to find a lower overall *threshold* for class membership than for word identification. This implies that the "subceptively" accurate judgments of class, made with *in*correctly identified words, must have been canceled out by a corresponding number of inaccurate class judgments made with *correctly* identified words, in which the subject said something like "I think the word is 'murder' and judge it pleasant." Such reports are hard to imagine, and, in fact, they rarely occurred (Eriksen, personal communication, 1966). Hence, this experimental demonstration of subception remains ambiguous.

Eriksen (1958) treats this "semantic" subception—when and if it occurs—as similar in principle to that of Lazarus and McCleary. In both cases, there is a response (the GSR in one case, a class-membership judgment in the other) which is only partially correlated with verbal report of the stimulus-word. To my mind, his argument only illustrates the ease with which correlational statistics can obscure underlying processes. There are several real differences between the two paradigms. In the Lazarus-McCleary design, subception without perceptual defense (i.e., without a lower threshold for the GSR) is easily understood. For every trial on which the subject reports a nonshock word despite a twinge of alarm, there may be another in which he chooses a shock word and yet remains relatively unperturbed. But as I have argued above, no such symmetry can be expected for judgments of "pleasant" and "unpleasant," and so subception without perceptual defense becomes statistically absurd.

The other difference between the two forms of subception lies in the ability of fragment theory to cope with them. The Lazarus-Mc-

Cleary design is easily understood in terms of part-perception. However, as we have seen, fragment theory cannot account directly for congruent prerecognition hypotheses where ordinary words are involved. If a seen fragment of the word *EASTER* leads the subject to report *SACRED,* as in Postman, Bruner, and McGinnies (1948), some kind of recognition of *EASTER* must have taken place first.

However, it is not necessary to suppose that *EASTER* was recognized by a special and superdiscriminative mechanism. We need only assume what introspection confirms—that subjects do not report every hypothesis that they form. If *EASTER* occurs to the subject only as a tentative possibility, the usual mechanisms of word-association may easily lead him to consider related words as other possibilities and occasionally to report one. Thus, common associates of the stimulus word should appear as prerecognition hypotheses relatively often. Since associates tend to belong to the same meaning-class (pleasant or unpleasant) as their stimulus, his guess about the class-membership of the stimulus will be often right even when he does not identify it correctly. If my interpretation is correct, congruent prerecognition hypotheses are essentially based on verbal processes and should not appear in the visual descriptions given by carefully interrogated subjects.

Before concluding the discussion of subception, we must briefly consider a third class of experiments which seem to implicate a superdiscriminating unconscious more directly. There have been many attempts to show that stimuli presented *very far* below the threshold of verbal report nevertheless are registered and play a subsequent role in the subjects' unconscious mentation. Those studies which depended on backward masking to conceal the critical stimuli were considered in Chapter 2, where it was argued that inferences from partial cues or from the demand characteristics of the situation were probably responsible for the results. It seems desirable to reaffirm this conclusion here with respect to briefly presented words. Since it would be impossible to review all the experiments which purport to demonstrate what may be called "radical" subception, we will consider only two—one in which the possible sources of artifact seem clear, and another where they are less obvious.

In the first of these (Dixon, 1958a), subjects were given very short exposures of a number of words, including several taboo items—so short that they insisted they had seen nothing at all. Nevertheless, they were forced to guess at the words, and a week later they matched up their guesses with the (now supraliminal) stimuli. They were able to do this more accurately than chance would allow. But, as Fuhrer and Eriksen (1960) point out, the subjects may have become dark-adapted during the progress of the experiment and on later trials been able to make out at least the length of the exposed words, which had been invisible at first. Furthermore, the experimenter was evidently present while the subject did the subsequent matching and may have provided unintentional cues. An attempted replication by Fuhrer and Eriksen (1960) did not succeed. Dixon has reported a great many other studies which seem to show the effects of subliminal perception in a number of ways (e.g., Dixon, 1958b; Worthington & Dixon, 1964), but in none of them does he seriously consider the possibility that an experimenter may unwittingly provide cues for a subject.

As a second example, we can consider the experiment of Spence and Holland (1962). While half the students in a classroom turned their back to the screen, the other half were exposed to several 7-msec. flashes of the word *CHEESE,* under illumination conditions such that "the general reaction of the group was that nothing had been flashed." Then the experimenter read a list of words, including ten associates of *CHEESE* (*MOUSE, GREEN, COW,* . . .) and ten control words, and immediately tested for recall. It turned out that the "experimental group" (those who had not turned around during the brief stimulation) recalled more cheese-associates than control words, while no such trend appeared in the subjects who had not been "exposed," nor in another group to whom *CHEESE* had been flashed above threshold! Spence and Holland are delighted with the paradoxical character of these results, which they take as proof that the unconscious has laws of its own.

In a group experiment of this kind, the results cannot easily be ascribed to demand characteristics. Nevertheless, it is difficult to take them at face value, and easier to agree with Bernstein and Eriksen's (1965) doubts as to whether the critical stimulus was really below threshold for all the subjects. These authors found no effects of "subliminal" stimuli when really careful threshold measurements were made in an experiment of similar design. Their interpretation seems preferable to that of Spence and Holland, since it does not force us to assume that the discriminative capacities of man have been grossly underestimated by all other procedures.

## *READING FOR MEANING*

In the two preceding sections, I have taken on the role of debunker and tried to show that neither perceptual defense nor subception are in any way mysterious. Both phenomena are readily observed, but they can be accounted for in terms of fragment theory, expectation, response suppression, word-association, and other principles of which we have a reasonable understanding. Before concluding this chapter, it is appropriate to mention a more mysterious phenomenon, which is far less easily explained. Most people—and surely most readers of this book—can understand what they read without actually identifying many of the individual words. How is this possible?

It is very clear that this kind of reading—often called "reading for meaning"—does occur. The evidence is not merely introspective but quantitative. By definition, to "identify" a word or a letter is to pronounce its name in inner or outer speech, and thus to store it in verbal immediate memory. We have seen that even the words of an overlearned phrase cannot be pronounced in less than 100 msec. apiece (600 per minute). The maximum scanning rate through a word list, where individual meanings must be taken into account, is only half that fast (Neisser & Beller, 1965). Since many people read appreciably faster than 300 or even 600 words per minute, they surely do not identify every word (unless Sperling's 1967 model, which allows 100 letters to be identified every second, is to be accepted. See Chapter 2). For that matter, even people who read more slowly do not usually report word-for-word encoding. Most literate adults resort to individual words only when the material is very difficult, or when viewing conditions are poor.

The usual explanation of this kind of reading appeals to the "redundancy" of language. It is well-known that readers (and listeners) can "fill in" missing letters and words in English prose with remarkable success. The "redundancy" of English has been estimated by various methods to be as high as 50 percent. (For a sophisticated discussion of this concept in information-theory terms, see Garner, 1962.) In some way, this "redundancy" enables the reader to supplement what he sees with information drawn from his past experience.

Despite the quantitative precision of information theory, such an account of reading for meaning leaves something to be desired. It suggests that a reader sees half the words on the page and infers the others, like a subject in a "filling-in" experiment. But rapid reading is no more limited to 1200 or 600 words a minute than to 300. Moreover, in reading one does not seem to "see" only a few words, separated by blank spaces and blurs. Verbal memory does not seem to contain an irregular sample of items, leaving to some other process the task of completing the sense; neither does it contain the whole sequence, some words having been seen and others inferred.

There is a somewhat plausible analogy between reading sentences without attending to specific words and recognizing words without attending to specific letters. It is easy, and perhaps even helpful, to say that reading for meaning is "at a higher level" than recognizing words, just as words themselves are at a higher level than letters. This comfortable simile should not blind us to a real difference between the two relationships. Word-recognition and letter-recognition are often very similar processes. In both cases, the end product is a *name,* a structured verbal pattern in inner or outer speech. Given a cognitive system capable of constructing individual letters visually, and of verbalizing their names, no giant step is required for it to use the same methods to identify whole words. That is, the recognition of a word is not always "at a higher level" than the recognition of a single letter. The same methods can lead from the same kind of elementary information to the same sort of result. To be sure, there are many cases when recognition of letters *does* precede the recognition of words, but then the mediating role of verbal inference is usually obvious.

Where rapid reading is concerned, the situation is quite different. The end product of cognitive activity is not a bit of verbal behavior but a deep cognitive structure; not a verbalized name but a continuing silent stream of thought. Reading for meaning seems to be a kind of analysis-by-synthesis, a construction which builds a non-sensory structure just as "lower levels" of cognition synthesize visual figures or spoken words. Reading is externally guided thinking. Perhaps we should not be surprised that it is so poorly understood; we may not understand it until we understand thought itself.

In rapid reading, we attain a meaning without identifying individual words. In this respect it bears some resemblance to subception, and some of the impetus for the study of subception may have come from the observation that meaning can be somehow attained without attending to individual words in the reading process. Nevertheless, I believe that the two phenomena are very different. The conditions of subception are diametrically opposed to those which facilitate rapid reading. Brief, dim exposures lead to subception because they interfere with accurate identification, but they do not lead to rapid reading. In reading for meaning, we continuously take account of *new* constellations of words to construct *novel* thought processes. In subception, on the other hand, a *familiar* but indistinct constellation of letters leads to the verbal representation of an entirely *familiar* word, or to an equally familiar nonverbal response. Finally, the results of the subception experiments can easily be explained without leaving the framework of visual synthesis and verbal memory, while the existence of rapid reading apparently cannot be understood within this frame of reference at all.

Until some understanding of reading for meaning is achieved, we will remain embarrassingly ignorant about questions that appear superficially easy. How fast is it possible to read? However dubious we may be about the extravagant claims of reading-improvement courses, we cannot refute them. Indeed, we cannot even *define* "reading" (as distinguished from "skipping," for example), let alone set a maximum to its speed. What role do the meanings (in a dictionary sense) of individual words play when we grasp the meaning of a paragraph? Why is high-speed reading unpleasant, leading many persons who have learned it to drop back soon to intermediate speeds? Does reading for meaning bypass verbal immediate memory altogether, or does it only make use of that memory in a novel way? The discussion of linguistics in Chapter 10 may clarify some of these questions, but they will not be answered. For the present, rapid reading represents an achievement as impossible in theory as it is commonplace in practice.

## Chapter 6

# Visual Memory

This chapter begins with the integrative process that transforms a succession of fleeting and discontinuous retinal snapshots into a stable perceived world. Eidetic and dream imagery may well represent extensions of the same constructive activity; at least they seem to involve similar eye movements. The symbolic function of imagery and dreaming is then considered, along with "dream-incorporation" and related phenomena. Schizophrenic, hypnotic, and drug-induced hallucinations are discussed. Finally, the sensory experiences produced by electrical stimulation of the brain, sometimes presented as evidence for a "permanent record of the stream of consciousness," are given a different interpretation.

Previous chapters have dealt only with two kinds of memory. The first of these is the brief persistence of "iconic storage," which lasts for one or two seconds at best. While it lasts, we can focus and refocus our attention several times, on different parts of the field, and construct a number of visual figures, letters, or words. The other kind of memory is verbal: we can also *name* the figures we construct, thereby entering a different storage medium called "verbal" or "auditory" memory. Important as these two processes are, however, they are by no means the only ways to store visually-presented information. It is impossible to suppose that all visual memory really stops with the icon; that we preserve nothing except what we have time to describe. One does not synthesize visual figures only for the sake of naming them. Everyday experience provides many proofs that visual information can outlast the stimulus almost indefinitely. Perhaps the most obvious way to make this point is to note that animals and young children can learn from visual experience. Since they do not use words, some nonverbal storage medium must be available to them.

There are many phenomena in ordinary adult cognition which force us to postulate a visual memory. Imagery is perhaps the most obvious of these, but recognition, perceptual learning, and similar processes should not be ignored. However, direct "reproduction" has a more dubious status. A request to reproduce visual information does not necessarily restrict the subject to visual memory. He may also base his response on such other sources as verbally-coded information, stereotypes, or motor habits (Carmichael, Hogan, & Walter, 1932; Bartlett, 1932). It is important to realize that the influence of stereotypes on reproduction need not imply that visual memory itself has been affected by them. The subject can often *recognize* the original picture although he has produced a distorted version of it (Prentice, 1954), and he may even be able to draw an undistorted copy if the experimenter explicitly demands one (M. T. Orne, personal communication, 1966). Thus, experiments using the method of reproduction give only equivocal evidence about visual memory, and will not be considered in this chapter. On the other hand, it seems necessary to begin our discussion with a process in which the contribution of memory has gone almost entirely unnoticed.

## *VISUAL SNAPSHOTS AND THEIR INTEGRATION*

In normal use, the eyes can shift to a new fixation point several times every second. As Lashley put it, "Visual perceptions are rarely based upon a momentary stimulation of the fixed retina . . . most of our perception of objects is derived from a succession of scanning movements, the succession of retinal images being translated into a single impression of form" (1954, p. 432). This act of "translation" has hardly ever been studied, but it is evidently among the most fundamental cognitive processes. It is not restricted to human beings; every animal with eyes like ours must carry out the same kind of integration. Nor is it a process that can occur in vision alone. When we feel an object with our hands, the succession of *tactile* stimuli is "translated into a single impression of form" by a process which seems closely analogous to the visual one (Gibson, 1962).

As you read this page, your eyes make dozens of discrete fixations, perhaps averaging about 300 msec. in length. As many as three separate fixations, taking about one second in all, may be occurring for each line of print. Yet you do not experience a rapid and bewildering succession of visual experiences; you see the whole page continuously, though your attention may be focused only on a part of it. This suggests that a residue of information extracted from earlier fixations remains available, and helps to determine what is seen in the present. The residue cannot just be a series of copies, or "afterimages," of previous patterns; successive copies would only overlap in a confusing manner. Indeed, confusion often results if the *stationary* eye is presented with a rapid series of different figures, although other consequences are also possible in such a case.

It is sometimes assumed that eye movements go unnoticed because each one is precisely compensated by some innate mechanism, which can project every successive "snapshot" onto the right place in a higher-level "map" of phenomenal space. This seems very unlikely. Not only does recent work in motion-perception give us reason to doubt the existence of such a mechanism (Stoper, 1967), but its usefulness would be limited in any case. Movements of the head and body, and especially motions of the object itself, change the proximal stimulus somewhat as eye movements do, but stable objects are seen nevertheless. Proximal changes actually *aid* in the perception of depth and solidity, a fact long recognized as the effect of "movement parallax" or "gradients of motion" (Gibson, 1950). They are also critical in what Wallach has called the "kinetic depth effect" (Wallach & O'Connell, 1953). However, the motions of external objects could hardly be "compensated" by any innate mechanism. The conclusion seems inescapable: if we see moving objects as unified things, it must be because perception results from an integrative process over time. The same process is surely responsible for the construction of visual objects from the successive "snapshots" taken by the moving eye.

Under normal conditions, then, visual perception itself is a constructive act. The perceiver "makes" stable objects, using information from a number of "snapshots" together. Such a process requires a kind of memory, but not one which preserves pictorial copies of earlier patterns. Instead, there is a constantly developing schematic model, to which each new fixation adds new information. The individual "snapshots" are remembered only in the way that the words of a sentence are remembered when you can recollect nothing but its meaning: they have contributed to something which endures. Every successive glance helps to flesh out a skeleton which the first already begins to establish.

When the notion of "figural synthesis" was introduced in Chapter 4, we were primarily concerned with the isolated retinal patterns produced by tachistoscopic exposures. With such stimuli, it seemed almost a matter of taste whether one spoke of "analyzing" the input or "synthesizing" a perceptual object. Here, however, the terminology of synthesis becomes far more compelling. Given a succession of different input patterns, the perceiver constructs something. If eye movements intervene between related patterns, the constructed object may be seen as stationary; otherwise it will probably seem to move or change its shape. Depending on the particular relations between "snapshots," it may or may not be perceived as having three-dimensional depth. Unfortunately, the limitations of this book do not allow us to consider the classical problems of space and motion perception, though they obviously fall within the compass of cognitive psychology. In principle, *all* perceptual phenomena arise from transformations of input information.

Before leaving the question of visual integration, it seems appropriate to raise some additional questions. One of these concerns iconic memory (Chapter 2), which preserves visual information for a second or so after a single brief exposure. In normal vision, we often take several glances at an object in a second: what role do the iconic representations of earlier "snapshots" play in the constructive process? Is iconic memory the mechanism by which integration is achieved, or does it act as an obstacle to that integration if it persists long enough?

The second hypothesis is perhaps the more plausible of the two. If the icon is a retinally-fixed representation of a single visual "snapshot," it could only cause confusion by overlapping with subsequent glances. Just this kind of confusion does result from ordinary negative afterimages. For example, if you look first at the center of a bright light and then at its edge, you will probably see a grey area (the afterimage from the first fixation) superimposed on the light itself. If we are willing to generalize from afterimages to iconic memory, we must conclude that the latter has little or no role in visual integration. At most, it could preserve each "snapshot" long enough for some information to be assimilated. Thereafter, a more schematic memory, not tied to retinal position, would have to take over.

While this interpretation may be persuasive, it is not the only possible one. Iconic memory may not be related to the afterimage at all; this is one reason why I felt compelled to invent a new name for it. Perhaps *all* useful visual memory is of the integrative, schematic sort, and the icon only *seems* like a fading retinal image because it has always been studied with flat stimulus objects and without eye movements. We could hardly expect the subject's process of visual synthesis to function normally in tachistoscopic exposures. Although the icon does look like a rather literal copy of the retinal input, it may seem literal merely because it has only a single "snapshot" to integrate. Perhaps it really represents a limiting case of the synthesis that ordinarly unites different retinal patterns. For the present, this question must remain undecided.

Equally unknown is the relation of these two types of visual memory—iconic storage and the integration of snapshots—to a further kind of perceptual learning, which also involves short-term storage of visual information. At issue here is the effect of recent past experience on the organization of ambiguous visual patterns. This effect was first demonstrated by Leeper (1935), with the aid of the famous *wife/mother-in-law figure* (Figure 29a). He was not able to influence his subjects' perception of this figure by a preliminary verbal description, but could easily do so by first showing a biased version of it, like those in Figures 29b and 29c. Apparently, some organizational tendency persisted between trials.

An ingenious demonstration by Epstein and Rock (1960) shows

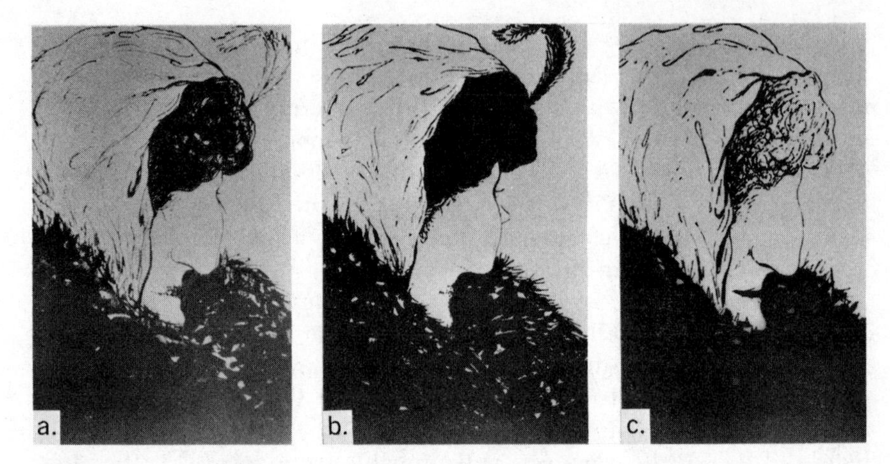


Figure 29a. "My wife and my mother-in-law." This ambiguous figure, used by Leeper (1935), was first described by Boring (1930). 29b. A version which is unambiguously the "wife." 29c. A version which is unambiguously the "mother-in-law."

that this kind of visual memory can be more powerful than mere "set" in determining how an ambiguous figure will be organized. Using the *wife/mother-in-law* and other figures, they preceded the ambiguous pattern with an alternating series of biased versions. After a sequence like *W–M–W–M–W–M–?,* the subjects *expected* the *W* but had *most recently seen* the *M*. If the ambiguous figure appeared at this point, *M* was generally seen: a clear victory for recency over expectation. It seems evident that this aftereffect represents a kind of short-term perceptual learning, which may well be related to the integration of successive retinal patterns, to iconic memory, or to both. Unfortunately, neither its time-course nor its limitations are known.

Why have these phenomena been so little studied? The general lack of interest in them is especially striking where "snapshot" integration is concerned, since it underlies virtually all ordinary vision. Perhaps the reason is the efficiency of the process itself. Our eye movements generally have no counterpart in phenomenal experience. We are not aware of the succession of different inputs in our own perception, so the issue does not force itself upon us. It is this very unobtrusiveness of the movements that seems to demand explanation. The integrative process is so efficient that a radical realignment of the input several times each second can go completely unnoticed!

In contrast to the general neglect of the problem is one very substantial attempt to deal with it directly: that of Hebb (1949). His interpretation is, however, quite different from the one I have given. He argues that one can perceive objects as wholes only after familiarity with them has made it nearly irrelevant where the eye fixates. The organized central activity (or "phase sequence," in his terminology) which corresponds to seeing any particular sort of object can arise only through extensive visual experience. During this experience, fixation on one part, followed by an eye movement, has frequently then been followed by fixation on another part, and then another and another. Eventually,

> . . . the various sets of assemblies (of neurons which correspond to various retinal patterns) would gradually acquire an interfacilitation—if sight of the object from one angle is often followed by sight of it from another. Arousing one set would then mean arousing the others, and essentially the same total activity would be aroused in each case (Hebb, 1949, p. 91).

According to this theory, the integration of retinal patterns does indeed involve visual memory, but it is not primarily a short-term memory for immediately preceding retinal input. Instead, a long-term and slow-growing "interfacilitation" among the memory-representations of individual "snapshots" is held to be responsible. If you see the printed page as a stable and single visual object, despite the rapid succession of retinal images, it is only because you have often experienced such a succession before. Any one of the present fixations would presumably suffice to arouse the neural system created by these earlier experiences.

In my opinion, such a model does not do justice to our perceptual capabilities. It is reminiscent of those theories of speech perception which try to explain our understanding of sentences in terms of previous familiarity with the words of which they are comprised, and of associations between these words. Chapter 10 will show that such theories do not account for our understanding of *novel* sentences (and nearly every sentence we hear is novel), and do not give a good account of linguistic structure. It seems, at least intuitively, that an associative model of visual integration must encounter similar difficulties.

Although Hebb's view may be uncongenial, it must be admitted that there are not many data which might decide between it and the notion of figural synthesis. Although innumerable tachistoscopic experiments have limited the subject to one fixation, none seem to have limited him to two. Such everyday processes as tracking, typing, reading, and visual search have been studied in terms of *motor* integration, but rarely with respect to its visual counterpart. Thus, it is hard to be sure if successive retinal patterns are related in an interactive, constructive way, or whether each "snapshot" acts independently to arouse a central representation that already exists. However, there are at least two sources of suggestive evidence: apparent motion and visual imagery.

We have already noted that the field of movement perception is too complex to be dealt with here. Nevertheless, a few passing remarks about apparent (or "stroboscopic") motion may not be out of place. This phenomenon, which underlies the ordinary "moving picture," can be produced very easily. One simple way is to light two small lamps in alternation, with a time interval of about 300 msec. between them (the exact interval for optimal movement depends on many variables). The observer sees one lamp moving back and forth, in an illusory motion which he can follow with his eyes if he wants to. This was the first phenomenon studied by the Gestalt psychologists (Wertheimer, 1912), and with good reason. The perceived motion is not inherent in either stimulus alone, but only arises by virtue of the relation between them; it is a whole very obviously different from either of its parts.

Apparent motion occurs normally even if, due to an intervening eye movement, the images of both lamps fall on the same retinal position (Rock & Ebenholtz, 1962). Moreover, the perception of apparent motion is innate, not only in lower animals (Rock, Tauber, & Heller, 1965), but also in human beings (Tauber & Koffler, 1966). Hence, we have at least one instance in which the integration of successive retinal "snapshots" demonstrably occurs *without* the benefit of past experience. It is perhaps noteworthy that Hebb's (1949) book omits all discussion of the perception of movement, whether real or apparent.

Moving objects are, then, "constructed" by the perceiver on the basis of several "snapshots" together. A phenomenon described by Kolers (1964a, 1964b) provides a particularly good illustration of this constructive process. If a Necker cube is set into apparent motion back and forth (Figure 30), it will undergo occasional reversals of perspective

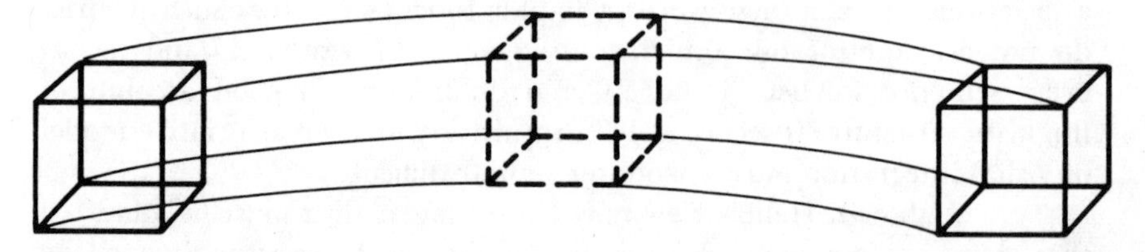

Figure 30. Kolers (1964b) found that when a Necker cube is set into oscillating apparent motion, it may undergo spontaneous reversal of perspective while apparently in midflight.

just as a stationary cube does. The important point is that some of these reversals occur *in midflight,* at moments when the cube seems to be halfway between its two terminal positions. To be sure, the perceived cube is a product of figural synthesis even at its end points, but its synthetic nature is especially obvious when the apparent cube is at a place where the real cubes never go. The reversal of perspective at that point emphasizes that figural synthesis is not a matter of cold-blooded inference but of genuine construction.

The example of apparent motion gives us good reason to believe that perception involves a genuine integration of successive patterns. If this is true, some kind of schematic visual memory, readily modified by information from further glances, must endure at least through a number of "snapshots." The term "schematic" does not imply anything less real than ordinary perceptions—indeed, these *are* the ordinary perceptions. But what is seen is not the product of any single glance; it must be both less than this, and more.

What happens to these integrated perceptions when the subject turns elsewhere? Are they simply lost, as construction of a new visual figure begins? One might think so. It turns out, however, that they are often preserved, and a "schematic" visual object can sometimes be recovered after long periods of time. This sort of recovery is what is called a "visual image." We shall see that images are indeed constructs, rather than replicas of isolated stimulus patterns.

### *VISUAL IMAGERY AND VISUAL SYNTHESIS*

There is no getting around the fact that people often see things which are not physically present at all. We can try to exclude this fact from consideration by distinguishing "hallucination" and "imagery" from "perception," but the phenomena themselves remain: dreams, hypnagogic images, eidetic images, psychotic hallucinations, and so on. It is with these sorts of imagery, as well as with the more mundane visual images of ordinary memory, that we are here concerned. (Of course, this does not imply that all "ordinary memory" includes visual images. There are wide individual differences in this respect, as was first noted by Francis Galton: see Woodworth, 1938.)

Although the difference between hallucination and perception is clear enough in extreme cases, it does not represent a sharp boundary. The preliminary definition above, phrased in terms of "not physically present," is evidently inadequate. If a man dreams about his wife, his dream is not less a hallucination because she actually lies beside him. On the other hand, watching a movie is surely perception and not imagery, even though none of the perceived objects are really there. For these reasons, the definition of imagery is usually stated with respect to *stimuli* rather than objects; one is said to have an image whenever one's visual experience does not correspond with what is "present to the senses," i.e., with the retinal "snapshot." But this more sophisticated definition does not really help; some of its difficulties have already been mentioned. Our visual experience is never the stimulus directly. It is always a construction, based only in part on currently arriving information. What we hallucinate, on the other hand, may also incorporate some stimulus information, as when a blast of cold air from the window leads to a dream in which we are trapped with Scott at the South Pole. The arguments of the last section strengthen this point still more. Perception is generally the result of an integration of many "snapshots," which creates something different from any of them; seeing itself is a matter of visual memory.

With such a premise, one can plausibly think of the various forms of imagery as if they were closely related to the processes of perception. This is the viewpoint to be explored here. It is hardly a new idea: such otherwise different theorists as Freud (1900) and Newell, Shaw, and Simon (1962) have held that images make use of the perceptual apparatus. My application of the same principle means that images will be treated here as products of visual synthesis. If visual cognition is an active and constructive process in "perceiving," when there is much relevant information in the retinal image, it must continue to be so when stored information is primarily involved. Imagery is not a matter of opening old file drawers, but of building new models.

Terms like "hallucination" and "image" have been used in different ways by different authors. My own usage will be as follows: "visual image" is a partly undefined term for something *seen* somewhat in the way real objects are seen, when little or nothing in the immediate or very recent sensory input appears to justify it. Imagery ranges from the extremely vivid and externally localized images of the Eidetiker—to be described below—to the relatively hazy and unlocalized images of ordinary visual memory. I hope the reader has at least as much imagery as I do, which is just enough to persuade me that those who report these phenomena are not simply telling tall stories. Believing that the processes of imagery are also those of perception, I will use the verb "see," hereafter without quotation marks, with respect to them. Believing that these processes also create the vivid visual phantasms of dreams and psychoses, I will occasionally use the term "image" in this connection as well. An image, even an unclear one, is called a "hallucination" if the subject believes that what he sees really exists; otherwise it is just an image, no matter how vivid it happens to be.

If images are the product of visual synthesis, we must conclude that one phenomenon, often thought of as related to them, belongs in a separate category entirely. This is the so-called "afterimage," negative or positive, which may appear after one has been staring at bright lights or colors. Afterimages apparently have little to do with visual synthesis; at most, they are the dregs of single "snapshots." That is the reason why, unlike perceived objects and genuine imagery, they move with every shift of the eyes. The afterimages apparently play no important role in vision; they are only the senile vestiges of once-useful processes. They are significant chiefly because they may be responsible for a number of visual disturbances studied by psychologists, perhaps including the so-called "figural aftereffects" (Ganz, 1966a, 1966b).

Neither vision itself, nor its resurrection in imagery, seems to owe much to these phenomena. By the same token, afterimages themselves seem almost invulnerable to the higher processes of vision. One can ignore them, by focusing attention on other things, but it is apparently impossible to produce them directly by expectation, learning, or intent. To be sure, we may elaborate an afterimage into a rich and genuine imagined visual object, but then it is functioning more as a stimulus than as part of the process of synthesis. The occasional reports of afterimages produced by hypnotically-hallucinated colors have not stood up to careful scrutiny (Barber, 1964). Figural aftereffects, which Ganz (1966a, 1966b) interprets as dependent on afterimages, also cannot be produced without actual stimulation. Reported results to the contrary have probably been due to demand-characteristic effects like those demonstrated by Singer and Sheehan (1965).

However, there is one role which afterimages have often played in studies of genuine images: they have been used as vehicles of communication between experimenter and subject. This has been especially common in experiments on *eidetic* imagery (Jaensch, 1930). An image is called "eidetic" when (1) the subject describes it as having a clarity and definiteness comparable to that of external objects; (2) he "projects" it, i.e., sees it as occupying a particular place in space; (3) he can "examine" it as he might examine a real picture; and (4) it does not shift its position with eye movements as an afterimage would. One obvious source of difficulty in studying these images is that the "Eidetiker," generally a child, may be quite unpracticed at the art of describing his own experience. He may even be reluctant to do so lest he be thought crazy or foolish, since he sees things that are not really present. To overcome these problems, studies of eidetic imagery generally begin by inducing some predictable negative afterimages, which the subject is encouraged to describe carefully. Only then is he asked to look at a picture, and to report whether he can still see it after the experimenter has taken it away.

While this method may indeed overcome the observer's reluctance to describe images of any kind, it has its own problems. In particular, it may change the demand characteristics of the situation so radically that the subject will feel he *ought* to report images, even if he doesn't have any! Moreover, it points up another difficulty which would exist in any case: how are genuine eidetic images to be distinguished from afterimages at all? As Klüver pointed out in his thorough review (1931), the classical studies of eidetic imagery were not carried out with sufficient consideration of these (and other) possible artifacts. Partly for this reason, the phenomenon was little studied in the 30 years between

1934 and 1964. Apparently no one doubted the fact itself—that some children can essentially see a picture even after it is no longer present, and read off details that they had not mentioned during the original presentation—but it seemed too elusive and ill-defined for systematic study.

The subject of eidetic imagery has recently been revived in a careful study by Haber and Haber (1964), noteworthy both for its method and for its results. The Habers relied systematically on a criterion which had been used only haphazardly in the classical eidetic work: eye movements. In the preliminary trials (intended to produce negative afterimages), the subject was told to fixate, both during the exposure of the colored square and when the image was expected. But later, when pictures were presented, he was told ". . . move your eyes around so that you can be sure you can see all the details." At the end of the instructions, the experimenter repeated ". . . be sure, while the picture is on the easel, that you move your eyes around it to see all of the parts." At the point when the eidetic image was expected, scanning movements of the eyes were permitted to continue: "When I take the picture away, I want you to continue to look hard at the easel where the picture was, and tell me what you can still see after I take it away. After I take it away, you also can move your eyes all over where it was on the easel" (p. 134). Moreover, the experimenter watched the subject's eyes carefully to make sure that the scanning instructions were obeyed during the 30-second presentation of the picture, and to see whether any scanning took place while the image was being reported.

Haber and Haber individually tested 151 children—almost the whole enrollment of a New Haven elementary school. After the preliminary afterimage trials, each child was given four complex pictures (e.g., an Indian fishing in a canoe, with many fish in the water) in the test for eidetic imagery. Their image reports were scored for accuracy (by a method of judgment, for which satisfactory reliability is reported). In addition, it was noted whether scanning occurred, whether the images were positively or negatively colored, and how long they lasted. By these criteria, 12 children stood out sharply as Eidetikers. There was a sharp discontinuity between their performance and those of the other 139 subjects on every measure. They were far more accurate; their images always lasted much longer (at least 40 seconds); nearly all their images were positively colored. Most impressive of all, the eidetic children all scanned each of their images, which the other subjects virtually never did.

The most interesting of these findings, at least from the present point of view, is the implication that eye movements play an important role in eidetic imagery. Eidetic reconstruction is of integrated visual scenes, not of retinal "snapshots." And the act of constructing the image evidently involves—indeed, may require—further eye movements like those originally made in perceiving. It is important to note that the eidetic children could distinguish clearly between "having an image" of the picture and just "remembering" it, which they could do after the image had disappeared. There was no question about the visual character of the eidetic process.

> The most striking aspect of the eidetic child's report was the vividness and completeness of an image that was "out there" in front of him. There was no qualification in his speech, such as "I think I see," nor did he ever use the past tense as he might have if he were combining image and memory. He was able to report very fine detail, such as the number of feathers worn by each of ten Indians in one pretest picture, the different colors in a multi-colored Indian blanket, the expressions on the faces, and the various poses of the persons, and all from the same image (Haber & Haber, 1964, p. 136).

With their rather strict criteria, Haber and Haber found that only 8 percent of the sample was eidetic. There was no hint of correlation with other obvious variables, such as age or sex. Since eidetic imagery seems to be almost nonexistent among American adults, the capacity must somehow decrease with age, but it is not known why or when the decline takes place. It is easy to suggest cultural reasons for it; Holt (1964) is one of many who have done so.

> In a factually-oriented, skeptical, anti-intraceptive, brass-tacks culture like ours, where the paranormal is scoffed at and myth and religion are in decline, the capacity for vivid imagery has little survival value and less social acceptability. We live in an age of literalism, an era that distrusts the imagination, while at the same time it develops its beat fringe of avid seekers after drugs that may artificially restore the capacity for poetic vision. It is little wonder that our children rapidly lose their eidetic capacity and that adults are made uneasy by the admission that they can experience things that are not factually present (p. 262).

This view receives apparent support from a recent study by Doob (1964), who used Haber's method to study eidetic imagery among adults of the Ibo tribe in Nigeria. While circumstances prevented Doob from making observations as carefully as might be desired, the main outlines of his findings are clear. Among *rural* Nigerian adults, eidetic imagery was extremely common: ". . . again and again informants who were utterly illiterate could trace correctly the license numbers in the last picture" (Doob, 1964, p. 361). However, *urban* members of the same tribe, living in the provincial capital of Enugu (population 15,000), showed very few traces of eidetic ability. While there were differences in the experimenter's rapport with the two samples which may have contributed to this result, it does tend to confirm the view that acculturation to adult urban life is somehow incompatible with eidetic ability. Further material appears in Doob (1965). Nevertheless, it would be hasty to conclude, with Holt, that the incompatibility stems from philosophical attitudes. Some visual factor connected with literacy may be responsible instead, or perhaps some gross physiological change is involved. Klüver (1965) believes there may be an intimate relation between eidetic images and the endocrine system. Siipola and Hayden (1965), in a very interesting study using the Habers' procedures, found that eidetic imagery is far more prevalent among brain-damaged, retarded children than among either normals or "familial" retardates of the same mental age.

Neither the children of the Habers' study nor Doob's Africans were asked to reinstate an image after it had once faded; they demonstrated only a capacity to hold on to a visual scene for a short period, generally a matter of minutes. Anecdotal evidence cited by Doob and by earlier workers in the field (Klüver, 1931) do suggest that some persons can recreate an eidetic image after months or years, but we have no experimental information about this possibility. However, one kind of imagery that reaches far into the past is familiar to all of us: our dreams.

## *DREAMING AND RELATED STATES*

Most dreams are primarily visual in content, although other modalities do appear (Oswald, 1962a). But though they are visual they are not always clear or vivid, as an eidetic image is. To be sure, dream images are hallucinatory: the subject believes that they are real objects. It is important to realize, however, that their experienced "realness" does not depend on their vividness. This point is often misunderstood. The use of such phrases as "hallucinatory clarity" by many writers is a mistake; hallucinations are not necessarily clear. In general, the perceived "realness" of things is not determined by their visual properties. We do not doubt the existence of a distant mountain whenever atmospheric conditions make it appear hazy, any more than we doubt the existence of Mt. Everest which we have never seen at all, or of a host of other unseen things: a round Earth, calories, or Eskimos. On the other hand, as we shall see, the images produced by certain drugs (misnamed "hallucinogens") are perceived as *un*real by most American users even when they are clear and vivid.

Thus, it is not surprising that hallucinating schizophrenics, like many dreamers, believe completely in the reality of images which are quite indistinct: voices heard only as murmurs, or faces seen only as blurs. They may also *dis*believe in the reality of things they see very well, including themselves or the people around them. Reality-testing is not primarily a matter of clarity; it involves questions of coherence, predictability, and sensibleness. Dreams and schizophrenic hallucinations seem real because these are questions which dreamers and lunatics do not ask. As Kolers has remarked: ". . . there is nothing in an experience that testifies to its correspondence with 'reality,' nothing in a perception that guarantees its truth. Judgments of reality and truth must come from other sources than the experience or the perception" (1964a, p. 99).

In recent years, the study of dreaming has been greatly accelerated by a series of exciting discoveries. The fundamental finding is that dreaming occurs primarily during a specific phase of sleep (variously called "stage 1," "paradoxical sleep," "REM-sleep," etc.) which recurs at regular intervals during the night. Subjects awakened from this stage very often report dreaming, even if they never recall any dreams under more ordinary circumstances. An enormous research literature has appeared in this area since the mid-1950s; for surveys see Oswald (1962a) or Foulkes (1966). Many points remain in dispute, but there is no doubt that most dreams are accompanied by a definite syndrome of physiological activity which includes both characteristic patterns of electrical activity in the brain and rapid movements of the eyes (REMs).

Are the rapid eye movements of a dreamer directly related to the visual nature of his dreams? Sometimes they seem to be. Roffwarg, Dement, Muzio, and Fisher (1962) compared the directions of successive glances in dreams (as inferred from the dream reports obtained subsequently) with the recorded eye movements of the sleeper, and found considerable correspondence. One subject, who was dreaming of walking up five or six steps, made five distinct upward deflections of the eyes spaced two or three seconds apart. This and similar instances suggest that the dreamer, like the eidetic child, moves his eyes normally around the imagined visual field.

On the other hand, it is perfectly clear that not all the rapid eye movements occurring in sleep can play this role. Similar movements have been observed in sleeping decorticate cats, newborn infants, and—though this point has been the subject of dispute—congenitally blind adults who have no visual dreams (Gross, Feldman, & Fisher, 1965). Moreover, many of the movements normally observed are much too extensive and violent to represent normal visual synthesis. Thus, eye motion can evidently occur during sleep for reasons that have nothing to do with imagery, as is also true in the waking state. Nevertheless it seems likely that vivid dream imagery, when it occurs, tends to be accompanied by suitable eye movements just as eidetic imagery is. What is reconstructed in a visual dream is not a single "snapshot" but an integrated visual event.

Related to the dream is the *hypnagogic* state which just precedes falling asleep. This transitional stage is notorious for the richness of its imagery. In a review of recent work, Holt (1964) estimates that half the population experiences hypnagogic images, though he does not say how he arrives at this proportion. Such images are often extremely vivid and compelling, and may be bizarre as well. McKellar (1957) quotes a report of "successive hypnagogic images that comprised a camel standing on a hilltop, fountain pens being filled, a screen composed of turkey feathers, a rowing eight on a river, an ice cream cornet, and so on" (p. 36). Often they are terrifying: "a large, bloated, yellow face, pouting, red lips, wild, blue eyes rolling, hair dishevelled . . ." (p. 37). These are not dreams, because the subject still knows who and where he is, and consequently knows that what he sees is imaginary. It is worth emphasizing again that the vividness of the hypnagogic image does not convince him of its real existence; conversely, the vagueness of many dreams seems to provide no grounds for doubt.

Recently there has been a revival of interest in the hypnagogic state. For example, Foulkes and Vogel (1965) found that conscious experiences during "falling asleep" (i.e., as the EEG shifted from a waking pattern to a sleeping one) were very like those of actual dreaming. Surprisingly, a dreamlike belief that the imaginary events were really occurring could be accompanied even by a *waking* EEG: "REM-sleep" is apparently not necessary for this kind of consciousness. Foulkes and Vogel also found that, while bizarre and exciting images were indeed experienced by some subjects as they fell asleep, much of the hypnagogic imagery reported—like many dreams—was relatively prosaic.

It is likely, as Oswald (1962a) and Holt (1964) suggest, that some of the imagery which has appeared in studies of *sensory deprivation* is essentially hypnagogic in nature. Witkin and his associates (Bertini, Lewis, & Witkin, 1964; Witkin & Lewis, 1965) have successfully used a background of "white" noise and homogeneous visual stimulation to induce hypnagogic phenomena, as will appear below. However, much recent work shows that reduction of sensory input, by itself, does not necessarily result in hallucinations or other perceptual phenomena at all. Although such effects do appear in "sensory deprivation" studies, they are partly a function of overt suggestion (Jackson & Kelly, 1962; Schaefer & Bernick, 1965) and of the implicit demand characteristics of the situation (Orne & Scheibe, 1964). Nevertheless, given the current interest in all these phenomena, we can expect increasing information about the processes involved in vivid imagery. So far, there seem to have been no explicit studies of the relation between directed eye movements and the content of a hypnagogic image (except for a brief study reported by Dement, 1965), but it seems likely that some relationship exists for these processes as it does for eidetic and dream imagery.

There is even evidence that eye movements are involved in another, less dramatic kind of imagery: the ordinary memory image which most people can summon up, at least crudely, when they want to. For example, Hebb reports:

"I find it very difficult to have a clear image of a triangle, square, or circle without imagining or actually making a series of eye movements. Several others, asked to make observation on this point, have reported the same thing. It is hard or impossible, that is, to have a clear image of a triangle fixated at one point. Eye movements definitely improve the 'image.' They do not take the form, necessarily, of following the figure's contours, but are apt to jump from point to point, perhaps three to four points in all." He adds ". . . approximately the same series of eye movements may contribute to a good image either of circle or square" (Hebb, 1949, p. 34).

A systematic study of this question was carried out by Antrobus, Antrobus, and Singer (1964), who also cite published reports similar to Hebb's as early as 1903. Their method followed the lead provided by Roffwarg *et al.* (1962), who had found it easiest to match eye movements and dreams when the content of the imagery included systematic *movement* (like climbing stairs). Thus, the subjects of Antrobus *et al.* were sometimes asked to imagine static scenes (e.g., an illuminated face in a dark empty room) and sometimes active movements (a tennis match observed from the net). The result was a great increase in eye movements during the active scenes as compared to the passive ones.

There is some danger of a contradiction here, which should not go unnoticed. If eidetic images are distinguished from the images of ordinary memory because they can be scanned, then ordinary imagery cannot very well depend on scanning too. I suspect that the difference is a matter of degree. The comments of Hebb and the study by Antrobus *et al.* only demonstrate a *tendency* to move the eyes during imagery, not a really systematic scanning process. Moreover, we do not know how "good" the images of the Antrobus subjects (or of Hebb and his associates) actually were. It seems likely that there is a continuum of the vividness of images, which is loosely correlated with the extent to which scanning eye movements are involved in them. One would not expect the correlation to be perfect. Even in perceiving real objects, where a similar correlation exists (one generally makes appropriate eye movements in attending to objects) shifts of attention without ocular motion can occur. Visual synthesis of an image without eye motion may be possible, but the better the image the more likely it is to involve some sort of scanning.

It is reasonable to conclude that all types of imagery do involve a process of visual synthesis, of construction, much like the one used to attend to objects and to integrate successive snapshots in ordinary vision. The emphasis given to eye movements in this discussion is not meant to imply that the construction is primarily of a movement-pattern;

obviously, an image is a *visual* and not merely a motoric structure. Its intimate association with ocular motion has been stressed primarily to show that imagery is a coordinated activity, like perception, and not just a revival of stored pictures.

There is another sense in which much imagery is obviously "constructive": its content. In dreams and in hypnagogic reverie, one frequently sees objects that one has never seen before, and even things that could never be encountered in the real world. While the components of such an image may all be traceable to one or another previous experience, they often appear to the perceiver in new and bizarre combinations. The explanation of these images demands something more than a theory of visual information processing. We would like to know what they mean, why they appear, and whether they serve any purpose. These questions may be asked about every sort of imagery, even the more mundane kinds, and they deserve consideration even if satisfactory answers are hard to find.

## *THE FUNCTIONS OF IMAGERY*

On first consideration, the varieties of visual imagery seem to divide naturally into two different kinds. In this dichotomy, one side would be represented by the unrealistic, unpredictable, and apparently novel images of hypnagogic reverie and sleep, while the other consists of realistic (and apparently reproductive) images like those of the eidetic child or the waking, remembering adult. Images of the first kind reflect what Freud (1900) called the "primary process" of thinking—primary not only because he thought it appeared in the child before any other sort of mentation, but also because he believed that it remained in close touch with the basic drives throughout life. The more practical images of memory, on the other hand, seem to be part of the "secondary process," in the service of normal adaptation. (For a review of the primary-secondary process distinction in terms familiar to the experimental psychologist, see Hilgard, 1962; for a recent presentation in psychoanalytic language, see Rapaport, 1951b. We will consider it further in Chapter 11.)

The primary and the secondary processes are said to differ not only in their characteristic operations—which produce a rich chaos in the first case and a dry logic in the other—but also in their motivation. Certainly, the two sorts of images we are comparing do seem to serve different functions. The purpose of the fantastic imagery that comes at the edge or in the depths of sleep is obscure. It is widely supposed that the meaning of such images, if they have any at all, can be discovered only by subtle psychoanalytic interpretation, following rules that are hard to understand and impossible to verify. On the other hand, eidetic imagery and memory imagery have usually been studied in subjects who are trying to remember something. As a result, there has been little doubt about their function; they apparently carry practical information, which the subject needs for his recall and "summons up" accordingly.

The distinction between these two kinds of imagery has been implicitly accepted in many quarters, but perhaps we should beware of drawing it too sharply. The waking image is not so functional a reproduction as has often been supposed, nor is the hypnagogic phantasm always unintelligible. For example, there are many reports that even eidetic images can be deliberately altered by the subject. "Objects can be made to change in color or size, and can be made to move about in the image" (Woodworth, 1938, p. 46). Meenes and Morton (1936) asked eight apparently eidetic children whether they could "make the dog move" in the image of a picture including a conspicuous dog. Not only did all the children succeed in this task, but "When asked what they had done to bring this about all subjects reported that when the eyes were moved to the left the dog jumped to the left, and when moved to the right, the dog jumped to the right" (p. 378). In fact, imagery which is apparently eidetic—as far as its clarity, apparent external position, and usefulness in recall are concerned—need not copy the originally perceived form at all! This is illustrated by the case of Salo Finkelstein, the "lightning calculator," who always imagined the numbers he worked with as written with chalk on a blackboard *in his own handwriting,* regardless of how they had been presented to him (Hunter, 1957, p. 151).

Thus, even eidetic imagery is not reproductive, not "photographic." Of course, the very notion of a "photographic memory" is based on the false assumption that there is "photographic perception"—that we see what is in the retinal "snapshot." Since this is not true, the most accurate visual memory imaginable could only reproduce the result of earlier integrative processes, and not the stimulus pattern itself. But it appears that even this degree of literalness is rarely or never achieved by the Eidetiker. What he has is a reconstruction—incredibly accurate in many cases, but a reconstruction nevertheless—on a continuum with other kinds of imagery that are more plastic and therefore less dependable.

The function and practical value of eidetic and memory imagery seem obvious—it provides information to the subject at the time of recall. But, while this may be true to a limited extent, it is by no means indisputable. Haber and Haber (1964) found eidetic recall more accurate than ordinary remembering (while the image lasted), but several other experimenters—Meenes and Morton (1936), Saltzman and Machover (1952), Siipola and Hayden (1965), Doob (1965)—report smaller differences or none. The negative results may stem from methodological weaknesses, and with careful procedures (such as those of Sheehan, below) a consistent difference should appear. Nevertheless, the information which the image provides is evidently not irreplaceable. It is even possible to be a "lightning calculator" without any imagery at all, judging by a case recently described by Hunter (1962).

When we go from eidetic imagery to the more common experience of adults with "good visual imagery," it is even more difficult to prove that images serve any immediate practical purpose. One might have supposed that persons who could summon up images would recall better than others who lack this talent, but in most cases this is not so. Bartlett's (1932) rather informal studies of this question showed that visualizers are often more *confident* than other subjects in describing a picture they have seen earlier, but not more *accurate*. The confidence (which everyone who interrogates a visualizer about such matters will encounter) is easy to understand, since the subject with a good visual image is describing an experience in the present—the image he currently sees. The lack of accuracy arises, according to Bartlett, because many details of the image may be importations and additions. We noted above that even eidetic images are subject to change; for ordinary memory images this is even more true. Woodworth (1938) gives an account of many attempts to separate visualizers from nonvisualizers in terms of the accuracy or richness of their recall, all of which ended in failure. (For a good example of lively and impressive recall in a nonvisualizer, see the quotation from Huxley in the next section.)

Very recently, Sheehan (1966) has demonstrated that vivid images do tend to be relatively accurate reproductions of the original "percepts" in at least some instances. His procedure forced the subject to examine the original material very closely at the time of presentation; it consisted of a design which had to be duplicated with blocks when it was first presented, and again later as the test of recall. With this method, the subject could not avoid carrying out complex processes of visual integration while the stimulus was still present. But even if the quality of imagery makes a difference under such conditions, they are hardly typical of daily life, or even of experimental procedures. It seems safe to say that ordinary visual images do not often play a critical part in purposive remembering.

It is true that when a good visualizer tries to remember something, a train of images generally appears before his "mind's eye." Asked to recall the syllables in a rote-learning experiment, for example, he may summon up an image of the memory drum. But in most cases, the syllable in the imagined drum will not be clear enough to read; he must still recall it nonvisually. For another example, the reader may try to remember who discovered the famous theorem about the square of the hypotenuse of a right triangle. He will probably have an image of a right triangle as he recalls the name of the right Greek philosopher. But the triangle itself does not provide the answer: the name required is not part of that image. What purpose, then, does it serve? The image hardly seems to be a step in the recall process at all, but rather a kind of cognitive "luxury," like an illustration in a novel.

This is not a new argument. Years ago, the introspective psychologists who studied the thought process came to the same conclusion. Images seemed to arise during thinking, but they did not generally do the substantive work. As Woodworth put it, "Images could occur as associative byplay without furthering the progress of thought" (1938, p. 788). If I am adding anything to these familiar observations, it is only to stress the continuity between images of this sort, arising in the course of directed thinking, and the phantasms of the "primary process." The memory images of waking thought are neither exact reproductions of earlier experiences nor useful sources of information for recall. Like the images of reverie and sleep, they serve primarily a "symbolic" function. (A similar argument has been made by Oswald, 1962a, but he seems to believe that images serve no function at all.)

To examine the symbolism of images more closely, it will help to examine some instances from the hypnagogic state. We can begin with a well-known retrospective report by Silberer.

> One afternoon I was lying on my couch. Though extremely sleepy, I forced myself to think through a problem of philosophy, which was to compare the views of Kant and Schopenhauer concerning time. In my drowsiness I was unable to sustain their ideas side by side. After several unsuccessful attempts, I once more fixed Kant's argument in my mind as firmly as I could and turned my attention back to Schopenhauer's. But when I tried to reach back to Kant, his argument was gone again, and beyond recovery. The futile effort to find the Kant record which was somehow misplaced in my mind suddenly represented itself to me—as I was lying there with my eyes closed, as in a dream—as a perceptual symbol: I am asking a morose secretary for some information; he is leaning over his desk and disregards me entirely; he straightens up for a moment to give me an unfriendly and rejecting look (1951, pp. 195–196).

Similar experiences are not uncommon; at least, I have had them myself. In the twilight stage between wakefulness and sleep, an abstract idea like "I am unable to obtain the necessary information" is transformed into the concrete vision of the morose secretary; a plan to improve a badly-written passage in an essay becomes an image of planing a piece of wood; the experience of taking a deep breath, with chest expanding, is represented by a hallucination of lifting up a table (these examples are also from Silberer). It seems that these images are simply appropriate concrete representations of thoughts which would otherwise be too abstract to pictorialize, as argued by Hall (1953a, 1953b), in his "cognitive theory of dreams."

Such transformations of ideas into somehow appropriate visual symbols are, of course, familiar in clinical settings. A therapist skilled in divining the more abstract ideas which symbols represent may use them to understand the patient's concerns, and perhaps to illustrate these concerns to the patient himself. But the success of clinical interpretation does not constitute proof that symbolic transformation has occurred. The fact that a symbol can be illuminatingly interpreted as representing a certain idea does not necessarily mean that it stood for this idea when it first appeared in the patient's awareness. Its apparent fittingness may be only *post hoc*. A cloud pattern in the sky may fit in well with your daydreams, but you do not usually conclude that the daydreams were its cause.

Even if it be granted that images result from the symbolic transformation of nonvisual mental processes, there is no doubt that experimental study of these transformations is badly needed. Such research might not only allay doubts like those expressed above, but could show where doubt is appropriate. For it is one thing to agree that symbolic transformation frequently occurs, but quite another to accept (or even to choose among) the intricate systems of dream interpretation proposed by psychoanalysts. If we are to find out more about these transformations, an experimental method seems to be necessary. People must somehow be induced to dream (or have hypnagogic images) about some *predetermined topic*, so we can see in what form it reappears in their imagery. There are several ways to do this, but all have their own disadvantages.

## *THE EXPERIMENTAL CONTROL OF DREAMING*

The most obvious approach to the problem is by direct instruction: the subject can be told what to dream about. To make the instruction more effective, it may be given hypnotically. Either of two hypnotic procedures may be and has been used for this purpose. The subject may be given a topic *X* and told to "dream" during the trance itself; alternatively, he may be given a posthypnotic suggestion to have a dream about *X* the next night. Several psychoanalytically-inspired studies using the first method appear in Rapaport's (1951a) collection, and many of the reported dreams include obvious symbolic transformations. However, these and similar studies have been justly criticized by Tart (1965a), in the first of two lucid reviews (see also Tart, 1965b). Hypnosis is not really sleep, although they may be somehow related to one another; in particular, the electroencephalogram during a hypnotic trance is like that of wakefulness. Hence the "dreams" which occur during trance cannot be exactly the dreams of true sleep, and Tart (1964) has shown experimentally that there are differences between them.

This objection alone would not make the symbolic transformations observed in hypnotic "dreams" uninteresting. A more serious problem with such experiments, and also with studies in which normal night dreams are influenced by suggestion, lies in the possible effect of demand characteristics. It is well known in clinical circles that patients have the sort of dreams that their psychoanalysts expect. The patients of Freudians have Freudian dreams, the patients of Jungians have Jungian dreams, and so on. In the early studies collected by Rapaport (1951a) a similar phenomenon may have been taking place; certainly the experimenters made it quite clear that a particular kind of dream report was wanted. In Tart's own study (1964), no symbolic transformations appeared; but this, too, may have been due to implicit suggestion. It is true, of course, that a dream image produced only to satisfy an experimenter or a therapist has still been produced and it proves that such representations can occur. What it does *not* prove is that transformation is a normal mode of mental life.

The same objection can even be made to the recent and rather spectacular work of Witkin and his associates, referred to earlier (Bertini *et al.,* 1964; Witkin & Lewis, 1965). These studies avoided the use of hypnosis. Instead, the authors attempted to influence the content of dreams and hypnagogic imagery by showing an emotionally charged film to the subject just before he retired. (One of their films shows the birth of a baby, aided by a childbirth device called a "vacuum extractor," in detail and color.) After the film, the subject was put in a situation designed to encourage hypnagogic imagery, and asked to describe his experiences continuously as he fell asleep. He was also awakened during every episode of dreaming sleep (determined by EEG and eye-movement criteria), to report his dreams.

With this procedure, some subjects had hypnagogic fantasies "permeated with imagery which can be traced to the film." One subject's protocol included the following reports, among others.

(1) "I just bit into an apple, and there was a worm inside of it, and . . . and half of the worm . . . the head and the first was inside the piece that I ate. And just the other half is sticking up outside the apple and it's . . . I spit it out and I got very nauseous and I throw up." (2) "See a volcano . . . or a Polynesian islands . . . erupting . . . and the black smoke is billowing up from the mouth of the volcano and the red lava is pouring down the sides on it, steaming and thick and jelly-like. And it's just pouring down the sides." (3) "See a lot of tourists leaving a country and the customs inspector wants to see this lady's suitcase. So he's suspicious and she's taking some jewelry or diamonds or liquor or perfume out of the country and she goes to open up the suitcase and the

whole bag opens up. And all the contents fall out all on the floor." (4) "There's a man trying to cross a ravine or a mountain pass by hanging hand over hand across a wire. To get from one side of the precipice to the other side. And he's just about in the middle of the . . . distance between the two cliffs, when his hands slip and he falls down, down, down, down, and he just disappears and you can hear . . . and his screams get lower and lower and lower, and he falls deeper and deeper and deeper into this pit" (Bertini *et al.,* 1964, pp. 518–519).

The relation of these passages to the birth film is obvious indeed, and they provide rich and vivid illustrations of the mechanisms which Freud attributed to the primary process: symbolism, displacement, condensation, and the like. Before taking them at face value, however, it is worth noting that very different results were obtained by Kubie (1943), using a similar procedure as an aid to psychoanalysis. A great many childhood memories appeared (as had been expected) but little imagery of the sort described by Bertini *et al.* Do the demand characteristics of these situations help to produce the reported experiences? The problem is a difficult one, especially since the line between spontaneous mental activity and deliberate cooperation is far from sharp.

One possible way to deal with this issue might be with the aid of "dream incorporation." If stimuli presented *during sleep itself* were to undergo symbolic transformation, it would be hard to imagine that deliberate cooperation with the experimenter was responsible. So far, however, studies of the effects of external stimuli on dream content have rarely succeeded in demonstrating such transformations. Tart (1965b) reviews these studies briefly, as does Foulkes (1966). While a heroic study by Rechtschaffen and Foulkes (1965) failed to demonstrate any effect of *visual* stimuli on dreams (the subjects had to sleep with their eyes taped open!) there is no doubt that auditory and tactile stimuli are often incorporated. However, they generally appear in the dream content rather directly without much evidence of symbolic change. Perhaps the most intriguing of these experiments is that of Berger (1963). He played tape-recorded *names* to dreaming subjects, sometimes using names with emotional significance (former girl friends, etc.) and sometimes neutral ones. Twenty seconds later the subject was awakened and asked for a dream report. The resulting protocols included many clear-cut cases of incorporation. Some were quite direct, as when the dream included the name itself; others seemed to be based on auditory similarity. One subject dreamed of a *jemmy* (burglar's tool) when the name was *Jenny,* and another of an old teacher named *More* when the name was *Maureen.* There also seemed to be a few cases of more symbolic incorporation. Clearly, this method is worth exploring further; other relevant material appears in the discussion of auditory synthesis (Chapter 8).

In addition to hypnosis, the use of strong emotional material, and the presentation of stimuli during sleep itself, there is a fourth method which has repeatedly been used in attempts to control the content of dreams. This is the use of subliminal, or at least "incidental" stimuli, as first proposed by Pötzl (1917, republished 1960). Pötzl gave his subjects a very brief exposure of a picture, and asked them to describe it. On the following night, material from the picture often turned up in their dreams, as reported to him a day later. In many cases, items that had gone *unreported* in the subject's direct description dominated the dream. Thus, it seemed to Pötzl that the primary process can and does use material that has never appeared in consciousness at all! Fleeting, incidental stimuli, which a mechanism more sensitive than ordinary perception somehow "registers" even though they never reach waking consciousness, can influence our dreams.

Pötzl's procedure has been elaborated in a number of recent experiments. Many have used electrical and eye-movement criteria to identify the dreaming sleep, and improved dream recall by awakening the subject immediately. Others have searched for the unconsciously "registered" information in such places as waking imagery, or free association. Fisher (1960) has provided an enthusiastic review of this work. Moreover, a series of studies by Shevrin and Luborsky (e.g., 1961) has imputed still more complexity to the primary process. These experimenters tachistoscopically expose a single "rebus," such as a picture of a *pen* and a *knee*. Subsequently, they find dream-content and associations somehow related to the word *penny,* even in subjects who deny having seen anything at all!

In Chapters 2 and 5, we considered a number of attempts to demonstrate the effects of subliminal stimuli on primary process thinking and found their claims unjustified. The same skeptical attitude is appropriate here. There are logical, psychological, and methodological grounds for doubting the genuineness of the Pötzl phenomenon. To see the logical difficulty, suppose for a moment that unnoticed stimuli do tend to appear in dreams, and calculate how many such stimuli there are. Pötzl used a single fixation in a tachistoscopic exposure, but our eyes make about a *hundred thousand* fixations daily. It follows that the chances of finding a randomly chosen "unnoticed stimulus" in any given dream must be so small as to vanish entirely. If Pötzl's subjects did dream about the picture, it cannot have functioned as just another unnoticed stimulus; it must have been singled out in some special way.

Psychological considerations substantiate this argument. The subject knows perfectly well that the tachistoscopic material has been presented for some definite reason; he is almost certain to go on thinking about it after finishing his verbal report. Far from being at the margin of attention, then, the exposed material is at its very center. In many cases, the demand characteristics of the situation indicate unambiguously that the reported images and dreams *ought to be* somehow related to the tachistoscopic exposure. In short, the experiments do not deal with "incidental" but with heavily emphasized material, albeit unclearly seen.

Methodologically, there are many reasons to doubt that the material recovered from the dreams and images of these subjects was really absorbed, unconsciously, during the brief exposure of the stimulus. A systematic critique of the method has been made by Johnson and Eriksen (1961), who tried unsuccessfully to repeat Pötzl's basic finding. They point out that apparent similarities between a dream element and a part of the stimulus may arise by chance. Moreover, an experimenter who knows what the dream ought to contain may unwittingly guide the subject toward suitable responses. These variables have been taken into account in more recent research. The subject may get a blank slide one day and the critical picture on the other, with the experimenter who obtains the dream "blind" as to which had been presented the day before. Nevertheless, a methodological problem remains; the subject will often have seen *something* different in the presentation of the critical picture than in the exposure of the blank slide. (Of course, he will be discarded from the experiment if he actually identifies the picture. Short of identification, however, he may well see a vague outline of its form.) As he works over this "something" mentally, in the period between the stimulus and the attempt to recover it, he may well develop images and ideas different from those which would follow the blank. Thus, even when it occurs, the Pötzl effect probably depends on elaborating stimuli which are anything but incidental, in a manner which is anything but unconscious. It seems entirely inappropriate as a method for the study of spontaneous symbolic transformations.

## *SPECIAL KINDS OF IMAGERY: DRUGS, SCHIZOPHRENIA, HYPNOSIS*

The attempt to treat various forms of imagery systematically, as forms of visual synthesis, has left a few loose ends. One of these concerns the visual experiences induced by certain drugs, the so-called "hallucinogens"; a second deals with the genuine hallucinations of schizophrenia; the third, with hallucinations brought about by hypnotic suggestion. Finally, we must consider the vivid imagery sometimes produced by electrical stimulation of the brain, often believed to be a kind of photographic recall of earlier experiences.

The effects of drugs such as mescaline or LSD often include imagery that is vivid, compelling, and bizarre. The images are projected —that is, they have a location in perceptual space—but they are not "hallucinations" in a strict sense since the subjects rarely believe they are real. (At least, this is true in laboratory experiments. When mescal is used in religious ceremonies, other criteria for reality may apply.) Real or not, they often seem very beautiful, and indeed the drug-taker may find the whole visual world invested with rare beauty, even to its most mundane and ordinary parts. For a compelling description of the state of mind in which everything appears rich and deep and wonderful beyond comparison, see Huxley's (1959) *Doors of Perception* and *Heaven and Hell.*

All who take these drugs do not have the same experiences. The moods which are induced may be terrifying as well as rapturous. (Moreover, they may be long-lasting or even partly irreversible, which makes popular use of the drugs quite dangerous.) Even where the perceptual phenomena themselves are concerned, there are wide individual differences in the effects produced. Huxley, for example, had relatively few images, and minimized their importance:

> Half an hour after swallowing the drug I became aware of a slow dance of golden lights. A little later there were sumptuous red surfaces swelling and expanding from bright nodes of energy that vibrated with a continuously changing, patterned life. At another time the closing of my eyes revealed a complex of grey structures, within which pale bluish spheres kept emerging into intense solidity and, having emerged, would slide noiselessly upwards, out of sight. But at no time were there faces or forms of men or animals. I saw no landscapes, no enormous spaces, no magical growth and metamorphosis of buildings, nothing remotely like a drama or parable (1959, p. 16).

Several points about this account should be stressed. First, Huxley makes it very clear that he had *expected* to see visions, on the basis of what he had read, but his expectations were disappointed. Second, the drug was anything but ineffective with him; his whole manuscript testifies to the immense significance and value of the experience in his case. Third, he did see at least something—"bright lights," "patterned nodes of energy," "grey structures." Why, then, were his visions relatively unimpressive? He gives us a possible clue by reporting that, in normal life, his visual imagery was meager:

> I am, and for as long as I can remember, I have always been a poor visualizer. Words, even the pregnant words of poets, do not evoke pictures in my mind. No hypnagogic visions greet me on the verge of sleep. When I recall something, the memory does not present itself to me as a vividly seen event or object. By an effort of the will, I can evoke a not very vivid image of what happened yesterday afternoon, of how the Lungarno used to look before the bridges were destroyed, of the Bayswater Road when the only buses were green and tiny and drawn by aged horses at three and a half miles an hour. But such images have little substance and absolutely no autonomous life of their own. They stand to real, perceived objects in the same relation as Homer's ghosts stood to the men of flesh and blood, who came to visit them in the shades. Only when I have a high temperature do my mental images come to independent

life. To those in whom the faculty of visualization is strong my inner world must seem curiously drab, limited, and uninteresting (pp. 15–16).

This passage is worthy of note in its own right. Huxley obviously knew vivid images when he saw them, as in fevered states, so he must be believed if he reports their absence. Yet it is hard to think that his inner life was "uninteresting" when he describes it in a passage as exciting as this one. If he lacked imagery, he did not lack imagination. Moreover, his memory was excellent (Erickson, 1965). But, not having imagery under ordinary conditions, he had little even under the influence of mescaline.

It is not known whether this correlation is generally valid, but certainly not everyone who takes a "hallucinogen" can expect to see vivid images. For those who do, the imagery produced is mostly visual. "Hallucinations" of hearing, smell, and taste rarely occur (Malitz, Wilkens, & Esecover, 1962), although changes in the body image are described as common by Klüver (1942). In nearly every case, the imagery begins as it did for Huxley, with geometrical patterns, spots of light, and the like. These appear regularly even in subjects who then go on to have more elaborate visual experiences. The consistency of this finding, in one study after another of supposedly unpredictable phenomena, is remarkable. The figures which Klüver (1942) called "form constants"—lattice work, cobwebs, tunnels, alleys, vessels and spirals—are seen in nearly every case where imagery appears at all. Other kinds of visual experience are also consistently reported: an increased vividness and impressiveness of real colors, and fluctuations in the apparent sizes and shapes of real objects.

It is plausible to explain these observations by assuming that the drugs act to create or emphasize certain *stimuli,* possessing genuine patterned structure. The more spectacular visions then result from the elaboration of these inputs by good visualizers. Indeed, it has often been suggested that the internal structures of the eye itself, which usually go unnoticed, may provide the stimuli in question. The "pale bluish spheres," for example, may be corpuscles in the capillaries which supply the retina. We do know at least that phosphenes—sparks perceived because of pressure on the eyeball—can serve as nuclei for images in this way. Whether the "stimuli" for mescal imagery actually have such obvious external origins may be doubted; Klüver (1942) considers this possibility and comes to a negative conclusion. However, this does not affect the basic hypothesis being advanced. Such drugs do not just disturb the mechanism of visual construction; they also provide unusual but specific inputs to it.

LSD was formerly called a "psychotomimetic drug," i.e., one which causes effects like those of mental illness. Whatever the other grounds for this term may be, it is misleading with respect to the "hallucinations" involved. The hallucinations of schizophrenics actually represent a type of imagery very different from that produced chemically. For one thing, they are primarily auditory. Schizophrenic patients, at least chronic ones, tend to hear voices rather than see visions. It is not clear why this should be true (Feinberg, 1962, lists a number of speculative hypotheses) but the trend is a very striking one. In the study of Malitz *et al.* (1962), 50 of 100 patients had auditory hallucinations and only 9 had visual ones; in 8 of these 9 the visions appeared in intimate association with voices. Similarly, Feinberg (1962) notes the great difficulty of finding as many as 19 schizophrenics having visual hallucinations when he wished to compare these with the imagery produced by LSD. However, Havens (1962) remarks that visual hallucinations are characteristic of acute (i.e., early) schizophrenia, and tend to be replaced by auditory ones only as the disease becomes chronic. He asserts that the same progression appears in alcoholism also, as *delirium tremens* gives way to chronic alcoholic psychosis.

When visual phenomena do appear in schizophrenia, they are not at all like those of the "hallucinogens"; they are more like dream-images. Feinberg makes the comparison explicit:

> (1) The visual hallucinations of schizophrenia appear suddenly and without prodromata; those of mescaline and LSD are heralded by unformed visual sensations, simple geometric figures, and alterations of color, size, shape, movement, and number. Certain visual forms (form-constants) almost invariably present during the development of the drug-syndromes, are almost invariably absent in schizophrenic hallucinations. (2) In schizophrenia, hallucinations occur in a psychic setting of intense affective need or delusional preoccupation . . . The mescaline and LSD hallucinations appear to develop independently of such emotional conditions, or else they produce their own affective alterations . . . (3) Schizophrenic hallucinations may be superimposed on a visual environment that appears otherwise normal, or, more rarely, they may appear with the remainder of the environment excluded. The drugs produce diffuse distortions of the existing visual world . . . (4) Schizophrenic hallucinations are generally seen with the eyes open; those of mescaline and LSD are more readily seen with the eyes closed or in darkened surroundings (1962, pp. 70–71).

To these differences, we may add one more. The schizophrenic often hallucinates people or objects which make some sense to him; they fit into his delusions as more normal imagery seems to fit the thinking of more normal people. Thus, schizophrenic hallucinations seem to represent a species of visual memory, continuous with the memory images of ordinary life (but more dreamlike, since the patient believes them to be real). Drug-induced "hallucinations," on the other hand, are more often experienced as incomprehensible, alien, or unfamiliar. While visual memory may play a part in the formation of these images also, they apparently include a novel element, a genuinely unusual stimulus, which is much more likely to surprise the perceiver.

In our discussion of various types of imagery, hypnotic hallucination should not be overlooked. The topic is unfortunately a complex one, partly because positive responses to a hypnotic suggestion may arise in more than one way. Orne (1962b) has analyzed some of these possibilities. His example is the typical demonstration in which the hypnotist suggests that person *X* is sitting in a particular (actually empty) chair, and then asks the subject to describe what *X* is wearing, fix *X*'s necktie, converse with *X*, etc. This is a relatively difficult suggestion, but "good subjects" can comply with it, and to the observer their behavior seems strange indeed. Orne points out, however, that not all those who comply actually have a visual hallucination. One characteristic of the hypnotic state is a compulsion to obey such suggestions. This compulsion can lead the subject to carry out an elaborate pretense of seeing, even when he lacks the suggested visual experience. (See Chapter 5 for a discussion of the difference between visual experience and verbal report.) More interesting for present purposes, of course, are the subjects who really do see something. *What* they see can range from a vague phantom at one end of the scale to a full-bodied image, apparently indistinguishable from a real person, at the other. It seems likely that the subjects who can experience really lifelike hallucinations have a good capacity for imagery also in the waking state, but this has never been demonstrated. It seems likely, too, that their eye movements are as appropriate to the imaginary object as those of the Eidetiker or the dreamer.

As in other cases, we must distinguish between the clarity of the image and the subject's belief that it represents a real person. One may believe in the reality of something only vaguely visible, or disbelieve even what is seen clearly. However, hypnotized persons, like dreamers, do not demand the usual degree of sensibleness from the world, and carry out relatively little reality-testing. Orne (1959) refers to this characteristic of cognition in the hypnotic state as "trance logic." If the real *X* walks into the room while the subject is hallucinating his presence, a situation is created in which *X* seems to be at two places simultaneously. This would create grave problems for anyone in a normal state, and indeed it is very disturbing for "simulating" subjects who are only pretending to be hypnotized. Since it would make no sense to see *X* twice, simulators typically find some explanation which permits them to deny what they see. A genuinely hypnotized and hallucinating subject, on the other hand, is much less disturbed; he just sees two *X*'s.

Under hypnosis, it is also possible to produce "negative hallucinations," in which the subject is told not to see something which is actually present. Perhaps the success of such a suggestion (as distinguished from pretense and simulation) can be understood in terms of the process of focal attention discussed in Chapter 4. We might suppose that the subject withdraws his attention from the critical part of the visual field; that is, he does not carry out any visual synthesis there. Hence he does not identify the object in question, has no detail vision for its parts, and can legitimately insist that he does not see it. Nevertheless, the preattentive mechanisms continue to function. The subject does not bump into the object (unlike persons only simulating hypnosis, who often do), and probably its sudden motion would lead to the usual automatic eye movements. Thus, at least as far as present evidence goes, the positive and negative hallucinations of hypnosis can both be explained in terms of the normal constructive processes of vision and visual imagery.

### *ELECTRICALLY INDUCED IMAGERY AND OTHER EVIDENCE FOR "HYPERMNESIA"*

The images occasionally produced by electrical stimulation of the brain have been described as very different from the others we have considered. Penfield's reports of these phenomena (e.g., 1952, 1954, 1958; also Penfield & Roberts, 1959) have been widely read, and his assumption that they represent the rearousal of specific memories has often been taken at face value. Specifically, the observations consist of spontaneous reports given by epileptic patients, who are on the operating table so that parts of their temporal lobes (in which the focus of the epilepsy seems to lie), may be removed. Because brain tissue lacks receptors for pain or touch, these operations can be carried out in fully conscious patients, with only a local anesthetic to numb the scalp and skull. Before removing any tissue, Penfield regularly applies a gentle electric current to the cortex at various places. In some patients, this has led to rather spectacular results.

Such patients are startled by vividly clear images, either visual or auditory (the latter apparently more frequent). These experiences have the force of actual perceptions, even though awareness of the operating room is not lost. Some examples are worth quoting:

> . . . while the electrode was being held in place, "Something brings back a memory. I can see Seven-Up Bottling Company . . . Harrison Bakers." He was then warned that he was being stimulated, but the electrode was not applied. He replied "Nothing."
>
> In another case . . . the patient heard a specific popular song being played as though by an orchestra. Repeated stimulation reproduced the same music. While the electrode was kept in place, she hummed the tune, chorus, and verse, thus accompanying the music she heard. After a point in her temporal cortex had been stimulated, [the patient] observed with some surprise "I just heard one of my children speaking . . . it was Frank, and I could hear the neigh-

borhood noises" . . . She said that it was not like a memory, "It seemed more real than that. But, of course, . . . I have heard Frankie like that many, many times, thousands of times."

[A 12-year-old boy], with stimulation, . . . heard a telephone conversation between his mother and aunt. When stimulation was carried out at [a neighboring cortical point] immediately afterward, he said "the same as before. My mother telling my aunt to come up and visit us tonight." When he was asked how he knew this was a telephone conversation he replied that he did not see them but he knew that his aunt was speaking on the phone by the way her voice sounded when she answered. In the original experience he must have stood very close to his mother as she telephoned [!] After a lapse of time, [an intervening point] was stimulated. The recollection mentioned above was no longer available to the electrode. This time he said "My mother is telling my brother he has got his coat on backwards. I can just hear them." He was asked whether he remembered this happening. "Oh yes," he replied, "just before I came here." He was then asked whether these things were like dreams, and he replied "No . . . It is just like I go into a daze" (Penfield, 1952, pp. 179, 182, 183).

What are we to make of these observations? Penfield's interpretation is straightforward: they are reactivations of specific previous experiences, revived in the patient's mind as one might replay a conversation on a tape recorder. In a paper entitled "The Permanent Record of the Stream of Consciousness," he states his conviction that ". . . nothing is lost, that the record of each man's experience is complete . . . that the brain of every man contains an unchanging ganglionic record of successive experience" (1954, p. 67). Actually, there are three steps in Penfield's argument, although he does not make them explicit: (*a*) These images must be reproductive memories (rather than fantasies) because the patient experiences them as familiar; (*b*) they must be accurate (rather than confabulated) because they are so vivid and subjectively real; (*c*) the "record of the stream of consciousness" must be complete (rather than fragmentary) because it evidently includes trivial events.

It seems to me that all three of these inferences are unjustified: (*a*) the feeling of familiarity may be misleading, as it often is in daily life; (*b*) in some subjects hypnagogic imagery is equally vivid, but obviously does not represent accurate recall; (*c*) the fact that some events are remembered without apparent cause hardly proves that no events are forgotten. As a matter of fact, most of the cases described by Penfield seem more like generic and repeated *categories* of events than specific instances—a voice calling a familiar name, a piece of music being played, friends laughing. In the very few which seem to be specific (such as the last quoted above), it is not clear whether any check on their accuracy was made. Moreover, there are at least some instances, like the one in which both sides of a telephone conversation were heard, which seem better described as "fantasy" than as "reproductive memory."

In short, the *content* of these experiences is not surprising in any way. It seems entirely comparable to the content of dreams, which are generally admitted to be synthetic constructions and not literal recalls. Penfield's work tells us nothing new about memory. Whatever it proves about the completeness of the "record of successive experience" follows just as convincingly (or as unconvincingly) from everyday recall in dreams or while awake. What is surprising is only the *vividness* of the imagery, which is seen or heard as clearly as if real objects were being actually perceived. (Images of equal clarity, generally bizarre rather than familiar, can occur spontaneously as a result of epilepsy or brain tumor—see Baldwin, 1962.) Indeed, far from locating a new sort of memory, Penfield's electrodes may have touched on the mechanisms of perceptual synthesis. It is regrettable that the present state of neurology suggests no way to pursue his work further in that direction.[1]

This argument does not prove that there is no "permanent record of the stream of consciousness," but only that the results of brain stimulation provide no particular evidence for one. It is sometimes suggested that the existence of such a record can be independently demonstrated by another dramatic technique: recall in the hypnotic trance. However, examination of the evidence for "hypnotic hypermnesia" shows it to be an even weaker reed. Although hypnotized subjects asked to recall or relive former experiences often produce a wealth of recollections, much of this material is usually fabricated. There is no good reason to believe that recall is more accurate or complete in trance than under suitably motivated waking conditions (Barber, 1965; Fisher, 1962). Despite recent claims (Reiff & Scheerer, 1959), it is unlikely that so-called "hypnotic age-regression" constitutes a genuine return to a fully preserved earlier state of mind (Orne, 1951; Orne & O'Connell, 1961). Hypnosis can be remarkably effective in freeing *repressed* memories, as an adjunct to psychotherapy or as a treatment for amnesic fugues. But what is recaptured in these instances is only what the patient might have been expected to remember anyway, had repression not occurred. It is not a fully accurate copy of earlier experience.

If the "permanent record of the stream of consciousness" is a fiction, there is still no doubt that our memories can store a great deal of information for very long periods of time. In general, the stored information does not manifest itself as frequently in imagery or direct recall as in the simple recognition that something or someone is familiar, discussed in Chapter 4. Some of the experiments cited there show very substantial mnemonic capacities, although none covered prolonged periods of time. If anecdotal evidence is to be trusted—and stories about

[1] A similar point of view toward Penfield's findings has been expressed by Mahl, Rothenberg, Delgado, and Hamlin (1964), who present an experimental case to support their interpretation. In this connection, see also Horowitz (1967).

dogs who recognize their masters after 20 years are as old as the *Odyssey* —a familiar face may stay recognizable forever. Skilled performance, too, does not seem to be lost, even over decades without practice. This category includes not only gross motor skills like bicycle-riding or piano-playing, but well-rehearsed verbal performances as well. Old actors slip easily into parts they learned decades ago, and tales of dying atheists who recite long-forgotten biblical passages are legion (e.g., Erickson, 1962).

For the most part, all these phenomena represent so many unsolved problems. Despite the effort that has gone into the study of memory for many years, we know very little about how stored information is organized and about what can happen to it. My own view, as the reader has already discovered, is that both memory images and percepts are constructed anew on every occasion when they are experienced. The same principle applies to other feats of memory, including verbal recall and skilled performance, although the principles and mechanisms of construction are different. This approach (which obviously owes much to the influence of Bartlett, 1932) necessarily is unsympathetic to the notion of a fixed and segmented record of the past. But there can be no disputing that information about past events is somehow stored, and to this extent those who argue for the existence of "memory traces" are surely correct. The present point is only that the information is not stored in the form of images, visual or otherwise. When an image is constructed, the operations of synthesis *use* the information, which otherwise is carried silently, unconsciously, in ways which (by definition) we can hardly "visualize." However, we shall see in Chapter 11 that some notion of how it is organized can be inferred from its manifestations in recall, problem-solving, and thinking. Meanwhile, we must undertake a four-chapter digression into another sense-modality. Auditory information, too, undergoes a series of complex cognitive operations before it is used or stored.

# *Part III*

# *Auditory Cognition*

# Chapter 7

# Speech Perception

This chapter begins the discussion of auditory cognition by considering how speech is understood. An elementary presentation of certain phenomena in acoustics and linguistics is followed by an examination of the cognitive units involved. Distinctive features, phonemes, words, and linguistic constituents are all considered. Certain hypothetical mechanisms of speech perception are discussed and related to the theories of pattern recognition reviewed in Chapters 3 and 4. Once again, the most satisfactory theory turns out to be "analysis-by-synthesis." Like its visual counterpart, auditory synthesis requires two stages: a relatively passive, preattentive phase during which some units are tentatively identified, and an active process which makes words and sentences out of them. Auditory imagery and hallucination are to be understood as products of this constructive activity.

In our discussion of visual cognition, there were many opportunities to emphasize that all knowledge of the world is mediated rather than direct, that no royal road to reality bypasses the need for analysis of the input. The same principle applies to hearing, and in particular to the perception of speech. The words we hear do not exist as separate and sharply defined units in the stimulus pattern; the meaning of a sentence cannot leap directly from the speaker's mind into the listener's. But, at a critical point, all the information to be transferred is briefly embodied in the physical sound wave itself. The dance of the air molecules which constitutes the "proximal stimulus" for hearing is the most accessible stage of the process of communication, and therefore the most appropriate starting point for a study of auditory cognition.

## *SOME VERY ELEMENTARY ACOUSTICS*

A sound wave in air is a succession of compressions and expansions. The succession impresses itself on the eardrum as a series of back-and-forth movements. The motions of the eardrum are transmitted by the bones of the middle ear to an organ called the *cochlea,* where a preliminary transformation of the input pattern is carried out. (Actually, the transmission to the cochlea introduces distortion into the sequence of pressures, and does *not* depend only on the drum and the middle ear, but these nuances can be ignored here.) The important point is that the auditory input consists of a temporal sequence of events. All the information is carried by the intensity of the successive pressures and their spacing in time. The most straightforward description of the input is a graph of pressure against time like Figure 31.

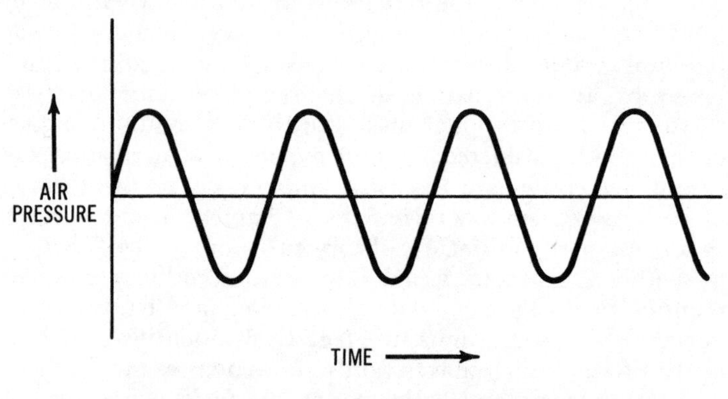


Figure 31. A sinusoidal sound wave.

The wave form in Figure 31, called a "sinusoid," is unusually simple and regular. It represents a "pure tone," like the sound of a tuning fork. Most sounds, even musical ones, have far more complicated wave forms. A signal like that in Figure 32a cannot be described by a single frequency. However, the effect of a complex wave is no different from the combined effect of a set of simultaneous sinusoids, provided that their frequencies, intensities, and relative phases are suitably chosen. This equivalence permits us to make a very different description of the auditory stimulus. Since any wave can be thought of as the sum of sinusoids, one need only display the "components" of a sound, with their intensities, in order to describe it almost completely. A description in terms of frequency-components is called a "spectrum": Figure 32b shows the spectrum of the complex wave in Figure 32a.

The analysis of complex sounds into frequency-components is not merely an abstract possibility or a mathematical trick. It can also be realized by physical devices called "filters." In general, a filter is a device whose output accurately reflects any input that has certain critical characteristics but remains uninfluenced by other kinds of stimuli. The filter is said to "pass" one sort of input and "reject" the other, much as a

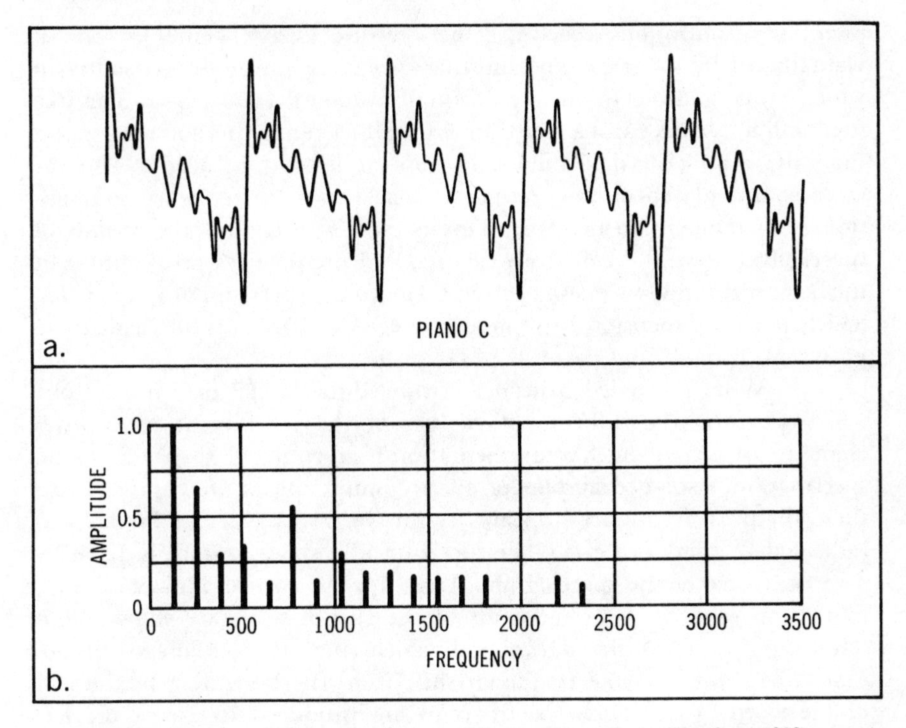


Figure 32. A complex wave form and its spectrum (from Fletcher, 1929).

sieve passes pebbles that are below a certain size and rejects those that are too large. Our sense organs are often thought of as filters, each of which passes a certain kind of energy—light for the eye, sound for the ear, and so on. Broadbent has made this metaphor central to his cognitive theory, which will be considered in the next chapter. I find it less congenial, because it interprets cognition as a passive rather than a constructive process.

In actual practice, acoustic signals are usually converted to electrical form by a microphone before a frequency analysis is made. Various electronic devices then do the actual filtering. Often a whole bank of so-called "band-pass" filters is used: one sensitive to sinusoids with frequencies below, say, 200 c.p.s. (cycles per second), the next limited to the range between 200 and 500, and so on until the limit of audible sound is reached between 16,000 and 20,000 c.p.s. The outputs of these filters indicate the amount of acoustic energy in corresponding "regions" of the input spectrum.

It is fortunate that electronic filters exist, for complex sounds could hardly be studied without them. Most of the sounds we hear do not have spectra as clear and discrete as the one in Figure 32b. That is, they are not mixtures of a few sharply-delineated frequencies. Many have essentially continuous spectra, some acoustic energy being present at virtually all frequencies. The limiting case is "white noise"—a sound in which every audible frequency is equally present. It sounds rather like the "sh-h-h" which can be heard in sea shells. Even white noise is simpler than the most everyday sounds, because at least it is steady. The ear more commonly encounters sounds which change in frequency composition from moment to moment. This is especially true of the sounds of speech. In the word "you," for example, high frequencies predominate at the beginning and low ones at the end. Hence the spectrum of frequencies, which has no dimension to represent irregular change, is an inadequate portrayal of the sound patterns of language.

What is needed instead is a three-dimensional description: one which portrays the different *intensities* of the component *frequencies* changing over *time*. Such a representation is given in the so-called "sound spectrogram." Some examples of spectrograms appear in Figure 33. In these pictures, frequency appears on the vertical axis, and intensity is indicated by shades of grey. The spectrum at a single instant is given by a vertical slice of the spectrogram. Time appears on the horizontal axis, so that successively later moments of the speech wave are shown from left to right. Thus the dark band which angles down diagonally in Figure 33 represents the frequency shift from the beginning to the end of the word "you." Such spectrograms are produced by banks of electronic filters. With their aid, serviceable descriptions of the auditory input become possible. It has even been claimed that deaf persons can learn to "read" the speech they represent (Potter *et al.*, 1947), and a computer program designed for visual pattern recognition has been able to identify spoken digits from them (Uhr & Vossler, 1961). Because they reflect the idiosyncratic characteristics of the speaker's voice, as well as his words, spectrograms have sometimes been used for identification in courts of law.

## *AUDITORY MECHANISMS*

The first important transformation of the auditory input is carried out by the cochlea of the inner ear, which acts as a "frequency analyzer." Rapid fluctuations of pressure set up *traveling waves* in the fluid medium which the cochlea contains, and the place where these waves reach a peak depends on the input frequency. Since the endings of the auditory nerve lie on a membrane running the length of the cochlea, different frequencies effectively stimulate different nerve endings. The presentation of a complex tone excites a whole array of endings, corresponding to its components. It is interesting that the function performed by the cochlea, though outside the central nervous system, is essentially a cognitive anal-

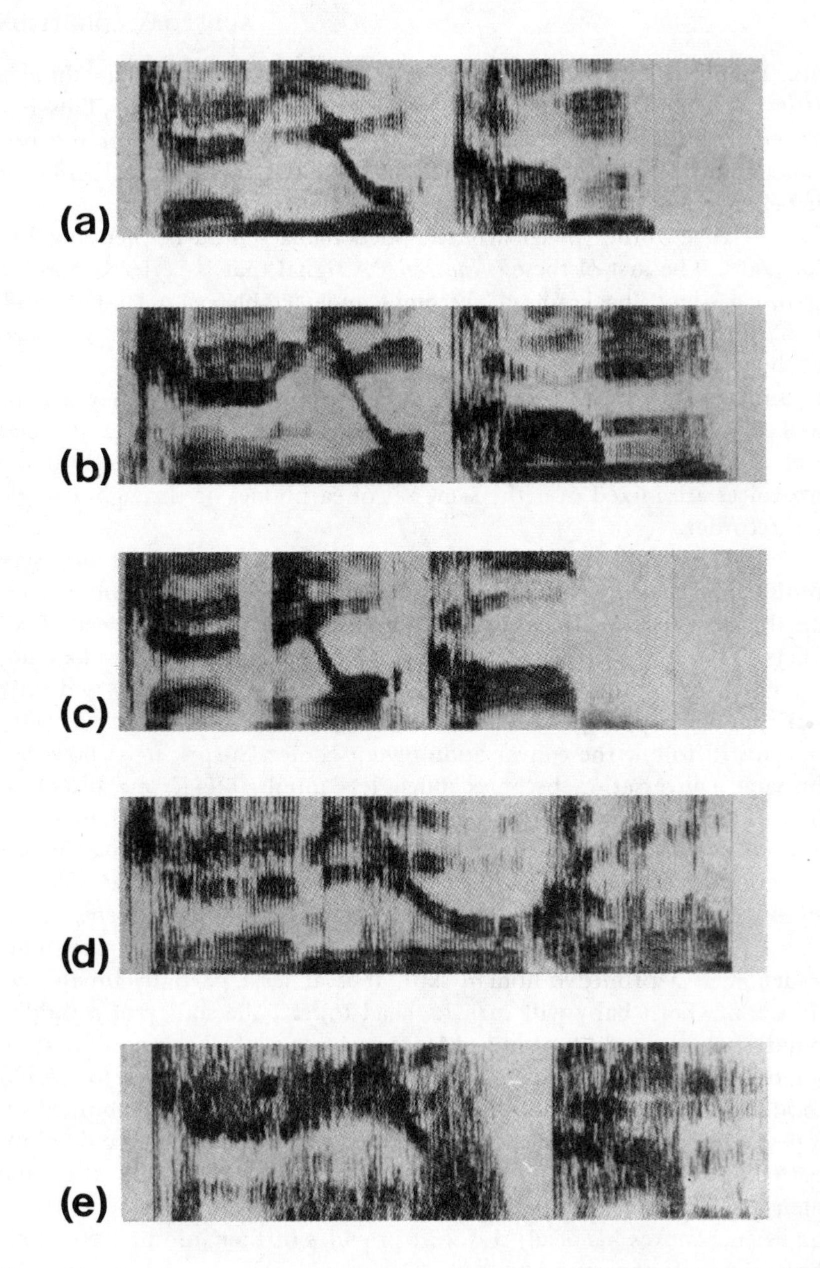


Figure 33. Speech spectrograms of the phrase "Can you come?" All samples are from the same speaker, using (*a*) normal intonation; (*b*) positive nasality; (*c*) negative nasality; (*d*) aspirate; (*e*) whisper (from Potter *et al.*, 1947).

ysis. Taking a sequence of pressures as input, it produces something a little like a neurally represented spectrogram for an output. (This is a gross oversimplification, of course. More adequate accounts of the psychology and physiology of hearing can be found in many textbooks, or in Békésy, 1960).

A few other psychoacoustic phenomena should be mentioned at this point. The first of these is *masking.* A signal that is perfectly audible against a silent "background" becomes undetectable or at least unintelligible in noisier situations. The masking of speech by noise has been much studied, in part because it has obvious implications for telephone transmission and other practical problems. However, speech may also be masked by sounds other than white noise. In particular, an additional irrelevant stream of speech can mask rather effectively, especially if the two voices are mixed over the same set of earphones or through a single tape-recorder.

Curiously, such masking of one voice by another is not very troublesome in daily life. Even in a crowd we have little trouble following the conversation in which we are interested, to the neglect of all others. This is the so-called "cocktail party phenomenon." It does not depend primarily on the meaningful content of what is said, and only partly on voice quality. Nor is it based on visual cues; with our eyes shut, we can still follow the conversation of our choice. Surprisingly, however, the same conversation becomes much less intelligible if one listens to the cocktail party only via a single microphone and a tape! (Many social psychologists with painstakingly recorded group interactions have already made this discovery.) The main basis of auditory selection is that different voices come from different *places* in our environment (Broadbent, 1954).

Auditory localization, which underlies the cocktail party phenomenon, is a primitive human skill. It is at least partially innate, because a newborn baby will turn its head toward the source of a sudden sound. (It is also readily modified by experience, as Held showed in 1955, but this is a tangled topic which the present volume hopes to avoid.) Localization is possible primarily because we have two ears, mounted on opposite sides of our heads. The sound from a particular source does not reach both ears at exactly the same instant, nor with exactly the same intensity. Moreover, the pattern of interaural differences must change as the listener moves his head; this shift provides further information about the position of the sound source.

The mechanisms by which the nervous system takes advantage of these minute time and intensity differences (and their changes) is not clear. Whatever it may be, there is no doubt that it plays a major role in overcoming masking. When we follow the conversation of a single person in a crowd, we are essentially following the sound coming from a particular place, i.e., the voice which has a certain arrival-pattern at the two ears. In fact, localization can be a big advantage even in simpler detection situations. A subject with a loud noise at both ears can detect a faint tone more easily if it comes to one ear only than if it (like the noise) comes to both. Under these conditions the noise is heard as if "centered in the head," while the signal appears from the side of the relevant earphone (Hirsh, 1950; Licklider, 1951). Auditory localization of speech has also been used as a crucial variable in a number of studies that will be discussed in Chapter 8.

## *PHONEMIC DESCRIPTION*

When the stream of speech is displayed in spectrograms like those of Figure 33, it displays a rather disconcerting continuity. We think of speech as made up of successive words, and words as composed of successive "sounds," but such parts are by no means always obvious when a spectrogram is examined. To understand the intuitive feeling that speech has components, we must begin with another kind of analysis, developed by linguistic science long before spectrograms were available. For the linguist, the basic unit of speech is the "phoneme," sometimes said to be as fundamental to auditory cognition as contours and shapes are in vision. This may not turn out to be true; evidence for the functional value of phonemes will be considered a little later. Nevertheless, we cannot omit at least a brief account of phonemics. Without it, much current work in auditory cognition would be incomprehensible. For a more thorough exposition of the subject, the reader should consult a textbook of linguistics (e.g., Gleason, 1961) or one of Roger Brown's discussions (1956, 1958).

Speakers of English tend to agree that words are made up of sequences of more elementary "sounds," which seem to recur in various combinations. "Lick," is easily analyzed into three successive units: /l/, /i/, and /k/. A change in any one of these elements can produce a different word: "kick," or "luck," or "lid." A different word is also produced if the elements are assembled in a different order, as in "kill." But it is not quite accurate to call these elements "sounds." The spectrograms corresponding to, say, /k/ may be quite different for different speakers, and for the same speaker on different occasions. The symbol /k/ really stands for a whole *class* of sounds which are (*a*) acoustically similar, and (*b*) more or less interchangeable so far as their use in English is concerned. (Actually there are several subclasses of /k/, which occur in different phonemic environments, but these differences are not important here.) Classes of sounds that are roughly equivalent in this way are called "phonemes." Although all instances of a phoneme must be acoustically similar, the criteria of similarity are not the same in all languages (nor are all languages based on the same set of phonemes). Spaniards do not make the distinction between /s/ and /z/ that we have in "zeal" and "seal"; we do not notice the difference between the /k/ in "cool" and the /k/ in "keep," but it matters in Arabic. Note that although phonemes serve to distinguish between words of different meanings, they have no meaning of their own. As Jakobson and Halle put it, "All phonemes denote nothing but otherness" (1956, p. 11).

It is obvious that ordinary English spelling does not generally give a good account of phonemic structure. For this reason, a separate "phonemic alphabet" has been developed. Symbols from this alphabet are usually set off by slashes, as in "/k/." The phonemic symbols used in the examples so far have been easily understood because they were adapted from English printed letters, but many others are not. The first consonant in "thigh," for example, is written /θ/. The initial consonant of "thy" is a different phoneme, written /ð/. In fact, it is the existence of pairs like "thigh" and "thy" which provides the demonstration that /θ/ and /ð/ are separate phonemes despite their acoustic similarity. The difference between the initial consonants is the only distinction between the pronunciations of "thigh" and "thy," whatever the spelling may suggest. Altogether, English is said by Gleason (1961) to have 21 consonant phonemes. In addition, there are 12 vowels or semivowels (/w/, for example, is a semivowel). Even these 33 do not cover quite everything that may determine the meaning of an utterance. The so-called "suprasegmental phonemes"—which are essentially patterns of stress, pitch, and rhythm—may be important as well. It is such patterns which distinguish the question "You can come?" from the assertion "You can come!" or the noun "con′vert" from the verb "con vert′."

Although the phoneme is a small unit indeed, it does not represent the limit of linguistic analysis. The dissection of phonemes themselves is also possible, because they fall naturally into several categories. One grouping, for example, divides the *voiced* from the *unvoiced* consonants. It is evident that /z/ and /s/ are different phonemes; so are /b/ and /p/. Acoustically, the difference is the same in both pairs: the first phoneme has some tonality which the second lacks. The "voicing" of such consonants as /z/ and /b/ originates in a vibration of the vocal cords which does not occur in their unvoiced counterparts. Of course, /z/ and /b/ are by no means identical. They differ on another dimension, i.e., in terms of another feature. The first is a so-called *fricative,* with a "noisy" spectrum produced by the rush of outgoing air through some narrow space in the oral cavity; the second is a *labial stop.*

Such considerations suggest that phonemes are distinguished from one another on the basis of certain *distinctive features,* which are the elementary components of speech. In recent years, the theory of distinctive features has become closely associated with the work of Roman

Jakobson and his associates (Jakobson, Fant, & Halle, 1961; Jakobson & Halle, 1956). According to these authors, nearly all the distinctive features are binary; every speech sound is either voiced or voiceless, nasalized or nonnasalized, tense or lax, etc. Moreover, each feature has both an articulatory and an acoustic definition. That is, each is produced because the speech mechanism—vocal cords, mouth, lips, etc.—is in one of two states and results in a speech wave which has one of two characteristics.

> In a message conveyed to the listener, every feature confronts him with a yes-no decision. . . . The listener is obliged to choose between two polar quantities of the same category, as in the case of grave vs. acute, or between the presence and absence of a certain quality such as voiced vs. voiceless, nasalized vs. nonnasalized, sharp vs. plain. (1956, p. 4)

Figure 34 shows the distinctive features proposed by Jakobson and Halle. It will remind the reader of Figure 25 in Chapter 3, which illustrated

a. **Some characteristics of the distinctive features on the acoustic level**

**1. Vocalic/nonvocalic**
Presence vs. absence of a sharply defined formant structure

**2. Consonantal/nonconsonantal**
Low vs. high total energy

**3. Compact/diffuse**
Higher vs. lower concentration of energy (intensity) in a relatively narrow, central region of the spectrum, accompanied by an increase (vs. decrease) of the total energy

**4. Tense/lax**
Higher vs. lower total energy in conjunction with a greater vs. smaller spread of the energy in the spectrum and in time

**5. Voiced/voiceless**
Presence vs. absence of periodic low-frequency excitation

**6. Nasal/oral**
Spreading the available energy over wider (vs. narrower) frequency regions by a reduction in the intensity of certain (primarily the first) formants and introduction of additional (nasal) formants

**7. Discontinuous/continuant**
Silence followed and/or preceded by spread of energy over a wide frequency region (either as burst or a rapid transition of vowel formants) vs. absence of abrupt transition between sound and such a silence

**8. Strident/mellow**
Higher intensity noise vs. lower intensity noise

**9. Checked/unchecked**
Higher rate of discharge of energy within a reduced interval of time vs. lower rate of discharge within a longer interval

**10. Grave/acute**
Concentration of energy in the lower (vs. upper) frequencies of the spectrum

**11. Flat/plain**
Flat phonemes in contradistinction to the corresponding plain ones are characterized by a downward shift or weakening of some of their upper-frequency components

**12. Sharp/plain**
Sharp phonemes in contradistinction to the corresponding plain ones are characterized by an upward shift of some of their upper frequency components

b. **Distinctive-features pattern of English phonemes**

| | o | a | e | u | ə | i | l | ŋ | ʃ | ʃ̂ | k | ʒ | ʒ̂ | g | m | f | p | v | b | n | s | θ | t | z | ð | d | h | # |
|---|---|---|---|---|---|---|---|---|---|---|---|---|---|---|---|---|---|---|---|---|---|---|---|---|---|---|---|---|
| 1. Vocalic/nonvocalic | + | + | + | + | + | + | + | − | − | − | − | − | − | − | − | − | − | − | − | − | − | − | − | − | − | − | − | − |
| 2. Consonantal/nonconsonantal | − | − | − | − | − | − | + | + | + | + | + | + | + | + | + | + | + | + | + | + | + | + | + | + | + | + | − | − |
| 3. Compact/diffuse | + | + | + | − | − | − | | + | + | + | + | + | + | + | − | − | − | − | − | − | − | − | − | − | − | − | | |
| 4. Grave/acute | + | + | − | + | + | − | | | | | | | | | + | + | + | + | + | − | − | − | − | − | − | − | | |
| 5. Flat/plain | + | − | | + | − | | | | | | | | | | | | | | | | | | | | | | | |
| 6. Nasal/oral | | | | | | | | + | − | − | − | − | − | − | + | − | − | − | − | + | − | − | − | − | − | − | | |
| 7. Tense/lax | | | | | | | | | + | + | + | − | − | − | | + | + | − | − | | + | + | + | − | − | − | + | − |
| 8. Continuant/interrupted | | | | | | | | | + | − | − | + | − | − | | + | − | + | − | | + | + | − | + | + | − | | |
| 9. Strident/mellow | | | | | | | | | + | + | − | + | + | − | | | | | | | + | − | − | + | − | − | | |

Key to phonemic transcription: /o/—pot, /a/—pat; /e/—pet, /u/—put, /ə/—putt, /i/—pit, /l/—lull, /ŋ/—lung, /ʃ/—ship, /ʃ̂/—chip, /k/—kip, /ʒ/—azure, /ʒ̂/—juice, /g/—goose, /m/—mill, /f/—fill, /p/—pill, /v/—vim, /b/—bill, /n/—nil, /s/—sill, /θ/—thill, /t/—till, /z/—zip, /ð/—this, /d/—dill, /h/—hill, /#/—_ill.

Figure 34. The distinctive features of English, as proposed by Jakobson and Halle. (The figure is taken from Lindgren, 1965b.)

Gibson's suggested distinctive features for letters; that proposal was explicitly modeled on the Jakobson-Halle theory.

The hypothesis that distinctive features are the critical stimuli in speech perception is attractive, but it has complexities of its own. Ideally, one might have supposed that each feature would be regularly represented by a definite property of the acoustic stimulus. This is not the case. Even this minute dissection of spoken language fails to reveal invariant units. Each feature is defined only in relation to its opposite, and in terms of the particular context in which it occurs. "In some languages . . . the same sound . . . in one position implements the diffuse, and in another, the compact term of the same opposition [of features]" (Jakobson & Halle, 1956, p. 14). If we recognize words in terms of distinctive features, it is also true that we can recognize distinctive features by means of the words in which they occur.

Figure 33 makes the difficulty apparent to the eye. The five spectrograms of this figure represent the same phrase, spoken intelligibly by the same speaker, with various mannerisms and intonations. Some common properties are indeed discoverable in all five versions: the downward sweep of frequencies as the speaker says "you," and the break before the /k/ of "come." Nevertheless, the differences among the spectrograms are so great that it seems impossible to discover any string of units that would identify all these patterns as the same. This is the paradox which has made the mechanical recognition of speech so difficult. Despite years of intensive work, and some limited success with restricted vocabularies, no devices or programs exist which can identify words as they are spoken in ordinary speech. (For an informative review of this field, see Lindgren, 1965a, 1965b.) A generation ago, when trips to Mars and the moon were still in the realm of fantasy, the so-called "speech typewriter" seemed to be just around the corner. As it turned out, the spaces between words are more stubborn obstacles than the space between the planets.

### *SEGMENTATION*

Despite its elegance and widespread influence, the theory of distinctive features leaves one critical question open. What are the features *of*? That is, what units are identified by them? The most common answer has been in terms of phonemes. Halle says explicitly ". . . it is by knowing which of these properties [the distinctive features] are actually present in the signal that we can determine which phoneme was uttered" (1956, p. 511). Jakobson and Halle write "The distinctive features are aligned into simultaneous bundles called phonemes; phonemes are concatenated into sequences; the elementary pattern underlying any grouping of phonemes is the syllable" (1956, p. 20). But if the syllable is "elementary," the phoneme may be less than crucial after all. In fact, Jakobson and Halle manage to repeat the argument on the same page without mentioning the phoneme at all: "The pivotal feature of syllable structure is the contrast of successive features *within the syllable*" (1956, p. 20; italics mine).

The notion that speech is understood in terms of phonemes is uncomfortably reminiscent of the proposition that reading consists of identifying letters. As we saw in Chapter 5, the letter-by-letter hypothesis must be abandoned in favor of a more flexible view. The size of the cognitive unit in reading depends on how the subject deploys his attention. It may be the letter, the spelling-pattern, the word as a whole, or even (in "reading for meaning") something larger. We will soon find that a similar flexibility characterizes the perception of speech. Phonemes, syllables, words, morphemes, phrases, and linguistic constituents may all act as functional segments under appropriate circumstances.

One set of results frequently cited to demonstrate the psychological reality of the phoneme was obtained by Liberman and his associates at the Haskins Laboratories. Their experimental materials were prepared with the aid of a device that can "read" a sound spectrogram, producing roughly those sounds which the spectrogram describes. Presented with spectrograms like those in Figure 35, it puts out speechlike

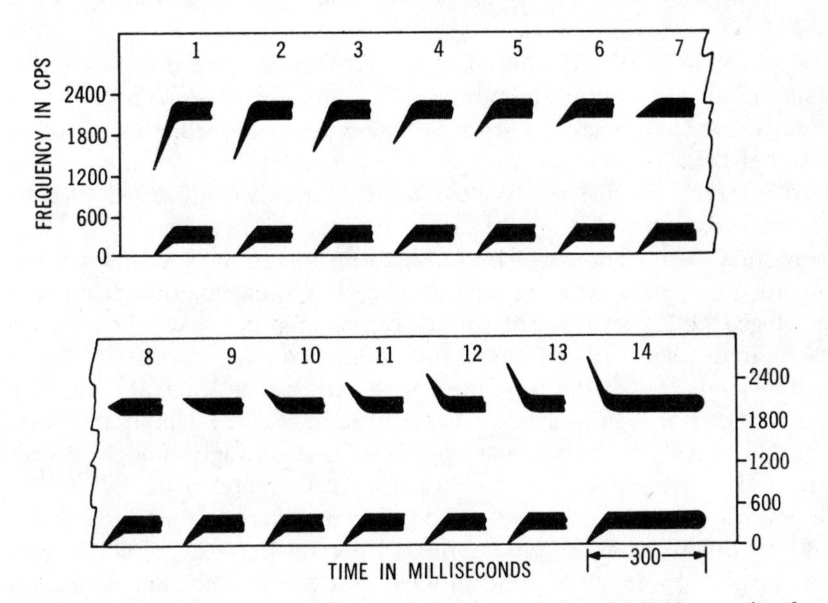


Figure 35. Spectrographic patterns used to produce a series of syllables ranging from "ba" to "ga" (from Liberman, Harris, Hoffman, & Griffith, 1957).

sounds. Those produced from Figure 35 resemble a series of syllables that ". . . start with 'ba' and then shift rather abruptly to 'da' and again to 'ga'" (Cooper, 1959, p. 413). Now, when listeners are given the task of discriminating such sounds from one another, it is much easier to distinguish between instances of different phonemes than between two sounds that belong to the same phoneme class.

This experiment has been interpreted as a proof that the auditory apparatus is tuned in terms of phonemes, and that the phoneme is the functional category for the analysis of speech. But it need not carry this implication. Ladefoged (1959, p. 416) points out that the subjects were actually presented with *syllables* rather than phonemes, and the results imply nothing about the units of which those syllables may have been composed. The same point applies to the work of Miller and Nicely (1955). They prefixed a number of consonants to the vowel /a/, buried the resulting syllables in noise, and presented them to listeners for identification. The distinctive features turned out to be excellent predictors of the listeners' confusion patterns. Syllables like /na/ and /ma/, which differ on only one feature (place of articulation) were more often mistaken for one another than those which, like /na/ and /ba/, differ on two features (place and nasality); syllables with still more differences were still easier to distinguish. These findings, too, say a good deal for the importance of distinctive features but little for the phoneme. The subjects were presented with whole syllables and may have processed them as such.

Not only the identity of distinctive features, but also their order, is important for accurate recognition. The difference between "fits" and "fist" is that in one case the fricative follows the stop, while in the other it comes first. The critical sounds may last only 20 to 30 msec. These short intervals are perilously close to Hirsh's (1959) measured minima for the perception of temporal order. Indeed, children frequently make errors in pronunciation which are based on inversion of successive consonants, or even of syllables. In studying this problem, Broadbent and Ladefoged (1959) synthesized simple consonants and asked listeners to discriminate their order. Persons unfamiliar with the particular sounds used generally failed the task, even with rather long intervals (e.g., 150 msec.). However, well-practiced observers achieved the temporal resolution that Hirsh's data would have predicted. Interestingly enough, Broadbent and Ladefoged report that "Introspections were to the effect that the sounds were discriminated on the basis of differences in quality, and not by a difference of the type normally described as a difference in perceived order" (p. 1539). It does not seem that the listener isolates /s/ and /t/ before examining their order. Instead, he gradually acquires a capacity to distinguish /st/ from /ts/.

For some reason, Broadbent and Ladefoged feel that their result supports a theory of discrete psychological "moments" like that of Stroud (1955). My own impression is just the opposite. The temporal complexity of speech perception, the varying sizes of units employed in different situations, the coexistence of brief distinctive features, longer syllabic rhythms, and still longer intonation patterns all argue against any discrete quantum of psychological time. Segmentation in auditory perception does not depend on the passage of time itself. If it did, tape recordings would become incomprehensible when their speed was slightly changed. In actual fact, they can be speeded up quite a bit and remain fully intelligible. Moreover, the elements critical for recognition *remain at the same relative positions* in the stream of speech under these conditions.

This indifference to tape speed was discovered by A. W. F. Huggins (1963, 1964), in his analysis of a phenomenon first reported by Colin Cherry (1953; also Cherry & Taylor, 1954). Cherry's subjects had been asked to "shadow" spoken prose which they heard through earphones, i.e., to repeat it aloud as they heard it. The speech was switched back and forth rapidly from one earphone to the other. This alternation did not interfere with shadowing if it was very rapid (20 times per second) or very slow (once each second), but it had a marked effect at intermediate rates. The worst performance was observed at 3 c.p.s., where comprehension dropped almost to zero. According to Cherry, this drop reflected a "dead-time" necessary to "switch attention" from one ear to the other. If such a dead-time were to last 1/6 of a second, then at 3 c.p.s. the message would always be gone from each ear just as "attention" arrived.

Cherry's explanation was unlikely from the first. The same critical rate of interruption appears even at a single ear without any alternation from side to side. As Broadbent (1958) pointed out, this means that a limitation on the "switching of attention" cannot be responsible for the effect. It was left for Huggins to administer the *coup de grâce:* minimal intelligibility is no longer at 3 c.p.s. if the speech is speeded up! As the number of words per second increases, the number of interruptions per second must likewise increase if intelligibility is to remain at its worst.

Huggins' own theory of the alternation and interruption effects can best be presented in terms of an analogy. Consider the difficulty of reading a series of printed words, broken up into two separate streams as in Figure 36. The message can be read at slow rates of alternation like (*a*), and at very rapid rates like (*e*), but between these extremes lies a critical range of rates which break up the basic units (letters or words), and make reading very difficut. If speech is perceived in terms of segments, of which many have roughly the same size, it should display a critical rate for similar reasons.

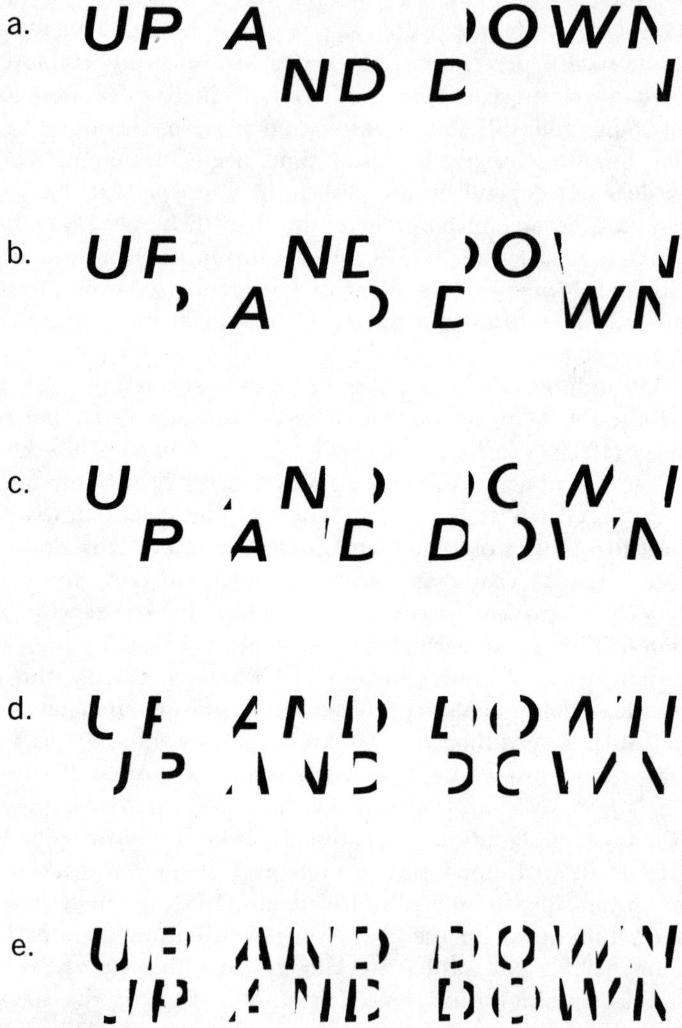

Figure 36. The effects of interruption and alternation on intelligibility, illustrated for the case of hand-printed text.

This theory explains why the worst rate of interruption is the same for monaural as for "dichotic" presentation, and why, as reported by Schubert and Parker (1955), this rate varies for different speakers (consider what would happen with different handwritings in Figure 36). We can also understand why the critical rate is speeded up by the same factor as the speech when rapid playback is used. Huggins reasoned that measurement of this rate, in terms of linguistic units, should enable him to pinpoint the critical segments. By analogy with Figure 36, one would expect comprehension to be poorest when each unit was split half-and-half between the two streams. In fact, the data of Cherry and Taylor, Schubert and Parker, and Huggins (two tape speeds) all agree rather closely on the rate which is most damaging: 0.36 words, or about 0.6 syllables, per uninterrupted half-cycle. These data tend to implicate the syllable itself as the cognitive unit. To be sure, they are also compatible with smaller, regularly-recurring units; Huggins himself argues for the importance of a certain class of phonemes, which he calls "transients."

These data seem to prove beyond reasonable doubt that some rather short segments, of syllabic size or smaller, function in normal speech perception. (Such units must be involved anyway, of course, whenever syllables are presented alone.) However, there is no implication that these are necessarily the *only* segments. Although Cherry found an almost complete loss of intelligibility at the worst alternation rate, this may have resulted from the demand characteristics of his experiment. That is, his subjects may have felt obligated to say nothing at all unless they were fairly sure of being right. With instructions specifically designed to encourage full reporting, Huggins found the maximum loss to be only about 30 percent. Apparently, it is not possible to destroy all of the segments by regular interruption. This suggests that they are not all of equal length.

Miller (1962b) gives an interesting argument for the existence of units much larger than the syllable. He points out that a cognitive unit involves a decision, and studies of reaction time (see Chapter 3) show that people cannot decide among alternatives in less than several hundred milliseconds. Moreover, such studies involve highly attentive subjects under ideal conditions, and a slower rate might be expected in ordinary casual conversation. A rate of one decision per second would suggest that the typical cognitive unit is about three words, i.e., a "phrase." Each such decision would have to be made among a great many alternative phrases, but we know that reaction time does not depend on the number of alternatives when they are highly familiar.

Miller's estimate is supported and clarified by the results of a different and extremely ingenious attempt to identify the units of speech perception, that of Fodor and Bever (1965), and Garrett, Bever, and Fodor (1966). Their work was based on a demonstration originally given by Ladefoged (1959; see also Ladefoged & Broadbent, 1960). In this demonstration, a brief click or hiss is superimposed on a tape-recorded sentence, and a subject must identify the exact point (word, or part of a word) at which it occurred. Ladefoged found that subjects often err by hundreds of milliseconds and several phonemes. This suggests that they are processing, or constructing, the sentence in rather large chunks that are difficult to interrupt.

With the aid of certain notions from linguistics, Fodor and Bever were able to make much more specific predictions of the error-patterns in this situation. We shall see in Chapter 10 that every sentence has a "structure"; it is divided into parts called "immediate constituents," each of these having constituents in its turn. The sentence *That he was happy was evident from the way he smiled* breaks first into *That he was happy* and *was evident from the way he smiled;* then the first part breaks into *That* and *he was happy,* and so on. The hypothesis of Fodor and Bever was that the constituent itself is the unit of speech perception. This suggests that Ladefoged's click should tend to be heard at the major grammatical break of the sentence—between *happy* and *was* in the example—rather than at other places. They succeeded in demonstrating that this is the case.

Given this finding, it was still possible to suppose that the effect of grammar might be only indirect. Perhaps speakers tend to pause longer, or accent more sharply, or to make some other distinctive vocal gesture at constituent boundaries. It might have been such a cue, rather than the grammatical division itself, which "attracted" the click to these positions. To eliminate this possibility, Garrett, Bever, and Fodor (1966) used pairs of sentences with a very special property. The final portions of the sentences in each pair were identical, and were *actually reproduced from the same strip of recording tape,* but different beginnings gave each sentence a different grammatical structure. For example,

(1) *As a direct result of their new invention's INFLUENCE THE COMPANY WAS GIVEN AN AWARD.*
(2) *The retiring chairman whose methods still greatly INFLUENCE THE COMPANY WAS GIVEN AN AWARD.*

In sentence (1), the major break is just after *INFLUENCE,* while in (2) it follows *COMPANY*. A click simultaneous with the first syllable of *COMPANY* was generally heard much earlier in (1) than in (2), near the deepest grammatical break in each case, even though the capitalized portions of the sentences were acoustically identical.

This result demonstrates that grammatical structure *alone* can be enough to determine where interruptions are heard, and presumably how sentences are segmented. The segments are not necessarily divided by any marker in the stimulus. They depend on a constructive process in the listener, and a grammar-dependent process at that.

Between the syllable and the phrase lies another obvious candidate for segmenthood, the word itself. The naive realist supposes that speech sounds must consist of a series of words separated by pauses, for this is what he hears. However, a moment of really careful listening (or a look at a spectrogram) will show that he is wrong. The blank spaces between printed words have no systematic equivalent in spoken language. In saying "His slyness made me suspicious," you probably pause longer in the middle of "sly-ness" than between most pairs of successive words.

The separateness of words in ordinary speech is not given in the stimulus, but supplied by the listener. It is partly because we cannot carry out this construction in an unfamiliar language that foreigners seem to talk so fast. (Of course, there may also be real differences among the average syllable-rates for various languages.) Persons with a poor command of English, such as recent immigrants and young children, have particular difficulty with word-segmentation. We often make it easier for them by introducing artificial gaps between words as we speak. We also pause between words to avoid certain ambiguities: "night rate" differs from "nitrate" only by a silent interval, which linguists symbolize as the phoneme / + /. In most cases, however, the listener hears words as separate to an extent which goes far beyond the corresponding gaps in the auditory input.

Perhaps it is obvious that words function as important cognitive units. Not only does speech seem to consist of separate words, but psychological experiments tend to be organized in the same way. Studies of immediate memory (see Chapter 9) tend to present isolated words for recall; studies of intelligibility have usually presented isolated words for recognition. Naturally, no larger units can become apparent as long as these procedures are used. Such studies of intelligibility are similar in nature to the tachistoscopic experiments reviewed in Chapter 5, and they produce similar results. A word-frequency effect appears in hearing as in vision (Howes, 1957; Savin, 1963), and can be interpreted in terms of a fragment theory. Whether the subject hears each word as a single unit, or tries to make inferences from heard fragments, probably varies from one situation to another.

In short, there seems to be *no* unit of fixed size on which speech perception depends. The scale of the segment which is recognized or constructed varies at least from the syllable to the phrase, with a flexibility comparable to that found in vision. But it is evident, in either modality, that the notion of a cognitive unit can make sense only in the context of some kind of theory. What are the mechanisms by which speech is perceived?

## *THEORIES OF SPEECH PERCEPTION*

The study of speech perception is a rich and complex field which can hardly be surveyed in a few pages. However, some basic principles deserve our attention. Licklider (1952) classified theories of speech perception into three kinds, which he called *correlation, filtering,* and *analysis-*

*by-synthesis.* The appearance of just these three possibilities suggests that the problems of pattern recognition are very general, and cut across the various sensory modalities. They are precisely the same as the alternatives considered for vision in Chapters 3 and 4, where they were called *templates, features,* and *figural synthesis* respectively.

In "correlation" theories, the listener is assumed to have a detailed, stored template of every possible speech segment ready in advance. Given a new input, he computes the correlation—i.e., the statistical cross-product—between the newcomer and each of his stored descriptions. Identification is determined by the highest of these correlations. Licklider points out that such a mechanism is somewhat implausible, because it would require precise temporal alignment between the two wave forms. This argument is essentially the same as the one made by Höffding for vision (Chapter 3): a template theory will work only if the input is perfectly aligned with the template. Other arguments against the template theory are equally applicable here. In particular, it seems impossible for a correlation theory to account for the recognition of ill-defined categories. And in speech perception, every segment seems to be ill-defined—that is just why mechanical recognition has proved so difficult. (Consider, in this connection, our remarkable ability to understand people with foreign accents.)

Licklider's "filtering" approach is like Selfridge's "Pandemonium" if the filters work in parallel, or like EPAM if they are in series. The parallel model, which is the more plausible of the two, assumes that the output of the cochlea goes to a bank of "filters," analogous to Selfridge's "demons" or Sutherland's "analyzers" (Chapter 3). The filters are selectively sensitive to certain intensity-frequency-time patterns like those recorded on the spectrograph. Linear combinations of the filters activate analyzers at a deeper level, which represent the syllables and words recognized by the listener. Any number of filters can examine the input in parallel, at the same time, without expenditure of energy.

We already know the advantages and disadvantages of this theory. Although much more powerful than a template model, and adequate for many kinds of pattern recognition, it will fail in the face of real complexity. In discussing visual cognition, I suggested that parallel analysis must be supplemented by a capacity for focal attention, and by an active process of *figural synthesis.* Licklider's third kind of theory, "analysis-by-synthesis," meets the same problem in the same way. In the case of speech perception, this approach is particularly compelling. It is also very old. Bergson (1911) stated the case for this approach in terms which seem very modern:

I listen to two people speaking in a language which is unknown to me. Do I therefore hear them talk? The vibrations which reach my ears are the same as those which strike theirs. Yet I perceive only a confused noise, in which all sounds are alike. I distinguish nothing and could repeat nothing. In this same sonorous mass, however, the two interlocutors distinguish consonants, vowels, and syllables which are not at all alike, in short, separate words. Between them and me where is the difference? . . .

. . . The difficulty would be insuperable if we really had only auditory impressions on the one hand, and auditory memories on the other. Not so, however, if auditory impressions organize nascent movements, capable of scanning the phrase which is heard and emphasizing its main articulations. These automatic movements of internal accompaniment, at first undecided or uncoordinated, might become more precise by repetition; they would end by sketching a simplified figure in which the listener would find, in their main lines and principal directions, the very movements of the speaker. Thus would unfold in consciousness, under the form of nascent muscular sensations, the *motor diagram,* as it were, of the speech we hear (pp. 134, 136).

In his emphasis on "muscular sensations," Bergson is advocating what is now called the *motor theory of speech perception:* a version of analysis-by-synthesis which lays particular stress on incipient movements of the articulatory muscles. Lane (1965) has recently reviewed the evidence for this view. Its most vigorous modern exponent has been Liberman (1957), who has presented some rather ingenious demonstrations in its support. He notes that certain syllables can be arranged into what seems (to the listener) like a continuous series. For example, the /g/ phoneme may be followed by various vowels in this way: /gi/, /ge/, /gɛ/, /ga/, /gɔ/, /go/, /gu/. The subjective continuity of these syllables is by no means apparent in the corresponding speech spectrograms, shown in Figure 37. The first four syllables show an increasing transi-

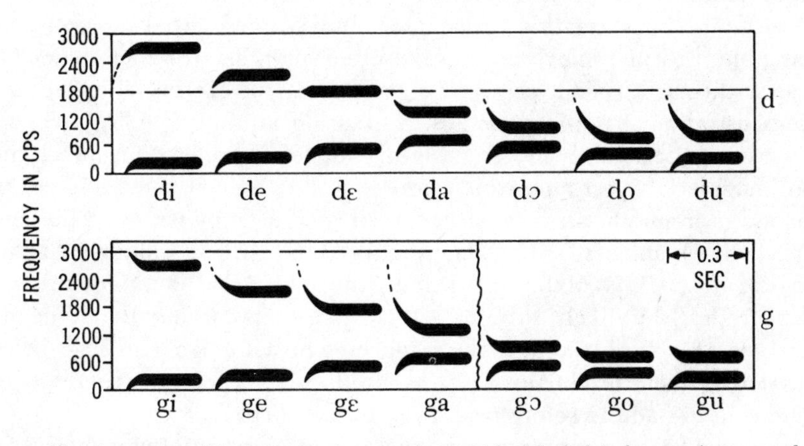


Figure 37. Spectrographic patterns that produce /d/ and /g/ before various vowels. The physical discontinuity after /ga/ is not represented in auditory experience, nor in the articulatory movements (from Liberman, 1957).

tional phase between the consonant and the upper stable frequency in the vowel, but the fifth shows almost no transition at all. This acoustic discontinuity does not appear in perception, perhaps because it is also absent from the muscular movements involved in *speaking* the various syllables. Liberman believes that ". . . speech is perceived by reference to articulation—that is, that the articulatory movements and their sensory effects mediate between the acoustic stimulus and the event we call perception" (p. 122). Such an argument assumes the validity of what the Gestalt psychologists called "psychological isomorphism": a continuity in experience is thought to reflect an underlying continuity in the perceptual mechanisms. Without isomorphism, Liberman's demonstration would not be relevant to the motor theory.

Another argument for the motor theory is that it gives a plausible account of auditory hallucinations. In hearing, as in vision, imagery and perception seem to lie on a continuum. It is often difficult to decide, over the rush of water into the bathtub, whether someone is really calling our name or if we are imagining it. In such a case, when we hear a voice that has no counterpart in reality, must it not be our own? There is even some direct evidence that the auditory hallucinations of schizophrenics have a motor component. Both Gould (1949, 1950) and McGuigan (1966) were able to amplify subvocal activity in patients who were actively hearing "voices"; they found a close correlation between what the patient actually said and what he heard the voices say. Small movements of the larynx have also been observed during verbal thinking (see experiments reviewed by Humphrey, 1951); they may be analogous in some ways to the eye movements which accompany vivid visual imagery.

Nevertheless, we must be wary of accepting this view uncritically. Hallucinatory phenomena certainly suggest some kind of constructive or "synthetic" interpretation of listening, but synthesis need not consist of tangible muscular movements. Like other peripheralist hypotheses, the motor theory of speech perception goes too far; it can be refuted just by demonstrating that the responses in question are not actually necessary. One need not actually move laryngeal muscles to understand speech, nor to imagine it. Speech remains comprehensible even if these muscles are removed or anesthetized; it can be understood even by persons who never speak, like Lenneberg's (1962) eight-year-old boy with an unknown "neurological deficit." Jakobson and Halle, who regard the motor theory as a "theoretically unlikely surmise" (1956, p. 34), point out that one may become able to distinguish the phonemes of a foreign language before mastering their production, just as children often can discriminate the phonemes of adults before beginning to use them.

The proponents of the theory are aware of these difficulties. Quite naturally, they resort to the postulation of "fractional" or "implicit" movements, familiar to psychologists from their use in theories of learning. Thus Liberman writes "The process is somehow short-circuited—that is, the reference to articulatory movements and their sensory consequences must somehow occur in the brain without getting out into the periphery" (1957, p. 52). This makes the theory difficult to test, of course, but not more so than other cognitive theories. In addition, it takes the motor theory perceptibly closer to a more flexible model of speech perception, which we must consider next.

### *THE ANALYSIS-BY-SYNTHESIS MODEL*

Even if we were to grant that speech perception depends on an intervening stage of articulatory movements, we would still have to explain just how the listener knows what movements to make and how he comes to make them. That is, we would like a theory of speech-synthesis that explains the selection of the items to be synthesized. Suppose we did have a mechanism that could produce speech; how would we instruct it? Would we have to specify (*a*) the actual successive adjustments of its "speaking tube"? Would it be enough to list (*b*) a succession of syllables or phonemes, or (*c*) a succession of words or phrases, or even (*d*) the sentence itself, or perhaps just (*e*) the substance of what was to be said? Obviously, this would depend on the mechanism itself. It seems clear that (*a*) through (*e*) would require successively more complicated machines. In fact, each machine in the series would have to incorporate most of the previous ones somehow within itself. That is, a device of type (*c*), which could simply be told to say a particular word, would have to be equipped with rules that could program its "speaking tube" appropriately as in (*a*). (It might or might not go through a stage like (*b*) to reach these rules.) A machine of type (*e*) would have to know how to construct sentences (*d*), which in turn would be strings of smaller units. This means that any "device" which produces spoken language, including man himself, must have a hierarchical set of rules for getting from an *intended* message to an actual *articulated* signal.

If it must incorporate these rules anyway, such a "device" could also apply them to get from a *guessed* message to a *hypothetical* signal. But then, given a way to generate guesses and a means of comparing the hypothetical signal with a real one, our "device" would be able to understand speech as well as to produce it! This mode of understanding is "analysis-by-synthesis," in the sense of Halle and Stevens (1959, 1964). As a psychological theory, it closely resembles Bruner's (1951) "hypothesis testing" or Solley and Murphy's (1960) "trial and check," and it is certainly congenial to the general approach of this book. We have met it before, in Eden's program for the automatic recognition of handwriting (Eden & Halle, 1961), which is explicitly based on the same principle.

It goes beyond the motor theory by being more abstract, by permitting construction to occur at many levels other than muscular activity. As Halle and Stevens remark, ". . . it does not regard perception as a covert form of motor behavior; instead it views perception as a variety of silent calculation, a type of calculation at which man is particularly adept" (1959, D-7). One makes a hypothesis about the original message, applies rules to determine what the input would be like if the hypothesis were true, and checks to see whether the input is really like that.

Auditory synthesis, like its visual counterpart, can apparently produce units of various sizes. The listener can ask himself "What sounds were uttered?" or "What words were spoken?" or "What was meant?" and proceed to synthesize accordingly. In each case, he must have a set of rules: phonetic, phonemic, syntactic, semantic, or what you will. It is the employment of these rules that makes analysis-by-synthesis more powerful than such methods as correlation or filtering. Stevens (1960) is explicit on this point. While other approaches would require the listener to store all possible acoustic inputs, in analysis-by-synthesis

> . . . *rules* for generating spectral patterns rather than the entire catalog of patterns themselves are stored, with a resulting large saving in storage capacity. Furthermore, if a proper strategy is devised for selecting the order in which patterns are synthesized for comparison with the input, then the number of patterns which must be generated and compared may be of orders of magnitude less than the total number of patterns that could be generated by the rules (p. 53).

The last point is crucial. Without a "proper strategy . . . for selecting the order in which patterns are synthesized" the notion of analysis-by-synthesis would reduce to the crudest kind of trial and error. No one seriously proposes that the listener keeps on synthesizing words or phonemes at random until he happens on a match. What form of strategy would be helpful here? Stevens lists a number of possibilities: "The order in which different articulatory descriptions are tried may depend in part on data from a preliminary analysis of the signal, in part on data from previous spectra, and part on the results of previous trials on the spectrum under analysis" (1960, p. 50).

The first two of Stevens' proposals are particularly interesting. "A preliminary analysis of the signal" must be a kind of processing which, by definition, is *not* analysis-by-synthesis. There must be mechanisms able to pick out portions of the input that are worth synthesizing, and to arrive at preliminary identifications of these portions. Such preliminary mechanisms play a role very like that of the preattentive processes described in Chapter 4. In the case of vision, it seemed best to think of them as feature-sensitive systems, organized in parallel like

"Pandemonium," and primarily concerned with wholistic, gross properties of the input. The same interpretation seems appropriate here.

Stevens' second proposal, that the listener uses "data from previous spectra," is an appeal to context and expectation. Indeed, perhaps the most powerful argument for the analysis-by-synthesis approach is that it provides a coherent account of the way listeners make use of contextual information. We must not suppose that contextual cues are just minor ways to "supplement" perception. Denes, an advocate of the motor theory, makes this point vigorously:

> The basic premise of [most speech-recognition] work has always been that a one-to-one relationship existed between the acoustic event and the phoneme. Although it was recognized that the sound waves associated with the same phoneme could change according to circumstances, there was a deep-seated belief that if only the right way of examining the acoustic signal was found, then the much sought-after one-to-one relationship would come to light. Only more recently has there been a wider acceptance of the view that these one-to-one relations do not exist at all: the speaker produces acoustic signals whose characteristics are of course a function of the phoneme to be currently transmitted, but which are also greatly affected by a variety of other factors such as the individual articulatory characteristics of the speaker, the phonetic environment of the sound to be produced, linguistic relationships, etc. As a result, the acoustic characteristics of the sound to be produced do not identify a particular phoneme uniquely, and the listener resolves the ambiguities of the acoustic signal by making use of his own knowledge of the various linguistic and contextual constraints mentioned above. The large part that is played by these nonacoustic factors in the recognition of speech is best shown by the remarkably small loss of intelligibility produced by quite serious distortions of the speech wave. It is becoming clear that automatic recognizers or synthesizers cannot hope to operate successfully unless they make use of these nonacoustic constraints of the speech mechanisms (1963, p. 892).

An early and important demonstration of the importance of context was given by Miller, Heise, and Lichten (1951). Their subjects were to identify words and nonsense syllables in a noisy background. Simple knowledge of what to expect made an enormous difference: "At a signal-to-noise ratio where practically no nonsense syllables were reported correctly, nearly all the (spoken) digits were correctly communicated" (p. 330). When whole sentences were presented, intelligibility was very much higher than for separate words. Similar gains appeared if the subject had advance knowledge of a restricted vocabulary, from which the spoken word was to be selected. Miller *et al.* interpret all their findings in terms of the size of the set of alternatives from which the subject chooses. Sentences restrict this set by a context effect, while specified vocabularies reduce it explicitly.

It is not necessary to assume that the alternatives are reduced word by word. Miller (1962a, 1962b) found that strings of words which form grammatical sentences, like *Don brought his black bread,* were more accurately reported than ungrammatical strings *(Bread black his brought Don)* even by subjects who were extremely familiar with the restricted set of words used in the experiment and the orders in which they could occur. Evidently the process of synthesis is partly under the control of the principles of grammatical organization. This kind of control is already familiar to us from the click-localizing experiments of Garrett, Bever, and Fodor (1966).

Such results lend themselves easily to interpretation in terms of analysis-by-synthesis. Hearing an utterance, the listener constructs one of his own in an attempt to match it. Such matching may go on at "several levels"—that is, in terms of different segment-sizes. If a single noise-masked word is presented, the listener's preliminary speech analysis may pick out a few distinctive features or syllables which suggest a tentative answer; various related words are then synthesized until one of them fits. If the stimulus is an entire sentence, a few words tentatively identified by the preliminary system may guide the synthesis of whole constituents as units, or even of the whole sentence. In this way the listener often manages to hear words which were not in the input at all, just as Pillsbury's (1897) subjects saw letters that were never presented (Chapter 5). It is this synthesis which creates the spaces between words in perception, which accounts for the prevalence of plausible substitution errors in listening, and which makes it hard to understand French when one expects English even if one knows both languages well.

The relevant context is not limited to the preceding words of the speaker. Any factor which predisposes the listener to synthesize one utterance rather than another will affect speech perception. Expectation, familiarity, and perhaps preference can play the same roles in hearing that they do in vision. To the best of my knowledge, there is no study of these variables in auditory perception which cannot be understood within the conceptual framework developed for printed words in Chapter 5.

In everyday life, the role of motives in speech perception is a matter of common observation. We tend to listen to, and thus to hear, primarily what interests us; we may even distort what is heard in the direction of our interests. Generally, however, we check our constructions against the input. When there is no input, this cannot be done. Under these conditions synthesis may yield more or less vivid auditory imagery, just as it does in the analogous visual case. In auditory dreams, and in the "voices" heard by schizophrenics, the products of synthesis are believed to be real, and so may be called "hallucinations" (see Chapter 6). Hallucinated voices can take many forms. The source may seem to be inside the patient's head, or outside; the hallucinated speaker may "take over" the patient's own voice for "its" purposes, or may have a voice of its own; it may be clear and sharp, or merely a murmur which is nevertheless understood. However, none of the reported varieties of auditory hallucination seem to invalidate the hypothesis that they are formed by the normal mechanisms of auditory synthesis.

There is no reason to suppose that the synthetic activity is always "motor" in character, though it may be. Nearly everyone can "hear" (there is no auditory equivalent of "visualize") the general tone-pattern of familiar voices just by thinking about them, though few of us are accomplished mimics. Musicians can certainly imagine sounds that they cannot produce vocally. Unfortunately not many can equal Mozart, who heard whole symphonies in his mind before ever committing them to paper (Humphrey, 1951, p. 53).

Recently, Warren and Gregory (1958) have reported a phenomenon that vividly illustrates analysis-by-synthesis; it has become known as the "verbal-transformation effect." (See also Warren, 1961a, 1961b; Taylor & Henning, 1963; Skinner, 1936.) When a single word or a short phrase is repeated over and over again, as by a tape loop, the listener may hear some rather surprising changes in what is said. If the recorded voice is saying "rest, rest, rest, . . ." it may suddenly become "stress, stress, stress, . . ." or "tress, tress, tress, . . ." or even "Esther, Esther, Esther, . . ." The changes seem abrupt, like the reversals of a Necker cube. They may include additions and omissions as well as changes of accent. In some cases they even have a hallucinatory quality, being experienced as "out there," or "real."

Several clinical observations provide a bridge between the relatively minor perceptual changes of the verbal transformation effect and the more radical illusory experiences of psychosis. Dr. Julio Dittborn (personal communication, 1966) explored the effects of a 30-second tape loop, with a simple verbal text, that repeated all night as he slept. On one occasion he woke up and heard the tape saying something quite different; it continued for seven minutes (by the clock), while he made notes. The message he seemed to hear was closely related to the dream from which he had awakened. Later, he gave tape loops to six of his private patients. Two of them had similar experiences, although they had not been led to expect any. Oswald (1962a, p. 118; 1962b) has reported similar phenomena in patients undergoing rather heroic forms of behavior therapy.

Transformations of this kind are to be expected if listening is a constructive process. Nevertheless, as long as normal waking subjects are used, the stimulus input is usually a primary determinant of the course of construction. Except in the case of true imagery, auditory synthesis is constrained by the signal, or—more precisely—by the "preliminary analysis of the signal" on which analysis-by-synthesis depends. There must be a kind of filtering, of feature-detection, which precedes the active construction of detail. Listening has both a passive and an active mode. This distinction will prove very helpful as we turn to the next chapter, and the problem of selective listening.

*Chapter 8*

# *Echoic Memory and Auditory Attention*

Since the auditory input is always extended over time, some kind of transient memory must preserve it long enough for the processes of speech perception to operate. As long as this "echoic" memory lasts, the listener can select portions of its contents for special attention. Here, attempts to measure the duration of echoic memory are reviewed, together with various examples of selective listening. The hypothesis that attentive selection involves a "filter" is considered and rejected in favor of an interpretation based on analysis-by-synthesis. This "constructive" view is applied to a number of experimental findings, including studies of shadowing and of stimulation during sleep.

As we have seen, the notion of analysis-by-synthesis leads to a distinction between two levels of auditory processing. A preliminary analysis, made by a relatively passive, preattentive stage, provides information which guides the more active process of synthesis itself. This distinction leads naturally to certain hypotheses about memory and attention. For example, each process may well have a separate medium of storage (a "memory") available to it. Moreover, it seems intuitively plausible to identify the synthetic process rather closely with the act of "paying attention" to any auditory stimulus. These arguments will be made more explicit later on. For the present, it seems better to begin anew with certain primitive auditory phenomena; they may lead to the same conclusion in their own right.

## *ECHOIC MEMORY*

Perhaps the most fundamental fact about hearing is that sound is an intrinsically temporal event. Auditory information is always spread out in time; no single millisecond contains enough information to be very useful. If information were discarded as soon as it arrived, hearing would be all but impossible. Therefore, we must assume that some "buffer," some medium for temporary storage, is available in the auditory cognitive system.

This conclusion can be applied specifically to the perception of speech. We have already seen that the cognitive units of language may be of various lengths. Some, like the shorter syllables, endure only for a small fraction of a second; others take much longer. But even the short ones have some finite duration, and their distinctive features take a certain amount of real time to come into being. If these features are to play their part in speech recognition, auditory information must be preserved in some *unsegmented* form, at least while each segment endures.

Like the visual short-term storage discussed in Chapter 2, this fleeting memory needs a special name. I will call it "echoic memory." Other designations are possible; such terms as "stimulus trace" (Hull, 1952; Peterson, 1963) and "raw storage" (Yntema, Wozencraft, & Klem, 1964) have been used to refer to the same medium. Both may be somewhat misleading: there is no raw, uncoded, tapelike record of the acoustic stimulus. The input has been transformed at least by the cochlear mechanisms, and perhaps by other processes, before this stage of processing is reached. However, while it does presuppose some recoding, we can be sure that the "grain," or unit size, of echoic memory is finer than the segmentation of speech which it makes possible.

In many ways, the echoic medium corresponds to what William James (1890, p. 643) called "primary memory." He used this phrase to describe the stability of the "specious present," the brief integrated portion of time which the perceiver experiences as "happening now" rather than as "already over." Almost by definition, a single segment of perceived speech must fall within this span. If part of it were to appear as "past" and another part as "present," it would be two segments rather than one. However, we will see below that echoic storage can substantially exceed the specious present; it may last for seconds and include several segments of speech. In addition, Waugh and Norman (1965) have used "primary memory" with a rather different concept in mind, so the phrase is better avoided altogether. For want of an alternative, then, I will continue to use "echoic." Its similarity to "iconic" is not inappropriate; both terms represent preliminary and transient storage mechanisms for sensory information.

How long does echoic memory last? Usually it is not needed for long: material that has been segmented and organized can be stored in what seems to be a different medium, which we will consider in Chapter 9. This would suggest that the "echo" is only useful for a relatively short time. Of course, it might be preserved even without being needed, and Penfield has suggested that ". . . there is, hidden away in the brain, a record of the stream of consciousness. It seems to hold the detail of that stream as laid down during each man's waking conscious hours. Contained in this record are all those things of which the individual was once aware . . ." (1958, p. 58). But even if Penfield were right—which we found reason to doubt in Chapter 6—his "record of the stream of consciousness" would not correspond to echoic memory, because it is not available for analysis by the processes of speech perception. So far as direct control over the listener's experience and behavior is concerned, the echo certainly disappears rather quickly.

It is possible to suppose that echoic memory is discarded immediately after each segment of speech; that the act of segmentation somehow destroys the less coded information on which it is based. However, this seems unlikely, for a number of reasons. New modes of organization could hardly be learned if inappropriate ones destroyed the basis for learning. The foreigner who is told "No, not zeal, *seal!*" could not benefit from this advice unless an echoic memory preserved the initial /z/ for comparison with the subsequent /s/. Moreover, the so-called "suprasegmental phonemes" seem to depend on a relatively long echoic memory. If the difference between the rising inflection of "You can come?" and the level "You can come!" is to be detected, the acoustic basis of "you" and "can" must still be available when "come" appears. The same argument can be made with respect to the recognition of individual voices, moods, etc., and for the appreciation of music. All these feats apparently require a fine-grained or echoic memory of appreciable length that persists through a number of cognitive units.

We noted earlier that the mechanisms of analysis-by-synthesis depend on guidance from the "context," particularly from words already identified. But in ordinary speech the context necessary to identify a segment may come *after* it, so segmentation itself can often be profitably delayed. Or, if it has not been delayed, it may still be corrected by information arriving subsequently. Some persistence of the echo would greatly facilitate this retrospective analysis of what has been heard. Miller suggests as much:

> If complete storage is necessary even after lower-level decisions have been tentatively reached, why bother to make the lower-level decisions first? Why not store the message until enough of it is on hand to support a higher-level decision, then make a decision for all levels simultaneously? [This would account for our subjective feeling that . . .] the larger more meaningful decisions are made first, and that we pursue the details only so far as they are necessary to serve our immediate purpose (1962b, p. 81).

Of course, we must admit that context can still be useful even if it comes after the echo has faded and only labeled segments remain. In such cases it helps by suggesting how to reinterpret them. It will be far more helpful, however, if the unsegmented information is still accessible and can be restructured.

The most direct attempt to measure the duration of echoic memory is perhaps that of Guttman and Julesz (1963; see also Julesz & Guttman, 1963). They played repetitive segments of white noise, prepared by a computer so that the end of the segment blended smoothly into the beginning of its next occurrence. The experimental question was whether the repetition would be noticeable. The results showed that with very short segments, a fraction of a second long, the listener regularly hears a repetitive "putt-putt" or "woosh-woosh." When the cycle is many seconds in length, the repetition is not noticed at all, except by deliberate search for particular codable fragments of sound. The longest segments heard as repetitive without such an effort were about one second long; Guttman and Julesz estimate the duration of "auditory memory" by this figure.

Echoic storage was tapped in a very different way by Pollack's (1959) study of poststimulus cueing. His procedure was analogous to that used with visual stimuli in a number of experiments reviewed in Chapter 2 (e.g., Lawrence & Coles, 1954). The subjects had to identify words spoken in a noisy background. They knew that the stimuli would come from a certain large set of possibilities. Just *after* each presentation, they were shown (visually) a small set of alternatives from which that particular stimulus word had actually been drawn. The size of this second set (the so-called "response alternatives") turned out to be crucial for the accuracy of identification.

To some extent, the effect of the response alternatives can be accounted for without reference to echoic memory, simply in terms of guessing. A subject who is told that the preceding stimulus was one of two words—say, either *backbone* or *doorstep*—can be correct half the time without any stimulus information at all. This 50 percent may represent a substantial improvement over his performance when there were 16 alternatives to listen for. It is not entirely clear how one should correct for such "guessing." According to the theory of signal detectability (now widely accepted in psychophysics—see Swets, 1964, for a review), the weighing of alternative possibilities is an integral part of the listening process. That theory provides a measure of signal discriminability, usually called $d'$ or $d_s$, which is independent of "guessing." When Pollack applied $d_s$ to his data, he found that the actual discriminability of the words did not depend on the number of subsequently presented alternatives after all.

More important for the study of echoic memory is a part of Pollack's experiment in which a set of (two) "response alternatives" was presented only after varying delays. Rapid presentation turned out to be extremely important, as Figure 38 makes clear. Although Pollack

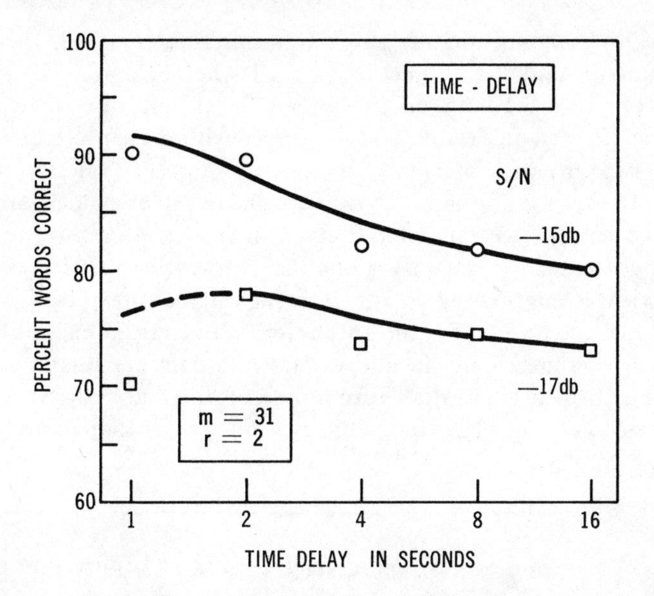


Figure 38. Decay of echoic memory as measured by Pollack (1959). The message was one of 31 alternative words presented at the indicated signal-to-noise ratio. After the delay shown on the abscissa, the number of alternatives was reduced to two by giving the subject a pair of words to choose from.

has drawn continuously decreasing functions through these data, the points themselves suggest that performance leveled off after about four seconds. Another portion of the experiment may explain why this "leveling off" occurred. In this condition, listeners were allowed to make *written notes* describing the sound of the stimulus-word as soon as it was over, but were not given the two "response alternatives" until hours later. Scores achieved with the aid of notes in this rather unusual procedure were quantitatively equal to those after four seconds of delay (Figure 38). Apparently the echo was "richer" than coded, segmental memory for the first few seconds and could be used to decide between the response alternatives if they came soon enough. With longer delays the coded units, which could be preserved indefinitely by written notation, proved to be more dependable. I suspect that if Pollack had applied the theory of signal detection to the delay conditions, a genuine drop in discriminability would have appeared in the first few seconds, and not thereafter.

Still another estimate of the length of the echo can be based on the work of Eriksen and Johnson (1964). Their subjects, more pleasantly engaged than participants in most psychological experiments, were told to spend two hours reading a novel. A signal tone was sounded occasionally during this period; it was loud enough to be easily detectable under ordinary conditions. A short time after each signal, the reading lamp went off and the subject was asked whether a tone had just occurred. The interval between the signal "beep" and the query was the experimental variable. Catch trials–queries without a preceding signal–were occasionally presented to check on the subject's honesty.

If we assume that attention to the novel precluded any encoding of the "beep," we can infer that recall in this procedure must have been based on echoic memory alone. Consequently, any decrease of accuracy with a lengthening of the interval can be interpreted as due to the decay of the echo. This interpretation is not unchallengeable, but it is noteworthy that a decrease did occur. The data are presented in Figure 39. The two curves in the figure represent different subjective criteria: the lower shows how often the subjects were *certain* that there had been

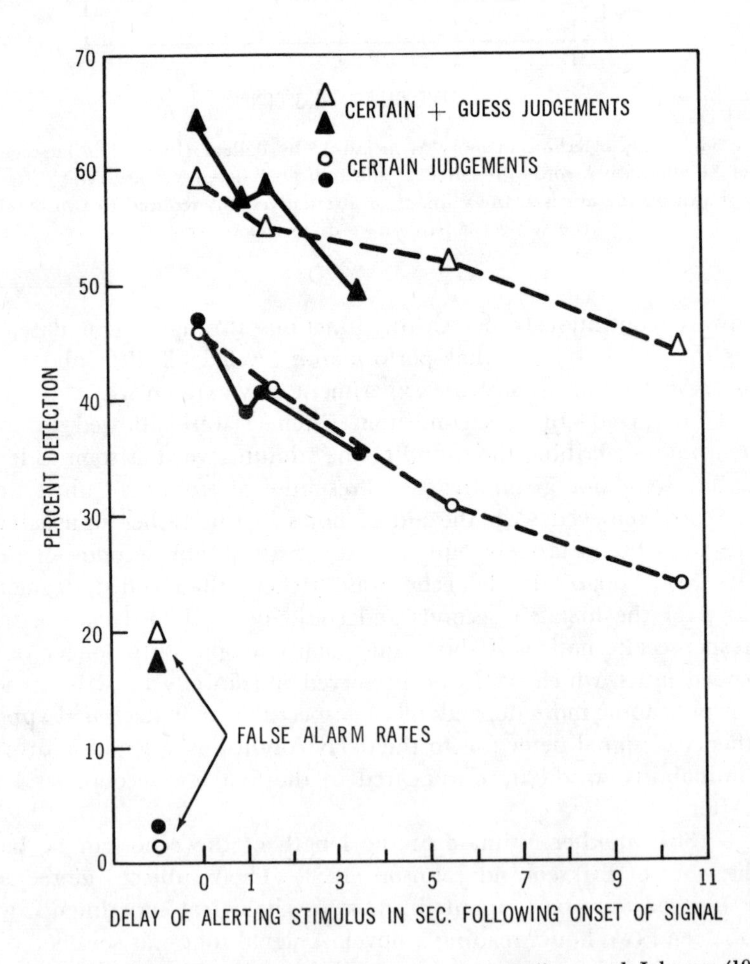


Figure 39. Decay of echoic memory as measured by Eriksen and Johnson (1964).

a signal, while the upper shows how often they were willing to say that one had *probably* occurred. The criterion of certainty was reached in 50 percent of the trials on which "beep" and the query were simultaneous; the proportion dropped 30 percent when the query was delayed by ten seconds.

It is interesting that only half the tones were detected even with a simultaneous query. This may mean that lack of attention can prevent stimuli from even entering echoic memory; that attention can "filter out" irrelevant stimuli entirely, as maintained by Broadbent (1958). Although many arguments against the filter theory will be presented below, this finding will have to be kept in mind. A similar result of Peterson and Kroener (1964) suggests that it was no accident.

The findings of Eriksen and Johnson indicate that the echo may contain useful information as long as ten seconds after the original stimulus. At first glance, this seems in contradiction with the four-second estimate from Pollack's (1959) data or the single second which was critical in the method of Guttman and Julesz (1963). However, we must realize that the durations measured by such techniques will depend on the difficulty of the experimental task. The spontaneous detection of periodicity, in the Guttman-Julesz procedure, may require a great deal more detailed information than is needed to distinguish between silence and a "beep." If echoic memory decays only gradually, its apparent duration will vary inversely with the difficulty of the task used to measure it.

We have already inferred the necessity for an echoic memory from the simple fact that the stimuli for speech perception are extended in time. The same argument applies to another, particularly interesting auditory phenomenon: the perception of *rhythm.* When successive taps or drumbeats are separated by alternately long and short intervals (** ** ** **), we nearly always hear a series of *pairs.* Each pair is a segment, a cognitive unit, functioning much like the syllable or the word or the constituent in speech. The "distinctive feature" involved seems to be the repetition of a sharp discontinuity at a fixed time interval, relative to neighboring intervals. This kind of segmentation obviously requires an echoic memory. It can only take place after several taps have appeared; their occurrence and the intervals between them must have been preserved in an unsegmented medium long enough for the rhythm to be defined and detected. Thus, another estimate of the duration of echoic memory can be made if we see at what intertap interval the rhythm seems to disappear entirely. Fraisse, who has carried out extensive studies of rhythmic structure (1956, 1963), reports that this happens when the taps are about two seconds apart. While this limit cannot be a sharply defined one, it is comfortingly within the range of echoic durations estimated by other means.

There are many striking similarities between the phenomena of rhythm and those of speech, and we will return to them repeatedly in the next two chapters. For the present, it is enough to remark that motor theories of the perception of rhythm have often been proposed (Stetson, 1905; Boring, 1942) and are supported by many casual observations (for example, by the prevalence of foot-tapping during band concerts). Again, however, it seems likely that actual muscular involvement is not necessary; the complexity and speed of rhythmic structures in music strongly suggests an abstract rather than a motoric form of analysis-by-synthesis. It is also interesting that we can "follow" individual rhythms just as we can follow individual conversations at a cocktail party. As noted earlier, the latter ability depends primarily on auditory localization, and thus also on repetitive time-differences (between the two ears). It has been the subject of considerable research in its own right.

### *THE SHADOWING EXPERIMENTS*

The chief tool for the study of selective listening in recent years has been the method of "shadowing," first described by Cherry (1953). To shadow a spoken prose message is to repeat it aloud *as it is heard,* staying as "close behind" the speaker as possible. If the speaker does not go too fast, shadowing is relatively easy and can be performed almost without error. In one particularly important series of experiments, Cherry asked his subjects to shadow a voice presented to one ear while a different, unrelated message appeared at the other. Even this task was not very difficult; "attention" can be successfully "tuned" to one message, leaving the other almost completely ignored.

Cherry treated this phenomenon as if the cue which distinguished the irrelevant message from the relevant one was the ear at which it arrived. "The processes of recognition may apparently be switched to either ear at will" (p. 977). We saw in Chapter 7 that a similar "switching" between ears played a crucial part in Cherry's theory of the alternation effect, later refuted by Huggins (1964). So far as simultaneous messages are concerned, it was already clear to Broadbent (1958) that selectivity is *not* based on the ear at which the message arrives, but on the perceived location of the sound source. The two-earphone situation serves only to make localization particularly easy. Selectivity occurs also when *both* messages reach *both* ears, provided that their sources are somewhat separated in space. So effective is the selective process that even the inhibiting effects of "delayed auditory feedback"—the briefly delayed playback of one's own voice which causes such remarkable difficulties in speaking—are much reduced if the feedback is arranged to sound as if it were coming from a different place (Hochberg & Berko, 1965).

Spieth, Curtis, and Webster (1954) showed that selective listening was possible with loudspeakers placed only ten to twenty degrees apart. The same authors also showed that messages coming through a low-pass filter could be followed in preference to those sent through a high-pass filter, so localization is not the only possible basis of selection. Egan, Carterette, and Thwing (1954) extended these findings and report that intensity, as well as frequency, can serve this function. Thus the mechanisms which react to *localization, voice quality,* and *intensity* all seem to operate prior to those involved in selective attention.

Cherry himself showed that voice quality could be detected outside of attention. The unshadowed message did not go entirely unheard: the subjects noticed when it gave way to a 400 c.p.s. tone, or when a man's voice was replaced by a woman's. Moreover, if the rejected message was actually the *same* as the one being shadowed, all subjects noticed the identity, even when one message was delayed by several seconds with respect to the other. His finding bears directly on the question of auditory memory, since there could have been no identity to notice unless the earlier message had been stored at least temporarily.

The experiment was repeated by Treisman (1964a; 1964b) in a systematic effort to determine the critical time intervals for the recognition of identity. Her subjects did not expect the two messages to be the same. They were told that the irrelevant one was only a distraction to be ignored, and it was "faded in" gradually after they had begun shadowing. In successive trials, the time lag between the two messages was systematically reduced from 6 seconds to zero. At some point, every subject noticed that they were identical. When the shadowed message was "ahead of" the irrelevant one, the average lag at which identity was noticed was 4.5 seconds. When the irrelevant message was leading, it was only 1.4 seconds. As Treisman realized, these two values differ because they represent two different kinds of memory. Echoic storage for unsegmented and unattended material lasts only one or two seconds, while segmented memory (for the shadowed text) survives much longer. Interestingly enough, the 4.5-second lag (when the shadowed message was leading and presumably being stored in segmental memory), included about 12 words, which is close to the ordinary memory span for this type of material. When the subject was shadowing isolated words, however, the critical lag was much smaller (about six words); this corresponds to the shorter memory span for unrelated items. On the other hand, the number of words by which the *irrelevant* message led when identity was noticed did not depend on the kind of material used at all, as one would expect in an echoic memory.

In an interesting experiment with bilingual observers, Treisman played a *translation* of the shadowed message into the rejected ear. Surprisingly enough, a few subjects noticed the identity. This result says nothing about the exact duration of memory, since a translation cannot be matched word-for-word with the original and so cannot be given a fixed amount of "lag." But it says a good deal about selective attention, which we must now consider more systematically.

## *THE FILTER THEORY*

At first glance, the experiments on selective listening suggest that attention behaves very like a filter. Some signals are "passed" for further processing, while others are rejected. This concept is the core of Broadbent's very influential theory of cognition. His approach has a good deal in common with the one adopted here, and in fact his phrase "the flow of information in the organism" (1963) sums up the definition of cognitive psychology used in this book. *Perception and Communication* (Broadbent, 1958) presents a general theory of attention, memory, learning, and related phenomena, in terms of information theory and filtering. (Oddly enough, speech perception is hardly mentioned, despite his interest in it—e.g., Broadbent, 1962.)

I am more skeptical than Broadbent about the value of information *measurement,* as earlier chapters have made clear. He argues that the cognitive mechanisms must have a finite informational capacity —in terms of bits per second—and that filtering mechanisms are needed if their capacity is not to be overloaded. This is surely true in some sense, but it does not help us to understand the mechanisms in question. One might as well say that the heart, which pumps only about 100 cc. of blood per stroke, has limited capacity compared with, say, a fire engine. This would also be true, but by itself would be of little help in understanding the physiology and "hemodynamics" of the heart. Perhaps it is for this reason that Broadbent's later papers (e.g., 1963) have emphasized flow charts rather than "bits."

Broadbent assumes that the hypothetical filter can be "tuned" by the observer to any of a large number of "channels." It will only pass information from the channel to which it is tuned. Possible channels include sense organs, directions in auditory space, particular voice qualities, etc. Only information that has been passed by the filter can affect the subject's response, or be long remembered. A diagram of the system appears in Figure 40. Actually this diagram is not an entirely fair representation of Broadbent's views, since he feels that response to several channels simultaneously *is* possible when the rate of information flow is low. Nevertheless, it is a satisfactory approximation.

Cherry's work on selective listening is entirely compatible with this model. To be sure, some features of the rejected voice apparently get through the filter, but as Broadbent points out: ". . . the features

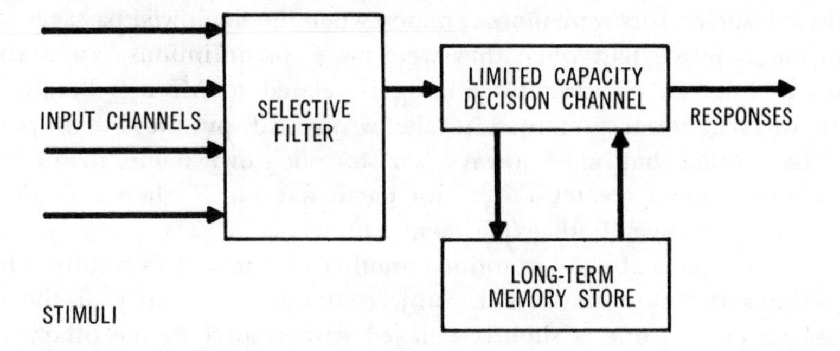


**Figure 40.** Flow chart for Broadbent's "filter theory" (taken from Treisman, 1964b).

of the rejected voice which are observed are those which are useful for picking out relevant from irrelevant words in . . . other [selective listening] experiments. Differences in voice are useful when one wants to ignore some words: equally, differences in voice are noticed even when the words are ignored" (1958, p. 23). That is, such characteristics as voice quality and location are detected in the box marked "selective filter" in Figure 40. while the words themselves are identified only in the box marked "limited capacity decision channel." This channel is never reached by voices with the wrong pitch or the wrong spatial location.

The trouble with the filter theory, as a number of critics have pointed out, is that under some conditions the meaningful content of the rejected message *does* make an impression. Moray (1959) was the first such critic. He found that, although instructions read to the unattended ear are generally ignored, they do come to the subject's attention if they are prefaced with *his own name*. Related findings have been made by Treisman (1960, 1964a, 1964b) under rather carefully controlled conditions. In one of her experiments, subjects were instructed to shadow a prose passage, in, say, the left ear while ignoring another message in the right. At a certain moment, the passages reaching the two ears were interchanged! Although no subject was so context-bound that he switched sides permanently, it was common for a few words from the wrong ear (which continued the passage previously shadowed) to intrude into the responses. An example will clarify this result. Line (1) is the input to the left ear, which the subject was to shadow; line (2) is the input to the right ear; the slash shows the point at which the messages were interchanged, and the capitalized words are the subject's responses (after Treisman, 1960, p. 246).

1. ". . . SITTING AT A MAHOGANY / three POSSIBILITIES . . ."
2. ". . . Let us look at these / TABLE with her head . . ."

In this example, the word "Table" was heard even though it came to the wrong ear, because the subject was expecting it. As might be expected, such errors were more common when the shadowed passages were continuous prose than when they were more discontinuous "approximations to English." Treisman's finding is related to Moray's because in both cases material presented to the wrong ear produced a response. If it be granted that one is always "set" for one's own name, in the same sense that context creates a "set" for particular words, then a single explanation can cover both experiments.

We have already examined another of Treisman's results, which is perhaps the most important. Subjects notice an identity of the two messages, even if one is slightly delayed with respect to the other. The detection of identity does not depend only on simple acoustic cues, because it occurs also if the rejected (and identical) message is read by a different speaker, and some bilingual subjects even notice identity between a shadowed message and a translation of it. These instances all suggest an inadequacy in the filter theory. If names, probable words, and identical meanings in the rejected message can force themselves on the subject's attention, he must be listening to it in some sense. For these reasons both Moray (1959) and Deutsch and Deutsch (1963) find it necessary to assume that *all* inputs are analyzed rather completely, with "filtering" or selection taking place only subsequent to the analysis. Such a solution is unsatisfactory, because it only moves us from one horn of the dilemma to another: why then does so *little* of the rejected message make an impression?

In 1960, Treisman suggested a theoretical way out of this difficulty which seemed plausible, and by 1964 Broadbent appeared to have come round to her point of view (Broadbent & Gregory, 1964, p. 316). Her suggestion was that the "filter" *attenuates* signals rather than eliminating them, and that the weakened signals can still be picked up by specially attuned cognitive systems.

## *THE FILTER-AMPLITUDE THEORY*

Treisman's theory is best explained in terms of three related experimental findings. All deal with the perception of one's own name. The first is Moray's (1959) result, already mentioned, that a subject who is shadowing prose at one ear will react to the presentation of his name at the other, even though he hears little else. This is congruent with common experience. One is sensitive to the use of one's own name, even in an irrelevant conversation.

A second experiment in this vein is that of Oswald, Taylor, and Treisman (1960). A recorded sequence of names was played to subjects while they were asleep, as determined by electroencephalographic criteria. Before going to sleep, the subjects had been instructed to close one fist whenever they heard their own name, and also for one other specified name. Both relevant names produced far more sleeping fist-clenchings than the irrelevant ones, and the subject's own name produced the most of all. Moreover, the two critical names often resulted in a characteristic EEG pattern (the so-called "K-complex"), even when no overt behavior could be seen. This finding is not unexpected; it is common knowledge that people can be aroused from sleep by certain specific sounds, such as a child's cry, even when the sounds are faint. Nevertheless, a well-controlled demonstration of the effect is worth having, especially since the results dovetail with a third experiment, by Howarth and Ellis (1961).

These authors used spoken names (in a noisy background) as the stimuli in a recognition experiment. It was found that subjects could recognize their own name 77 percent of the time at a signal-to-noise ratio where other names were heard only 50 percent of the time. Moreover, Howarth and Ellis were able to compare the advantage of one's own name in their situation with its advantage in the two other experiments just described, by converting all the data to z-scores. In these terms, the results of the three experiments were quantitatively equivalent. Following Treisman, Howarth and Ellis assumed that sleep simply attenuates or weakens the strength of external stimuli, and that one's own name can be heard at a fainter level than most other words. The argument is that inattention to one "ear" (i.e., to one perceived direction) in a shadowing experiment also simply weakens the signal arriving there. Unattended channels are not "switched off," as Broadbent had proposed, but attenuated.

With this theory, Treisman seems to have no difficulty in accounting for the experiments on selective attention. She need only assume that different words require different signal intensities for recognition. The threshold mechanism is described as follows:

> A possible system for identifying words is a hierarchy of tests carried out in sequence and giving a unique outcome for each word or other linguistic unit. The decision at each test point could be thought of as a signal detection problem . . . a certain adjustable cut-off or criterion point is adopted on the dimension being discriminated, above which signals are accepted and below which they are rejected as "noise." The criteria determining the results of the tests would be made more liberal for certain outcomes if favoured by contextual probabilities, by recent use, or by importance. Messages attenuated by the filter [i.e., presented to the unattended ear] would pass the tests only if the criteria had been lowered in their favour and, if not, would pass no further through the hierarchy. This would be more economical than Deutsch's full analysis, since most irrelevant words would fail tests early in the hierarchy (1964b, p. 14).

This view is related to that of Hebb. His "cell-assemblies" are sets of interrelated neurons that can act briefly as a unit and represent some well-established cognitive element by their action. In auditory attention, the cell-assemblies must represent words or other segments of speech perception. Attention operates by a sort of internal priming: "Each assembly action may be aroused by a preceding assembly, by a sensory event, or—normally—by both. The central facilitation from one of these activities on the next is the prototype of 'attention'" (Hebb, 1949, p. xix). Hebb's "facilitation" corresponds to Treisman's "liberalizing of criteria."

Certainly the filter-amplitude theory has an element of plausibility. It is true that we tend to hear loud messages rather than faint ones, and that even faint ones can be heard if we are prepared for their content. From those facts it seems an easy step to the proposal that the difference between attended and unattended messages is one of "attenuation," i.e., of loudness.[1] Nevertheless, it seems to me that this hypothesis cannot be correct. Surely, selective attention is not just a matter of selective attenuation. The irrelevant voices at the cocktail party do *not* seem faint. As hard as we may concentrate on our partner's conversation, the other voices are loudly present. We ignore their content, but they do not seem less loud on that account. The classical psychologists knew very well that "vividness" or subjective clearness was different from subjective intensity. Titchener warned his readers to *"Be careful not to confuse vividness with intensity:* when you are listening intently for a very faint sound, the sound, as it comes, is the most vivid experience you have, although it is near the lower limit of intensity . . ." (1915, p. 92, italics his).

So far, no one has asked subjects to judge the loudness of stimuli presented to the unattended ear in a shadowing experiment. According to the filter-attenuation theory, these judgments should not be hard to make and should reveal a large difference in favor of the shadowed message. I suspect, however, that they would prove to be very difficult, and that only small differences would appear. In this connection, the fact that one message can be selected in preference to another on the basis of intensity alone (Egan, Carterette, & Thwing, 1954) is also important. It is hard to see how this would be possible if the act of selection itself altered the relative loudnesses of the two messages.

### *ATTENTION AS AUDITORY SYNTHESIS*

If attention is not a way of making one message louder than the others, what is it? This question may profitably be considered in terms of the basic processes of speech perception. The previous chapter ended by iden-

[1] In personal communication, Treisman has argued that only the information content of the message is attenuated, not its loudness. This protects her hypothesis against the present critique, but also seems to give up much of its content.

tifying two hypothetical stages in the perception of speech. At one level, preliminary identification of words and other cognitive units is carried out by a passive filter system, which may indeed resemble Treisman's "hierarchy of tests." But this preliminary system does not do the entire job; it is normally supplemented by an active process of analysis-by-synthesis, in which the listener produces "inner speech" (at some level of abstraction) to match the input. I suggest that *this constructive process is itself the mechanism of auditory attention.*

On this hypothesis, to "follow" one conversation in preference to others is to synthesize a series of linguistic units which match it successfully. Irrelevant, unattended streams of speech are neither "filtered out" nor "attenuated"; they fail to enjoy the benefits of analysis-by-synthesis. As a result, they are analyzed only by the passive mechanisms, which might be called "preattentive processes" by analogy with the corresponding stage of vision (see Chapter 4). Like their visual counterparts, these processes can establish localization, form crude segments, and guide responses to certain simple situations. However, their capacity for detail is strictly limited.

The constructive theory of attention has much to recommend it besides its congruence with the account of visual perception put forward earlier. It has little difficulty in accounting for most of the phenomena of selective listening. (1) Since analysis-by-synthesis is normally controlled by contextual cues, extracted preattentively, we can understand why context sometimes overrode localization in Treisman's (1964a) switching experiment. (2) Because unattended speech is not systematically segmented, it is stored only in echoic memory. It remains available only for the one or two seconds during which the echo is still useful; features which are identical with those in the shadowed input must appear within this time if the identity is to be noticed. This is precisely Treisman's finding, for the case where the shadowed message lags behind the unattended one. (3) Longer delays can be tolerated if the shadowed message leads, since it *is* segmented, and the results are being stored in ordinary verbal memory. (4) There is no reason to doubt that the preattentive mechanisms can pick out simple units, such as the subject's own name in Moray's (1959) experiment. These are not synthesized, but detected like simple features. Similar "sets" could probably be established for other simple words as well. On the analogy of my own search experiments (Chapter 3), I would not expect the *number* of such "target" words to matter, in practiced subjects. The preattentive filters surely operate on echoic memory in parallel.

The results of Oswald *et al.* (1960), on the perception of names during sleep, require slightly more consideration. It is easy to suppose that the preattentive mechanisms, being essentially passive, are on 24 hour duty. But it is not safe to assume that auditory attention, the synthetic process, is completely inactive throughout the night. In Chapter 6, the imagery of dreams was ascribed to visual synthesis. In effect, this means that one pays attention in one's dreams. If dreaming sleep permits visual construction, why not auditory synthesis as well? During non-dreaming sleep (stages 2, 3, and 4 on the EEG), one can presumably detect only simple segments, like one's name or a child's cry, which activate the preattentive mechanisms. As always, the activity of these mechanisms can only lead to simple forms of behavior—gross body movement, fist-clenching, and especially waking up. If the process of awakening takes longer than the duration of echoic memory, the sleeper may not even know what awakened him. During stage 1 ("REM-sleep"), on the other hand, analysis-by-synthesis can apparently occur, and a sleeper may be able to hear and understand even whole sentences. However, what is heard may not rouse him to action; instead, it is likely to be incorporated into his dream.

The foregoing paragraph is speculative, but its general theme is supported by several recent experiments. Response thresholds have often been reported as *higher* in "REM-sleep" than in nondreaming sleep, which at first seems paradoxical since that state is the nearest to wakefulness. The resolution of the paradox (as others have already suggested) may be that dream incorporation *prevents* reaction to the stimulus. Similarly, while hearing one's name from a remote conversation at a party generally causes an alerting reaction, hearing it spoken by one's own conversational partner may produce no specific response at all, the name being directly incorporated into the ongoing synthesis.

The evidence for dream incorporation has already been reviewed in Chapter 6. Even the possibility that whole sentences might be understandable in dreaming sleep is not without some hint of confirmation. In work at the Unit for Experimental Psychiatry in Philadelphia, repeated success has been achieved with complex suggestions ("When I say the word 'itch,' your nose will itch and you will want to scratch it"), given verbally during uninterrupted "REM-sleep." In later recurrences of this stage of sleep, cue-words such as "itch" led to appropriate nose-scratching. This finding is compatible with the notion that complex auditory analysis-by-synthesis can occur during dreaming. However, the results should still be regarded as tentative; see Cobb, Evans, Gustafson, O'Connell, Orne, and Shor (1965), and Evans, Gustafson, O'Connell, Orne, and Shor (1966).

The hypothesis that auditory attention is the process of synthesis also explains how attention can be withdrawn from *every* external channel and focused on the subject's own train of thought. This common experience seems to pose grave difficulties for Broadbent's filter theory, and insuperable ones for the filter-amplitude theory of Treisman; inner speech is surely not louder than an external stimulus! The present theory suggests that inner speech is necessarily attention-compelling, since it is produced by the mechanisms of synthesis. Because the constructed sequence is entirely under the guidance of stored memories in such a case, it does not match the current input. As a result, the latter remains "unheard," like the irrelevant message in a shadowing experiment. People wrapped up in their own thoughts in this fashion are much like dreamers and can also be roused by calling their names. Of course, inner speech is not thought itself, as can be shown in many ways: consider how often one struggles to put a thought into words! But when thinking is not verbal, it cannot control auditory attention. Thus, it is peculiarly vulnerable to distraction. Indeed, the trouble with auditory distractions is not so much that they are irresistible, as that in order to resist them we must channel our thoughts along familiar verbal lines.

Do the results of the preattentive analyses have any long-run effect, in cases when attentive synthesis does not take over? Are they remembered? In considering a similar question about the preattentive processes in vision (Chapter 4), we came to a tentatively negative conclusion. The answer for hearing seems to be in the same vein. For example, Moray (1959) was unable to find any trace of retention for the material presented to the unattended ear. To be sure, one such result is hardly conclusive. In particular, it remains possible that unattended material is somehow incorporated into "primary-process" thinking, even though its effects do not appear on direct examination. This is essentially the assumption defended by Pine (1960). Pine used the method of the "Thematic Apperception Test" (TAT) to encourage the production of expressive fantasy. His subjects first made up two stories, then read a brief, specifically constructed essay aloud several times, and finally made up two additional stories. While they were reading aloud, a different essay was being read by an assistant in the next room. Although it was clearly audible, the circumstances were arranged so that the subject did not suspect it of having anything to do with his own experiment. One of the two essays, about cows, was deliberately filled with oral-passive imagery ("The cow is warm; it is soft . . ."), while the other dealt in a phallic-aggressive way with a steel hook ("The hook's unbending arc is a bulwark of the power required for the immense tasks it must perform. . ."). Pine predicted that the TAT stories told after this experience would be affected in different ways by the two essays. Elements of the one which the subject read himself, and thus paid attention to, should be directly incorporated in the stories, while the unattended one should be represented by relatively indirect, transformed incorporations. His prediction was confirmed: the stories told by subjects who had only incidentally heard the "cow essay" contained more oral-passive imagery (an indirect effect) than those of subjects who read the same story aloud, and similarly for the phallic themes of the "hook essay."

It could be argued that the preattentive processes are not really implicated in this experiment. The subjects may have briefly paid attention to the second essay from time to time, in the active mode of analysis-by-synthesis, even without thinking it was important. Such an argument would be irrelevant for Pine, who does not define attention in the way proposed here. However, there are other reasons for being unconvinced by the results. As in many similar experiments discussed in Chapters 2 and 5, it is possible that the experimenter unconsciously provided cues which encouraged the subject to continue an appropriate series of responses to the TAT card. Moreover, the trends in the stories may well have represented *negative* reactions to the focal essay instead of positive incorporation of the incidental one. A desire to avoid a theme which has been overdrawn could easily lead to imagery of an opposite kind. Lacking a control group with no irrelevant essay at all, we cannot tell.

In concluding this chapter, we must consider a few findings which tend to complicate the picture presented so far. In the first place, I may have dismissed the filter theory, and its revision by Treisman, somewhat too cavalierly. There *is* some evidence for a genuine shutting-off of sensory input under certain circumstances. Thresholds even for unattended stimuli are higher asleep than awake, after all. Moreover, some introspective reports suggest that one can be *so* deep in thought that sounds do seem attenuated, whether or not this happens in ordinary selective attention. Possibly related to this observation is a famous physiological experiment on the cochlear nucleus of the cat, by Hernández-Peón, Scherrer, and Jouvet (1956). They showed that the amount of electrical activity produced by a sound was sharply reduced when the cat became interested in a visual or an olfactory stimulus. This has often been interpreted as a "closing down" of the auditory channel, due to a shift in attention. Psychologists should not jump to conclusions on such a point; the "filter" interpretation of this experiment has been vigorously disputed by other neurophysiologists (e.g., Hugelin, Dumont, & Paillas, 1960). Nevertheless, we should not exclude the possibility that a modality *as a whole* can be partially closed off, especially in view of the results of Eriksen and Johnson (1964). As noted earlier, their subjects missed 50 percent of even those "beeps" which came simultaneously with the query. The filter theory may be appropriate, then, for cases where an entire sense-modality is to be ignored, even if analysis-by-synthesis is preferable as an account of selective listening itself.

An unexpected finding reported by Treisman (1964c) poses another problem for the view being advanced here. Noting that the presence of a message at the unattended ear makes shadowing more difficult, she contrived a situation with *three* spatially distinct messages. One appeared at the left ear, one at the right, and one at both—the last being subjectively localized in the center of the head. The subject was always to shadow the speech at the right ear, and ignore the others. Shadowing efficiency was much lower in this condition than when only a single irrelevant message was presented. Moreover, the same pair of irrelevant messages caused much less difficulty when they were superimposed on a *single* "channel" (either the left or the center) than when they were kept spatially distinct. While the filter theory can probably accommodate this result rather comfortably, I would not have predicted it from considerations of analysis-by-synthesis. If unattended messages are simply remaining unsynthesized, it is not obvious why a spatial separation between them should make a difference of any kind.

Certain other observations introduce a different kind of complication. In discussing the analysis-by-synthesis approach to speech perception, we distinguished between the "motor theory," which emphasizes real (though covert) articulatory movements, and a more abstract view in which the synthesis is only of linguistic forms. The same distinction must be made here. Although the shadowing experiments, and other work cited so far, are compatible with a strictly motor theory of attention, some phenomena cannot be reconciled with such a view. People can pay attention to sounds which they cannot literally imitate. One may listen selectively to a particular instrument in an orchestra, to an unusual rattle in an engine, or to the relentless drip of water from a leaky faucet. Indeed, the drip of the faucet may force itself on one's attention willy-nilly. What is being synthesized in such instances?

In some cases, even when the mechanism of attention cannot be a linguistic analysis-by-synthesis, it may nevertheless be a motor pattern of another kind. In particular, *rhythm* suggests itself as a plausible medium. The "motor theory of rhythm perception," mentioned earlier, suggests a possible interpretation of such cases. The listener can be thought of as actively "following" the rhythm of the attended sound. But this extension is not fully adequate, because we can attend to nonrhythmic aspects of the input as well. Melodies can be followed as well as rhythms. A melody surely has a structure, but it seems to be one without a motor analogue. It seems, then, that auditory synthesis can develop "structures" of an abstract sort, without any motor involvement at all. This should not surprise us, in view of what we already know about figural synthesis in vision. While the construction of visual objects and images tends to be accompanied by suitable eye movements, it is by no means only a motor activity.

For a conclusive—and extremely interesting—demonstration that neither a "motor theory of attention" nor a "motor theory of speech perception" is tenable, we need only consider the remarkable activity known as *simultaneous translation.* Such translations have become widely known through their use a' the United Nations, where diplomatic words may be converted from (say) Russian into English even as they are uttered, with the translator rarely far behind. In a sense, simultaneous translation is a form of "shadowing." However, it is not words, or articulatory movements, that are shadowed. The translator, who is obviously attending to and understanding the incoming stream of speech, cannot possibly be imitating the speaker's vocalizations. His own vocal tract is continuously occupied with an entirely different output. It follows that motor imitation *cannot* be a necessary condition for attention or understanding, at least in adults. Auditory synthesis can proceed at completely abstract levels. (For a direct experimental comparison between shadowing and simultaneous translation, see Treisman, 1965.)

The analysis-by-synthesis approach has still other implications. In particular, it leads rather directly to certain hypotheses about memory. We have already seen that there must be a brief, transient "echoic" memory for brief storage of the input. Once analysis-by-synthesis has taken place, however, an organized series of segments exists which must also be preserved. Their storage seems to require another, nonechoic form of memory. Like the verbal encodings of visual objects described in Chapter 2, attended speech has entered the system of "verbal traces," "chunks," "auditory information storage," and "rehearsal" which plays such a crucial role in cognitive theory. This system is treated in the next chapter.

*Chapter 9*

# *Active Verbal Memory*

This chapter deals with what is usually called "immediate memory," interpreted as a manifestation of auditory synthesis extended over time. The effects of rate and serial position in the memory span are considered, together with recent work showing that what is stored is auditory and linguistic in nature. There are two major theories of the organization of immediate memory, one of which postulates a certain number of preexisting "slots" that can each hold a chunk of information, while the other assumes that all connections are associative. Neither seems fully satisfactory; and the possibility that the memory span is basically a rhythmic structure is put forward here as an alternative. In a similar vein, the two principal accounts of the fate of the stored information—simple decay and active interference—are considered, and an alternative is advanced which, in a sense, combines them.

It is not difficult to repeat back a short string of digits that one has just heard. Of course, short-term memory is not restricted to digits; any series of unrelated words may be stored in the same way. The number of items that can be repeated successfully is known as the "span of immediate memory." It is about seven in a normal adult, though there is a good deal of individual variation. Wechsler notes, "Except in cases of special defects or organic disease, adults who cannot retain 5 digits forwards and 3 backwards will be found, in nine cases out of ten, to be feeble-minded" (quoted in Horrocks, 1964, p. 195). Verbal memory plays a crucial role in many cognitive processes. To understand a sentence, for example, one must remember a good deal about the beginning when one has reached the end. Echoic memory alone would not be enough for this purpose, since many sentences are much too long to be stored echoically. Another medium, which may conveniently be called *active verbal memory,* must be involved. This medium is also used for the storage of information recoded from the visual input. As noted in Chapter 2, such recoding plays an important part in preserving tachistoscopically exposed material. Even under normal visual conditions, one often uses verbal descriptions to recall what one has seen.

In addition, it seems likely—although it has never been proven—that all verbal material to be long remembered must first pass through such a stage. If so, its ultimate fate may depend largely on what happens to it in the first few seconds. In retrospect, it is surprising that long-term learning and memory have so rarely been studied as continuations of this initial process. Perhaps one reason for the neglect of this approach is that the memory span itself has remained something of an enigma until very recently. However, while some problems remain unresolved, genuine progress toward understanding active verbal memory has been made in the last few years.

### *RECODING*

The memory span is about the same size whether the subject is tested with strings of digits, letters, or monosyllabic words. Indeed, there is little reason to expect that it would be different, since "two, nine, one . . ." and "ex, jay, cee . . ." (*XJC*) are themselves strings of words, not very different from "bat, log, tin . . ." The near equivalence of these spans is disturbing only if, like some theorists, one expects "information" measures to be meaningfully related to human performance. In terms of information, a single digit (as one of ten alternative possibilities) conveys fewer "bits" than a letter (taken from 26 alternatives), or a word (one of many thousand possibilities). From this viewpoint—but from no other—some *ad hoc* hypothesis is needed to account for the near-invariance of the memory span. Since it is easier to assume that information measurement is irrelevant in the first place (see Chapter 1), such hypotheses will not be considered here. An explanation for the slight differences between various materials that do appear (Crannell & Parrish, 1957) will be considered later.

If the memory span has a roughly fixed capacity, and if this capacity is not measurable in the "bits" of information theory, in what terms shall it be described? What is it that the normal adult can remember seven of? From what has been said so far, it might be thought that the limit on capacity is seven *words,* but this is not true in general. Many more than seven words can be recalled easily after one presentation if they form a sentence. (The reader may use the preceding sentence as a test, if he likes—or this one.) This effect is not limited to sentences; we shall see in a moment that even random strings much longer than seven can be remembered if they are properly coded. For this reason, Miller (1956a) introduced the concept of the "chunk," which is a cognitive unit created by the subject himself. Immediate memory is said to hold from 5 to 9 chunks of this sort. In Miller's apt phrase, the "magic number" is $7 \pm 2$.

Often the "chunks" which the subject stores and recalls are not those which were presented, perceived, or originally stored. For this reason, we must assume that there is a verbal memory which is not simply echoic. The most elegant demonstration of this kind of recoding—and at the same time the clearest indication of the need for some such concept as the "chunk"—is S. L. Smith's experiment, reported in Miller's (1956a) paper. Smith tested his own memory span for "binary digits," i.e., strings of zeros and ones such as *011001011101001*. Having established his span (about 12), he deliberately memorized various methods of reading binary digits into other number systems. When he had learned "octal" numbering (*001 = 1,* etc.; see Chapter 2), his memory span for binary digits rose to nearly 36! In effect, he was translating every triad of zeros and ones into a single octal digit and then storing 12 of those. Similar results have been obtained by Pollack and Johnson (1965).

Smith's rather drastic method of recoding may not be typical of the processes used in most memory-span experiments. Nevertheless, there is reason to believe that material is generally reformulated as it is stored. This does not mean that echoic memory plays no role in a typical memory-span experiment (indeed, it surely does) but it cannot be the only medium involved. Even items as intractable as ordinary digits are subject to a reformulation called *grouping,* in which the subject introduces rhythmic clusters and gaps into an evenly spoken list. It is important to note that a grouped memory is not echoic: tape-recorders do not form groups. In my opinion, segmenting, grouping, recoding, and all inner repetition are essentially forms of auditory synthesis. The mechanisms involved may well be the same as those which underlie speech perception and attention (Chapter 7, 8). One might say that these mechanisms take information "out of" echoic storage and put it "into" the system here called active verbal memory. Another way of describing their function, perhaps more realistic, is that they "convert" information from echoic to linguistic form: they prolong its life at the cost of changing its nature.

The recoding which partially protects information against the passage of time must also take a certain amount of time to carry out. The effect of this requirement ought to appear in studies which vary the *rate* at which items are presented for immediate memory. If the time needed for recoding is substantial, rapid presentation might be expected to impair recall. However, this result should appear only to the extent that the span depends on *en*coded information. Since echoic memory seems to fade with time, high speed should improve whatever recall depends on *un*coded information. Given two mechanisms running in such opposite directions, we must not be surprised to find contradictory results in studies of memory span as a function of rate.

Perhaps the most common finding has been that rapid presentation impairs performance. A number of experiments with this outcome have been reviewed by Posner (1963). It appears impressively in a study by Yntema, Wozencraft, and Klem (1964), who had a computer that could "speak" at the incredible rate of ten digits per second. At this speed a string of digits sounds like a piece of cloth ripping, but each one is clearly intelligible. However, they are remarkably hard to remember. When seven digits are presented at ten per second, only three or four can be correctly recalled; at two per second, the number is nearly six. Yntema *et al.* drew a simple conclusion: ". . . during the presentation of a slow list the subject performs some sort of process that makes it easier for him to recall the list a moment later; but there is not enough time for him to perform this process when the list is presented rapidly" (1964, pp. 3–4).

The sharp drop in recall at high speeds is not nearly so pronounced when the items have been *grouped* for presentation to the subject, either by a slight pause interpolated after the third of six digits, or by playing the first three to one ear and the last three to the other. That is, subjects are not much hampered by a lack of time so long as grouping has been made easy for them. This confirms the hypothesis that the advantage of slow presentation lies in the active reorganization which it permits.

On the other hand, slow presentation is not always better than fast. Results to the contrary have been obtained under various conditions by Conrad and Hille (1958), Posner (1964b), and Mackworth (1965). While not all the data can be fitted into a single formula, they suggest that increased speed improves recall primarily when the digit-strings are short and have much internal structure (pauses, rhythms, etc.), or when the order of report is fixed. These are just the conditions which minimize the subject's opportunities for recoding. He has to place relatively greater reliance on echoic memory as a medium of storage, and relatively less on active verbal reformulation.

The notion that two different processes are involved in the memory span is also supported by the positions at which errors tend to appear. If only echoic memory were operative, the most recent digits should be best recalled, having had the least time to decay. In fact, however, the serial position curve is U-shaped. That is, the beginning and the end of a string of digits are both better remembered than the middle; there are both "primacy" and "recency" effects. (This finding holds only when the order of recall follows the order of presentation; otherwise, different serial position curves may appear, as in Kay & Poulton, 1951; Posner, 1964b.)

The active process in verbal memory is often called "rehearsal." Waugh attributed the primacy effects in her (1960) experiments to this source; when Waugh and Norman (1965) failed to find a rate effect, lack of rehearsal was cited as the probable cause. However, "rehearsal" itself is not as well-defined as it might seem to be. A subject can repeat a list to himself in many different ways, with different groupings, and at different speeds. Sanders (1961), who found that "rehearsal has a strengthening and stabilizing effect on retention" (it makes a series more resistant to interference, for example), goes on to say that

> . . . It seems doubtful, however, whether this improvement results from rehearsal in the sense of a mere automatic repetition . . . the main activity of the organism during the rehearsal period seems to be the assimilation of the material by means of interpretation, imposition of rhythms, finding of rules, etc. . . . Only during the period immediately after memorizing a digit combination does rehearsal approach automatic repetition . . . subjects tended to slow down their rehearsal rates after they had rehearsed for some time (p. 33).

This suggests that "rehearsal" is not very different from "recoding" or "grouping." Wickelgren (1964) asserts the same equivalence: "Whatever else a grouping method is, it is a method of rehearsal" (p. 414). He shows that rehearsing in groups of three is more effective than other groupings.

In short, it is characteristic of active verbal memory that information is recoded rather than simply echoed. It would be easy to conclude that the medium of storage was therefore nonauditory in character; that sound itself was lost in process of abstraction. Such a conclusion would be unwarranted, as the next section will show.

## *AUDITORY CHARACTERISTICS OF VERBAL MEMORY*

A number of experiments have shown that the information stored in short-term memory is still very much *auditory* information. This is particularly clear in Conrad's (1959, 1962, 1964) studies of errors made in immediate recall. Although the most common kind of mistake is a change in the order of the elements, substitutions of one for another also frequently occur. The important point for theory is that substitution errors tend to involve units that sound alike, even when the original stimuli are visual. Conrad (1964) found that the substitution errors made in *recalling* visually presented letters were just like those made in *identifying* letters spoken in a noisy background. This suggests that the visual letters are recoded into auditory representations, which may subsequently be confused with one another. Conrad's own interpretation goes further: following Brown (1959), he believes that the auditory representations undergo gradual decay over time. This remains unproven; his experiment does not show that the changes are gradual or progressive.

Earlier, we noted that the memory span was about the same size for letters and words as for digits. However, slight differences do appear, generally in the direction of shorter spans for items chosen from larger vocabularies. The work of Conrad and Hull (1964) suggests that these differences are due to the greater possibility of acoustic confusions in a larger vocabulary. Because there are more letters which sound somewhat alike than there are confusable digits, for example, letters are a little harder to remember. In a partial test of this hypothesis, Conrad and Hull studied the recall of seven-letter strings that had been drawn from four different vocabularies. Two of the vocabularies were made up of letters which a previous experiment had shown to be highly confusable in ordinary listening: *F, S, X* in one case, and *B, C, D, G, M, N, P, T, V* in the other. The two remaining vocabularies—*J, K, N* and *C, D, F, H, L, N, Q, Y, Z*—were composed of letters less easily confused with one another. The difficulty of recalling a string of letters turned out to depend more on the confusability than on the size of the vocabulary from which they were drawn. That is, strings like *SFSXXFS* were harder than ones like *DFQLYDN*.

Many experimenters have observed auditory confusions in immediate memory. The appearance of these errors in reports of tachistoscopically presented stimuli led Sperling (1960a, 1963) to postulate an "auditory information storage," similar in some respects to the active verbal memory under discussion here. Wickelgren (1965c) has shown explicitly that letters tend to be confused if their names have a phoneme in common, as *F, L, M, N, S,* and *X* share an initial /e/. Such findings leave no doubt that the information is preserved in a medium which is as auditory as language itself. It seems likely that the mechanism involved is the same one used in the analysis-by-synthesis of ordinary speech. Synthesis that occurs while the input continues is called "perception," while what occurs later is called "rehearsal." In this light, Hintzman's (1965) contention that the confusions are more "articulatory" than "auditory" boils down to an argument for the motor theory of speech perception, reviewed in Chapter 7.

The auditory—or at least linguistic—character of immediate memory has been impressively documented in a series of studies by Wickelgren. In a demonstration of "retroactive inhibition," for example (Wickelgren, 1965a), the subjects heard four letters they were to remember, then eight more they had to copy, and finally were asked to recall the first four. Their ability to do so was markedly impaired if the interpolated letters were similar in sound to the original ones. In a "proactive inhibition" study (1966a), he found that phonemically similar (but irrelevant) letters also disturb recall if they are presented *before* the to-be-memorized list. "Intralist inhibition" appeared in the study already cited (1965c), which found a high error rate in lists composed of letters that sound somewhat alike. Auditory similarity even affects short-term memory when a method of "recognition" is used, so that the subject need only say whether a particular test letter was or was not present in a preceding series (Wickelgren, 1965e, 1966c).

This work represents an explicit link between speech perception and immediate memory. The confusions among similar sounding letters cannot be ascribed to errors made in hearing them originally, since Wickelgren's subjects always begin by copying the stimulus as it is presented. (Only correctly copied letters are considered in the analysis of data.) Nevertheless, the items which interfere with one another consistently tend to have phonemes in common. For that matter, they have distinctive features in common also, and in two very sophisticated papers (1965b, 1966b) Wickelgren pushes the analysis to this level. He uses confusions in recall to validate particular hypotheses about the distinctive features of speech, exactly as Miller and Nicely (1955) had used confusions in listening. Essentially the same distinctive features are identified by both procedures.

Wickelgren assumes that immediate memory is mediated by "internal representations" of phonemes. Associations between phonemes are supposedly formed when a string of letters is heard and are subsequently responsible for recall. However, we noted in Chapter 7 that while such data can demonstrate the reality of distinctive features, they do not perform the same service for phonemes. There still seems little reason to interpose a hypothetical phonemic level between the spoken letters themselves and the distinctive features which identify them. If the units of verbal memory were phonemes, as Wickelgren suggests, its capacity ought to be measurable in terms of the number of phonemes stored. This does not seem to be the case: Miller's "magical number $7 \pm 2$" is not measured in phonemes but by words or larger units.

It may be appropriate to review the argument that has been presented so far. On the one hand, active verbal memory cannot be simply echoic, since what is remembered has typically been grouped and recoded until it is quite different from what was presented. On the other hand, the material is evidently stored in a form similar to that in which words are perceived, since the same confusions occur in both cases. This seeming paradox is resolved if both speech perception and verbal memory involve the same active process of synthesis, or auditory attention. This is the reason why active verbal memory can contain only attended messages—the shadowed but not the unshadowed material in Treisman's (1964a) experiments, for example. As William James put it, ". . . we cannot deny that an object once attended to will remain in the memory, whilst one inattentively allowed to pass will leave no traces behind" (1890, Vol. I, p. 427).

The distinction between echoic and active memory is central to this argument, and in many respects it seems clear enough. One is passive, the other active; one is continuous, the other segmented; one is composed of sounds, the other of speech; one seems to decay rapidly, the other can be renewed indefinitely through rehearsal. Nevertheless, both seem to be basically auditory. It is at least possible that, in some sense, they share a common medium. If so, rehearsal could be thought of as a way of recirculating transformed information back to the "place" from which it came. This hypothesis has been advanced by Broadbent (1958). It is an attractive notion, but one which faces serious difficulties. For example, it suggests that echoic memory is overwritten and destroyed by the act of segmentation, which we have reason to doubt. In the absence of clear-cut evidence on this point, echoic and active verbal memory will be distinguished here only when necessary, and otherwise will be referred to indiscriminately as "auditory memory."

Having established that short-term memory is essentially auditory, we can turn to three more specific questions. First, how is the memory organized? The two major competing theories about its organization will be considered in the next section, where they are called the "slot theory" and the "association theory" respectively. Since neither seems to be entirely adequate, a third view, based primarily on the organizing properties of rhythm, will also be presented. Second, what happens to items in auditory memory? Do they simply wither away if they are not rehearsed, or do they endure until new material obscures them? Finally, what is the relation between this short-term auditory memory on the one hand, and more permanent storage of auditory information on the other?

## *SLOTS OR ASSOCIATIONS?*

One way of thinking about auditory memory is to suppose that the subject has some number of slots, bins, boxes, or "neuron pools" into which he can put successive chunks of input. The span is limited to seven items because there are only that many slots. The slots exist before the stimuli appear (otherwise we would have a different, organizational theory like the one to be discussed later), and by definition each holds exactly one chunk. When we hear *6497825* we put *6* into slot #1, *4* into slot #2, etc. Forgetting then results from the gradual fading of each slot's contents and can be prevented by active rehearsal. With this model, Miller (1956a, 1956b) was easily able to explain S. L. Smith's results: having learned the octal code, Smith could simply put an encoded digit into each slot instead of a binary digit. In general, intellectual efficiency increases as ". . . we develop representational techniques such that the magic number 7 ± 2 is filled with purer and purer gold" (Bruner, 1966, p. 20).

One striking observation which fits well into a slot theory is that subjects usually know the serial position of the items they can still remember, even when they have forgotten intervening material. To account for this, we need only assume that they know from which slot each retrieved digit has come. The same assumption explains the curious "serial order intrusions" of Conrad (1960a). When subjects are repeatedly tested with eight-digit series, they sometimes err in the following way: instead of reporting the sixth digit (say) of the series just presented, they report the sixth digit of the *immediately preceding series.* To explain these intrusions, we can suppose that vestigial remains of digits from previously tested arrays still linger in their slots, whence they are sometimes mistakenly retrieved.

According to Conrad (1959), transpositions of order—recalling "VNSBPX" when the actual series was *VNSPBX*—are the most common errors in immediate memory. This poses a problem for slot theory: can stored items really change places? Very recently, Conrad (1965) has put forward an explanation of the transpositions which at least partially accounts for them within the framework of a slot theory. He begins by showing that, in immediate memory for letters, transpositions do not occur at random. Instead, it is primarily letters which *sound alike* that are transposed. This suggests that a transposition might just be a double substitution that happens to look like an inversion of order. Conrad gives an ingenious reason why substitutions might tend to occur in pairs. He points out that stimulus-lists prepared by psychologists usually contain no doubled letters. Subjects know this, and tend to avoid doubled letters in their own responses. Hence, a subject who has made a simple substitution error of B for P (as in the example above) will not go on to say another B ("VNSBBX") but will probably make a second substitution instead; this time a P will replace a B. The results of these two successive substitutions is an apparent inversion.

Depite this and other arguments in favor of a slot theory, its adherents have always been in the minority. Some of the opposition to it is based on other theoretical commitments. Those who hold an interference theory of forgetting tend to oppose the slot notion because interference between slots is hard to imagine. Those seeking a unified account of short-term and long-term memory reject it because the latter has no definite "span." Psycholinguists, interested in natural languages, also have little use for slots: subjects can remember sentences far longer than seven words. (To be sure, one may assume—with Miller, 1956b, and Tulving and Patkau, 1962—that a sentence is made up of successive multiple-word phrases or "chunks," each of which uses up just one slot. As we shall see, however, linguistic structure is too complex to be successfully treated this way.) For my part, the slot concept seems much too passive to do justice to the synthetic nature of verbal memory and attention.

What is the alternative to a slot theory? How else can each stored digit be kept in its place? One possibility, which appeals greatly to many experimental psychologists, is that this and all other memory may simply depend on "associations." The successive items we hear—or the chunks we create—may just be bonded together so that each tends to elicit the next one in recall. On this view, when we hear *6497825,* we acquire new or strengthened associations between *6* and *4, 4* and *9,* etc. When we recall the series, our responses are determined by these bonds.

What entities are actually associated in such a theory? In principle, there seem to be two possibilities: (*a*) the *response* of saying "4" may be associated with the *stimulus* of hearing "6"—where both the responding and the hearing may go on subvocally—or, (*b*) as Wickelgren (1965a; 1965f) puts it, an *internal representation* of *4,* such as the firing of a specific group of neurons, may be associated with an internal representation of *6.* These views are analogous to the S–R and S–S models once so hotly debated in learning theory. There is little difference between them here, since the stimuli and responses of the first alternative are inaudible anyway. (*Overt* stimuli and responses cannot be what are generally associated, in view of evidence for recoding.) Furthermore, the analysis-by-synthesis theory suggests that "hearing" a word involves saying it, in some sense, so the distinction between stimuli and responses cannot be meaningfully upheld at all.

A principal advantage of the association theory is the continuity between short- and long-term memory which it suggests. Associations can function over long periods as well as short ones, and there is no specific limit to their number. But precisely this advantage creates a difficulty: why then is the memory span so specific and fixed? Why does the whole string of seven digits seem to be stored, and eventually to disappear, almost as a unit?

The response of an association theorist to this question is to deny its premise. The memory span may *not* have any special status. With respect to forgetting, for example, it is simply not true that material amounting to less than the span must be learned and forgotten as a unit. This has been established with a widely used technique due to Peterson and Peterson (1959). A subject is given a subspan series of, say, three chunks. It does not much matter whether presentation is auditory (Peterson & Peterson, 1959) or visual (Hellyer, 1962), nor whether the three chunks are consonants or disconnected monosyllables (Murdock, 1961). Immediately after the series, the subject carries out a paced and complex activity: typically, he is asked to count backwards by threes from a presented number. After a period of time, this activity is terminated, and he tries to recall the original series. Under these conditions a decrement in performance appears after only a few seconds and becomes steadily more pronounced with longer delays of recall. The main result is illustrated in Figure 41.

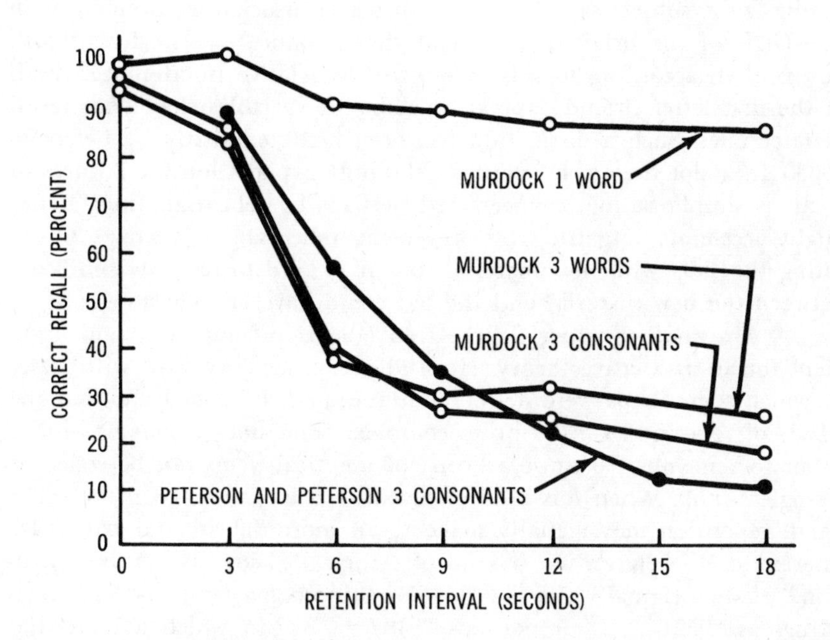


Figure 41. Loss of items from immediate memory as a function of the amount of interpolated counting activity before recall (from Peterson, 1963). The data are from Murdock (1961) and Peterson and Peterson (1959).

Many experiments have been carried out using this paradigm (for summaries, see Peterson, 1963; Postman, 1964). The amount of retention has been shown to depend on the number of chunks in the original list (Murdock, 1961), the number of trials given before the retention interval begins (Hellyer, 1962), acoustic similarity between the interfering activity and the critical series (Wickelgren, 1965a), etc. The implications of these results for a theory of forgetting will be considered in a later section. Here they are cited only to show that the discontinuity between material "within" and "exceeding" the memory span disappears with certain methods of measurement. Perhaps, then, the "span" is just the number of associations still strong enough to produce accurate responses, under the conditions usually used.

Wickelgren (1965a) argues for an association theory over a slot theory on the basis of the interfering effects of auditory similarity. Subjects have more trouble recalling *DGCV* after interpolated copying of *PTBPZBTZ* than after copying *FSMSNFNM*. In terms of association theory, their difficulty stems from generalization. The /iy/ sound, common to *D, G, C,* and *V,* becomes associated with incorrect letters during the copying of *PTBPZBTZ*. When this sound occurs again in the act of recall, as the subject says "D–," the incorrect associations compete with the–*GCV* of the original series and thus produce errors. (It is worth noting that, according to this account of associative interference, recall of the first letter should depend on different variables than does recall of later ones. Such a distinction has been made explicitly by Peterson, 1963.) In a slot theory, by contrast, the only explanation for failures of recall is simple fading, counteracted perhaps by rehearsal. Interference might accelerate forgetting by preventing rehearsal, or perhaps by refilling the slots with new material, but it is hard to see how similarity between the new material and the old could have any effect.

In another paper, Wickelgren (1965f) presents a second argument for an associative theory. He studied the memory span with series in which some items were deliberately repeated. It turned out that the effects of repetition can be quite complex. Sometimes it makes a series easier to remember, because a "run" of identical items can be coded as a single chunk. When this kind of recoding is impractical, on the other hand, repetition may actually make recall more difficult. Of particular interest to Wickelgren was a kind of error called an "associative intrusion." If the original series is *92953874,* subjects may respond with such strings as "9591 . . ." or perhaps "9192 . . . ," in which a digit that should have followed one of the *9*'s appears behind the other instead. Wickelgren found that associative intrusions occurred more frequently than would be expected by chance. Moreover, they did not seem to be produced by complex processes of rehearsal and recoding, for they were even more common at a high rate of presentation (five digits per second) than at one digit per second. Such intrusions are to be expected on an associative theory, since the two different digits associated with *9* would necessarily interfere with one another. In terms of a slot theory, they are inexplicable.

These specific and ingenious experiments seem to favor an associative theory of auditory memory, but it must not be thought that such a theory encounters no difficulties. One problem arises directly out of Wickelgren's repetition experiment. Instead of asking "why do associative intrusions occur?" we may ask "how are they ever avoided?" The stimulus recurs; why doesn't the response? An appeal to "remote associations" does not provide a satisfactory reply, because the same problem is raised in a different form by other observations. Subjects usually know when they have left out a digit, and they generally know to what part of a series a fragmentary recollection belongs. It is simply impossible to suppose that each digit in the response is determined by the preceding items alone. This is generally admitted by association theorists, who often explain such phenomena by assuming that serial position itself is a kind of stimulus:

> The fact that memory for the items following the separated occurrences of repeated items is not disastrously impaired [i.e., that associative intrusions are generally avoided] is evidence for the existence of some kind of serial order cues (such as: beginning, next to beginning, middle, next to end, end) in addition to prior-item cues for the ordered recall of ordered lists (Wickelgren, 1965f, p. 24).

The notion that serial position is a "stimulus" has been used in other contexts, as by Ebenholtz (1963). It is much in need of clarification. Although "end" and "beginning" are simple concepts when the series is thought of as a unified structure, they cannot be treated as if they were external stimuli. To see the problem, try to imagine how an associatively organized system could know just when it was coming to the end of a list. To be sure, *after* the stimulus series there will be a period of silence, or a special tone from the tape recorder, or a remark by the experimenter. But none of these events can be cues for the recall of the last item, for they do not precede it. Moreover, the problem would only be rephrased, not eliminated, by the common appeal to hypothetical "cue-producing" responses. Even if we suppose that the subject tends to say "end" in synchrony with the last stimulus, and again at the point where the final digit is to be recalled, how can he recognize these points in the first place? It would be just as difficult to determine when "end" was appropriate as to know which digit was going to be the last one.

In short, serial positions are not stimuli. Nevertheless, they do play an important part in auditory memory. Subjects know that a given item was the last on the list, or the first, or near the beginning; on occasion their knowledge can even lead to "serial intrusions." The failure of association theory to account for these phenomena should not incline us back to the slot model, in face of the evidence that has already been reviewed. The kind of theory that seems necessary is one in which the structure of the series as a whole can play some meaningful part. A proposal of this kind will be made later on, but some other problems of association theory must be considered first.

The notion that the subject of a memory-span experiment merely associates each stimulus with its neighbors remains simple only so long as the span is measured by direct recall. Other measurements are perfectly possible, however, and yield sensible results. Wickelgren himself (1965e) has successfully used a "recognition" procedure, in which the subject need only indicate whether or not a given test letter was on the initial list. More complex is Buschke's (1963a; 1963b) "missing span." In this method, the subject must report which of the numerals from *1* to *n* was not included in a series of (*n*–1) presented numerals, so that the correct response to *6, 10, 5, 7, 2, 9, 4, 3, 1* is "8." Here, the correct "association" can hardly be strengthened during presentation, since it does not even occur. One might imagine that the recalling subject first examines the strength of his various associations and then makes appropriate inferences, but these inferences would be circuitous indeed.

The important point here is not just that different ways of measuring memory lead to different results. The mere fact that tests like "recognition" are relatively easy to carry out already has a serious implication. It means that the subject does not only acquire new or temporarily strengthened links *between* verbal items, but also records the identity of these items *per se*. This finding is far from a mortal blow to association theory (the distinction between response learning and associative learning is an old one—see Underwood, 1964, for example), but it should not be ignored. Although association theory is often placed in opposition to views which refer to the storage of stimulus information (Postman, 1964), it is hard to see how one can avoid the notion altogether.

Perhaps for these reasons, Wickelgren is willing to assume that the internal representations of digits not only have associations to one another, but also "strengths." In a very interesting paper, Norman and Wickelgren (1965) study recognition memory for *pairs* of digits, as well as single digits, from this point of view. The rather complex formal models which the authors propose for their data need not be considered here. It is their result which is important: apparently the ability to recognize a digit-pair does not result from the recognizability of its members. Pairs are recognized as wholes, much as individual items are. If this result is sustained in further experiments, it represents an almost unbearable complication for a purely associative approach.

It appears that neither the slot theory nor the associative theory gives an adequate account of the way "chunks" are organized in the memory span. Some structural principle of organization seems to escape them both. The next section presents some tentative suggestions as to the nature of this principle.

## *RHYTHM AND STRUCTURE IN AUDITORY MEMORY*

One of the most pervasive phenomena in auditory memory is subjective grouping. Every subject with an introspective bent is eager to tell the experimenter that he does not remember the series directly, say as "61935827," but rather as "619–358–27," or in some other segmented sequence. If no groups are present in the input, the subject creates them by rehearsal. As noted earlier, the decline in performance at high rates of presentation, which appeared so markedly in the study of Yntema, Wozencraft, and Klem (1964) is apparently due to a failure of the grouping process and can be prevented if segments are introduced artificially. The usefulness of grouping is somewhat perplexing, however: why should it help the subject to remember? After all, the rhythm gives no cue to the identity of the digits; any eight numbers could appear in the pattern "***-***-**." One might even expect the pattern to act as an additional burden on memory, but it does not. When the subject stores a grouping pattern *as well as* eight digits, he finds his task easier than the eight digits would be alone! There are two questions here. First, how is the rhythm itself stored and recalled? Second, why does it help with the digits?

With respect to the first question, it is apparent that a rhythmic pattern is a single structural unit. In a well-known paper, Lashley (1951) argued that rapid, temporally integrated responses, like those of speech, typing, piano-playing and the like, must be structured in advance. It is impossible to suppose that a pianist strikes each piano key as a response "conditioned" to the preceding note, or that each successive movement of the vocal cords depends on an S–R bond with the one before. Conduction times in the nervous systems are simply not rapid enough; succeeding responses are triggered before feedback from prior ones has had time to arrive. Miller, Galanter, and Pribram (1960) have extended Lashley's model in a far-reaching way to many areas of behavior. For present purposes, however, no wide generalization is necessary. A rhythm is just the sort of structured response that Lashley had in mind; rhythmic patterns like "***-***-**" must be represented by simple unitary codes in the response system. Moreover, since the essence of rhythm is repetition, it is easy to repeat a rhythmic pattern just heard or produced; indeed, we can hardly help following and repeating the rhythms we encounter. Of course, they must not be too long if we are to repeat them accurately. Thus a subject can easily repeat the rhythm of a series he hears, or modify it if he wishes, and then repeat the modification. Remembering a rhythm in this way does not take up room in the memory span—on the contrary, it *creates* room in an active memory which otherwise would hardly exist.

One way to think of the effect of rhythm is that it may provide a set of reference points, to which digits or words can be attached. This solves the problem of serial position, which was so difficult for association theory. A subject knows when he is at the end of the list because he himself has produced a rhythmic pattern with an end prefigured in its beginning. Once he has initiated the pattern, it "runs automatically," and he can learn that *7* occurs at the end of it, or that *9* is the middle digit of the second group. Such positions simply do not exist unless they form part of a subjectively created organization. In a sense, this is a slot theory in which the subject makes up his slots as he goes along.

Even this interpretation may be too limited. Like the old theory of the *Gestaltqualität* (reviewed in Boring, 1950), it treats the whole pattern as existing independently of the digits which compose it, so that they can be inserted in the slots it provides. We might do better to follow the Gestalt psychologists all the way, and think of the digits as integral parts, visible tips, of the entire rhythmic structure. On either interpretation, however, the limit on the memory span (Miller's $7 \pm 2$) can be seen essentially as a limit on our capacity to organize extended rhythmic sequences. (See Fraisse, 1956, for a related view.)

A number of phenomena in auditory memory can be interpreted on a rhythmic basis. For example, it explains how subjects with only partial recall can still know from what part of the series the recalled digits have come. It also accounts for the difficulty of backward recall. An ordinary slot theory does not explain this at all, except *ad hoc,* while association theory can only do so by assuming that backward associations are weaker than forward ones. Perhaps the opposite is more nearly correct: backward associations are difficult because they demand rearrangement of a rhythmic pattern.

The theory also explains why the "running memory span" is so much poorer than the standard kind. In this method (Pollack, Johnson, & Knaff, 1959; Waugh, 1960) the subject hears a long string of digits which eventually stops; at that point he is to write down as many from the end of the string as he can. Under these conditions he must constantly form and re-form new relations between the digits and his rhythmic structures. Neither beginning nor end are defined for him until the series is over. As in other procedures which interfere with grouping (e.g., high-speed presentation), however, these negative factors can be counteracted if temporal grouping is deliberately provided by the experimenter. And indeed, Pollack *et al.* found that explicit stimulus-grouping improves the running span substantially, while it has little effect in the fixed-length procedure. There was also a differential effect of rate. Slow presentation turned out to be more help in the fixed span, where the subject can make good use of extra time, than in the running span, which must rely relatively more on echoic memory anyway.

If a rhythmic structure underlies immediate verbal memory, interruption of the rhythm should have serious effects on retention. To some extent, any activity interpolated between stimulus and response will tend to disturb it, and we have seen that interpolations do interfere seriously with recall. To be sure, interpolation may have a number of other effects—preventing rehearsal, supplying associative interference—in addition to the disruption of a rhythmic sequence. However, the present hypothesis may explain why very brief activities, far too short to cause much interference or prevent much rehearsal, can sometimes produce substantial losses. A startling example of this phenomenon was observed by Conrad (1960b). He found that simply by saying the digit "nought" between an 8-digit series and its recall reduced scores in his subjects from 73 percent to 38 percent. This may be because *any* verbal response must be somehow incorporated in the rhythmic, semilinguistic structure which the subject elaborates around the items, and thus "takes up space" in it.

A rhythmic pattern is a structure, which serves as a support, an integrator, and a series of cues for the words to be remembered. At the risk of being old-fashioned, it is worth emphasizing that such a structure is a whole, greater than the sum of its parts. The parts (individual beats) get their meaning (relative position) from the whole, even though that whole does not exist at any moment of time. It exists, as one might say, in the subject's mind, as an intent, a Gestalt, a plan, a description of a response that can be executed without further consideration. Are there any other temporary structures of this kind? Indeed there are; we make use of them whenever we speak. Spoken language is built upon "syntactic" organizations of this sort, whose complexities are currently being unraveled by linguists. This is no coincidence. My hypothesis is that the processes of spoken language are continuous with those of active verbal memory; that the "synthesis" postulated in certain theories of speech perception involves the same capacities and mechanisms as the synthesis of a rhythmic pattern in a memory-span experiment. However, grammatical organization is complex enough to deserve a chapter of its own, which it will get shortly. First, we must turn to some other questions about auditory memory. What happens to stored auditory information, rhythmic or otherwise, as time goes by?

### *DECAY vs. INTERFERENCE*

The recent upsurge of interest in immediate memory has been much influenced by the work of J. Brown (1958, 1959), and of Broadbent (1958). Both support a decay theory, but while Broadbent restricts decay to short-term memory, Brown applies it more widely. He believes that all forgetting reflects a single decay process. All stored information degenerates, rapidly at first and then more slowly. Long-term memory survives this decay only if the items have been encoded in a sufficiently "redundant" way, so that they remain identifiable even after much "degradation" of their specific features. Because of these redundant encodings, and also because a subject may make plausible reconstructions from what remains even after much loss, ". . . the time course of forgetting does not necessarily follow the time course of decay" (Brown, 1959, p.

738). Information about the *order* in which items or lists were presented is said to be especially vulnerable to decay. So-called retroactive and proactive inhibition may be due to loss of order-information (the subject cannot remember which list was which), with consequent confusions in recall.

Although Brown's views are phrased in the metaphors of "information theory," the memory-organization he envisages is not very different from that assumed by association theorists like Wickelgren, who oppose the decay theory vigorously. Brown's "traces" correspond to Wickelgren's "internal representations," his "signal-to-noise ratio" for a fading trace is like "strength," and his "order-information" is not described in any way which would distinguish it from "associations." Moreover, Brown's argument that the serial position curve is due to "variations in the use of storage space," because the ends are used as "reference points" (1959, p. 742), is not really different from the associative explanation of the same phenomenon. The two theories differ substantively only in their account of forgetting. Brown ascribes it primarily to decay with the passage of time, although he does allow for occasional "confusions in recall." For an association theorist, on the other hand, all failure to recall is due to interference.

In weighing these opposing views, we may well begin with studies of the rate of presentation. Earlier in this chapter, we found that rapid rates can produce better performance than slow ones, but only where other factors limit the possibility of, or the need for, active recoding and rehearsal. In the absence of such factors, slow presentation is generally better. Moreover, the last part of a series seems to have an advantage due to its recency, while the first part has an advantage which might possibly be ascribed to rehearsal during the presentation of the rest. At first glance, all of these observations seem to fit Brown's assumptions that (*a*) items in verbal memory are available for the first few seconds no matter what may intervene, and (*b*) thereafter they simply decay, unless reimpressed through rehearsal.

However, certain quantitative considerations complicate this interpretation. Rehearsal, in the literal sense of an inner repetition, must take a certain amount of time. We saw in Chapter 2 that the rate of inner speech cannot possibly exceed about ten words per second, or 100 msec. per word. Taken together with the normal length of the memory span—say, seven words—this sets a limit to the possible rate of trace decay. If traces were to decay in less than 700 msec., no amount of rehearsal could produce a seven-item span, since the trace of the first item would be gone before the last had been rehearsed. It seems that decay must proceed relatively slowly, as our review of echoic memory in Chapter 8 has already suggested. But if this is admitted, the decay theory is unable to explain the results of Yntema, Wozencraft, and Klem (1964), discussed earlier. At a presentation-rate of ten per second, a string of five digits is complete within 500 msec., yet subjects are unable to recall such strings without error! Decay theories can hardly deal with this finding except *ad hoc*.

To be sure, the negative effects of high-speed presentation also complicate a simple interference theory; why should rapidly formed associations be especially vulnerable? However, association theories have encountered rate effects before, in the case of ordinary rote learning. Presumably the theoretical devices developed for those problems—chiefly the notion of an inhibition that decays with time—would be useful here also. This hypothesis also seems somewhat unsatisfactory (to me), but before considering an alternative view, we must look at some other experiments.

A subject who hears a string of digits shorter than the memory span can remember them for a relatively long time if he is undistracted, but loses them soon if he turns his attention elsewhere. In Brown's theory, the prolonged remembering depends on more or less continuous rehearsal, while the loss is due to a decay which starts as soon as rehearsal is terminated. According to the interference theory, on the other hand, remembering continues unchecked so long as no interference takes place, and forgetting is a direct result of the distracting material. Thus, both theories predict rapid forgetting as a result of interfering activity, but arrive at this conclusion by different routes. The result itself has by now been well established by many experiments, including Brown (1958), Peterson and Peterson (1959), and others. The basic findings have already been presented. As illustrated in Figure 41, extensive loss can occur within a few seconds while a subject is engaged in backward counting. Although the decay and interference theories can both account for this finding, they make rather different predictions about the effect of certain variables on the amount that is lost. These variables include the amount of interfering material, the time at which it is presented, and its nature.

1. *Amount of interpolation.* According to decay theory, the crucial parameter in such an experiment is *how long* the interpolated activity lasts. According to interference theory, the important factor is the *number* and *kind* of interfering items presented. Although it would seem easy to settle this question by manipulating the rate at which subjects count backward (for example), such an approach encounters difficulties. Opportunities for covert rehearsal increase as the rate of counting decreases, so neither theory can make an unambiguous prediction. In fact, studies of this variable have led to conflicting results.

Murdock (1961, Experiment III) read a list of words to his subjects, who were instructed to remember both the first word and the last three. Since the subjects did not know the length of the list in advance (a "running span" method), the effort to remember the last three "seemed to prevent rehearsal of the first." He found that recall of the first word varied substantially with the *interval* between presentation and recall, but did not depend on the rate at which the other words were presented. Rates ranging from 0.5 to 2.5 words per second were explored. The implication of this finding seems to be (although Murdock does not give data for individual intervals) that a seven-second interval is equally damaging whether it is filled with 7 words at 1/sec., 13 to 14 words at 2/sec., or still more words at a higher rate. Such a result would support the decay theory. So would the preliminary results reported by Broadbent (1963) in a rate-of-interpolation experiment: subjects had to say "ABC" at various speeds before recalling a list, and slower rates led to poorer recall.

Waugh and Norman (1965) presented their subjects with 15 digits followed by a single "probe digit," which had occurred once before in the sequence. The subjects were only to recall what digit had *followed* the probe on its earlier appearance. They were asked to control rehearsal by "thinking only of the last digit you have heard and never of any earlier ones." Thus the presentation of a probe digit from the tenth position in the list was essentially a request to respond with the eleventh digit, with digits 12–16 acting as interpolated items. In this situation, the decay theory was *not* supported. The probability of correct recall depended sharply on the number of interpolated items, but there was little or no effect of presentation rate. Recall was as good after eight digits at 1/sec. (eight seconds) as after eight digits at 4/sec. (two seconds).

None of these experiments is conclusive. Waugh and Norman's subjects were asked to rehearse individual items and had more time to do so at the slower rate; the extra rehearsal may well have made up for a greater delay of recall. In Murdock's experiment, the critical source of interference was surely not the words actually presented, but the subjects' continuous recoding as they tried to keep the "last three words" in mind. Finally, Broadbent's method must have disturbed the subject's rhythmic organization of the list. So far, the rate-of-interpolation studies have been ambiguous.

2. *Proactive inhibition.* A number of experiments have shown that extra material presented *before* the critical items has a damaging effect on immediate memory: Brown himself (1958), Murdock (1961), Wickelgren (1965d). For example, in Murdock's experiment, several irrelevant words were read to the subject before the single one he was to remember; after the critical word, he counted backwards for, say, 18 seconds before attempting to recall it. Accuracy in this condition was only 80 percent, while it was 91 percent when the irrelevant words were omitted. The difference was small but consistent. Proactive interference also appeared in the intrusion data from the experiment. When subjects recalled an incorrect word, it often (40 percent of the time) came from the list presented just previously. Such effects are embarrassing to a

pure decay theory, since preceding stimuli can hardly disturb subsequent rehearsal.

3. *Similarity.* Although it was formerly believed that every kind of interpolated activity produced the same decrement in recall so long as it prevented rehearsal (Broadbent, 1963), recent work does not support this view. Particularly Wickelgren (1965a, 1966a, etc.) has shown that the amount of interference depends on the auditory or linguistic similarity between the series to be recalled and the interfering material. Of course, copying either *PTBPZBTZ* or *FSMSNFNM* makes a prior presentation of *DCVG* hard to recall, but the former, dominated by the sound of /iy/, does appreciably more damage. If interference appeared only because subjects cannot rehearse while they copy, one would expect both to have equal effects. An account of this finding in terms of associative interference was given earlier; it is very difficult to reconcile with decay theory.

The results on proaction and similarity speak rather decisively for some kind of interference effects in immediate memory. At least, forgetting cannot be *exclusively* due to decay. If the notion of decay is to be preserved at all, we must turn to a two-factor model of some kind. Precisely such a theory suggests itself in connection with the difference between echoic and active verbal memory. However, it would be too simple to suppose that the former decays while the latter suffers only interference. I would prefer to formulate a different hypothesis. Where the interference theory suggests that items in active verbal memory survive indefinitely if they are not explicitly destroyed, and the decay theory proposes that they survive only if they are rehearsed, it seems to me that they do *not* survive, under any circumstances whatever, except as rapidly-fading echoes.

The original content of echoic memory is information that has not been segmented or organized. It is possible, however, that the products of auditory synthesis also have echoic status and are equally subject to decay. They only *seem* to survive; actually they are replaced by new constructions based on information supplied by the earlier ones. If a construction follows the main lines of what was heard before, it is called a "rehearsal." If it follows different lines—perhaps because the subject is counting backwards in an interpolation experiment—it is called "interference." Rehearsal and interference are the same process seen from different points of view, the former emphasizing the similarities among successive constructions while the latter stresses the differences between them. Of course, rehearsed or interpolated material will leave its own temporary residue in echoic memory. This may indeed cause "confusions in recall," as the subject tries to make something new with what is now available. Such "confusions" are especially likely if the two sets of material are phonemically similar.

This account of forgetting in immediate memory is very like that of Brown (1959). However, I do not conceive either rehearsal or decay as he does. Rehearsal is not the invigoration of an old structure but the synthesis of a new one, typically rhythmic in experiments like those under discussion. (When whole sentences are to be remembered, the structure is grammatical in nature, like those described in the next chapter.) As for decay, Brown's hypothesis that "order-information" is subject to unusually rapid decay becomes less *ad hoc* and arbitrary if "order-information" is carried by rhythm. A rhythm is a creature of time, formed out of temporal relationships, living only while these relationships endure, dying in as little as two seconds (see Chapter 8) if it is not reborn. A rhythm can be preserved over time only by replicating it, which necessarily changes its character.

It seems obvious that rhythm can be a factor in supporting memory only over the short run, though it may have some effect on the long-run stability of learned series. Hence my hypothesis suggests that there is at least some difference between the mechanisms of short-term and long-term memory. Others have reached this conclusion on different grounds, but their opinion is not undisputed.

## *TWO KINDS OF MEMORY OR ONE?*

The hypothesis that short- and long-term memory operates on different rules—sometimes called the "duplexity theory of memory"—has long been implicitly accepted in psychology. In most textbooks, "memory span" is not treated in the same chapter with "learning" or "forgetting," and the same questions are not raised about it. The duplexity theory has a certain intuitive plausibility, just as decay theory does, and indeed the two are based on the same kind of observations. Immediate memory seems to have an all-or-none character and a short time constant. Material that has once been "really learned," on the other hand, tends to be lost only bit-by-bit, over extended periods. This obvious difference is the basis for theories which assume a "temporary store" or "buffer," from which favored or fortunate items of information sometimes pass to a "long-term store"; items which are not thus transferred soon meet with a sticky end. The most influential theory of this kind is that of Broadbent (1956, 1957, 1958), which deserves careful review.

Broadbent's theory of short-term storage was designed especially to incorporate the results of his work with simultaneous stimulation. In a series of experiments, he presented pairs of spoken digits simultaneously to the two ears of his subjects. A series such as *6–4–9* would be presented to the left ear in perfect synchrony with another series, say, *2–8–3,* at the right. When the subject was asked to recall these numbers, he nearly always reported all the numbers from one ear before any from the other; i.e., he would say "649–283" or "283–649," not "62–48–93" or "26–84–39." If compelled to report by pairs, his performance was much worse than when he was allowed to report by ears. The report by ears clearly involves a kind of memory: the three digits reported last must be stored during the period that the others are heard and recalled. As one might expect, retention was better for the digits reported first.

These experiments raise two questions. Why did the subjects violate the temporal sequence of presentation, to report by ears instead of by pairs? And what are the properties of the memory-system involved? To the first of these questions, Broadbent proposed an answer which has turned out to be wrong. He believed that the subject could not "switch attention" from one ear to the other in the half-second available between pairs of digits. In the language of filter theory, the "filter" could not move rapidly enough to another "channel." Several experiments refute this view. Moray (1960) showed that rapid "switching" does not necessarily create difficulties: if the two members of a pair are separated by 250 msec. (instead of being simultaneous) the effect disappears. Yntema and Trask (1963) showed that sensory "channels" need not be involved; the effect appears as markedly, or more so, when different *classes* of items (i.e., digits and nondigits in the sequence *two-coil-six-roam-four-good*) are used instead of different *ears*. The real basis of the effect is that recall is better when items which "belong together" by any principle of grouping can be recalled together. The same point was also made by Gray and Wedderburn (1960), and is now generally conceded (Broadbent & Gregory, 1964).

There remains the fact that some of the digits are stored during the period when the others are heard and reported. This suggested to Broadbent that there was a storage mechanism (the "*S* system") which could accept information from several sources simultaneously, and store them for brief periods, acting in concert with a perceptual mechanism (the "*P* system") which took items from *S* one at a time. Decay in *S* was rapid, but material could be recirculated through *P* (rehearsal) and then replaced in *S*. The *S* system is very like "auditory memory," in the sense of this chapter. There is one major difference: Broadbent does not consider the possibility that information might be changed, reorganized, and grouped on its way through *P*, i.e., during resynthesis.

How is Broadbent's position to be described in terms of the basic theoretical issues? He is a decay theorist: the contents of *S* are assumed to disappear spontaneously. He is not specific about the organization of material within *S*. (The sequence of successive items is preserved isomorphically in *P*, but it must be somehow represented in *S* as well.) A slot theory would hardly be possible, since items can arrive in *S* simultaneously. Perhaps an association theory would be attractive to Broadbent in this respect. It is unlikely that he would accept the structural notions proposed here, since they are linked to a theory of attention very different from his own.

Finally, Broadbent is the best-known duplexity theorist. Long-term storage is not in the *S* system, but somewhere else. It is not clear where else; Broadbent is surprisingly vague about "the long-term store" considering how certain he is that it differs from "the short-term store." Or perhaps it is not surprising—the reader will find a good deal of vagueness in my own Chapter 11. We just do not know very much about long-term memory, at least in terms that seem helpful here. Consequently, the duplexity theory remains a matter of opinion. For some psychologists, duplexity is just a fact of life: recent material disappears very quickly unless it is constantly rehearsed, while older material seems to hang on for long periods without any special attention. Others don't see it that way: weak associations, based on a single trial, are very easily wiped out by interfering material, while stronger ones are much more resistant.

A satisfactory account of the relations between short- and long-term auditory memory will have to reckon with one particularly interesting phenomenon, which deserves mention even though its theoretical basis is obscure. Hebb (1961) tested immediate memory with strings of nine digits, giving each subject many such strings to recall. Unknown to the subject, every third string was the same. By the twenty-fourth trial, which was the eighth with the critical string, about 26 subjects got it right; only five had succeeded with it on the first presentation. Interestingly enough, about the same number of subjects reported noticing "some repetition," but Hebb does not say whether the successful subjects were just those who noticed. On the basis of recent work on "learning without awareness" (see Eriksen, 1962), one would expect so. Melton (1963) has recently extended and confirmed Hebb's finding. It seems that a string of digits can, at least on occasion, make a relatively permanent impression under surprisingly adverse circumstances.

Although some questions, especially about decay and about duplexity theory, remain unanswered, this survey of data on immediate memory has not been in vain. It has suggested that the content of this memory is essentially inner speech, acoustic in character and highly vulnerable to mnemonic interference. Its vulnerability is lessened by organization around a rhythmic structure. In the next chapter we will see that it becomes still less vulnerable when it is organized around the deeper structures of language.

*Chapter 10*

# *Sentences*

This chapter extends the account of speech perception begun earlier. The concept of "structure" used by contemporary linguists is examined and shown to have much in common with the notion of "Gestalt" familiar to students of visual perception. A general discussion of the relation between linguistics and psychology is followed by a more specific presentation of the principles of "phrase-structure grammar" and its implications. It is suggested that the surface structures of sentences have much in common with rhythmic patterns, and that their psychological effects can be understood along similar lines. However, consideration of "transformational grammar" complicates this picture considerably.

One of the points stressed in the last chapter was that items are not stored in auditory memory as isolated units. The subject creates a structure—usually a rhythmic one—as he rehearses and reformulates the information presented to him, and his subsequent recall is based on that structure. This point seems clear enough to me, but it will not find unanimous acceptance among psychologists. There are bound to be many who would rather deal with the phenomena of immediate memory without invoking any structural concepts. When we turn from random strings of digits to the sentences of naturally spoken language, however, the role of structure is much less likely to be disputed. Current developments in linguistics have made it especially clear that sentences are far more than the sum of their parts, and some consideration of sentence structure is surely required here. In any case, it would be hard to justify a treatment of "cognition" that did not deal with the understanding of ordinary language.

There have been many recent attempts to acquaint psychologists with the major insights of contemporary linguistics (e.g., Miller, 1962a, 1965). Nevertheless, it would not be safe to assume that every reader of this book is familiar with them, and so another presentation, even by an amateur like myself, may have some value. Moreover, many of these insights can be seen as natural extensions of other psychological principles. The exposition which follows will take this point of view wherever possible. It is a continuation of the argument from Chapter 7, where we saw that speech perception involves an active process of synthesis on the part of the listener, and that the course of synthesis seems to follow grammatical structure at least to some extent.

Perhaps the most perplexing thing about verbal behavior is its irrepressible novelty. Most of what we hear and understand, like most of what we say, is new to us and unique to the occasion. Each sentence in this paragraph will be new to you as you read it, as it was new to me when I wrote it. This creates difficulties for theories which explain speech with the aid of concepts like habit, reinforcement, or conditioning. As Chomsky has put it:

> The central fact to which any significant linguistic theory must address itself is this: a mature speaker can produce a new sentence of his language on the appropriate occasion, and other speakers can understand it immediately, though it is equally new to them. Much of our linguistic experience, both as speakers and hearers, is with new sentences; once we have mastered a language, the class of sentences with which we can operate fluently and without difficulty or hesitation is so vast that for all practical purposes (and, obviously, for all theoretical purposes) we can regard it as infinite . . . a theory of language that neglects this "creative" aspect of language is only of marginal interest (1964a, p. 50).

However, speech displays regularity as well as novelty. Natural sentences tend to follow certain rules of formation, and they are understood in terms of these rules. The rules are *structural.* That is, they do not dictate what particular words are to be used, but rather how they are to be related to each other and to the sentence as a whole. The meaning of a sentence depends not only on the words which compose it but on their complex interrelationships. This is true even though meanings seem to be given "directly," without any mediating mental steps. All perceptual and cognitive processes involve analysis and transformation, and the understanding of speech is no exception to this principle.

As a simple example, consider the sentences *Paul saw Mary* and *Mary saw Paul.* We distinguish their meanings effortlessly, unsurprised that the same three words can stand for very different states of affairs when their order is changed. So easy is this kind of understanding that study of grammar has a very bad reputation, especially among schoolchildren. It seems pedantic to dismember what is so intelligible as a whole.

The use of this example should not imply that syntactic structure is simply a matter of word order. In English, word order is a rather important *indicator* of structure, but by no means the only one. We can paraphrase *Paul saw Mary* as *Mary was seen by Paul,* reversing the order completely. In certain other languages, such reversals can be made very freely. *Paul saw Mary* goes into Latin as *Paulus vidit Mariam,* or *Mariam vidit Paulus,* or *Mariam Paulus vidit,* or in any of three other orders. In the Latin sentences the specialized endings *-us* and *-am* indicate the underlying structure regardless of the order in which the words appear.

The meaning of a sentence does not depend only on its component words or their order, but on an overall structure. A sentence is more than the sum of its parts. This is not an unfamiliar slogan. Long ago, the Gestalt psychologists used it to describe the wholistic aspects of visual perception. In many respects, their arguments were strikingly similar to those used by today's "psycholinguists." An explicit comparison between the two movements may help bring linguistic theory into a relevant frame of reference for psychologists. In addition, the reinterpretation of some Gestalt concepts suggested in Chapter 4 may turn out to have a linguistic counterpart.

### *LINGUISTICS AND GESTALT PSYCHOLOGY*

The Gestalt psychologists had innumerable examples to prove that the figure as a whole, rather than its parts individually or additively, determines what we see. Such phenomena as apparent movement, color contrast, the perceptual constancies, visual grouping, and physiognomic perception are cases in point. Similarly, linguists insist that the sentence as a whole, rather than its words individually or additively, determines what we understand. This principle, too, is easily illustrated; consider Lashley's (1951) classical example *Rapid righting with his uninjured hand saved from loss the contents of the capsized canoe.* In its spoken form, this sentence is usually understood in a way that requires a full and surprising reorganization when the end is reached.

The Gestalt psychologists made particularly effective use of *ambiguous figures* to illustrate the importance of structure. All figures are organized, with shape and contour, but the changing organization of a reversible one like the Peter-Paul Goblet (Figure 26, Chapter 4) shows immediately how crucial this organization is. The directionality of the contours, and indeed the significance and depth of all parts of the picture, depend on the structure which is dominant at the moment. In the face of such an example, it would be difficult to maintain that structural organization is irrelevant to the process of seeing.

Interestingly enough, *ambiguous sentences* play a role in modern linguistics very like the one which ambiguous figures had for Gestalt psychology. *They are eating apples* is such a sentence. It can have two very different meanings, depending on whether *eating* is seen structually as related to *apples* (as in *Eating apples cost more than cooking apples*) or to *are* (as in *They are eating too many apples*). (For a more spectacular case of ambiguity, consider *The police were ordered to stop drinking after midnight*!) In the face of such examples, it is again difficult to maintain that structural organization is irrelevant to the processes involved.

Gestalt psychology and the new linguistics are even similar in their reaction to a common "enemy." The "behaviorists," the "associationists," and the "stimulus-response theorists" seem every bit as benighted and reactionary to Chomsky as they ever did to Wertheimer or Köhler. Chomsky's 32-page review (1959) of Skinner's *Verbal Behavior* is far more than an effective refutation of the behavioristic approach to language. It is an extraordinarily powerful critique of the underlying assumptions of stimulus-response psychology, carried out with a vigor and enthusiasm perhaps unmatched since Koffka's (1935) *Principles of Gestalt Psychology*.

It is not surprising that both these two movements have negative reactions to behaviorism. Each emphasizes the importance of structure, as against momentary or fragmentary stimuli taken alone. For both, the structures are created anew by the perceiver on every occasion. Behaviorism, on the other hand, is a systematic attempt to explain psychological phenomena in terms of responses previously attached to some of the current stimulus cues. Thus, novelty is explained away, and the whole is interpreted in terms of its parts.

The Gestalt psychologists were successful in many respects, and the importance of pattern and structure in perception is now generally taken for granted. Nevertheless, there is one point on which they are generally thought to have been mistaken. They were "nativists," believing that the perceptual processes were largely determined by necessary and innate principles rather than by learning. The proper figural organization —into depth, or movement, or constant size, etc.—was not the result of suitable previous experience. Instead, it was due to processes in the brain, which followed unvarying (and wholistic) laws of physics and chemistry. The perceived world always took the "best," the "structurally simplest" form, because of an equilibrium principle that transcended any possible effects of training or learning or practice. They did not believe that learning (conceived as the formation of traces and bonds between traces) could ever account for visual organization, which seems immediate and spontaneous even when the presented figure is entirely novel.

We know now that the effects of experience on perception are very substantial. These effects have been demonstrated by numerous studies (of animals reared with restricted visual experience, of human beings adapting to distorting spectacles, etc.) which seem to fit sophisticated empirical theories like that of Hebb (1949). The "pendulum" has swung back toward empiricism, and we tend to think of the Gestalt psychologists as "naive" in this respect.

However appropriate empiricism may be for visual perception, it has long seemed the only possible approach to language. Children acquire the language of the community where they happen to grow up, and it seems a truism that this acquisition must result from experience rather than innate endowment. Yet precisely this truism is vigorously denied by Chomsky and other contemporary linguists. Their insistence on the importance of innate factors in determining the structure of language is particularly noteworthy because it moves against the current empiristic tide. Like the Gestalt psychologists, contemporary linguists find it impossible to believe that learning could ever account for structure. In sentences too, organization seems immediate and spontaneous even when the input is new and unfamiliar. Can we really suppose that the entire grammatical apparatus, only now being gradually uncovered by linguists, is acquired effortlessly by children before the age of three?

Lenneberg (1964a, 1964b) argues that children all over the world acquire languages with the same basic characteristics, in about the same sequence, at about the same age, almost regardless of their intelligence and almost regardless of their environment. If this is true, it suggests that the basic forms of language—the duality between phonemic and morphemic levels, the organization of utterances into phrases, the transformations of phrase structure—are somehow genetically inevitable. They are a model which experience can clothe, but cannot reshape. Just this was also the nativism of the Gestalt psychologists. They never argued that experience had *no* effects, but only that its effects were organized and determined by the deeper requirements of structure.

These impressive similarities between the new linguistics and the old Gestalt psychology should not lead the reader to identify the two. Apart from their different subject matter, there is a crucial difference of method between them. The Gestalt psychologists were never able to provide any satisfactory description or analysis of the structures involved in perception. The few attempts to specify "fields of force" in vision, or "ionic equilibria" in the brain, were *ad hoc* and ended in failure. In linguistics, by contrast, the study of "syntactic structures" has a long history. The field has recently acquired new vigor from the remarkable theoretical work of Noam Chomsky (1957, 1963, 1964a, 1964b). Chomsky is by no means the first linguist to concern himself with questions of structure, but his precise and vigorous formulations of the questions, and of the alternative answers, have made his work particularly important for psychologists. George Miller saw the relevance of Chomsky's work some years ago (Miller, Galanter, & Pribram, 1960; Miller & Chomsky, 1963) and has examined its bearing on various cognitive processes in a series of experiments.

Any review of the effects of linguistic structure on cognition must begin with a preliminary account of modern linguistics itself. Unlike Gestalt psychology, which had only to be believed, linguistics must be learned. Although the exposition which follows is adequate for the purposes of this book, it is necessarily oversimplified. Linguistic structure is far too complex to be adequately represented in a nontechnical account by a nonlinguist. The reader should not make the mistake of supposing that he has a grasp of structural linguistics just because he has read this chapter. More adequate presentations appear in Fodor and Katz (1964) and the Miller-Chomsky chapters in Luce, Bush, and Galanter (1963).

### *GRAMMATICAL STRUCTURE: GENERAL CONSIDERATIONS*

As everybody knows, grammar consists of rules. In this respect at least, the conception of grammar held by modern linguists is like that held by schoolteachers and their pupils. However, rules can be stated in two different ways: either *restrictively* ("Do not smoke.") or *positively* ("First beat together three eggs. . . ."). Although children and teachers tend to think of grammatical rules as restrictive ("Don't say *ain't*."), linguists prefer to formulate them in a positive way, as descriptions of allowable sentences. In fact, linguistic rules do more than describe sentences; like the recipe above, they actually show how the desired result can be brought about. Whatever the practice in "grammar school," a theoretical grammar can hardly be other than *generative*. A grammar, then, is a system of rules that "generates" all the sentences of some language, together with their structural descriptions; it must not "generate" any nonsentences.

The rules of grammar are scientifically interesting because they seem to govern a large class of human behavior. If a man speaks grammatical sentences one after the other, and avoids ungrammatical ones, he is following these rules, and in some sense he must "know" them; they must be represented somehow in him. Moreover, if your understanding of his sentence depends on a grasp of its structure, and in particular on its *grammatical* structure, then the grammar must be represented inside you as well. Thus, linguistics assumes that each user of a language somehow incorporates or "has" its grammar. The assumption can hardly be avoided; it is little more than a definition. Nevertheless, it brings up a number of problems, including: (1) the infinity of possible sentences; (2) our inability to describe the grammar we "have"; (3) the existence of ungrammatical statements; (4) the role of a grammar in cognitive theory.

From the theoretical point of view, the number of English sentences is infinite. It is always possible to make new ones, if only by extending any existing sentences with clauses, conjunctions, and the like. Some of these theoretically possible sentences would become impractically long, but even the number of short sentences (say, under 20 words) is extremely large. Given this vast set of possibilities, it is not surprising that most of the speech we actually encounter is new to us. This fact creates grave difficulties for probabilistic theories in the psychology of language, but it poses no problem for psychology or physiology in general. There is no reason why a finite brain cannot store rules that define a potentially infinite set of products. Even very simple rules, like those which define the sequence of whole numbers, can "generate" potentially infinite sets.

The second problem is already familiar from other psychological contexts. How can it be supposed that a man "knows" or "has" a grammar if he can give no account of it; if, indeed, no fully adequate description of English grammar has ever been published? However, there is really no contradiction here. We need only conclude what we already knew: introspection is not always a good guide to the cognitive processes. That people speak grammatically without being able to describe their grammar is no more surprising than that they see without being perceptual theorists, or think in the absence of a theory of thinking.

The problem of ungrammatical speech is a more serious one. To be sure, the "incorrect" speech of persons with "bad grammar" creates no theoretical puzzles, however much it may disturb schoolteachers. People who regularly construct sentences like *That ain't no way for him to be!* have a grammar which is no less real for being unorthodox or disapproved. Scientifically, "grammar" has undergone the same change of meaning as "culture." Both were originally value-laden words ("Learn your grammar!", "Become a cultured person!") which have been neutralized through use in a technical sense ("The grammar of the four-year-old," "The culture of the aborigines"). But a more intriguing question arises when people produce speech which violates *their own* grammatical rules, either through carelessness or by deliberate intention. Even here, there is no difficulty as long as the problem is seen from the viewpoint of linguistics rather than psychology. The linguist can study the rules of grammar whether they are breakable or not. There is nothing paradoxical about breaking rules: every social situation has its conventions, every dance its steps, which can be acknowledged even when they are not always followed. In this sense a grammatical rule is a *custom,* like many others. The study of custom is the province of anthropology, of which linguistics is properly a branch. It is only for the psychologist that ungrammatical utterances are a problem, because he wishes to account for all behavior, whether customary or not.

This brings us to the fourth and subtlest of the problems raised by the definition of grammar as a set of rules for "generating" sentences: the relation between grammar and cognitive theory. Is a "generative" grammar a model of the speaker? Of the hearer? If it is not such a model, how is it important for psychologists?

Let us consider the speaker first. If a man consistently produces grammatical sentences, it can hardly be doubted that the rules of an appropriate grammar are somehow represented inside him. Nevertheless, these rules are not themselves a theory of the speech-producing processes. Chomsky is insistent on this point: "The attempt to develop a reasonable account of the speaker has, I believe, been hampered by the prevalent and utterly mistaken view that a generative grammar in itself provides or is related in some obvious way to a model for the speaker" (1964b, p. 126). A grammar regulates what can be said, but does not actually explain the activities involved in saying it. We might compare syntactic rules to government standards on the output of a meat-packing plant. If these standards are generally met, there must be someone or something inside the plant which takes account of them—but the standards themselves are hardly a good description of the meat-packing process.

Chomsky is fully justified in denying that a grammar is a model for the speaker (though it is hard to see how the development of such models has been "hampered" by the contrary view). It is safer to assume only that the grammar represents a "device" that is somehow "employed" in the production of speech. Miller and Chomsky put it this way: "How can we construct a model for the language user that incorporates a generative grammar as a fundamental component?" (1963, p. 465). Similarly one might ask "How can we construct a model of the meat-packing process that incorporates some mechanism for observing government standards?" But it is instructive to note, in this meaty analogy, that as government regulations become more complex an increasingly large portion of the plant's effort will necessarily be organized around them. Under these conditions, a good account of the regulations will look more and more like a description of meat-packing. Similarly, if grammar is so complex that obeying syntactic rules is a major part of the job in speaking, then an account of grammar is a major part of a theory of speaking.

Even in the complex case, where the rules of syntax must play a large role in speech production, there will always be many alternative ways to formulate these rules. A formulation drawn up to be *prescriptively* clear by grammarians may not be *descriptively* clear for psychologists. Even if government standards determine the meat-packing operation rather completely, the bureaucratic rulebook will probably require a good deal of reinterpretation before its impact on the production process is clear. As another example of this point, consider the behavior of a man filling out his income tax form. Here the Internal Revenue Act as passed by Congress is analogous to the grammar, and indeed it has a large effect on his actions. But the statute does not directly explain just why, at a given moment, he writes a certain number into a given space. To give that explanation, one must appeal to Form 1040 itself, and its accompanying instructions, which present the prescriptions of the Internal Revenue Act in a different form.

In summary, while it is true that the rules of a generative grammar must be somehow represented in the speaker, it does not follow that they should appear explicitly in a theory about his behavior. As Miller has remarked, ". . . it is by no means obvious *a priori* that the most economical and efficient formal description of the linguistic data will necessarily describe the psychological process involved when we actually utter or understand a grammatical sentence" (1962a, p. 756). At most, the grammatical operations may be regarded as hypotheses about the actual generative mechanisms.

Although these analogies have been more appropriate to the speaker than the hearer, it is the latter with whom cognitive psychology is first concerned. Here, the problem of the relevance of grammar is perhaps still more complicated. On the one hand, it is not as obvious *a priori* that the grammar must be represented in the hearer as it was for the speaker. The listener is hardly responsible for the fact that the sentences reaching his ears obey grammatical constraints! On the other hand, it is evident that sentences are understood as wholes, by grasping their underlying structure, and this seems to concede the relevance of grammar from the outset. But this conclusion is not entirely compelling, at least until we have shown that the "perceptual structure" which the listener uses is the same as the "syntactic structure" described by linguists. There could conceivably be more than one kind of structure.

This possibility—that grammatical structure is not what the listener uses—deserves a moment's consideration, even though we will eventually reject it. Just as the consumer of sausages may be blissfully ignorant of the regulations which govern their manufacture, so also the consumer of sentences might not need to know any syntax. We can even find cases of genuine communication which illustrate the same independence. In ordinary social dancing, for example, there is a great deal of communication between the partners, effected by means of slight anticipatory movements, pressures, and the like. We refer to these messages when we say the man "leads" the woman. Analysis of such communication would surely show that the woman responds to whole structured patterns of movement, not to isolated pushes or pulls. Yet all this has little relation to the formal rules governing the dance—to the fact that it is a fox-trot or a waltz or some other sequence of steps. An anthropologist who studied the dance as a custom might find a lot to say about the "generative" rules of the fox-trot, without ever discovering what really controls the leader's partner. He would be correct in assuming that the leader, at least, must "have" these rules, but incorrect if he assumed that the partner must have them also. Is language this kind of a dance? If it is, the cognitive psychologist need have little concern with the work of grammarians.

The question cannot be resolved without actually considering the grammars that have been proposed for natural language. If these turn out to be simple arrays of uninteresting rules, lacking in subtlety and indifferent to the meaning of what is said, the analogy of the fox-trot might become plausible. We would be tempted to look elsewhere for the structural basis of understanding. But if grammar turns out to be rich and intricate, and if its "generative" rules produce the very kind of structure the listener needs, the case will be different. The more complex the rules of grammar are, the more likely it is that they not only describe the cultural constraints on the speaker, but also provide the vehicle of understanding for the listener. Otherwise each of us would need *two* complex systems, one which enabled him to speak grammatically and another which permitted him to understand the sentences he heard. It is far simpler to suppose that each person has a single "grammatical system" which he uses both in speaking and in listening.

This brings the argument back to the attractive hypothesis of analysis-by-synthesis, which has appeared so often in this book. The hypothesis, as applied to linguistic processes, has already been used to deal with attention and immediate memory; here we find that it is also useful in dealing with the complexities of grammar. Consequently, Miller and Chomsky (1963, p. 465) are among those who support the Halle-Stevens proposal as the chief mechanism of speech perception. If it is accepted, there can no longer be any doubt that the study of syntax is an integral part of cognitive psychology. We deal with the sentences we hear by reformulating them for ourselves; we grasp their structure with the same apparatus that structures our own utterances.

In addition to these rather theoretical arguments, there are experimental reasons for supposing that syntax is crucial for the listener. Many experimenters have succeeded in manipulating perception, memory, and understanding by varying syntactic form. Here, too, the weight of their argument cannot be appreciated without considering the particular grammar, or *type* of grammar, on which it is based. Consequently, we must turn to a more specific account of the various forms which grammatical rules might take.

It is obvious that a set of rules appropriate for English would be inappropriate for Latin or Hopi or Sanskrit. The objectives of linguistic science might be set, rather modestly, at discovering the actual syntax governing each natural language. But this seems a pedestrian goal, and one of Chomsky's particular contributions was to set the sights of linguistics much higher. In his view, a fully satisfactory theory of grammar would indicate what *types* of rules we can expect to find; what properties must be shared by all natural grammars. The first step toward this objective was to enumerate and to analyze all imaginable types. Of these, three are particularly interesting: the so-called *Markov, phrase-structure,* and *transformational* grammars. A readable elementary account of them has been given by Miller, Galanter, and Pribram (1960, Ch. 11).

The Markov (or "left-to-right") grammars are so simple that they have never been taken seriously by linguists and are chiefly useful as negative examples. They are sets of rules in which the only constraints on each word to be uttered are the words that have been already spoken. Such a grammar might have a rule like: "after the sequence *The people . . .*, proceed with *are, who, of, you, . . .* but not with *the, car, am, . . . .*" It is clear that a person who used such a grammar would have to know an impossible number of cumbersome rules, if he were to deal with sentences involving long dependencies. In *The people who called and wanted to rent your house when you go away next year are from California,* the use of *are* depends on *people,* 15 words before.

The overwhelming arguments against Markov grammars are reviewed by Miller and Chomsky (1963), from whose article the foregoing example is taken. Chomsky has even given a formal proof that no such grammar could generate certain kinds of English sentences. A discussion of his proof is not necessary here, since it is clear intuitively that left-to-right rules do not provide "structure" in the sense we seek. If Markov grammars have any interest at all, it is because they are related to certain traditional hypotheses about verbal behavior, such as that words are conditioned responses, elicited primarily by earlier words functioning as stimuli. To the extent that Markov grammars are inadequate, these hypotheses are wrong.

Chomsky himself argues that only the transformational type of grammar, which is the most complex of the three possibilities, can actually deal with the regularities of English or any other language. Though he may be right—not all linguists agree with him—our discussion will begin with the simpler phrase-based grammars instead; i.e., with what is often called "surface structure." This level of analysis has a certain kinship with the grammar of "Grammar School" and will be relatively familiar to most readers. (To be sure, the traditional versions of phrase structure are unsatisfactory in many ways; for discussion see Rycenga and Schwartz, 1963.) Moreover, a number of psychological studies of grammar have been based on analysis into phrases or "constituents" and have shown that they play a significant role in cognition. Finally, even transformational grammars make use of phrase structure, so an understanding of transformations depends on a grasp of the simpler ideas at this level.

### *PHRASE-STRUCTURE GRAMMARS*

The claim that a set of elements is "structured" always means that a change in one element creates systematic changes in others, even if those others are remote from the first. The Gestalt psychologists pointed out that this is true of the visual field: contrast, grouping, and similar phenomena all represent remote effects of local variations. It is equally true of sentences: their elements are not independent, and the interdependence can extend over an essentially indefinite range. However, not all the interrelations are equally strong; the surface structure of sentences is *hierarchical.*

Visual organization is sometimes hierarchical also, and a visual example may help to make this notion clear. Consider the rolling wheel, which has been discussed by Duncker (1929), Metzger (1953), and many others. When a wheel rolls along a level surface, as in Figure 42a, a point

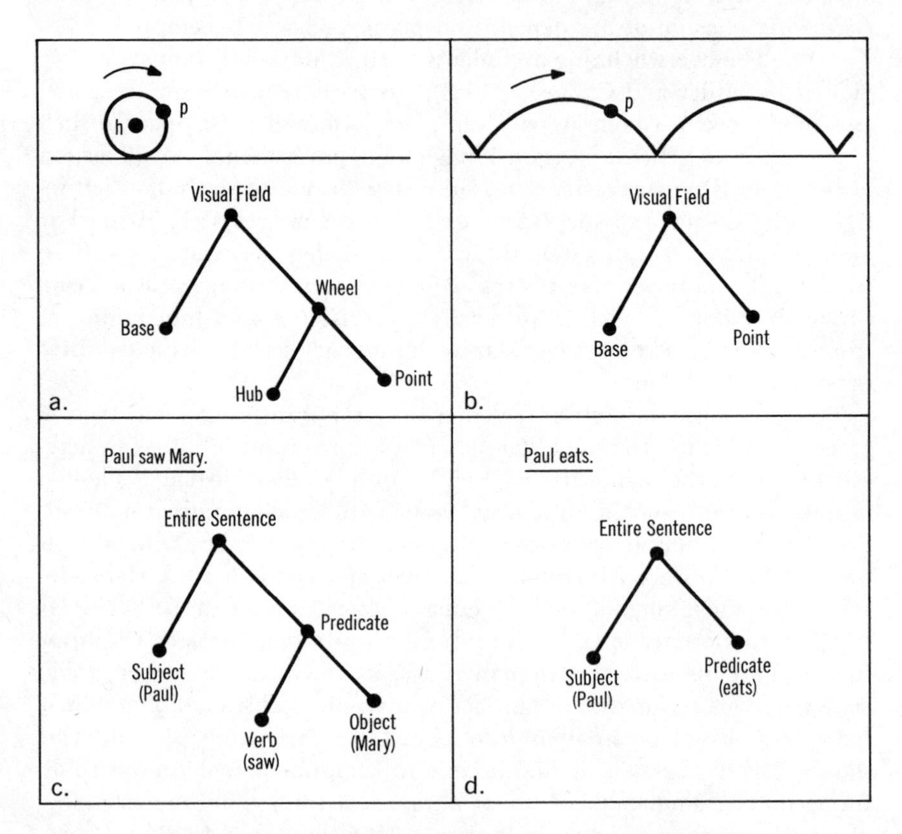


**Figure 42. Visual structure and sentence structure compared.**

on the circumference is seen as describing a circular path while the hub, with the wheel as a whole, is seen as moving horizontally. This experience is, in some sense, an illusion: the point *p* actually traverses the cycloidal path shown in Figure 42b with respect to the baseline. We can see this path if the wheel rolls in a darkened room, with only *p* illuminated. As soon as the hub *h* is also made visible, we stop seeing the cycloid and see the rolling motion of Figure 42a again.

When the hub is introduced, the perceiver immediately locates the peripheral point *p with respect to the wheel* rather than to the baseline; the wheel itself is then located with respect to the rest of the visual field. Such a "structure of reference" is represented by the abstract diagram in the lower part of Figure 42a, which shows that both the point and the hub belong to a hierarchically deeper unit, the wheel; the wheel and the baseline together make up the whole of the relevant visual field. When the wheel is made invisible so that only the cycloidal motion of *p* is seen, the structure of reference has the simpler form shown with Figure 42b.

A similar hierarchy of levels may be used to describe the surface structure of sentences. *Paul saw Mary* has a structure not unlike that of the visual example; it is diagrammed in Figure 42c. Again, there are three levels: *saw* and *Mary* are both part of the predicate, which together with *Paul* makes up the entire sentence. If a one-word predicate is used instead, say, *Paul eats,* we have the simpler structure of Figure 42d, which is like the simpler structure of reference for the cycloid.

The sentence diagrams contain one feature which is not provided for the visual case: each part, or "constituent," has a *label* ("subject," "predicate") indicating its structural role. Although such generic labels (perhaps "ground" for the baseline and "figure" for the wheel) seem superfluous in the visual case, they are very necessary in the sentence. To understand *Paul drinks,* one must know that *Paul* is the subject and *drinks* the predicate. This seems a trivial thing to know, until one considers examples such as *Time flies!,* which may be either a comment about subjective duration or an injunction to make speed measurements on a common species of insect.

Labeled sentence diagrams like those of Figures 42c and 42d are called "superficial phrase-markers." A phrase-structure grammar is a system of description which assigns at least one of them (i.e., at least one "constituent structure") to every proper sentence in a natural language. Those of Figure 42 are atypical, however, both because they are unusually simple and because they do not use standard linguistic notation. The "entire sentence" is usually represented by *S,* and terms such as *NP* (noun phrase) and *VP* (verb phrase) have become preferred to "subject" and "predicate." A typical phrase-marker for a simple sentence appears in Figure 43a, which represents *The rug covered the platform.*

There is, of course, nothing sacred about the form in which a phrase-marker is diagrammed. The surface structure of *The rug covered the platform,* represented by a tree in Figure 43a, can also be described by the labeled bracketing of Figure 43b. A linguist can provide such a description, in some convenient form, for every sentence. Because the "surface structure" described by the phrase-marker shows how words are related to one another, and what role each plays in the sentence, it seems to represent exactly what the listener needs. It defines the "constituents"

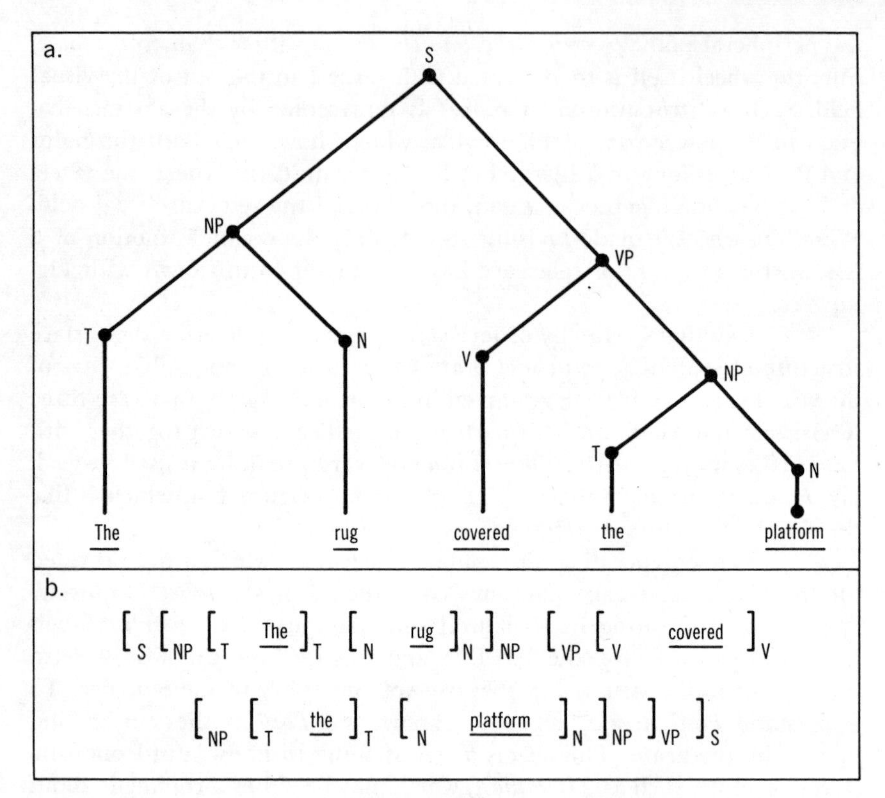


Figure 43. Two representations of a phrase-marker.

which were found by Garrett, Bever, and Fodor (1966; see Chapter 7 above) to function as cognitive units in the perception of speech.

The hypothesis that surface structure is crucial for understanding seems to be strengthened by consideration of certain kinds of ambiguity. Some sentences have more than one superficial phrase-marker. The two interpretations of *Time flies!,* for example, reflect markers which differ in the labeling of their branches. In the case of *They are eating apples,* the two alternatives even have differently shaped trees, as indicated in Figures 44a and 44b. Even with words *and word order* fixed, a sentence may be ambiguous until its structure is known.

It is important to note that this kind of ambiguity can be avoided in sentences which are spoken and heard. In speaking, we are able to emphasize or de-emphasize the relationship between *eating* and *apples* as necessary, with suitable stresses and changes of rhythm. Thus, the phrase-marker governs the pronunciation of sentences as well as their meaning.

There are many sources of ambiguity, and it must not be sup-

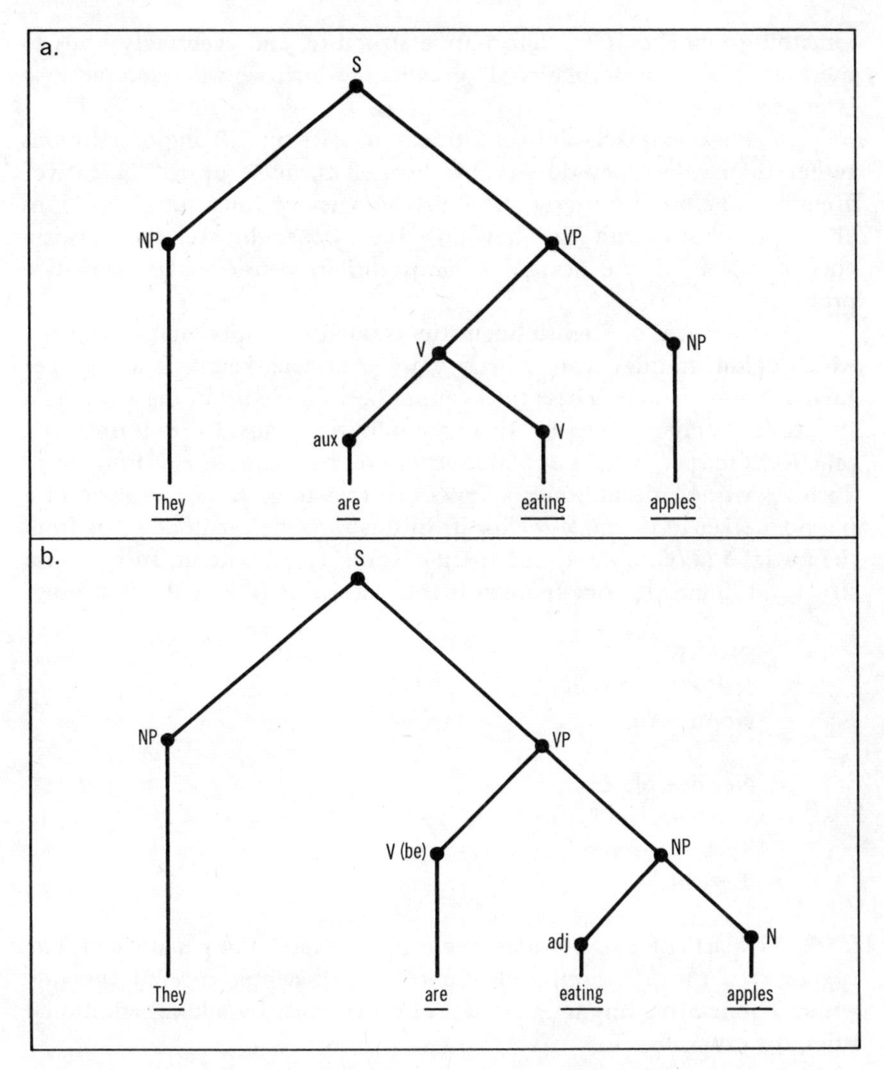


Figure 44. Two phrase-markers for an ambiguous sentence.

posed that all of them involve uncertainty about phrase structure. Some ambiguities (such as the meaning of *He is very wise*) have nothing to do with grammar at all. Others, which have played a crucial theoretical role in the recent development of linguistic theory, are grammatical and yet curiously subtle. The ambiguity of *Flying planes can be dangerous*, for example, cannot be resolved by examining its superficial phrase-marker. *Flying* and *planes* belong together whether the sentence refers to the act of flying an airplane or distinguishes between planes that fly and planes on the ground. An adequate account of this sentence seems to demand something more complex than phrase structure, and eventually leads to the notion of "transformational" grammar, which we will examine in a later section.

Phrase-markers are descriptions of structure. Being descriptions rather than rules, they do not, by themselves, make up a "generative" grammar. Before turning to the psychologically interesting questions about phrase structure (e.g., how does the listener discover the constituents of a sentence he hears?), we must briefly consider the generative problem.

One goal of English linguistics is the formulation of a set of rules which define and delineate exactly those phrase-markers that are proper English constructions. These rules cannot be a simple list of the acceptable structures themselves, because there are infinitely many. Current linguistic practice is to specify the acceptable structures by means of *rewriting rules.* Each rewriting rule indicates permissible ways to go from one node in a phrase-marker to the nodes below it; in this way one eventually gets from the initial *S* (a sentence) to the specific words at the bottom. In works on structural linguistics, one frequently sees "derivations" like the following:

S → NP + VP
NP → T + Noun
Noun → rug

Noun → platform
VP → Verb + NP
Verb → covered
T → the

With this particular set of rules, one can "generate" the p-marker of *The rug covered the platform,* and also of *The platform covered the rug,* without generating any ungrammatical statements. By adding additional rules, for example,

NP → T + Adj + Noun
T → a (in certain cases)
Adj → blue

the range of possible sentences is easily enlarged. As soon as *recursive* rules are included, such as (though this is a trivial example),

S → I + believe + that + S

the grammar becomes able to generate an infinite number of sentences: *I believe that the blue rug covered the platform,* and so on.

If the reader has skipped the preceding paragraph, he is probably a psychologist rather than a linguist. Intuition suggests that while such a system may define grammatical English, it is not the way people produce or understand sentences. Chomsky says so quite explicitly: "The . . . hypothesis . . . that the speaker produces the phrase-marker of a sentence *from top down*—that is, that he invariably selects grammatical constructions before he selects the words that he will use, etc.— . . . seems to me to have neither any particular plausibility nor any empirical support . . ." (1964b, p. 126). Nevertheless, we must not conclude that cognitive psychology is concerned only with the descriptive aspect of grammar and can avoid generative rules altogether. The constructive view of cognition in general, and "analysis-by-synthesis" in particular, must postulate some sort of generative mechanism. Since the number of possible sentences is infinite, it seems certain that phrase-markers are developed only as they are needed, in accordance with general principles known to the listener.

## *CUES TO PHRASE STRUCTURE*

There is little doubt that phrase structure is crucial for the listener. As Miller put it, "We cannot understand a sentence until we are able to assign a constituent structure to it" (1962a, p. 751). Nevertheless, one can hardly wait until he has the complete phrase-marker in hand, as it were, before trying to interpret what he hears. Most sentences are far too long for this to be practical; a dozen, or even several dozen, words can go by before the phrase-marker is fully determined. Moreover, we will soon see that phrase structure is responsible for the surpassing ease with which sentences (as opposed to random strings of words) can be remembered. This must mean that the listener begins to formulate the structure before the sentence is over; otherwise it would appear too late to be of any help! The synthesis involved is "local" at first, establishing the structure of a few words at a time. These "pieces" are then somehow integrated into a larger pattern, as the incoming information and the listener's cognitive resources permit.

Plausible as this model may be, we must not forget that an "analysis-by-synthesis" always needs some initial information on which to feed. Every constructive process in cognition must include a preliminary stage which provides it with cues; otherwise it will hallucinate rather than perceive. Where, in the stimulus, are the cues which suggest what sort of phrase-marker might be appropriate?

Perhaps the most obvious of the cues involved are the so-called "function words." Linguists have often pointed out that the vocabulary of English includes two different kinds of entries. The vast majority are so-called "content words," mostly nouns, verbs, adjectives, and adverbs, which (speaking very loosely) seem to "mean something." It is easy to coin new words of this sort, as new things to talk about make them necessary, and it is almost as easy to forget old ones. In contrast, the small set of function words changes so slowly that it is called a "closed class." In English, there are only one or two hundred of them: *the, in, however, we, any, that, who, but, and, after,* and so on. Although they lack clearly-defined "meanings" of their own, they have marked effects on the meanings of sentences. Examples are easy to find: compare *The ship sails* with *Ship the sails* or *The dog is the friend of man* with *Any dog is a friend of that man* (Francis, 1963). Most function words are short, and they occur very often in ordinary speech. It is widely agreed that they play crucial roles in delineating the structure of a sentence.

Very similar roles are played by certain *parts* of words, mostly endings, which also form a closed class: *-ly, -ment, -s, -tion, -ing,* etc. If one follows the linguistic usage of calling any fragment a "morpheme" if it has even a moderately consistent relation to the meaning of a sentence, then these fragments may be classed together with the function words as "closed-class morphemes." The positions of closed-class morphemes with respect to the sequence of words then define what some linguists call a "sentence frame."

As an example of a "frame," consider *All* ________*y were the* ________*s, and the* ________ ________*s* ________. While it does not fully determine the phrase-marker of the sentence, there are some fairly clear cues. The first ________*s* is probably a plural noun, since it is preceded by *the* and ends in *-s;* moreover, it must be the subject of the first half of the sentence, unless ________*y* can somehow be a plural noun agreeing with *were.* These and similar arguments suggest a structure like that of Figure 45, which would accommodate such sentences as *All gloomy were*

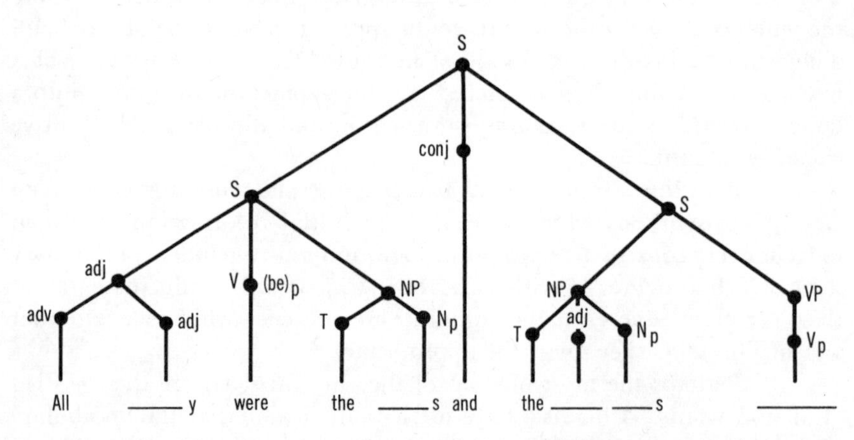


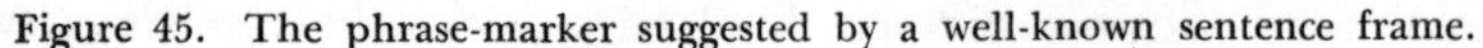


Figure 45. The phrase-marker suggested by a well-known sentence frame.

*the oracles, and the chief priests wept.* A few other phrase-markers are possible (as in *All twenty were the winners, and the forecast seems genuine*), but less plausible. Despite its minor ambiguities, this "frame" is a particularly good example of closed-class morphemes in action. In its best-known realization, the blanks are not filled with words at all. It is from Lewis Carroll: *All mimsy were the borogroves, and the mome raths outgrabe.* For a further discussion of its structure, see Francis (1963).

The "frame" of a sentence may be a useful clue to its structure, but it must not be confused with that structure itself. An illustration from Chomsky makes this point obvious. If we compare *Friendly young dogs seem harmless* with *Furiously sleep ideas green colorless,* we find that both have the same "frame," while only one has phrase structure. (The same is true if each string is read from right to left, but then the second one, *Colorless green ideas sleep furiously,* is the only English sentence.) Moreover, even as cues to structure, the importance of "sentence frames" must not be exaggerated. In cases like *I love cheese* (as opposed to *I love trees*) the "frame" is not even determined until understanding is complete. Some sentences, like Chomsky's *Sheep provide wool,* have no "frame" at all.

Whatever the available cues may be—and we will consider some others shortly—the listener uses them to guide his construction of fragmentary structures, and eventually of whole phrase-markers. These structures control and govern what he hears; one might say that they *are* what he hears. It is surely this possibility of construction which explains why words in sentences are easier to understand than the same words heard in isolation (Miller, Heise, & Lichten, 1951). In the experiment mentioned in Chapter 7, Miller (1962a, 1962b) showed that the perceptual effect of the phrase-marker is not just a matter of familiarity. Even when subjects were extremely familiar with all the strings of words that might occur, they could hear *Don brought his black bread* more easily than *Bread black his brought Don.* As an attempt to prove that structure is more powerful than simple repetitive experience, this experiment is again reminiscent of Gestalt psychology. Its logic is like that of Gottschaldt's (1926) embedded-figure study, which seemed to show that *no* amount of experience with a simple form could influence the subsequent perception of a complex one. Of course, neither experiment really proves that experience is unimportant for structure; only that certain kinds of experience are irrelevant for certain kinds of structural organization.

As we have seen, the listener's grammatical synthesis usually begins before a heard sentence has been completed. This means, among other things, that he can occasionally be fooled. A comedian with a good sense of timing can trick his listeners deliberately. This is particularly easy with cliches, as in *It isn't the heat, it's the timidity.* Here *timidity* is effective because it rhymes with another word, *humidity,* which exists only in the listener's covert synthesis. In this instance, the two alternative sentences have the same structure. When their phrase-markers are different, however, the result is not so much amusement as confusion. An example is: *Are you optimistic about the weather? Hope springs e-qually nice next year*. Here the change from the expected *Hope springs eternal . . .* converts *hope* to a verb and *spring* to a noun. The listener must reorganize the entire sentence, an activity which is usually attended by conscious effort. It is interesting that—to the best of my knowledge—a listener who is not paying attention cannot be either amused or confused in this way. This follows directly from the hypothesis that auditory attention is nothing but analysis-by-synthesis itself.

To say that the listener "constructs a phase-marker" does not mean that he visualizes a diagram like those which illustrate this chapter. Structure can be represented by many notations, and the internal representation of structure in a listener must differ in many respects from any that could be put into a book. To the extent that it is tangible at all, his representation must be *auditory,* making use of whatever resources are available to the sense of hearing. One of these resources was discussed at length in Chapter 9. The concept of a *rhythmic pattern* proved useful there to account for serial position effects, grouping, and the other phenomena of active verbal memory. Following up this lead, let us examine the possibility that phrase-markers are represented internally as rhythmic structures, or at least that they resemble rhythms in many respects.

A first consequence of this assumption is that the overt rhythms of speech, including stress, pause, and rate patterns, should be significant cues in the determination of the phrase-marker. There is little doubt that this is true. Because of the close relationship between phrase structure and pronunciation, pauses can easily resolve the ambiguities in *They are eating apples* or *Sam the mechanic can't come.* (In print, a comma in the second example can settle matters by telling the reader where to hesitate: *Sam, the mechanic can't come.*) Most linguists would probably agree that pronunciation ranks with "function words" and endings as an indicator of structure. In my view, it has more fundamental status than the others. They are merely cues to structure, and it is to be expected that different languages will emphasize different cues. The rhythm of speech, however, is very nearly the structure itself, corresponding intimately to the listener's internal representation. On this hypothesis, all languages should use pauses in about the same way: to indicate breaks between constituent phrases. Whether comparative linguistics supports this deduction, I do not know.

The hypothesis that phrase structure is closely related to rhythm and to grouping has a second consequence: variables which have been shown to depend on the latter should depend also on the former. Since rhythmic structure plays a large role in memory, phrase structure should have a similar—or even larger—effect. I argued earlier that gouping improves the memory span because the internally produced rhythm provides a way of producing the successive words at the right places. This should be true for phrase-markers as well; they provide and define structural nodes where words can be placed. Material with a definite surface structure should be particularly easy to recall or to learn.

Exactly this has been demonstrated in a series of experiments by Epstein (1961, 1962). Using material not unlike Lewis Carroll's, he showed that nonsense syllables are appreciably easier to learn when they appear in "sentence frames" than otherwise. The structured sequence *The yigs wur vumly rixing hum in jegest miv* is easier than *The yig wur vum rix hum in jeg miv,* despite its greater length. Moreover, the effect disappears when the items are exposed one-by-one in a memory drum, so the subject does not think of them as comprising a sentence. This is particularly interesting, because successive exposure of items in a drum has long been supposed to create "associations" between them. In Chapter 11, we will find reasons to doubt that "associations" exist at all, but, even if they do, we cannot ascribe sentence structure to their operation. Here is further evidence that sentences are not produced by a Markov "left-to-right" grammar; they have at least phrase structure.

The importance of phrase structure was not clearly understood at the time of the first studies in "psycholinguistics." In an influential experiment carried out a dozen years before Epstein's work, Miller and Selfridge (1950) obtained similar results with word-by-word "approximations to English." A second-order approximation, for example, is a string of words constructed by a Markov grammar to mirror the probabilities with which pairs of words occur naturally. Such a string is constructed by first choosing an initial item, say, *was.* The second is then selected with the aid of some device which reflects the transitional probabilities of the language (*was I* and *was he* are more common than *was dog* or *was is*), perhaps producing *he.* The third word is selected by using a similar device to establish the probability of pairs beginning with *he* (*he is, he went, he hated, he she, he extraordinarily* . . . ). In this way one may obtain *was he went to the newspaper is in deep end,* one of the strings used by Miller and Selfridge. Other orders of approximation reflect varying degrees of contextual determination. A fifth-order approximation like *they saw the play Saturday and sat down beside him* is produced with fidelity to the probabilities of five-word sequences; a first-order approximation like *abilities with that beside I for waltz you the sewing* only respects the probabilities of individual words.

Miller and Selfridge found that the higher approximations are easier to recall than the lower, which is not surprising since the higher ones look much more like ordinary English. They assumed that by quantifying the degree of sequential dependency, they were scaling the critical variable in "meaningfulness." But if people interpret sentences with a phrase-structure grammar rather than as a Markovian sequence, this is a misleading assumption. As Epstein has pointed out, the method of "approximations to English" confounds syntactic structure with other variables. It seems likely that *They saw the play Saturday and sat down beside him* is easier to remember than *was he went to the newspaper is in deep end* because it has a more coherent structure, not just because its sequences are more probable. This point is worth stressing because, although Miller has long since abandoned the Markov model in favor of transformational grammars, other psychologists still use "approximations to English" rather freely.

The importance of grammatical structure in organizing the way strings of words are learned is also illustrated by Thorndike's (1931, Chapter 2) classical experiments on what he called "belongingness." The subjects of these experiments listened 10 times to sequences like: *Alfred Dukes and his sister worked sadly. Edward Davis and his brother argued rarely. Francis Bragg and his cousin played hard. Barney Croft and his father watched earnestly. Lincoln Blake and his uncle listened gladly.* Afterwards they often knew *Barney's* last name, and what he had done, and how, but they almost never knew what word had followed *hard,* or *sadly.* No "associations" were formed between successive sentences, because the words involved did not "belong together," as Thorndike put it. Perhaps it would be better to say that they are not related by any syntactic structure. Indeed, McGeoch gave much this interpretation in 1942: "Subjects go with predicates, adverbs with verbs, last names with first ones. Sentences are closed units and lead on from each one to the next as from unit to unit, not as from one word to another" (p. 552).

The importance of phrase structure for memory is particularly clear in a recent experiment by Savin (personal communication, 1966). He studied the immediate recall of consonant trigrams (e.g., *B J Q*), using an interference method like that of Peterson and Peterson (1959). In one condition the subjects were simply given the trigrams, to be recalled after a few seconds of interpolated counting. In a second condition, they were given such sentences as *That man's initials are B J Q;* recall was significantly improved! This remarkable finding brings out the analogy between rhythmic structure and sentence structure. In Chapter 9, we saw that "adding" a rhythm to a series of digits does not seem to use up extra "storage space." In a sense it creates a more articulated space in which the digits can be stored, or of which they are a part. Here we see that "adding" a phrase-marker does not use up space either; it also seems to create positions where words can be put.

In a recent experiment related to Epstein's and Savin's, Glanzer (1962) found that even small pieces of a sentence frame can be helpful in learning. His subjects had to attach three-word responses to neutral stimuli. He found that triplets like *tah of zom* or *woj and kex,* containing function words, were easier to learn than control triplets like *yig food seb* or *mef think jat,* presumably because responses with function words in them could be learned as units more easily than the others. However, one would not expect such an effect to be substantial: three words are easily grouped even without any syntax. It will be recalled that Wickelgren (1964) found three to be the most effective group size in immediate memory. If even *yig food seb* can easily be perceived as a unit, there is little room for any effect of function words. Hence it is not surprising that other experimenters (Cofer, 1964; Marshall, 1965) have found Glanzer's effect weak and unreliable. Syntactic variables can have powerful effects only with material which otherwise overtaxes the subject's capacity.

It has long been known that meaningful sentences are easier to learn than random strings of words. Indeed, it was this phenomenon to which Miller and Selfridge related their work with approximations to English. From the present point of view, the explanation is simple enough; it has already been mentioned in connection with Epstein's work. Real sentences have a structure which nonsense does not, and thus permit the subjects to synthesize phrase-markers in which the words can be embedded. We can extend this approach further by taking account of the old observation that poetry is more easily learned than prose (McGeoch, 1942, p. 158). This superiority is hard to explain in terms of sequential probabilities, since poets tend to prefer *un*usual word combinations. It can be explained, however, if we assume that the rhythm of the poem provides additional structure, above and beyond the syntax of its sentences. This hypothesis would make some testable predictions about the *kinds* of poetry which ought to be easily memorizable, but apparently no such studies have been conducted.

In addition to function words, affixes, and rhythmic patterns, there is yet another cue to phrase structure which must be considered. This is *word position,* which, in a sense, is basic to all of the others. In *All mimsy were the borogroves,* we know that *borogroves* is a noun because it follows *the.* This is an argument for the importance of function words, but also for the importance of order. Function words and pauses serve as reference points, which help to indicate the syntactic roles of the words that follow or precede them.

In fact, according to some grammarians, the very definitions of "noun," "verb," and similar *word-classes,* must be formulated in terms of the positions where particular words can appear in sentence "frames." This version of grammar is not universally accepted, but it is surely better than the traditional definition of a noun as naming a "person, place, or thing." (It seems impossible to define "thing" at all, if it has to cover words as diverse as *growth, millisecond,* and *unicorn!*) Such a definition of the parts of speech is interesting, since word-classes themselves help to determine the phrase-marker. *Exterminate flies!* does not share the ambiguity of *Time flies!,* for example, because *exterminate* is unmistakably a verb. Even this cue becomes a matter of relative position (like all the others) if word-classes are fundamentally defined in a positional way.

To some extent, words preserve their character as nouns or verbs even in otherwise ambiguous contexts, or in isolation. *Sheep* and *wool* are always nouns; *provide* is a verb. If this character arises from the occurrence of the words at suitable positions in sentence frames, such positions must be learnable. An unknown word which repeatedly appears in "noun positions" should acquire the functional properties of a noun in other contexts, as when the subject attempts to define it, free associate to it, and so on. A number of experiments have confirmed these hypotheses: Werner and Kaplan (1950); McNeill (1963); Glucksberg and Cohen (1965). This kind of learning has been systematically exploited by Martin Braine (1963a, 1963b, 1965) as the basis for an ingenious theory of the development of grammatical understanding in children.

Position need not be defined only with reference to function words. In short sentences, such as the two-word constructions of young children, each word is either *first* or *last.* In studies using artificial languages, with "grammars" restricting some words to one position and some to another, Braine (1963a) has shown how readily children learn to follow positional rules and employ them in creating novel "sentences." In a developmental study (1963b), he has shown that such rules actually dominate the early speech of children, and that certain classes of words soon come to "fit" certain positions. His theoretical discussion (1963a) extends these notions to hierarchical structures and speculates on the role of pronunciation and function words in defining "learnable" positions. He also argues that some notion of word-association must supplement positional learning, but this argument would carry us too far afield here. From the present point of view, Braine's work is particularly interesting because it provides a bridge between rhythmic structure and phrase structure. In a two- or three-word sentence, "position" is a structurally defined concept (see Chapter 9), and the structure is very like a rhythmic one. It seems quite possible that the intricacies of phrase structure are produced by the gradual differentiation of sequences into such positions, first with respect to the ends of an utterance, and later in relation to specific words or word-classes.

At this point, it might seem that the aims of the present chapter have been accomplished. We have seen what superficial phrase structure is, how the listener uses it, what difference it makes, and even how it might develop. Once in echoic memory, auditory information is segmented and then resynthesized: a phrase-marker, or a succession of fragmentary markers, are developed to fit it on the basis of various available cues. The newly formed structure, including the words themselves, thereby finds its own place in auditory memory, where it can easily be renewed again and again.

Persuasive as this account may be, there are good reasons for remaining somewhat skeptical of it. Many linguists have argued (e.g., Bever, Fodor, & Weksel, 1965a, 1965b, in their dispute with Braine) that *no* account based only on the superficial phrase-marker can be satisfactory, because that marker itself is inadequate as a description of syntactic structure. To understand this claim, we must return to grammatical theory and examine Chomsky's conception of a "transformational grammar." The most radical—and also the most difficult—aspects of the "new linguistics" are its assumption that some phrase structures are actually transformations of others, and its elaboration of "deep structures" which this assumption makes necessary.

### *TRANSFORMATIONAL GRAMMAR*

The ambitions of the phrase-structure approach are limited to dealing with individual sentences. The grammar aims at providing an adequate description of the structure of each sentence and a set of rules which might "generate" it. Despite what has been said so far, a grammar limited to constituent analysis apparently cannot achieve either objective. Chomsky's notion of "grammatical transformation" is a suggestion that a higher ambition may actually be easier to fulfill. By examining the relations *among* sentences, the linguist may be able to describe their individual structures in a better way.

Consider such superficially similar sentences as *Growling lions can be dangerous* and *Subduing lions can be dangerous.* Both have essentially the same phrase-marker, in which *Growling lions* or *Subduing lions* is the noun phrase. Nevertheless, there is a sense in which they have very different structures. *Growling* is something that lions do, while *Subduing* is something which is done to them. A single phrase-marker can never represent facts of this kind, because the crucial data are in another sentence altogether, or at least would appear in another sentence if they were to be expressed overtly. The listener knows that there is a potential *Lions growl* but no *Lions subdue;* there might be *Tarzan subdues lions* but never *Tarzan growls lions.* The meaning of such a sentence as *Growling lions can be dangerous* is clear only because of what we know about other sentences with *growl,* or more exactly because we have some structure, "deeper" than a single phrase-marker, which is related to those other sentences as well as to the given one. Without guidance from such a deeper structure, ambiguity results. This is clear in *Flying planes can be dangerous,* where one cannot tell whether *flying* is used as in *planes fly* or as in *Tarzan flies planes.*

A great many potential sentences are interrelated by these "deep structures." Consider the differences among interrogative forms like *Are growling lions dangerous?* and *Is subduing lions dangerous?;* passive forms like *The lions were subdued* (but not *The lions were growled*); additional modifications like *Growling and snarling lions can be dangerous* (but not *Subduing and snarling lions can be dangerous*); negatives like *No growling lions can be dangerous*—at least if they are like barking dogs—and *Not subduing lions can be dangerous*—especially if you have once aroused their anger. These relationships are so systematic and far-reaching that it seems absurd not to represent them directly in the structural descriptions of sentences. They are regularities to which speakers conform, and which hearers expect.

The first systematic treatment of such relations was that of Chomsky (1957), following on an insight of Zellig Harris. He argued that many kinds of English sentences cannot comfortably be described by single phrase-markers. Such descriptions may work moderately well for simple, active, declaratory sentences like *Lions growl, Tarzan subdues lions,* or *The rug covered the platform,* but they cannot easily handle discontinuous constituents (*Turn the lights out*), passives, questions, and many other forms. It seems best to regard the more complex forms as versions of the simpler ones that have been *transformed* by various operations. This gives the "generative" aspect of grammatical description, which seemed almost like an unnecessary frill in our discussion of superficial phrase structure, a central role.

Some phrase-markers can, then, be derived from others with the aid of grammatical transformations. Apart from the surface structure described earlier, sentences have "deep structure," which indicates how and from what they are derived. The relatively uncomplicated examples in which these problems do not arise represent a special and simple type of structure called a "kernel." The deep structure of a kernel sentence does not differ in fundamental ways from its surface structure. Derived sentences, in contrast, have structures which include one or more "optional" transformations and cannot be adequately described without some kind of generative transformational grammar. Because the deep structures of meaningfully related sentences like *Tarzan subdued the lions, The lions were subdued by Tarzan, Did Tarzan subdue the lions?,* etc. have much in common, it can be argued that deep structure is more important, more fundamental than what appears on "the surface."

Chomsky's theoretical claims may be divided into two parts. First, he argued that there is more to sentences than a phrase-structure grammar can reveal; that a notion of deep structure is necessary as well.

Second, he advanced certain specific grammatical proposals for the description of deep structure. In his early work, he suggested that it was best represented as a series of phrase-markers related by transformations. More recently (1965), he has advocated a somewhat different grammar, and other linguists have also put forward proposals. The issues involved here are highly technical and need not concern us (see Clifton & Odom, 1966, for a partial review). But even Chomsky's first claim seems like strong medicine if it is relevant to the processes of cognition. Can we really suppose that the listener not only detects the surface structure of a sentence, but also its transformational history?

As noted earlier, we are not logically required to assume that grammatical structure is directly relevant to cognition. However, many lines of evidence have been cited to show that superficial phrase structure is relevant indeed: it seems to govern perceptual segmentation and sustain recall. Whether deep structure plays a similar role is an empirical question, and at the present time a hotly disputed one.

Before we review the research which is relevant to this issue, a historical parallel may help to clarify it. The idea of deep structure is not without precedent; like other linguistic concepts, it has an analogue in Gestalt psychology. The notion that sentences are understood by referring them to simpler kernels is reminiscent of the assumption that figures are perceived with reference to simpler or ideal figures. This point was made by Koffka in his discussion of Wulf's study of spontaneous changes in recall. In reproducing a jagged line from memory, most subjects erred by making the angles sharper than they should have been. One person, however, ". . . reproduced the figure with a progressive flattening. The reason . . . is clear . . . . Whereas the other subjects perceived this pattern as a zigzag or something similar, this one saw it as a 'broken line,' i.e., as a modification of a straight line" (1935, p. 499).

We know by now that the Wulf experiment has many pitfalls (see Riley, 1962, for a review). The quotation shows only that Koffka agreed with Chomsky in using more than one level of structure to account for cognitive processing. The area of agreement between them can also be illustrated with a more direct analogy. We have seen that two kinds of ambiguous sentences are important in linguistic theory. *They are eating apples* has two different surface structures (Figure 44), but *Flying planes can be dangerous,* with a single surface structure, has two alternative interpretations in depth. Similarly, there are two important kinds of ambiguous figures in vision. Some, like the Peter-Paul goblet (Figure 26, Chapter 4) have two alternative shapes even superficially. But others, like the Necker cube (Figure 30, Chapter 6) are *literally* ambiguous in depth. The surface organization of the drawing—the distinction between figure and ground—is perfectly definite; ambiguity arises only when it is referred to a constructed three-dimensional space. Thus, we can give at least an analogical interpretation of the claim that sentences are interpreted in terms of deep as well as surface structure. However, the evidence on this point is not entirely clear.

Perhaps the first relevant experiment was that of Mehler (1963; see also Miller, 1962a). His subjects were to memorize eight sentences. One of these was a kernel sentence like *The secretary has typed the paper,* but all the others incorporated the effects of one or more optional transformations. Only three transformations were used—passive, negative, and query—but these led to seven kinds of transformed sentences because they could appear in combination. *Hasn't the paper been typed by the secretary?* results from applying all three transformations to the phrase-marker that underlies the kernel sentence above. Figure 46b presents examples of the eight types of sentences used by Mehler, together with a list of the transformations (*P, N,* or *Q*) which must be applied to generate them. The subjects were given five "prompted" trials to learn the sentences; that is, each recall trial included a prompting word (e.g., "paper") for every sentence. Average learning curves for the eight types appear in Figure 46a.

Most of the errors, other than downright omissions of whole sentences, were "syntactic." The (phrase-markers of the) incorrect responses were usually transformations of the (phrase-markers of the) right ones: *The girl hasn't worn the jewel* instead of *Hasn't the girl worn the jewel?* In itself, this is not particularly interesting. Hardly any other kind of error is possible in a task where prompts are given and synonyms accepted as correct. More important is Mehler's discovery of a "shift toward the kernel." This shift expressed itself in several aspects of the data. Kernel sentences themselves were easier to learn than others (see Figure 46a); subjects frequently erred by replacing a transformed sentence with its kernel, but rarely in the other direction. To some extent, even errors which did not involve the kernel tended to "move toward" it, so that too few transformations were present in the recalled version.

Here again an analogy with Gestalt concepts seems apt. There may be a tendency to remember the simpler kernel rather than the transform, just as there was once said to be a tendency to remember good figures rather than poor ones. The quotation from Koffka given earlier is very much in this spirit. But as usual, structural linguistics offers far more detailed analysis than Gestalt psychology did. Miller (1962a) proposed a very specific model to fit such data, based on the assumption that the presence or absence of each transformation was remembered independently. Each sentence was thought to demand four independent feats of recall: say, *girl-wears-jewel, passive, negative,* and *no question.* Although this model fitted some of Mehler's preliminary data, Mehler himself backed off from the assumption of complete independence in his final (1963) report. Nevertheless, he also felt that grammatical trans-

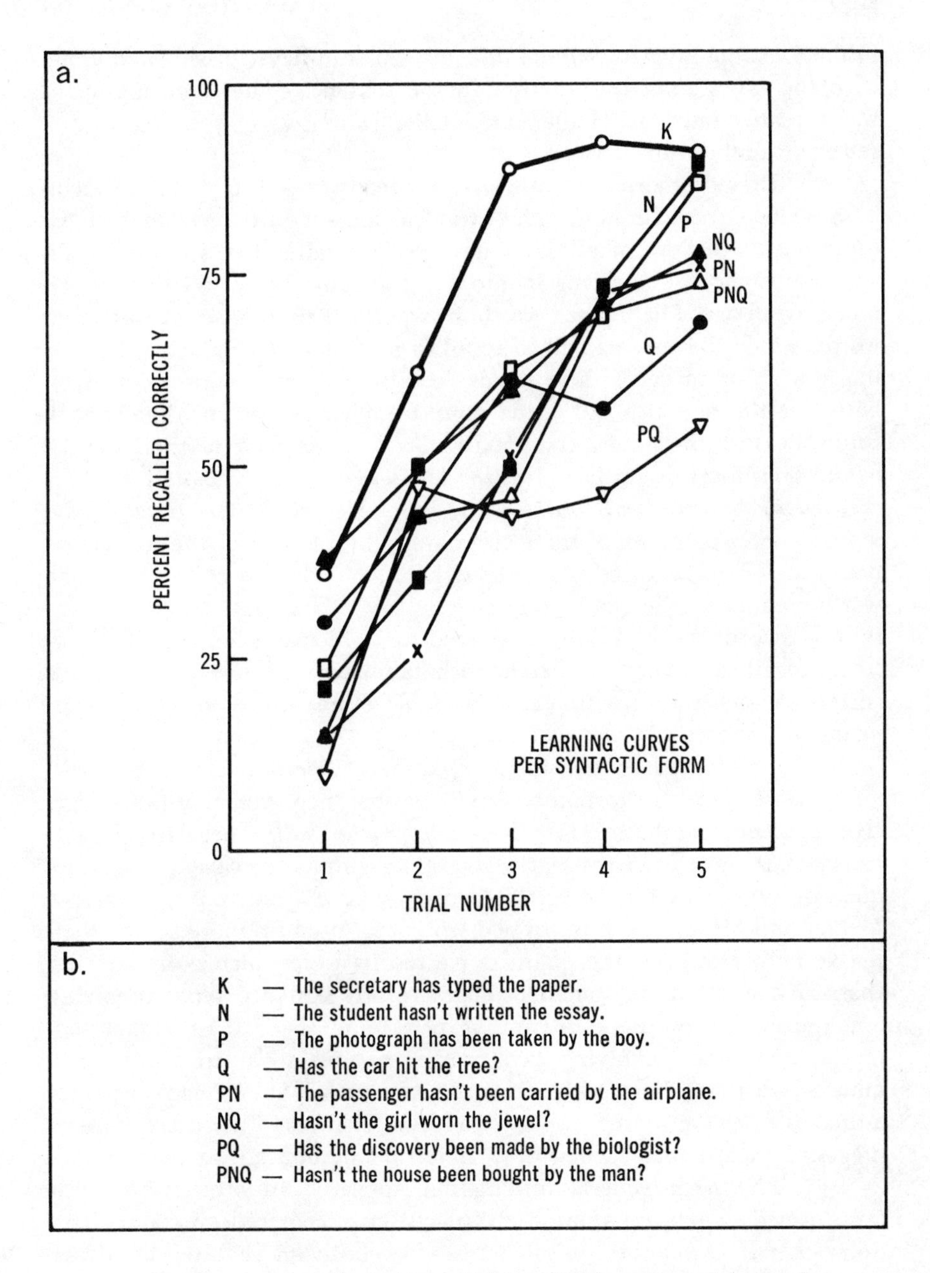


Figure 46. Sample sentences from Mehler's (1963) study, and its results.

formations represent *additional* information, and have to be stored *along with* the raw kernel information in the sentence. The same argument was repeated later by Mehler and Miller (1964), in connection with a retroactive-inhibition design.

Do grammatical transformations really "take up space" in memory? Savin and Perchonock (1965) tried to answer this question with an ingenious "overflow" method. One can determine the volume of an irregular object by dropping it into a full glass of water and noting how much overflows. The "water" in their experiment was a set of unrelated words, which the subject had to recall *in addition* to a sentence. By noting how many more of these words "overflowed" (i.e., were not remembered) as the sentence was made more complex, Savin and Perchonock could measure the added complexity. On a single trial of their experiment, the subject might hear *Has the boy been hit by the ball? . . . tree, cat, truck, month, lamp, rain, shirt, blue.* He tried first to recall the sentence, then as many of the words as possible. Recall of the words was not entirely unstructured: the subject knew that the list consisted of one word from each of eight categories ("nature," "animal," "vehicle," etc.) in a fixed order. Using only those trials on which the sentence was correctly recalled, Savin and Perchonock tabulated the number of words correct in each case, treating it as an inverse measure of the amount of memory "used up" by the sentence.

The sentences used included kernels (*The boy has hit the ball*) and a variety of transformation-types: passive, negative, question, negative question, emphatic (*The boy did hit the ball!*), negative passive, passive question, passive negative question, emphatic passive, and who-question (*Who has hit the ball?*). As one would expect from the work of Mehler and Miller, the transformed sentences "used up more space" than the kernels. However, the quantitative results were much more striking than such a summary statement suggests. All sentence types involving one transformation took up significantly more space than kernel sentences, and those involving two transformations took up significantly more space than those with either component alone. In fact, separate estimates of the amount of space used by each transform agreed closely, suggesting again that each was an independent burden on memory.

The same general finding has appeared in other work with transformed sentences, where the subjects' tasks centered on comprehension rather than memory. In one series of experiments reported by Miller (1962a), subjects were asked to make transformations of kernel sentences —to rephrase them as passive, as negative, or as passive-negative—and then to find the transformed sentence in a list of alternatives. In a related experiment by McMahon (cited by Miller, 1962a), subjects had to decide whether sentences of these various types were true or false. Similar research has been reported by Gough (1965). All of these studies found that subjects need more time to deal with transformed sentences than with kernels. Indeed, most of them found, as did Savin and Perchonock, that "transformation times" were *additive.* If one computes the time needed for the passive transformation (by subtracting the time needed for a kernel from the time needed for a passive) and the time needed for the negative transformation, one can predict the time required by the passive-negative by adding both to the kernel time. There are some exceptions to this principle where false statements are involved, and for the negative-question, but for the most part it has been confirmed in a number of studies.

Miller and his associates have a rather straightforward theoretical interpretation of these findings. More transformations take more "storage space," provide more opportunity for error, and take more time to unravel when the truth or falsity of a sentence is at stake. As Mehler (1963, p. 350) puts it: ". . . *S*s do not recall the answer verbatim, but rather . . . they analyze it syntactically and encode it as a kernel sentence plus appropriate transformation. For example, if the sentence is *The ball has been hit by the boy,* then *S* presumably codes it as an underlying kernel plus some 'mental tag' that indicates that the passive transformation must be applied for recall."

This view has not been universally accepted. Among those with a different approach are Martin and Roberts (1966), who have had some success with a nontransformational measure of the complexity of sentences. Their measure is based on the work of Yngve (1960, 1962), whose analysis of sentences uses only "constituent structure," i.e., only the superficial phrase-marker. Yngve argues that the construction of a phrase-marker by the listener (or the speaker) is an ongoing process which requires a certain amount of temporary memory if the subject is not to lose his place. In particular, phrase-markers with more "levels" are more demanding. In *The paper has been typed by the secretary* (diagrammed in Figure 47a), the speaker must know as he pronounces *has* that (1) it is part of the auxiliary verb, which (2) is part of the main verb, which (3) is part of the verb phrase; all of these constituents will have to be properly concluded before the sentence is over. Presumably, the listener must have a similar array of expectations as he hears *has.* This "depth" can be conveniently measured by counting the number of left branches in the tree which lead to *has,* in this case three. Martin and Roberts call this the "Yngve number" of *has* and index the depth of a sentence by the average of the "Yngve numbers" of its component words.

Figure 47a indicates that the mean "depth" of *The paper has been typed by the secretary* is 1.38. The active version of the same sentence, *The secretary has typed the paper,* is diagrammed in Figure 47b.

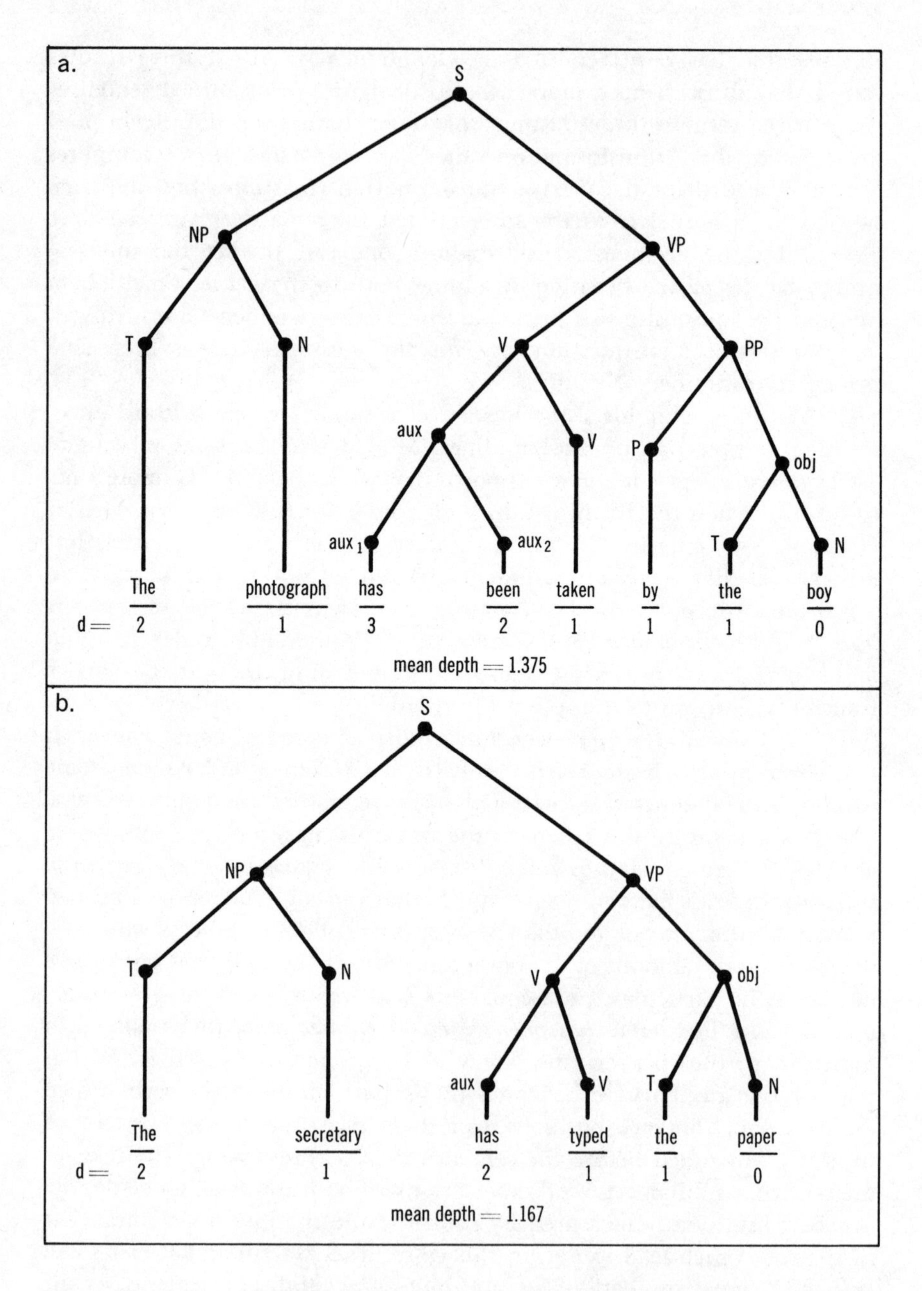


**Figure 47.** Active and passive versions of a sentence, showing how their mean depths are computed from the phrase-marker.

It never reaches a depth of three at any point, and so its mean depth is only 1.17. Martin and Roberts believe that this difference in depth, rather than the extra transformation in the deep structure, is responsible for the greater difficulty of the passive sentences in Mehler's study. In their own experiment, they varied depth and transformational structure independently. They found no increase in difficulty as transformations were added (in fact, passives, passive-negatives, and the like were somewhat *better* recalled than kernels!), but there was a distinct and consistent effect of increased depth.

It seems unlikely that the Yngve criterion of complexity will prove entirely satisfactory. It cannot possibly account for the results of Savin and Perchonock, for example. They found that even the question-transformations (*Has the secretary typed the paper? Who has typed the paper?*) add to what must be remembered; yet the phrase-marker of the direct question has the same depth as that of the active form (Figure 47b) and the "who-question" has even less. Moreover, this formulation sidesteps all the problems with which transformational grammars attempt to deal. It is indeed somewhat implausible to suppose that listeners strip sentences to their kernels one transformation at a time, only to reassemble them in the same way later. However, it seems equally hard to imagine them keeping track of the phrase-marker, node-by-node, as in Yngve's model.

In short, we do not yet understand the cognitive consequences of complex sentences. There can be no doubt, I think, that material is far more easily handled when it has phrase structure than when it has none. Sentences are better recalled than random strings because a phrase-marker can "carry" more words than a simple rhythmic pattern can. But as the syntactic structure becomes more complicated, along dimensions which are still controversial, it becomes a burden in its own right, and performance suffers accordingly.

As if this were not sufficiently confusing, we must face the fact that syntax is not the only variable which affects the way sentences are understood, remembered, and used. Not even psycholinguistics can ignore meaning indefinitely, however difficult it may be to treat. Some effects of meaning are even rather analogous to those of syntax. "Semantically anomalous" sentences like *Hunters simplify motorists across the hive* are harder to hear (Miller & Isard, 1963) and to remember (Marks & Miller, 1964) than sensible ones like *Gadgets simplify work around the house* or *Accidents kill motorists on the highways.* The reason is not because the sensible ones are more "predictable": nearly all sentences are unique. Rather, it is just because they make more sense; they fit better into something that might be described as a cognitive structure, though it is surely not syntactic.

Such effects of sensibleness on memory and perception have long been familiar to psychologists. Although they certainly occur in immediate recall of single sentences (Zangwill, 1956), they have mainly been described in connection with long-term memory (Bartlett, 1932). They surely involve more than one modality and more than one kind of psychological experiment. It would be misleading to deal with them as if they only concerned auditory memory. Such effects bring us directly up against the general problem of what people know, how they come to know it, and how they use their knowledge.

# *Part IV*

# *The Higher Mental Processes*

*Chapter 11*

# *A Cognitive Approach to Memory and Thought*

It is assumed that remembering and thinking are analogous to adaptive movement and motor skill; they also resemble the synthetic processes of visual memory and speech perception. Stored information consists of traces of earlier constructive acts, organized in ways that correspond to the structure of those acts. However, the "traces" are not dormant copies of earlier experiences, somehow aroused into consciousness from time to time. Stored information is never aroused, it is only used, just as stimulus information is used in the act of perception.

The processes of remembering are themselves organized in two stages, analogous to the preattentive and attentive processes of perception. The products of the crude, wholistic, and parallel "primary processes" are usually elaborated by the "secondary processes," which include deliberate manipulation of information by an active agent. An analogy to the "executive routines" of computer programs shows that an agent need not be a *homunculus.* However, it is clear that motivation enters at several points in these processes to determine their outcome. Thus, an integration of cognitive and dynamic psychology is necessary to the understanding of the higher mental processes.

This chapter will be concerned with relatively *delayed* vicissitudes of sensory information—with remembering events that happened more than a few seconds ago, or solving problems that require some use of stored information. The "constructive" view of these processes, which is to be presented here, has a long history. Bartlett, who demonstrated long ago that reorganization and change are the rule rather than the exception in memory, has been its outstanding advocate. At the end of *Remembering,* for example, he remarks:

. . . the description of memories as "fixed and lifeless" is merely an unpleasant fiction . . . memory is itself constructive . . . . I have regarded it rather as one achievement in the line of the ceaseless struggle to master and enjoy a world full of variety and rapid change. Memory, and all the life of images and words which goes with it, is one with the age-old acquisition of the distance senses, and with that development of constructive imagination and constructive thought wherein at length we find the most complete release from the narrowness of presented time and place (1932, pp. 311, 312, 314).

It is hard to disagree with these sentiments, especially after one has spent ten chapters expounding an active, constructive theory of the more immediate cognitive processes. Nevertheless, it must be admitted that this kind of theorizing deals at best with half the problem. Even if the constructive nature of memory is fully acknowledged, the fact remains that information about the past must be somehow stored and preserved for subsequent use. Today's experience must leave some sort of trace behind if it is to influence tomorrow's construction.

This problem was not central to earlier chapters of this book, because they dealt primarily with the cognitive transformations of *present* (or very recent) input. The question "what is being transformed" was easily answered in terms of stimulus information. Only in discussing imagery and hallucination (Chapter 6) did we consider processes that may be entirely "inner-directed." That argument attempted to show that visual memory is just as "constructive" as perception itself. However successful the attempt may have been, it left a whole series of questions rather awkwardly unanswered. If images are constructions, what is their raw material? How is this raw material organized? For that matter, how is the process of construction organized? What determines the particular image that is constructed; what purpose does it serve?

These questions do not apply to imagery alone but to all remembering, and to thinking and problem-solving as well. They can be answered only by an adequate theory of memory and thought. For various reasons—some of which will be discussed below—we are far from having such a theory today. The views to be presented here are not a theory either, and are offered only for their suggestive value. It is not even possible to review the experimental evidence that bears on them, in the manner of the earlier chapters, because there is far too much of it. The purpose of this epilogue is not so much to present a cognitive theory of the higher mental processes as to show that one is possible, consistent with the foregoing treatment of visual and auditory cognition.

## *THE REAPPEARANCE HYPOTHESIS*

Given the fact that information about the past is somehow preserved, it is important to ask what aspects of experience are stored, how the stored information is organized, how and why it is recovered, and by whom. As noted in Chapter 1, we are not primarily interested in the way information is physically stored by the brain. Psychology deals with the organization and use of information, not with its representation in organic tissue. Our question is the one which has been addressed in the past with such concepts as *traces, ideas, associations, schemata, clusters, habit-family hierarchies,* and *response-strengths.*

Perhaps the simplest and the most influential account of memory is that given long ago by the English empiricist philosophers. Hobbes, Locke, Hume, and Mill all assumed that one retains "ideas," or "conceptions," which are nothing but slightly faded copies of sensory experiences. These ideas are linked to one another by bonds called "associations." Ideas become "associated" whenever the original experiences occur simultaneously or in rapid succession ("temporal contiguity"), and perhaps also if they are similar. A person's ideas are not all conscious at any given moment. Instead, they become aroused successively, so that only one or a few are active at once. The order in which they "come to mind" is governed by the associative links, and therefore by prior contiguity in time. As James Mill wrote in 1829, "Our ideas spring up, or exist, in the order in which the sensations existed, of which they are copies" (Dennis, 1948, p. 142).

In this view, mental processes are by no means "constructive." Instead of the creation of something new in each act of remembering, there is only the arousal of something that already exists. The ideas lie dormant most of the time and spring to life intermittently when they are aroused or—as Freud put it—"cathected." Indeed, Freud's view of truly unconscious thinking, which he called the "primary process," resembled Mill's in many ways. He, too, supposed that ideas exist even when they are inactive, and that the flow of mental activity, or cathexis, tended to follow "association paths" (1900, p. 529). However, Freud did not leave this flow to its own devices as Mill had. Above it, he postulated elaborate subsystems like the ego, and executive functions like "censorship"; below, an internal source of excitation in the form of the sexual drive. Mill had resisted even this much inner-determination or spontaneity. Even where sex was concerned, he treated thinking as if it were entirely stimulus-bound: "The spot on which a tender maiden parted with her lover, when he embarked on the voyage from which he never returned, cannot afterwards be seen by her without an agony of grief" (Dennis, 1948, p. 145).

The notion that the stored information consists of ideas, suspended in a quiescent state from which they are occasionally aroused, has a very long history in psychology. It seems to me so important—and so misguided—that it deserves a special name. Here I will call it the "Reappearance Hypothesis," since it implies that the same "memory," image, or other cognitive unit can disappear and reappear over and over again. It has always had many supporters and a few beleaguered opponents, of whom William James is the most quoted: "A permanently existing 'idea' or 'Vorstellung' which makes its appearance before the footlights of consciousness at periodical intervals, is as mythological an entity as the Jack of Spades" (1890, Vol. 1, p. 236).

Despite James' opposition, the Reappearance Hypothesis has never stopped exerting a malevolent fascination over psychologists. It was adopted not only by associationism and psychoanalysis, but by behaviorism and even—as we shall see—by Gestalt psychology. The behaviorists introduced a new view of the elements involved—stimuli and responses were associated, rather than ideas—but they endowed the response with the same permanence that had once characterized the idea. Such terms as "habit strength" (which continues to exist even when the habit is dormant), "stimulus control" (of an independently existing response), and "stimulus generalization" (the response conditioned to one stimulus can also be elicted by another), all assume that something exists continuously and makes an occasional appearance "before the footlights." The stage on which it appears is observable behavior rather than consciousness, but the principle of Reappearance still applies.

This assumption is so ingrained in our thinking that we rarely notice how poorly it fits experience. If Reappearance were really the governing principle of mental life, repetition of earlier acts or thoughts should be the natural thing, and variation the exception. In fact, the opposite is true. Precise repetition of any movement, any spoken sentence, or any sequence of thought is extremely difficult to achieve. When repetition does occur, as in dramatic acting or nonsense-syllable learning or a compulsive sequence of actions, we ascribe it either to long, highly motivated practice or to neurotic defensiveness.

What *is* natural, on the contrary, is adaptive variation. We saw in Chapter 6 that visual images are not copies but suitably constructed originals, in Chapter 9 that verbal memory contains new rhythmic organizations rather than copies of stimuli, and in Chapters 7 and 10 that the words and sentences of normal speech are hardly ever duplicates of anything said earlier. The same generalization can be made about long-term memory, as Bartlett (1932) showed so vividly. Verbatim recall of a story occurs very rarely, while reorganization in line with the interests and values of the subject must be expected.

Even the simple conditioned response illustrates the weakness of the Reappearance Hypothesis. Although *theories* based on conditioning generally assume that "the response" is made conditional on a new stimulus through some form of reinforcement, no such "response" is observable. It is generally agreed that ". . . the CR and UCR are never strictly the same, and that the conditioned response is not simply a duplicate of the unconditioned one" (Kimble, 1961, p. 52).

Perhaps it is not surprising that behaviorists and psychoanalysts both continue to make Mill's Reappearance assumption; their historical roots in associationism are fairly clear. More striking is the degree to which their historical opponents, the Gestalt psychologists, adopted the same stance. In the Gestalt view, each perceptual experience lays down a "trace." Contiguous perceptions result in grouped *traces,* and associative recall consists of the rearousal of traces via these groups. To be sure, the aggregate, or "trace-field," was assumed to be active and self-organizing. Individual traces tend toward simpler forms, and groups like the successive nonsense syllables of a list form unified *structures,* which can submerge some of their parts (intraserial inhibition) and accentuate others (the isolation effect). Nevertheless, the Reappearance Hypothesis was not abandoned. Gestalt theory and its opponents agreed that stored information consists essentially of copies (traces) of earlier events (ideas, responses, perceptions). These copies are supposedly linked (associated) to form pairs or larger groups (complex ideas, response sequences), and they are aroused from time to time by means of these links. So great was the area of agreement that Osgood (1953) could find only a single testable difference between the Gestalt and the S–R theories of memory: the dubious hypothesis that memory traces change autonomously toward better form (see Riley, 1962, for a review of the inconclusive search for such changes).

In "Toward a Cognitive Theory of Associative Learning," Rock and Ceraso (1964) take a position very similar to that of Gestalt psychology. They advance forceful arguments against stimulus-response theory, pointing out that the very distinction between "stimulus" and "response" is artificial and confusing where verbal memory is concerned. However, they are unflinchingly loyal to the Reappearance Hypothesis.

A central feature of cognitive theory is the construct of a representational memory trace. This memory trace is conceived of as the product of learning, and serves as the basis of memory. The memory trace is taken to be representational in the sense that activation of a trace corresponding to a prior experience will give rise to a new experience similar to that prior experience (p. 112).

Although Rock and Ceraso choose to call their approach a "cognitive theory," it makes so little appeal to transformations and constructive processes that a better name might be "neo-associationism." They are not unaware of this:

Our intent in using the word "cognitive" is to do justice to the experiential aspects of learning and recall. If we do not give it any other surplus meaning (as, for example, notions about parts and wholes, emergentism, or the like) our meaning is approximately the same as that of classical association theory. Thinkers such as Locke, Hume, Titchener, and James were concerned with the association and recall of ideas. It is only the displacement of association theory by behavior theory that makes it necessary at this time to point up certain of its features that have been prematurely cast aside (p. 113). [They go on to say that their view differs from classical associationism in that certain perceptual organizing processes are assumed to precede the actual formation of the trace.]

The Reappearance Hypothesis has dominated not only theories about memory but also the experimental techniques used to investigate it. Studies of rote learning take for granted that the same nonsense-syllable response can be elicited over and over again, and ask only how its reappearance depends on certain variables. Similarly, studies of "concept formation" nearly always assume that the same classificatory response can occur repeatedly; the subject need only "attach" it to the proper stimuli. This theoretical commitment makes most of these studies difficult to interpret from a cognitive point of view. If "associations" (in the sense of connections between reappearing traces or responses) do not exist, it makes little sense to ask whether they are learned in a single trial, or more slowly in homogeneous lists, or more quickly with distributed practice. Experiments dealing with such questions have sometimes uncovered interesting phenomena, but they will not be reviewed here.

Of course, in an operational sense there is no doubt that responses *do* reappear. Subjects can be observed to press the same lever repeatedly, or to speak what sounds like the same syllable on many different trials. With prolonged practice, so much stereotypy may be created that the successive responses become indistinguishable in every respect, even in the subject's own awareness. But the fact that simple operations fail to distinguish between the complex problem-solving of the naive subject and the bored stereotypy of the sophisticated one does not make the distinction unimportant. Rather, it suggests that we should get better operations.

### *THE UTILIZATION HYPOTHESIS*

Is there an alternative to Reappearance? If the stored information does not consist of dormant ideas or images or responses, how are we to conceptualize it? Following Bartlett and Schachtel, we can agree that recall and thought are both constructive processes, but the metaphor of construction implies some raw material. Moreover, since repeated recalls of the "same event," or repeated appearances of the "same image" do have much in common, the raw material must exercise a good deal of control over the final product.

We have met this situation before. In fact, the same problem has arisen repeatedly throughout this book. Like recall, *attention* and *perception* are also constructive processes in which adaptive variation is the rule. Nevertheless, repeated perceptions of the "same event" may have much in common. This is easily explained by common properties of the *stimuli* in the two cases—properties which the mechanisms of cognition are prepared to seize on and elaborate. Perception is constructive, but the input information often plays the largest single role in determining the constructive process. A very similar role, it seems to me, is played by the aggregate of information stored in long-term memory.

This is not to say that the stimuli themselves are copied and stored; far from it. The analogy being offered asserts only that the role which stored information plays in recall is like the role which stimulus information plays in perception. In neither case does it enter awareness directly, and in neither case can it be literally reproduced in behavior except after rather special training. The model of the paleontologist, which was applied to perception and focal attention in Chapter 4, applies also to memory: out of a few stored bone chips, we remember a dinosaur. To assert otherwise, to defend the Reappearance Hypothesis, would be to adopt an attitude reminiscent of naive realism in perception. It represents a fallacy in both contexts. One does not see objects simply "because they are there," but after an elaborate process of construction (which usually is designed to make use of relevant stimulus information). Similarly, one does not recall objects or responses simply because traces of them exist in the mind, but after an elaborate process of *re*construction, (which usually makes use of relevant stored information).

What is the information—the bone chips—on which reconstruction is based? The only plausible possibility is that it consists of traces of *prior processes of construction.* There are no stored copies of finished mental events, like images or sentences, but only traces of earlier constructive activity. In a sense, all learning is "response" learning; i.e., it is learning to carry out some coordinated series of acts. In the case of a motor skill like bicycling or speaking, the acts include overt movements. In visual memory the construction is largely internal, except when it spills over into the eye motions discussed in Chapter 6. Recall, by way of an image, takes place when a new construction is largely under the control of what remains from an earlier one. Recall in words, on the other hand, is a new verbal synthesis which may be based on information from a number of sources, including not only traces of earlier verbalizations, but perhaps visual images and other constructions as well.

The present proposal is, therefore, that we store traces of earlier cognitive acts, not of the products of those acts. The traces are not simply "revived" or "reactivated" in recall; instead, the stored fragments are used as information to support a new construction. It is as if the bone fragments used by the paleontologist did not appear in the model he builds at all—as indeed they need not, if it is to represent a fully fleshed-out, skin-covered dinosaur. The bones can be thought of, somewhat loosely, as remnants of the structure which created and supported the original dinosaur, and thus as sources of information about how to reconstruct it.

### *COGNITIVE STRUCTURES*

When we first perceive or imagine something, the process of construction is not limited to the object itself. We generally build (or rebuild) a spatial, temporal, and conceptual framework as well. In previous chapters little has been said about this background; "construction" has meant construction in focal attention. But, when you see a friend across the street, you are not seeing only him. *He,* a person of a particular kind with a particular relevance to your life, is appearing *there,* a particular place in space, and *then,* at a certain point in time. Similarly, a spoken sentence is not just a string of words to be identified, but it has a particular meaning, is spoken by a particular person, at a particular time and place. These frames of reference can be thought of as a third level of cognitive construction. The preattentive processes delineate units, provide partial cues, and control simple responses; focal attention builds complexly structured objects or movements, one at a time, on the basis thus provided; the background processes build and maintain schemata to which these objects are referred.

Taken together, the activity of these background schemata creates what Shor (1959) has called the "generalized reality orientation." As he points out, it is not always with us, and its absence creates a rather peculiar state of consciousness.

I had been asleep for a number of hours. My level of body tonus was fairly high and my mind clear of dream-images so that I believe I was not asleep but rather in some kind of trance-like state. At that time I was neither conscious of my personal identity, nor of prior experiences, nor of the external world. It was just that out of nowhere I was aware of my own thought processes. I did not know, however, that they were thought processes or who I was, or even that I was an *I.* There was sheer awareness in isolation from any experiential context. It was neither pleasant nor unpleasant, it was not goal directed, just sheer existing. After a time, "wondering" started to fill my awareness; that there was more than this, a gap, an emptiness. As soon as this "wondering" was set into motion there was immediately a change in my awareness. In an instant, as if in a flash, full awareness of myself and reality expanded around me. To say that "I woke up" or that "I remembered," while perhaps correct, would miss the point of the experience entirely. The significant thing was that my mind changed fundamentally in that brief instant. In rediscovering myself and the world, something vital had happened; suddenly all the specifications of reality had become apparent to me. At one moment my awareness was devoid of all structure and in the next moment I was *myself* in a multivaried universe of time, space, motion, and desire (Shor, 1959, p. 586).

The "generalized reality orientation" described by Shor is only one example—though perhaps the most inclusive one—of the organized systems of stored information that we call "cognitive structures." In general, a cognitive structure may be defined as a nonspecific but organized representation of prior experiences. Our grasp of the surrounding geography, our understanding of American history, our "feel" for driving a car, our "intuitions" about linguistic form are all the result of a great number of individual experiences, but they do not reflect these experiences separately. One easily forgets the *occasions* on which one learned how the local streets are oriented, what the Civil War was about, how to shift gears, or how to speak grammatically, but they leave a residue behind. Because these residues are organized in the sense that their parts have regular and controlling interrelations, the term "cognitive structures" is appropriate for them. (This definition is meant to leave the question of empiricism and nativism open. It is very possible that the form and organization of at least some cognitive structures, especially those for space, time, and language, are determined genetically, or otherwise, before any experience has accumulated.)

Historically, a concern with these structures has been the distinguishing characteristic of "cognitive psychologists." The array of theorists who could be cited in this connection would have to include at least Bartlett, Piaget, Schachtel, Tolman, Lashley, Rapaport, and Bruner; many other names could be added as well. It is not possible to review all of their work here. The remainder of this section is only a commentary, from the viewpoint of the present author, on aspects of cognitive structure that have been treated far more extensively elsewhere.

Cognitive structures play a particularly interesting role in learning and remembering. In this connection, they are most frequently called "schemata," after Bartlett (1932). It is easy to see why the schemata control the fate of stored information; they are themselves information of a similar sort. The hypothesis of the present chapter is that cognition is constructive, and that the process of construction leaves traces behind. The schemata themselves are such constructions, elaborated at every moment in the course of attentive activity. Recall is organized in terms of these structures because the original experiences were elaborated in the same terms. It probably is unwise to think of them as filing systems into which specific memories can be put; they are integral parts of the memories themselves. In any case, it is easy to agree with Lashley's estimate of their importance:

> . . . every memory becomes part of a more or less extensive organization. When I read a scientific paper, the new facts presented become associated with the field of knowledge of which it is a part. Later availability of the specific items of the paper depends on a partial activation of the whole body of associations. If one has not thought of a topic for some time, it is difficult to recall details. With review or discussion of the subject, however, names, dates, references which seemed to be forgotten rapidly become available to memory. Head has given instances of such recall by multiple reinforcement in his studies of aphasia. Although there are no systematic experiments upon this "warming up" effect, it is a matter of common experience, and is evidence, I believe, that recall involves the subthreshold activation of a whole system of associations which exert some sort of mutual facilitation (1950, pp. 497–498).

Everyone recognizes the close relationship between interests and memory, which seems to result from the extensive schemata we build for material we care about. We have all known, or been, boys who could remember everything about baseball or fishing but not a bit of history. As adults, we can learn an endless variety of new facts that relate to our profession or our hobby, while everything else seems to go in one ear and out the other. In the same vein, Bartlett (1932) has described African herdsmen who were unable to give adequate testimony in a court of law, but could recall the details of cattle transactions for years with astonishing accuracy. The most important advice offered by the many practitioners of "memory improvement" systems (e.g., Furst, 1948) is to develop detailed and articulate schemata into which new material can be fitted.

If cognitive structures can facilitate recall, we should be able to work backwards from observations of recall to learn something about them. This aim has been extensively pursued in recent studies of clustering and word-association. In a method devised by Bousfield (1953), for example, subjects are asked to memorize a list in which all the words belong to certain categories—animals, cities, weapons, or the like—but are presented in a randomized sequence. The order of recall is left to the subject's own discretion, and thus it can reveal a good deal about the "subjective organization" of the information involved. The typical subject recalls first a cluster of words from one category, then some from a second group, and so on. (As a matter of fact, idiosyncratic clusters appear in recall even when the material has not been specially designed to encourage them, but in such instances they are more difficult to detect—see Tulving, 1962.) One might regard these studies as the definitive refutation of James Mill: the order of ideas does *not* repeat the order of sensations by any means. Instead, it follows lines determined by cognitive structure.

Similar analyses can be made of data obtained with the method of word-association: "Say the first word that comes into your mind when I say *black*." Deese (1965) goes so far as to define an "associative structure" as a group of words that are likely to elicit the same associates. In such experiments, the subject is generally instructed to avoid any purposeful or directed thinking, so that a relatively unclouded view of the organization of memory may be obtained. However, some caution should be exercised in the use of the method, for this is a difficult instruction to follow. Many people have distinct notions about the kind of responses expected of them in such tasks, and behave accordingly. Like other performances, word-association depends not only on the organization of memory but on what the subject is trying to achieve.

While cognitive structures (or "coding systems," as they are called by Bruner, 1957a) make recall possible, they also have some negative effects. By necessity, they tend to introduce bias and distortion into both the initial construction and the later reconstruction. Documentation of these changes makes up the bulk of Bartlett's *Remembering* (1932). They have also been studied in more conventional experimental situations, notably by Postman (1954). However, there is no doubt that more experimental studies of these phenomena are needed. Replication of Bartlett's findings is not easy (but see Paul, 1959) and other kinds of mnemonic biasing seem to be even more tenuously established (see Waly & Cook, 1966).

It has been repeatedly emphasized that stored information is not revived, but simply used, in the constructive activity of recall. This applies to background schemata as well as to recall of specific figures or events. When I try to recall my first day at college, I do so by means of complex frames of reference, arrays of information, in which that day is included: college life as a whole, myself as a young man, the geography of the town, and so on. It is because these schemata are being used that I will go on to remember other, related facts which are not directly germane to the question. However, the critical frames of reference do not literally come to life again; if they did, I would be seventeen once more. (This is precisely the miracle claimed for so-called "hypnotic age regression." As we saw in Chapter 6, the age of miracles is over.) Instead, they are *used* by the present me, via the schemata which I am *now* capable of constructing.

For the attempted recall to succeed, the schemata I develop now, in the attempt to recall, must not be too different from those whose traces were established long ago. They can differ, but not so much that the present ones cannot incorporate the information stored earlier. Otherwise, the stored fragments of structure will be unusable, and recall will fail. This is what happens when an inappropriate "set" produces failures of memory, as in problem-solving experiments showing "functional fixedness," or in trick sentences like *Pas de la Rhone que nous.*

Of course, loss of a cognitive system can have much more serious consequences than this. Knowledge about oneself, one's own personal history, also comprises a rather tightly knit cognitive system. When it becomes unavailable we speak of "loss of memory," or more precisely of a "fugue." Rapaport (1957) gives a detailed account of a fugue, to illustrate the dramatic effects of cognitive structuring. In such states, the reason for the patient's inability to reconstruct his own past is generally a dynamic one: he does not *want* to use the schemata which concern himself. The result is not only a loss of memory but a badly weakened sense of present reality, as Shor's argument would have suggested.

Fugues are often reversible, especially with the aid of special techniques such as hypnosis. So are inappropriate sets, of course: one need only be told that *Pas de la Rhone que nous* is an English sentence beginning with *Paddle.* However, the rather similar state of *infantile amnesia*—inability to recall one's own early childhood—is not reversible to any substantial degree. The reason, as Schachtel (1947) saw clearly, is that adults cannot think as children do; they no longer carry out attentive constructions in the way they once did. As a result, they cannot make use of any fragments of infantile constructions that they may still retain. Elsewhere (Neisser, 1962), I have considered this phenomenon in more detail.

A particularly important class of cognitive structures are those which represent arrangement in time. Except in unusual states of consciousness, adults—especially adults in our western, time-oriented culture—tend to construct the events of their experience in a temporal framework. I *am writing* these lines today (September 26, 1966), which is the day *before* I leave on a long-planned trip and several days *after* reorganizing this chapter into its present format. I *have been* at my office for several hours and *soon* it *will be* time to go to lunch. And, of course, the *I* to whom these experiences are referred is a temporally ordered entity, whose experiences are strung along a temporal line that begins hazily at about age five and continues without any serious disturbance of continuity far into the future. That (imagined) future is less definite than the (remembered) past, but the events foreseen in it—*next* Christmas, *next* summer—are for the most part in just as linear an array.

This temporal structuring is so pervasive for us that it has been given a central, primitive role in most theories of learning. The common assumption has been that the temporal succession of two stimuli, or of a stimulus and a response, automatically produces some inner representation in which their order is preserved. "Contiguity in time" has been taken as the basic principle of mental organization. In one sense, this is undeniable. Time must be important for the informational processes of cognition, as for any other processes in nature: whether and how two events interact depends in part on their temporal relations. But this does not mean that these temporal relations will be directly represented in recall or in performance. Conversely, the succession that *is* represented in recall need not result directly from the physical time-order of stimuli.

As an example of the first point, consider that I must have acquired my present vocabulary of English words in some order; in fact, the particular order was probably a factor in making some words easier to learn than others. However, this order of acquisition is not reflected in my current mental activity. It does not matter, nor do I know, which of the words "current," "mental," and "activity" I learned first. As an example of the second point, consider history. I know the sequence of American Presidents, or at least the first few, better than I know the sequence of my own grammar school teachers. This is not a matter of direct experience, nor even of having once chanted "Washington, John Adams, Jefferson, . . ." in order. I also know the sequence of recent American Secretaries of State beginning with Cordell Hull, although I have surely never recited their names successively until today. Historical and personal facts each have their own representation in a *temporal structure*. Once such a structure exists, the real time-order of stimuli may help to determine their temporal representation, but other factors, including instruction and anticipation, can play an important role.

There are many experimental illustrations of the distinction between real temporal contiguity on the one hand and functional, experienced contiguity on the other. Perhaps the best is Thorndike's "belongingness" effect, discussed in Chapter 10, which shows that "associations" are formed only between words that have been incorporated into a single cognitive unit. For another example, consider the astonishing errors of sequence made by children, especially in their use of language, where inversions of words and syllables are common. This is not surprising if, as argued in Chapter 7, the order of linguistic units is recovered by constructing a larger pattern into which they fit. Because cognitive development is outside the scope of this book, this question will not be pursued further here. For those who are concerned with it, Piaget's account of the child's conception of time (see Flavell, 1963) is particularly relevant.

*Space* is another cognitive dimension which is important but not as "primitive" as is sometimes supposed. It is obvious enough that generally we conceive of ourselves and of the world in spatial terms. The words on the printed page have location as well as identity: left or right, top or bottom, near or far. Information about these spatial aspects of construction remains available to recall, so that we often know on what portion of the page a certain argument is to be found. (For a related phenomenon in rote learning, see Asch, Hay, and Diamond, 1960.) Again, it is important to note that this kind of spatiality does not simply reflect the raw spatial organization of the input. Position on the retina is an important source of stimulus information, but it is not directly represented by a position in cognitively elaborated space. As we have seen (Chapter 6), perceived space itself is the result of an integration of numerous retinal "snapshots." Moreover, one's "cognitive map" (Tolman, 1948) of the surrounding environment may easily include "contiguities" that have *never* been directly experienced. In imagining my own house, I am just as aware of the relationship between the dining room and the bedroom (which are above one another, and thus never experienced in immediate succession) as of that between the adjacent dining and living rooms. The extent to which this spatial organization exists fully articulated in the newborn infant (as opposed to developing through commerce with the environment) is still a hotly disputed topic.

## *THE PROBLEM OF THE EXECUTIVE*

The cognitive approach to memory and thought emphasizes that recall and problem-solving are constructive acts, based on information remaining from earlier acts. That information, in turn, is organized according to the structure of those earlier acts, though its utilization depends also on present circumstances and present constructive skills. This suggests that the higher mental processes are closely related to skilled motor behavior—a relationship which Bartlett has explored and illustrated in two books, 26 years apart.

> Suppose I am making a stroke in a quick game, such as tennis or cricket. How I make the stroke depends on the relating of certain new experiences, most of them visual, to other immediately preceding visual experiences and to my posture, or balance of postures, at the moment. The latter, balance of postures, is the result of a whole series of earlier movements, in which the last movement before the stroke is played has a predominant function. When I make the stroke I do not, as a matter of fact, produce something absolutely new, and I never merely repeat something old. The stroke is literally manufactured out of the living visual and postural "schemata" of the moment and their interrelations. I may say, I may think that I reproduce exactly a series of textbook movements, but demonstrably I do not; just as, under other circumstances, I may say and think that I reproduce exactly some isolated event which I want to remember, and again demonstrably I do not (*Remembering,* 1932, pp. 201–202).

> . . . all skilled behaviour is set into a form of significant sequence within which it must be studied if understanding is to be reached . . . it submits to a control which lies outside itself and is appreciated, at the bodily level, by the receptor system . . . proper timing, the ways in which transition is made from one direction of move to another, "point of no return," and the character of direction and how it is appreciated are all critical features of skilled behaviour.

From time to time, and in relation to all the kinds of thinking which I have discussed, I have returned particularly to those properties of skill, and it has seemed not only that thinking of all kinds possesses them, but also that their study does throw some real light upon the thinking processes themselves.

. . . thinking is an advanced form of skilled behaviour . . . it has grown out of earlier established forms of flexible adaptation to the environment . . . the characteristics which it possesses and the conditions to which it submits can best be studied as they are related to those of its own earlier forms (*Thinking,* 1958, pp. 198–199).

For many kinds of thinking, this is a convincing argument. Rational problem-solving and deliberate recall do seem like purposeful and skillful actions. However, there is a major difference between these activities and simple bodily skills, as Bartlett realized. Mental activities are far less dependent on the *immediate* past, on "the last movement before the stroke" than simple movements are. To account for our ability to use earlier experience selectively, he suggested that "An organism has somehow to acquire the ability to turn round upon its own 'schemata' and to construct them afresh" (1932, p. 206). Other theorists have dealt with the same issue by speaking of *searches through memory, strategies, censorship,* and even *covert trial and error.* All of these concepts, like *turning round,* raise a very serious question. Who does the turning, the trying, and the erring? Is there a little man in the head, a *homunculus,* who acts the part of the paleontologist vis-à-vis the dinosaur?

Unpalatable as such a notion may be, we can hardly avoid it altogether. If we do *not* postulate some agent who selects and uses the stored information, we must think of every thought and every response as just the momentary resultant of an interacting system, governed essentially by laissez-faire economics. Indeed, the notions of "habit strength" and "response competition" used by the behaviorists are based on exactly this model. However, it seems strained and uncomfortable where selective thought and action are involved. To see the problem, consider an experiment proposed by Yntema and Trask (1963), which highlights the need for some kind of active executive process in a theory of memory. Suppose we read a list of five words to a subject, and shortly thereafter read four of them again, in a scrambled order. He is to tell us which one was omitted on the second reading. People can easily do this, but Yntema and Trask point out that ". . . *S* does not respond with the missing item because it has been reinforced most often, or because it is in any conventional sense the strongest response. Thus, it seems reasonable, indeed almost necessary, to assume that some sort of data-processing mechanism can intervene between memory and overt response" (1963, p. 66).

There are many mechanisms which might successfully carry out this task, but it is hard to imagine any which do not distinguish between a *memory* in which the first list is somehow stored, and an agent or *processor* which somehow makes use of it. Yntema and Trask suggest a number of alternative strategies; for example, the processor might check off each stored word as "repeated" when it appears in the second list, and subsequently skim through until it finds an unchecked item. Some kind of agent seems unavoidable here (as in Buschke's very similar "missing span" method, in which the subject must produce the digit that was *not* presented to him—see Chapter 9) simply because the correct response is not "in any conventional sense the strongest." This is true of many other situations as well. However, such responses are rarely thought to reflect only "memory." For the most part, experiments with this annoying property have been classed as studies of "thinking" or "problem-solving" or "reasoning" rather than "memory." This is virtually the definition of the "higher mental processes," as they appear in ordinary psychological texts. We credit a subject with something more than "remembering" when the response he makes is not the strongest in a conventional sense.

Most psychological theories are "conventional" in this respect. The notion of a separate processor, or *executive,* is rejected not only by classical association theory but by behaviorism, by the "trace theory" of Rock and Ceraso (1964), and by Gestalt psychology (except for a few cryptic passages in Koffka, 1935). It is also missing from Freud's notion of "primary-process thinking." Freud was quick to postulate executive processes of many kinds as well (e.g., the ego, the superego, the censorship) but he was usually more interested in what they suppressed than in what they produced.

A "conventional" theorist can deal with executive phenomena in two ways. First, he can classify them as "higher mental processes" and thus as outside his area of interest. Second, he can treat them directly, but this means that he must *reduce* them to conventional cases. He is obliged to argue that appearances are deceptive: what seems like an executive process is really the simple resultant of existing response strengths, and what seems like fresh and adaptive behavior is only the reappearance of previous elements. My own view is quite different. Appearances are indeed deceptive in many experiments, but they deceive at least as often in studies of "rote learning" as in work on thinking. What seems to be simple associative revival of earlier responses may actually be a complex process of search and construction; a subject instructed to memorize syllables by rote tends instead to construct complex rhythmic and semantic patterns which incorporate them. In this sense remembering is always a form of problem-solving, and therefore a higher mental process. That is why it is treated as one in this book. (A similar treatment appears in Miller, Galanter, and Pribram, 1960, Chapter 10.)

While there seems to be no justification for distinguishing remembering from other forms of thinking, there are certain problems of *retention* that must not be entirely overlooked. When information is stored over time, we have reason to ask a number of questions. For example, psychologists have long wondered whether long-term memory decays as a function of time alone ("simple forgetting"), or whether losses over time result only from interference by other material and other activities ("proactive inhibition" and "retroactive inhibition"). It has also been suggested that time can have a beneficial effect on stored information ("consolidation"), rendering it less vulnerable to such gross interventions as electroconvulsive shock. These are important issues, currently under intensive study. They will not be reviewed here, because (so far as I can presently judge) their resolution does not depend on the question of how memory is organized and used.

It is important to understand why the hypothesis of a separate executive process has always been rejected by the "conventional" theories. The most commonly cited ground is the law of parsimony, "Occam's Razor": constructs should not be elaborated more than is necessary. But this razor has two edges; Granit has remarked that ". . . the biologist's attitude should be humbler. His duty is to admit that he does not know nature well enough to understand her requirements or 'necessities.' That is why he experiments" (1955, p. 37).

In any case, the law of parsimony would hardly explain the very unparsimonious hypotheses erected by stimulus-response theorists to explain away what seem to be executive processes. Their real motive is a more serious one. They are afraid that a separate executive would return psychology to the soul, the will, and the *homunculus;* it would be equivalent to explaining behavior in terms of a "little man in the head." Such explanations seem to lead only to an infinite regress, which must bar further research and frustrate theory. If the actions of the executive account for behavior, what accounts for those actions in turn? Does the ego have an ego?

It now seems possible that there is an escape from the regress that formerly seemed infinite. As recently as a generation ago, processes of control had to be thought of as *homunculi,* because man was the only known model of an executive agent. Today, the stored-program computer has provided us with an alternative possibility, in the form of the *executive routine.* This is a concept which may be of considerable use to psychology.

Most computer programs consist of largely independent parts, or "subroutines." In complex sequential programs, the order in which the subroutines are applied will vary from one occasion to the next. In simple cases, a conditional decision can lead from one subroutine to the next appropriate one: "transfer control to register *A* if the computed number in register *X* is positive, but to register *B* if it is negative or zero." In other situations, however, the choice between register *A* and register *B* may depend on a more complicated set of conditions, which must be evaluated by a separate subroutine called "the executive." Common practice is to make all subroutines end by transferring control to the executive, which then decides what to do next in each case. One might well say that the executive "uses" the other routines, which are "subordinate" to it. Some programs may even have a hierarchical structure, in which routines at one level can call those which are "lower" and are themselves called by others which are "higher." However, the regress of control is not infinite: there is a "highest," or executive routine which is not used by anything else.

Note that the executive is in no sense a *programmulus,* or miniature of the entire program. It does not carry out the tests or the searches or the constructions which are the task of the subroutines, and it does not include the stored information which the subroutines use. Indeed, the executive may take only a small fraction of the computing time and space allotted to the program as a whole, and it need not contain any very sophisticated processes. Although there is a real sense in which it "uses" the rest of the program and the stored information, this creates no philosophical difficulties; it is not using itself. (As a matter of fact, some programs *do* have so-called recursive subroutines, which use themselves. An example is the "General Problem-Solver" of Newell and Simon, 1963, which Reitman, 1965, describes in some detail. However, we do not need to explore this possibility here.)

As noted in Chapter 1, the use of a concept borrowed from computer programming does not imply that existing "computer models" are satisfactory from a psychological point of view. In general, they are not. One of their most serious inadequacies becomes particularly apparent in the present context. The executive routine of a computer program must be established by the programmer from the beginning. Although artificially intelligent programs can easily "learn" (modify themselves as a result of experience), none so far can make major developmental changes in its own executive routine. In man, however, such functions as "turning round on one's own schemata" and "searching through memory" are themselves acquired through experience. We do not know much about this learning, but it poses no new problem in principle, if we already assume that human memory stores information about processes rather than about contents. Mental activities can be learned; perhaps they are the only things that are ever learned.

## *THE MULTIPLICITY OF THOUGHT*

We were led to the notion of an executive by Bartlett's analogy between thought and purposeful action. It is time now to admit that this is not all of the story. Thought is by no means always coordinated toward a particular goal. We are not forever engaged in "filling up gaps in the evidence" (Bartlett, 1958, p. 20), nor in following out some strategic plan. It is true that I may construct an image in the course of directed train of thought, but more often the image just "comes by itself," as if "I," at least, had not constructed it. As we saw in Chapter 6, even the images that do accompany purposeful thinking tend to have only a tangential, symbolic relation to it. This is even more obvious in dreams and fantasy, which seem to represent a mode of thinking and remembering quite different from the step-by-step logic of reason.

Historically, psychology has long recognized the existence of two different forms of mental organization. The distinction has been given many names: "rational" vs. "intuitive," "constrained" vs. "creative," "logical" vs. "prelogical," "realistic" vs. "autistic," "secondary process" vs. "primary process." To list them together so casually may be misleading; the "autistic" thinking of schizophrenics, as described by Bleuler (1912), is surely not "creative." Nevertheless, a common thread runs through all the dichotomies. Some thinking and remembering is deliberate, efficient, and obviously goal-directed; it is usually experienced as self-controlled as well. Other mental activity is rich, chaotic, and inefficient; it tends to be experienced as involuntary, it just "happens." It often seems to be motivated, but not in the same way as directed thought; it seems not so much directed toward a goal as associated with an emotion.

The distinction between these two kinds of mental organization is reminiscent of the difference between *parallel* and *sequential* processing which is already familiar. We saw in Chapter 3 that a sequential program can be defined as one that "makes only those tests which are appropriate in the light of previous test outcomes." Viewed as a constructive process, it constructs only one thing at a time. The very definitions of "rational" and "logical" also suggest that each idea, image, or action is sensibly related to the preceding one, making an appearance only as it becomes necessary for the aim in view. A parallel program, on the other hand, carries out many activities simultaneously, or at least independently. Their combined result may be useful, but then again it may not. This is just the chief characteristic of the "primary process," as it appears in dreams, slips of the tongue, "free association," and many forms of mental disorder. The very word "schizophrenia" refers to a state of mind in which ideas and trains of thought are *split* apart from one another, lacking any coherent sequence.

To call primary-process thought "parallel" may be misleading. The word tends to suggest straight lines that never meet, while the "wealth of trains of unconscious thought striving for expression in our minds" (Freud, 1900, p. 478) are not straight in any sense, and meet often. Selfridge's (1959) "Pandemonium" is tempting as an alternative term; Freud might not have objected to describing the primary process as a shouting horde of demons. This model, which was intended as an account of pattern recognition in the face of uncertainty and poor definition (see Chapter 3), has some merit as a description of uncertain and poorly defined thoughts also. Nevertheless, a less colorful term is desirable for everyday use. Elsewhere (Neisser, 1963a) I have suggested "multiple processing," as a phrase which seems appropriate to the ill-organized variety of dreamlike thoughts.

Multiple processing does not go on only in dreams, or in the minds of madmen. In waking life also, a hundred or a thousand "thoughts" appear briefly and are gone again even when we are primarily engaged in purposeful activity. The extent to which these fleeting thoughts are developed, and are permitted to interrupt the main direction of mental activity, varies from person to person and from time to time. For the most part, they are immediately forgotten, like the dreams they so strongly resemble. Occasionally they interrupt ongoing activity, and we recognize a "mental block," a "lapse of attention," or a "Freudian slip."

Without accepting Freud's claim that *all* such interruptions are the result of suppressed motives and ideas, we can acknowledge that at least some of them surely are. Freud's encounter with a young man on a train, reported in *The Psychopathology of Everyday Life* (Freud, 1904), provides a conveniently dramatic example. In the course of the conversation, the two travelers began to discuss, and to deplore, the difficult situation of European Jews. The young man concluded a particularly forceful statement with a Latin verse from the *Aeneid,* which expresses the hope that posterity will eventually right the wrongs of today. However, he cited the verse incorrectly, leaving out the single word *aliquis,* which Freud then supplied. Since he had heard of the psychoanalytic axiom that all errors are motivated, the young man immediately challenged Freud to explain his omission.

Freud accepted the challenge and encouraged his companion to free-associate to the word in question. After some associations like *liquid* and *fluid,* his thought turned to several Catholic Saints, including St. Simon (who was murdered as a child), St. Augustine (he had recently read an article entitled "What St. Augustine said concerning women"), and St. Januarius, whose blood was said to be preserved in a phial in Naples, and to liquefy miraculously each year on a certain holiday. Then he had a thought which at first he was reluctant to disclose; it turned out to be about a woman "from whom I could easily get a message that would be annoying to us both." To the young man's surprise, Freud immediately inferred the content of the feared message: that she had missed a menstrual period, i.e., was pregnant. He then pointed out that the first error and all the intervening associations had been related to this theme: the "liquid" in *aliquis;* the calendar-like names of two of the Saints; the child-murder of the other; the miracle of the blood. The original slip itself is also intelligible from this point of view. The Latin passage had expressed a wish for posterity, but the young man was not at all eager for any posterity that might arrive in nine months' time!

The thoughts involved here are evidently not sequential. They could have come in any order, and they lead nowhere in particular as far as the thinker is concerned. In short, they are multiple processes. To be sure, they are not truly simultaneous, at least as the young man describes them, but the definition of parallel or multiple processing does not require actual simultaneity so much as functional independence. Moreover, they may well have been simultaneous in fact, and only serialized for presentation aloud.

This example, in which every association is clearly related to a single theme, is an unusual one. Freud naturally used the best possible illustration of the point he wished to make: that even apparently undirected actions and thoughts are really drive-determined. The situation is not always so clear, and much primary-process thinking appears in such chaotic profusion that it can neither be adequately described nor easily accounted for. Nevertheless, it would be pointless to develop a theory of thought and memory that had no room for these phenomena.

## *PRIMARY AND SECONDARY PROCESSES RECONSIDERED*

We need a conception of the mind which allows for multiple activity at some levels, but also has a place for an executive process. Both kinds of operations seem to characterize human thinking. Moreover, neither one serves simply as a retrieval system, selecting and arousing particular "memory traces." Each is essentially constructive in nature, making use of stored information to build something new.

There are no adequate models of such processes among today's computer programs. Both parallel and sequential models have been proposed and programmed, as the examples of Pandemonium and EPAM illustrate, but none so far has done justice to the constructive character of thought. This critique applies even to an ingenious program which combines the two principles rather successfully: Reitman's "Argus" (Reitman, 1965, Chapter 8). Nevertheless, Argus is an interesting program, not so much because of what it can do (it solves analogies problems like *Hot is to Cold as Tall is to (Wall, Short, Wet, Hold)?)* as because of the way it is organized. Information is stored in the form of "semantic elements" like *Hot,* each represented by several lists of relevant data. The lists indicate the element's relations with other elements

(Which one is its *opposite?* its *superordinate?*), its threshold, its state of arousal, and the time when it was last "fired." Elements can "fire" each other via their listed relations, so the aggregate is spontaneously active. Its activity is organized in parallel. In addition, Argus has an executive routine, which can carry out various sequential strategies. It may fire the alternative answers, examine the relationships among recently-fired elements, and so on. Thus both parallel and sequential organization contribute to the system's effectiveness.

Intriguing as Argus is, it seems far too heavily committed to the Reappearance Hypothesis. Only those elements can be aroused which already exist in a dormant state; only those relationships can be employed which have been explicitly entered by the programmer. This may be why, as Reitman himself notes (1965, Chapter 9), it cannot solve more challenging analogies *(Samson is to Hair as Achilles is to (Strength, Shield, Heel, Tent)?)* except in a very artificial way. The programmer can, of course, include a relationship like *point of susceptibility to major negative influence from the environment?* in the original semantic descriptions of Samson and Achilles. However, he would hardly do this except to anticipate the specific analogy in question, and such anticipations would make the program uninteresting. Human beings do not solve challenging problems by reviving relationships that already exist, but by constructing new ones, just as they construct new sentences, new images, new rhythms, and new movements to suit the needs of the moment.

It is fair to say that no contemporary psychological theory and no existing program deals satisfactorily with the constructive nature of the higher mental processes. This deficiency will not be remedied here. As noted earlier, a serious theory of memory and thinking is beyond the scope of this book. I can, however, suggest an analogy which may be helpful. Like the Gestalt psychologists, though for different reasons, I believe that the processes of *visual cognition,* and perception in general, may serve as useful models for memory and thought.

To see why a perceptual analogy might be appropriate, let us briefly review the processing of visual information, especially in terms of the theory put forward in Chapter 4. The central distinction made there was between *focal attention* and the *preattentive processes.* There seem to be two distinguishable levels of visual activity. The first, preattentive stage is a parallel one. Stimulus information, arriving simultaneously all over the retina, is first used in the construction of separate visual figures, or objects. The processes involved are wholistic, both in terms of the stimulus information they use and of the properties of the constructed figures. This level of activity results in *iconic storage,* a transient persistence of the visual objects during which they are available for further analysis. If no additional processing takes place, only crude properties of the stimuli—movement, general location, brightness, etc.—can have any effect on behavior; often there is no effect at all. Like all parallel processes, preattentive activity is inherently "wasteful." Most of the visual figures thus formed never do receive additional processing, and disappear unnoticed.

The relationship of iconic memory to *consciousness* is particularly interesting. There is a sense in which we are aware of its contents, but the experience is a fleeting and tenuous one. After a tachistoscopic exposure in Sperling's (1960a) experiment, the subject feels that he "saw" all the letters, but he cannot remember most of them. The uncoded ones slip away even as he tries to grasp them, leaving no trace behind. Compared with the firm clarity of the few letters he really remembers, they have only a marginal claim to being called "conscious" at all.

A very different fate awaits that portion of the stimulus information which becomes the focus of attention. Attention is serial: only one object can be attended to at any given moment, and each attentive act takes an appreciable fraction of a second. Operating within the preattentively established boundaries, figural synthesis produces objects which may have considerable complexity, or be charged with considerable affect. The course of synthesis is partly determined by stimulus information, but it also depends on such factors as past experience, expectation, and preference. These nonstimulus variables play a dual role, since they influence the choice of one figure rather than another for attention as well as the details of the construction which then takes place.

Although the constructive processes themselves never appear in consciousness, their products do: to construct something attentively is to see it clearly. Such objects can then be remembered; that is, they can be *re*constructed as visual images. In addition, they may achieve representation in other modalities if an appropriate coding system exists. Verbal recoding is particularly common and has the effect of re-storing relevant information in auditory memory, where it is more easily available for use in later descriptions. (For a demonstration that auditory and visual memory are functionally distinct, see Wallach and Averbach, 1955.)

This general description of the fate of sensory information seems to fit the higher mental processes as well. Perhaps the most striking analogy is between the preattentive processes and the multiple thinking that is so prominent in dreams and fantasy. Both produce only fleeting and evanescent objects of consciousness, crudely defined and hard to remember. If their products are not seized on and elaborated by an executive process of some kind, they have little effect on further thinking or behavior. Such effects as they do have reflect only crude and global properties of the objects involved. The "symbolism" of primary-process thinking is based on overall shapes, simple movements, and gross sound patterns: just the properties to which the preattentive processes of vision and hearing are sensitive.

The executive processes of thought, whose selective function is indispensable for rational problem-solving, share many of the properties of focal attention in vision and of analysis-by-synthesis in hearing. In thinking, we construct mental "objects" (and overt responses) of great complexity, selecting one or another of the crude products offered by the primary processes and elaborating it as necessary. The constructed mental objects may be invested with affect, or they may be emotionally neutral. They can even be recoded into other systems, as when we imagine a scene and then describe it. The course of construction is governed by motives and expectations as well as by the "input," which here is the aggregate of stored information about earlier constructions.

Whatever its defects, this analogy at least avoids the Reappearance Hypothesis—the unpalatable assumption that memory traces exist continuously and are occasionally aroused to action. Attentive synthesis does leave traces of a sort behind, but these are never subsequently "aroused," they are only used. I am proposing that their use requires a two-stage mechanism, analogous to those of vision and hearing. First, the so-called primary processes make an array of crudely defined "objects" or "ideas," along lines which tend to follow the structure of the "input," i.e., the information in memory. Then, in alert and waking subjects, the secondary processes of directed thought select among these objects and develop them further. In this interpretation, the primary and secondary processes are by no means as antagonistic as Freud believed. One is essential to the other. Rational thought is "secondary" in the sense that it works with objects already formed by a "primary" process. If these objects receive no secondary elaboration, as in some dreams and disorganized mental states, we experience them in the fleeting and imprecise way that characterizes the uncoded figures of iconic memory. However, the same multiple processes that produce these shadowy and impalpable experiences are also essential preliminaries to directed thinking.

These are not entirely new arguments. The notion that memory retains information about mental *acts* rather than copies of experiences is, as we have seen, closely related to Bartlett's views. It may also remind the reader of modern stimulus-response theory, in which internal or implicit "responses" play a major role. However, I am not simply saying that learning consists of the acquisition of (covert) responses. Indeed, *no* learning consists of responses in this sense. A movement-pattern, or the construction of an image, is not a series of responses which the subject will later tend to repeat. A new movement may be synthesized with the aid of information about an old one, but the two are rarely identical. Indeed, the whole conception of a structured synthesis is very different from that of a response sequence. As we saw in the case of rhythmic patterns and sentences, mental constructions are wholes, whose ends are prefigured in their beginnings. They are not organized as, nor do they stem from, chains of connected units.

The notion that the secondary process can serve to elaborate primary-process material is an old one. It has often been advanced in connection with the problem of "creativity" (e.g., Kris, 1950; Maslow, 1957). However, the present suggestion goes further. It seems to me that *all* directed thinking is an elaboration of this sort, just as *all* visual and auditory perception depends on prior wholistic construction of some kind of unit.

Also familiar is the idea that the primary process, as defined by Freud, has a perceptual function; it is often said to manifest itself in such phenomena as "subliminal perception" and "perceptual defense." Some have even supposed that the primary processes comprise a separate cognitive system with supersensitive capacities, able to detect and react to stimuli that are otherwise subthreshold. This hypothesis must be rejected; in previous chapters, we have repeatedly found contaminating artifacts in the experiments which seem to support it. I am making a different suggestion. There is indeed a stage of perception which corresponds to the primary processes of thought, but the relation between them is one of functional similarity, not identity. In remembering and thinking, as in perception, the secondary process further examines and further develops the objects made available to it by the primary one.

Another similarity between perception and memory is also worth remarking. Just as iconically present figures may go undeveloped by the visual attentive mechanisms, so may a tentatively formed idea receive no further elaboration by the secondary processes of thought. In vision, this can occur for many reasons—because of a certain strategy of search, because of competing interest in something else, or even by deliberate instruction (or self-instruction) as in the negative hallucinations discussed in Chapter 6. The same kinds of factors can prevent us from remembering or thinking about things, even when the necessary information was stored, and is being touched on by the primary processes. Again, the executive may be using an inappropriate strategy of search, may be concerned with some incompatible activity, or may be deliberately avoiding construction in certain areas. In this last case we usually speak of "repression," or perhaps of "censorship."

## *A SUMMING UP*

At this point, it may be appropriate to review the speculative hypotheses that have been advanced. (1) Stored information consists of traces of previous constructive mental (or overt) actions. (2) The primary process is a multiple activity, somewhat analogous to parallel processing in computers, which constructs crudely formed "thoughts," or "ideas," on the basis of stored information. Its functions are similar to those of the preattentive processes in vision and hearing. Its products are only fleetingly conscious, unless they undergo elaboration by secondary processes. (3) The secondary processes of directed thought and deliberate recall are like focal attention in vision. They are serial in character, and construct ideas and images which are determined partly by stored information, partly by the preliminary organization of the primary processes, and partly by wishes and expectations. (4) The executive control of thinking in the secondary process is carried out by a system analogous to the executive routine of a computer program. It is not necessary to postulate a *homunculus* to account for the directed character of thought. (5) The secondary processes themselves are mostly acquired through experience, in the same way that all other memories—which also represent earlier *processes*—are acquired. (6) Failures to recall information which is actually in storage are like failures to notice something in the visual field, or failures to hear something that has been said. The executive processes of recall may be directed elsewhere, either deliberately or because of a misguided strategy of search; they may also lack the necessary constructive abilities altogether.

The reader who objects to the vague and speculative character of these hypotheses has good reason to do so. To be sure, he can be answered with the familiar excuse that psychology is a "young science," and that cognitive theory cannot be more explicitly formulated at the present time. But this reply may not satisfy him; he may legitimately ask why this should be the case. Why have the higher mental processes been so resistant to meaningful investigation? The earlier stages of cognition, which were the subject of the first ten chapters, made a different impression. The models proposed there were relatively specific; many pertinent experiments were considered; testable hypotheses were easy to formulate. What new difficulty appears in the study of thinking?

The problem can be phrased in terms of one particularly obvious weakness of the present approach. In accounting for the course of thought and action, there has been repeated reference to the subject's motives and expectations, and even to an "executive" that seems to have purposes of its own. We have seen that this leads to no logical impasse, to no *homunculus,* but it surely does raise a practical issue. If what the subject will remember depends in large part on what he is trying to accomplish, on his purposes, do not predictions become impossible and explanations *ad hoc?* If we give no further account of these purposes, how can we tell what he will think of next?

While this is indeed a weakness of the cognitive approach, it may be an inevitable one. In Chapter 1, the study of motives was assigned to dynamic rather than to cognitive psychology; thus, it could be conveniently set aside. This strategy worked well so long as we considered only the relatively "stimulus-bound" or "outer-directed" processes of perception and immediate memory. At those levels, motivation can select among a few alternative kinds of cognitive synthesis, but thereafter the constructive act is closely controlled by present or recent stimulus information. However, the course of thinking or of "inner-directed" activity is determined at every moment by what the subject is trying to do. Although we cannot always see only what we want to see, we can generally think what we like.

The classical procedures of experimental psychology attempt to avoid this problem by brute force. In an ordinary learning experiment, the subject is supposed to have only a single motive: he must get on with the experimental task, learn what he is told to learn, and solve what he is told to solve. If he has any other desires—to outwit the experimenter, to walk out, to ask what the answer is—he must do his best to act as if they did not exist. In this respect, experimental situations are very different from those of daily life. When I try to recall the name of the man who has just entered my office, it is for a number of partly independent reasons: I want to know who he is so I can have a meaningful relation with him; I don't want to offend him by having forgotten his name; I would prefer not to seem a fool, in his eyes or in my own. Moreover, one of my options would eliminate the necessity for remembering; I can ask him what his name is. Such multiplicity of motivation and flexibility of response are characteristic of ordinary life, but they are absent—or are assumed to be absent—from most experiments on the higher mental processes.

In itself, this is hardly a devastating criticism. Experiments need not imitate life. In fact, the art of experimentation is the creation of *new* situations, which catch the essence of some process without the circumstances that usually obscure it. The question in this case is whether the essence has truly been caught. The simplifications introduced by confining the subject to a single motive and a fixed set of alternative responses can be justified only if motivation and cognition are genuinely distinct. If—as I suppose—they are inseparable where remembering and thinking are concerned, the common experimental paradigms may pay too high a price for simplicity.

Thus, it is no accident that the cognitive approach gives us no way to know what the subject will think of next. We cannot possibly know this, unless we have a detailed understanding of what he is trying to do, and why. For this reason, a really satisfactory theory of the higher mental processes can only come into being when we also have theories of motivation, personality, and social interaction. The study of cognition is only one fraction of psychology, and it cannot stand alone.

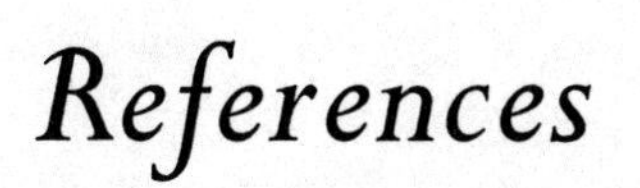

Alpern, M. (1952) Metacontrast: Historical introduction. *Amer. J. Optom., 29,* 631–646.

Alpern, M. (1953) Metacontrast. *J. opt. Soc. Amer., 43,* 648–657.

Antrobus, John S., Antrobus, Judith S., & Singer, J. L. (1964) Eye movements accompanying daydreaming, visual imagery, and thought suppression. *J. abnorm. soc. Psychol., 69,* 244–252.

Arbib, M. A. (1964) *Brains, machines, and mathematics.* New York: McGraw-Hill.

Arnheim, R. (1954) *Art and visual perception.* Berkeley, Calif.: Univer. of Calif. Press.

Asch, S. E. (1962) A problem in the theory of associations. *Psychol. Beiträge, 6,* 553–563.

Asch, S. E., Ceraso, J., & Heimer, W. (1960) Perceptual conditions of association. *Psychol. Monogr., 74,* No. 3.

Asch, S. E., Hay, J., & Diamond, R. M. (1960) Perceptual organization in serial rote-learning. *Amer. J. Psychol., 73,* 177–198.

Averbach, E. (1963) The span of apprehension as a function of exposure duration. *J. verb. Learn. verb. Behav., 2,* 60–64.

Averbach, E., & Coriell, A. S. (1961) Short-term memory in vision. *Bell Syst. tech. J., 40,* 309–328.

Averbach, E., & Sperling, G. (1961) Short-term storage of information in vision. In C. Cherry (Ed.), *Information theory: Proceedings of the Fourth London Symposium.* London: Butterworth.

Baldwin, M. (1962) Hallucinations in neurologic syndromes. In L. J. West (Ed.), *Hallucinations.* New York: Grune & Stratton.

Barber, T. X. (1964) Hypnotically hallucinated colors and their negative after-images. *Amer. J. Psychol., 77,* 313–318.

Barber, T. X. (1965) The effects of "hypnosis" on learning and recall: A methodological critique. *J. clin. Psychol., 21,* 19–25.

Bartlett, F. C. (1932) *Remembering.* Cambridge, England: Cambridge Univer. Press.

Bartlett, F. C. (1958) *Thinking.* New York: Basic Books.

Békésy, G. v. (1960) *Experiments in hearing.* New York: McGraw-Hill.

Berger, R. J. (1963) Experimental modification of dream content by meaningful verbal stimuli. *Brit. J. Psychiat., 109,* 722–740.

Bergson, H. (1911) *Matter and memory.* Trans. by N. M. Paul and W. S. Palmer. New York: Macmillan.

Bernstein, I. H., & Eriksen, C. W. (1965) Effects of "subliminal" prompting on paired-associate learning. *J. exp. Res. Pers., 1,* 33–38.

Bertini, M., Lewis, H. B., & Witkin, H. A. (1964) Some preliminary observations with an experimental procedure for the study of hypnagogic and related phenomena. *Arch. Psicol. Neurol. Psichiat., 25,* 493–534.

Bever, T. G., Fodor, J. A., & Weksel, W. (1965a) On the acquisition of syntax: A critique of "contextual generalization." *Psychol. Rev., 72,* 467–482.

Bever, T. G., Fodor, J. A., & Weksel, W. (1965b) Is linguistics empirical? *Psychol. Rev., 72,* 493–500.

Bleuler, E. (1912) Autistic thinking. In D. Rapaport (Ed.), *Organization and pathology of thought.* New York: Columbia Univer. Press, 1951.

Boring, E. G. (1930) A new ambiguous figure. *Amer. J. Psychol., 42,* 444–445.

Boring, E. G. (1942) *Sensation and perception in the history of experimental psychology.* New York: Appleton-Century-Crofts.

Boring, E. G. (1950) *A history of experimental psychology.* New York: Appleton-Century-Crofts.

Bousfield, W. A. (1953) The occurrence of clustering in the recall of randomly arranged associates. *J. gen. Psychol., 49,* 229–240.

Braine, M. D. S. (1963a) On learning the grammatical order of words. *Psychol. Rev., 70,* 323–348.

Braine, M. D. S. (1963b) The ontogeny of English phrase-structure: The first phase. *Language, 39,* 1–13.

Braine, M. D. S. (1965) On the basis of phrase structure: A reply to Bever, Fodor, and Weksel. *Psychol. Rev., 72,* 483–492.

Bricker, P. D., & Chapanis, A. (1953) Do incorrectly perceived tachistoscopic stimuli convey some information? *Psychol. Rev., 60,* 181–188.

Broadbent, D. E. (1954) The role of auditory localization in attention and memory span. *J. exp. Psychol., 47,* 191–196.

Broadbent, D. E. (1956) Successive responses to simultaneous stimuli. *Quart. J. exp. Psychol., 8,* 145–152.

Broadbent, D. E. (1957) Immediate memory and simultaneous stimuli. *Quart. J. exp. Psychol., 9,* 1–11.

Broadbent, D. E. (1958) *Perception and communication.* New York: Pergamon Press.

Broadbent, D. E. (1962) Attention and the perception of speech. *Scientific Amer., 206* (April), 143–151.

Broadbent, D. E. (1963) Flow of information within the organism. *J. verb. Learn. verb. Behav., 2,* 34–39.

Broadbent, D. E., & Gregory, M. (1964) Stimulus set and response set: The alternation of attention. *Quart. J. exp. Psychol., 16,* 309–312.

Broadbent, D. E., & Ladefoged, P. (1959) Auditory perception of temporal order. *J. acoust. Soc. Amer., 31,* 1539.

Brown, J. (1958) Some tests of the decay theory of immediate memory. *Quart. J. exp. Psychol., 10,* 12–21.

Brown, J. (1959) Information, redundancy, and decay of the memory trace. In *The mechanisation of thought processes.* London: H. M. Stationery Office.

Brown, R. (1956) Language and categories. In J. S. Bruner, J. J. Goodnow, and G. A. Austin, *A study of thinking.* New York: Wiley.

Brown, R. (1958) *Words and things.* New York: Free Press.

Brown, W. P. (1961) Conceptions of perceptual defense. *Brit. J. Psychol., Monogr. Suppl.,* No. 35.

Bruner, J. S. (1951) Personality dynamics and the process of perceiving. In R. R. Blake and G. V. Ramsay (Eds.), *Perception: An approach to personality.* New York: Ronald.

Bruner, J. S. (1957a) Going beyond the information given. In *Contemporary approaches to cognition: A symposium held at the University of Colorado.* Cambridge, Mass.: Harvard Univer. Press.

Bruner, J. S. (1957b) On perceptual readiness. *Psychol. Rev., 64,* 123–152.

Bruner, J. S. (1964) The course of cognitive growth. *Amer. Psychologist, 19,* 1–15.

Bruner, J. S. (1966) *Toward a theory of instruction.* Cambridge, Mass.: Harvard Univer. Press.

Bruner, J. S., Goodnow, J. J., & Austin, G. A. (1956) *A study of thinking.* New York: Wiley.

Bruner, J. S., Miller, G. A., & Zimmerman, C. (1955) Discriminative skill and discriminative matching in perceptual recognition. *J. exp. Psychol., 49,* 187–192.

Bruner, J. S., & Minturn, A. L. (1955) Perceptual identification and perceptual organization. *J. gen. Psychol., 53,* 21–28.

Bruner, J. S., & Postman, L. (1949) On the perception of incongruity: A paradigm. *J. Pers., 18,* 206–228.

Bruner, J. S., & Potter, M. C. (1964) Interference in visual recognition. *Science, 144,* 424–425.

Brunswik, E. (1956) *Perception and the representative design of psychological experiments.* Berkeley, Calif.: Univer. of Calif. Press.

Bryden, M. P. (1960) Tachistoscopic recognition of non-alphabetical material. *Canad. J. Psychol., 14,* 78–86.

Bryden, M. P. (1961) The role of post-exposure eye movements in tachistoscopic perception. *Canad. J. Psychol., 15,* 220–225.

Bugelski, B. R., & Alampay, D. A. (1961) The role of frequency in developing perceptual sets. *Canad. J. Psychol., 15,* 205–211.

Buschke, H. (1963a) Retention in immediate memory estimated without retrieval. *Science, 140,* 56–57.

Buschke, H. (1963b) Relative retention in immediate memory determined by the missing scan method. *Nature, 200,* 1129–1130.

Camp, D. S., & Harcum, E. R. (1964) Visual pattern perception with varied fixation locus and response recording. *Percept. mot. Skills, 18,* 283–296.

Carmichael, L. C., Hogan, H. P., & Walter, A. A. (1932) An experimental study of the effect of language on the reproduction of visually perceived form. *J. exp. Psychol., 15,* 73–86.

Cherry, E. C. (1953) Some experiments on the recognition of speech, with one and with two ears. *J. acoust. Soc. Amer., 25,* 975–979.

Cherry, E. C., & Taylor, W. K. (1954) Some further experiments on the recognition of speech with one and two ears. *J. acoust. Soc. Amer., 26,* 554–559.

Chomsky, N. (1957) *Syntactic structures.* 's-Gravenhage: Mouton.

Chomsky, N. (1959) Review of B. F. Skinner's *Verbal behavior*. *Language, 35,* 26–58.

Chomsky, N. (1963) Formal properties of grammar. In R. D. Luce, R. R. Bush, and E. Galanter (Eds.), *Handbook of mathematical psychology*. New York: Wiley.

Chomsky, N. (1964a) Current issues in linguistic theory. In J. A. Fodor and J. J. Katz (Eds.), *The structure of language: Readings in the philosophy of language*. Englewood Cliffs, N. J.: Prentice-Hall.

Chomsky, N. (1964b) On the notion "rule of grammar." In J. A. Fodor and J. J. Katz (Eds.), *The structure of language: Readings in the philosophy of language*. Englewood Cliffs, N. J.: Prentice-Hall.

Chomsky, N. (1965) *Aspects of the theory of syntax*. Cambridge, Mass.: M. I. T. Press.

Chomsky, N., & Miller, G. A. (1963) Introduction to the formal analysis of natural languages. In R. D. Luce, R. R. Bush, and E. Galanter (Eds.), *Handbook of mathematical psychology*. New York: Wiley.

Clifton, C., & Odom, P. (1966) Similarity relations among certain English sentence constructions. *Psychol. Monogr., 80,* No. 5.

Cobb, J. C., Evans, F. J., Gustafson, L. A., O'Connell, D. N., Orne, M. T., & Shor, R. E. (1965) Specific motor response during sleep to sleep-administered meaningful suggestion: An exploratory investigation. *Percept. mot. Skills, 20,* 629–636.

Cofer, C. N. (1964) Learning of content and function words in nonsense syllable frames: A repetition and extension of Glanzer's experiment. Paper presented to Psychonom. Soc., Niagara Falls, Ontario.

Conrad, R. (1959) Errors of immediate memory. *Brit. J. Psychol., 50,* 349.

Conrad, R. (1960a) Serial order intrusions in immediate memory. *Brit. J. Psychol., 51,* 45–48.

Conrad, R. (1960b) Very brief delay of immediate recall. *Quart. J. exp. Psychol., 12,* 45–47.

Conrad, R. (1962) An association between memory errors and errors due to acoustic masking of speech. *Nature, 196,* 1314–1315.

Conrad, R. (1964) Acoustic confusions in immediate memory. *Brit. J. Psychol., 55,* 75–83.

Conrad, R. (1965) Order error in immediate recall of sequences. *J. verb. Learn. verb. Behav., 4,* 161–169.

Conrad, R., & Hille, B. A. (1958) The decay theory of immediate memory and paced recall. *Canad. J. Psychol., 12,* 1–6.

Conrad, R., & Hull, A. J. (1964) Information, acoustic confusion, and memory span. *Brit. J. Psychol., 55,* 429–437.

Cooper, F. S. (1959) Discussion of Ladefoged's paper. In *The mechanisation of thought processes*. London: H. M. Stationery Office.

Crannell, C. W., & Parrish, J. M. (1957) A comparison of immediate memory span for digits, letters, and words. *J. Psychol., 44,* 319–327.

Crovitz, H. F., & Davies, W. (1962) Tendencies to eye movement and perceptual accuracy. *J. exp. Psychol., 63,* 495–498.

Crovitz, H. F., & Schiffman, H. R. (1965) Visual field and the letter span. *J. exp. Psychol., 70,* 218–223.

Davis, D. R., Sutherland, N. S., & Judd, B. (1961) Information content in recognition and recall. *J. exp. Psychol., 61,* 422–428.

Deese, J. (1965) *The structure of associations in language and thought.* Baltimore: Johns Hopkins.

Dement, W. C. (1965) Perception during sleep. In P. H. Hoch and J. Zubin (Eds.), *Psychopathology of perception.* New York: Grune & Stratton.

Denes, P. B. (1963) On the statistics of spoken English. *J. acoust. Soc. Amer., 35,* 892–904.

Dennis, W. (Ed.) (1948) *Readings in the history of psychology.* New York: Appleton-Century-Crofts.

Deutsch, J. A., & Deutsch, D. (1963) Attention: Some theoretical considerations. *Psychol. Rev., 70,* 80–90.

Dixon, N. F. (1958a) The effect of subliminal stimulation upon autonomic and verbal behavior. *J. abnorm. soc. Psychol., 57,* 29–36.

Dixon, N. F. (1958b) Apparent changes in the visual threshold as a function of subliminal stimulation. *Quart. J. exp. Psychol., 10,* 211–219.

Doob, L. W. (1964) Eidetic images among the Ibo. *Ethnology, 3,* 357–363.

Doob, L. W. (1965) Exploring eidetic and other imagery among the Kamba of Central Kenya. *J. soc. Psychol., 67,* 3–22.

Doyle, W. (1960) Recognition of sloppy, hand-printed characters. *Proc. West. Joint Computer Conf.,* San Francisco, Calif.

Dulany, D. E., & Eriksen, C. W. (1959) Accuracy of brightness discrimination as measured by concurrent verbal responses and GSRs. *J. abnorm. soc. Psychol., 59,* 418–423.

Duncker, K. (1929) Über induzierte Bewegung (Ein Beitrag zur Theorie optisch wahrgenommener Bewegung). *Psychol. Forsch., 12,* 180–259. Trans. and extracted in W. D. Ellis (Ed.), *A source book of Gestalt psychology.* New York: Humanities Press, 1950.

Eagle, M. (1959) The effects of subliminal stimuli of aggressive content upon conscious cognition. *J. Pers., 27,* 578–600.

Ebenholtz, S. M. (1963) Serial learning: Position learning and sequential association. *J. exp. Psychol., 66,* 353–362.

Eden, M. (1962) Handwriting and pattern recognition. *I. R. E. Trans. information Theory, IT-8,* 160–166.

Eden, M., & Halle, M. (1961) Characterization of cursive handwriting. In C. Cherry (Ed.), *Information theory: Proceedings of the Fourth London Symposium.* London: Butterworth.

Egan, J. P., Carterette, E. C., & Thwing, E. J. (1954) Some factors affecting multichannel listening. *J. acoust. Soc. Amer., 26,* 774–782.

Epstein, W. (1961) The influence of syntactical structure on learning. *Amer. J. Psychol., 74,* 80–85.

Epstein, W. (1962) A further study of the influence of syntactical structure on learning. *Amer. J. Psychol., 75,* 121–126.

Epstein, W., & Rock, I. (1960) Perceptual set as an artifact of recency. *Amer. J. Psychol., 73,* 214–228.

Erickson, M. H. (1962) Basic psychological problems in hypnotic research. In G. H. Estabrooks (Ed.), *Hypnosis: Current problems.* New York: Harper & Row.

Erickson, M. H. (1965) A special inquiry with Aldous Huxley into the nature and character of various states of consciousness. *Amer. J. clin. Hypnosis, 8,* 14–33.

Eriksen, C. W. (1956) Subception: Fact or artifact. *Psychol. Rev., 63,* 74–80.

Eriksen, C. W. (1958) Unconscious processes. In M. R. Jones (Ed.), *Nebraska symposium on motivation: 1958.* Lincoln, Neb.: Univer. of Nebraska Press.

Eriksen, C. W. (1960) Discrimination and learning without awareness: A methodological survey and evaluation. *Psychol. Rev., 67,* 279–300.

Eriksen, C. W. (Ed.) (1962) *Behavior and awareness.* Durham, N. C.: Duke Univer. Press.

Eriksen, C. W., Azuma, H., & Hicks, R. B. (1959) Verbal discrimination of pleasant and unpleasant stimuli prior to specific identification. *J. abnorm. soc. Psychol., 59,* 114–119.

Eriksen, C. W., & Collins, J. F. (1964) Backward masking in vision. *Psychonom. Sci., 1,* 101–102.

Eriksen, C. W., & Collins, J. F. (1965) Reinterpretation of one form of backward and forward masking in visual perception. *J. exp. Psychol., 70,* 343–351.

Eriksen, C. W., & Hoffman, M. (1963) Form recognition at brief durations as a function of adapting field and interval between stimulations. *J. exp. Psychol., 66,* 485–499.

Eriksen, C. W., & Johnson, H. J. (1964) Storage and decay characteristics of non-attended auditory stimuli. *J. exp. Psychol., 68,* 28–36.

Eriksen, C. W., & Lappin, J. S. (1964) Luminance summation—contrast reduction as a basis for certain forward and backward masking effects. *Psychonom. Sci., 1,* 313–314.

Eriksen, C. W., & Steffy, R. A. (1964) Short-term memory and retroactive interference in visual perception. *J. exp. Psychol., 68,* 423–434.

Evans, F. J., Gustafson, L. A., O'Connell, D. N., Orne, M. T., & Shor, R. E. (1966) Response during sleep with intervening waking amnesia. *Science, 152,* 666–667.

Evey, R. J. (1959) Use of a computer to design character recognition logic. *Proc. East. Joint Computer Conf.,* Boston, Mass.

Fehrer, E., & Biederman, I. (1962) A comparison of reaction time and verbal report in the detection of masked stimuli. *J. exp. Psychol., 64,* 126–130.

Fehrer, E., & Raab, D. (1962) Reaction time to stimuli masked by metacontrast. *J. exp. Psychol., 63,* 143–147.

Fehrer, E., & Smith, E. (1962) Effect of luminance ratio on masking. *Percept. mot. Skills, 14,* 243–253.

Feigenbaum, E. A. (1963) The simulation of verbal learning behavior. In E. A. Feigenbaum and J. Feldman (Eds.), *Computers and thought.* New York: McGraw-Hill.

Feigenbaum, E. A., & Simon, H. A. (1962) A theory of the serial position effect. *Brit. J. Psychol., 53,* 307–320.

Feigenbaum, E. A., & Simon, H. A. (1963) Brief notes on the EPAM theory of verbal learning. In C. N. Cofer and B. S. Musgrave (Eds.), *Verbal behavior and learning: Problems and processes.* New York: McGraw-Hill.

Feinberg, I. (1962) A comparison of the visual hallucinations in schizophrenia with those induced by mescaline and LSD-25. In L. J. West (Ed.), *Hallucinations.* New York: Grune & Stratton.

Fisher, C. (1960) Introduction: Preconscious stimulation in dreams, associations, and images. *Psychol. Issues, 2,* No. 3, 1–40.

Fisher, S. (1962) Problems of interpretation and controls in hypnotic research. In G. H. Estabrooks (Ed.), *Hypnosis: Current problems.* New York: Harper & Row.

Flavell, J. H. (1963) *The developmental psychology of Jean Piaget.* New York: Van Nostrand.

Flavell, J. H., & Draguns, J. A. (1957) A microgenetic approach to perception and thought. *Psychol. Bull., 54,* 197–217.

Fletcher, H. (1929) *Speech and hearing.* New York: Van Nostrand.

Fodor, J. A., & Bever, T. G. (1965) The psychological reality of linguistic segments. *J. verb. Learn. verb. Behav., 4,* 414–420.

Fodor, J. A., & Katz, J. J. (Eds.) (1964) *The structure of language: Readings in the philosophy of language.* Englewood Cliffs, N. J.: Prentice-Hall.

Foote, W. E., & Havens, L. L. (1965) Stimulus frequency: Determinant of perception or response? *Psychonom. Sci., 2,* 153–154.

Foulkes, D. (1966) *The psychology of sleep.* New York: Scribner.

Foulkes, D., & Vogel, G. (1965) Mental activity at sleep onset. *J. abnorm. soc. Psychol., 70,* 231–243.

Fozard, J. L., & Yntema, D. B. (1966) The effect of repetition on the apparent recency of pictures. Paper presented to East. Psychol. Ass., New York.

Fraisse, P. (1956) *Les structures rhythmiques.* Louvain: *Publications Universitaires de Louvain.*

Fraisse, P. (1963) *The psychology of time.* New York: Harper & Row.

Francis, W. N. (1963) Revolution in grammar. In J. A. Rycenga and J. Schwartz (Eds.), *Perspectives on language.* New York: Ronald.

Freeman, J. T. (1954) Set or perceptual defense? *J. exp. Psychol., 48,* 283–288.

Freeman, J. T. (1955) Set vs. perceptual defense: A confirmation. *J. abnorm. soc. Psychol., 51,* 710–712.

Freeman, J. T., & Engler, J. (1955) Perceptual recognition thresholds as a function of multiple and single set and frequency of usage of the stimulus material. *Percept. mot. Skills, 5,* 149–155.

Freud, S. (1900) *The interpretation of dreams.* In A. A. Brill (Ed.), *The basic writings of Sigmund Freud.* New York: Modern Library, 1938.

Freud, S. (1904) *The psychopathology of everyday life.* In A. A. Brill (Ed.), *The basic writings of Sigmund Freud.* New York: Modern Library, 1938.

Freud, S. (1915) Instincts and their vicissitudes. In *Collected papers of Sigmund Freud.* Vol. IV. London: Hogarth, 1956.

Fries, C. C. (1963) *Linguistics and reading.* New York: Holt, Rinehart and Winston.

Frohlich, F. W. (1925) Über die Methoden der Empfindungszeitmessung in Gebiete des Gesichtsinnes. *Arch. f. d. ges. Psychol., 208,* 131.

Frohlich, F. W. (1929) *Die Empfindungszeit.* Jena: Gustav Fisher.

Fuhrer, M. J., & Eriksen, C. W. (1960) The unconscious perception of the meaning of verbal stimuli. *J. abnorm. soc. Psychol., 61,* 432–439.

Furst, B. (1948) *Stop forgetting: How to develop your memory and put it to practical use.* Garden City, N. Y.: Doubleday.

Ganz, L. (1966a) Mechanism of the figural after-effects. *Psychol. Rev., 73,* 128–150.

Ganz, L. (1966b) Is the figural aftereffect an *after*effect? A review of its intensity, onset, decay, and transfer characteristics. *Psychol. Bull., 66,* 151–165.

Garner, W. R. (1962) *Uncertainty and structure as psychological concepts.* New York: Wiley.

Garrett, M., Bever, T., & Fodor, J. (1966) The active use of grammar in speech perception. *Percept. & Psychophys., 1,* 30–32.

Gerard, F. O. (1960) Subliminal stimulation in problem-solving. *Amer. J. Psychol., 73,* 121–126.

Ghent, L. (1960) Recognition by children of realistic figures presented in various orientations. *Canad. J. Psychol., 14,* 249–256.

Ghent, L., & Bernstein, L. (1961) Influence of the orientation of geometric forms on their recognition by children. *Percept. mot. Skills, 12,* 95–101.

Gibson, E. J. (1953) Improvement in perceptual judgments as a function of controlled practice or training. *Psychol. Bull., 50,* 401–431.

Gibson, E. J. (1963) Perceptual learning. *Annu. Rev. Psychol., 14,* 29–56.

Gibson, E. J. (1965) Learning to read. *Science, 148,* 1066–1072.

Gibson, E. J., Bishop, C. H., Schiff, W., & Smith, J. (1964) Comparison of meaningfulness and pronunciability as grouping principles in the perception and retention of verbal material. *J. exp. Psychol., 67,* 173–182.

Gibson, E. J., Gibson, J. J., Pick, A. D., & Osser, H. (1962) A developmental study of the discrimination of letter-like forms. *J. comp. physiol. Psychol., 55,* 897–906.

Gibson, E. J., Osser, H., Schiff, W., & Smith, J. (1963) An analysis of critical features of letters, tested by a confusion matrix. Final report on Cooperative Research Project No. 639, Office of Education, Department of Health, Education, and Welfare.

Gibson, E. J., Pick, A. D., Osser, H., & Hammond, M. (1962) The role of grapheme-phoneme correspondence in the perception of words. *Amer. J. Psychol., 75,* 554–570.

Gibson, J. J. (1950) *The perception of the visual world.* Boston, Mass.: Houghton Mifflin.

Gibson, J. J. (1962) Observations on active touch. *Psychol. Rev., 69,* 477–491.

Gibson, J. J., & Gibson, E. J. (1955a) Perceptual learning: Differentiation or enrichment? *Psychol. Rev., 62,* 32–41.

Gibson, J. J., & Gibson, E. J. (1955b) What is learned in perceptual learning? A reply to Professor Postman. *Psychol. Rev., 62,* 447–450.

Gilbert, L. C. (1959) Speed of processing visual stimuli and its relation to reading. *J. educ. Psychol., 50,* 8–14.

Glanzer, M. (1962) Grammatical category: A rote learning and word association analysis. *J. verb. Learn. verb. Behav., 1,* 31–41.

Glanzer, M., & Clark, W. H. (1963a) Accuracy of perceptual recall: An analysis of organization. *J. verb. Learn. verb. Behav., 1,* 289–299.

Glanzer, M., & Clark, W. H. (1963b) The verbal loop hypothesis: Binary numbers. *J. verb. Learn. verb. Behav., 2,* 301–309.

Gleason, H. A. (1961) *An introduction to descriptive linguistics.* New York: Holt, Rinehart and Winston.

Glucksberg, S. (1965) Decay and interference in short-term memory. Paper presented to Psychonom. Soc., Chicago, Ill.

Glucksberg, S., & Cohen, J. A. (1965) Acquisition of form-class membership by syntactic position: Paradigmatic associations to nonsense syllables. *Psychonom. Sci., 2,* 313–314.

Goldiamond, I., & Hawkins, W. F. (1958) Vexierversuch: The log relationship between word-frequency and recognition obtained in the absence of stimulus words. *J. exp. Psychol., 56,* 457–463.

Gottschaldt, K. (1926) Über den Einfluss der Erfahrung auf die Wahrnehmung von Figuren: I. Über den Einfluss gehäufter Einprägung von Figuren auf ihre Sichtbarkeit in umfassenden Konfigurationen. *Psychol. Forsch., 8,* 261–317. Trans. and extracted in W. D. Ellis (Ed.), *A source book of Gestalt psychology.* New York: Humanities Press, 1950.

Gough, P. B. (1965) Grammatical transformations and speed of understanding. *J. verb. Learn. verb. Behav., 4,* 107–111.

Gould, L. N. (1949) Auditory hallucinations and subvocal speech: Objective study in a case of schizophrenia. *J. nerv. ment. Dis., 109,* 418–427.

Gould, L. N. (1950) Verbal hallucinations as automatic speech: The reactivation of dormant speech habit. *Amer. J. Psychiat., 107,* 110–119.

Granit, R. (1955) *Receptors and sensory perception.* New Haven: Yale Univer. Press.

Gray, J. A., & Wedderburn, A. A. I. (1960) Grouping strategies with simultaneous stimuli. *Quart. J. exp. Psychol., 12,* 180–184.

Gross, J., Feldman, M., & Fisher, C. (1965) Eye movements during emergent stage-1 EEG in subjects with lifelong blindness. Paper presented to Ass. for Psychophysiol. Study of Sleep, Washington, D. C.

Guthrie, G., & Wiener, M. (1966) Subliminal perception or perception of partial cue with pictorial stimuli. *J. Pers. soc. Psychol., 3,* 619–628.

Guttman, N., & Julesz, B. (1963) Lower limits of auditory periodicity analysis. *J. acoust. Soc. Amer., 35,* 610.

Gyr, J. W., Brown, J. S., Willey, R., & Zivian, A. (1966) Computer simulation and psychological theories of perception. *Psychol. Bull., 65,* 174–192.

Haber, R. N. (1964a) A replication of selective attention and coding in visual perception. *J. exp. Psychol., 67,* 402–404.

Haber, R. N. (1964b) The effects of coding strategy on perceptual memory. *J. exp. Psychol., 68,* 357–362.

Haber, R. N. (1965) Effect of prior knowledge of the stimulus on word-recognition processes. *J. exp. Psychol., 69,* 282–286.

Haber, R. N. (1966) Nature of the effect of set on perception. *Psychol. Rev., 73,* 335–351.

Haber, R. N., & Haber, R. B. (1964) Eidetic imagery: I. Frequency. *Percept. mot. Skills, 19,* 131–138.

Haber, R. N., & Hershenson, M. (1965) Effects of repeated brief exposures on the growth of a percept. *J. exp. Psychol., 69,* 40–46.

Hall, C. S. (1953a) A cognitive theory of dream symbols. *J. gen. Psychol., 48,* 169–186.

Hall, C. S. (1953b) A cognitive theory of dreams. *J. gen. Psychol., 49,* 273–282.

Halle, M. (1956) Review of Hockett's *Manual of Phonology. J. acoust. Soc. Amer., 28,* 509–511.

Halle, M., & Stevens, K. N. (1959) Analysis by synthesis. In W. Wathen-Dunn & L. E. Woods (Eds.), *Proceedings of the Seminar on Speech Compression and Processing.* Bedford, Mass.: Air Force Cambridge Research Laboratories.

Halle, M., & Stevens, K. N. (1964) Speech recognition: A model and a program for research. In J. A. Fodor and J. J. Katz (Eds.), *The structure of language: Readings in the philosophy of language.* Englewood Cliffs, N. J.: Prentice-Hall.

Harcum, E. R. (1964) Effect of pre-recognition exposure on visual perception of words. Paper presented to East. Psychol. Ass., Philadelphia, Pa.

Harris, C. S., & Haber, R. N. (1963) Selective attention and coding in visual perception. *J. exp. Psychol., 65,* 328–333.

Haselrud, G. M. (1964) Perception of words as a function of delays between and summation of subliminal exposures. *Percept. mot. Skills, 19,* 130.

Havens, L. L. (1962) The placement and movement of hallucinations in space: Phenomenology and theory. *Int. J. Psychoanal., 43,* 426–435.

Havens, L. L., & Foote, W. E. (1963) The effect of competition on visual duration threshold and its independence of stimulus frequency. *J. exp. Psychol., 65,* 6–11.

Havens, L. L., & Foote, W. E. (1964) Structural features of competitive responses. *Percept. mot. Skills, 19,* 75–80.

Hebb, D. O. (1949) *The organization of behavior.* New York: Wiley.

Hebb, D. O. (1961) Distinctive features of learning in the higher animal. In J. F. Delafresnaye (Ed.), *Brain mechanisms and learning.* Oxford: Blackwell.

Hebb, D. O. (1963) The semi-autonomous process: Its nature and nurture. *Amer. Psychologist, 18,* 16–27.

Held, R. (1955) Shifts in binaural localization after prolonged exposure to atypical combinations of stimuli. *Amer. J. Psychol., 68,* 526–548.

Hellyer, S. (1962) Supplementary report: Frequency of stimulus presentation and short-term decrement in recall. *J. exp. Psychol., 64,* 650.

Hernández-Peón, R., Scherrer, H., & Jouvet, M. (1956) Modification of electric activity in the cochlear nucleus during "attention" in unanesthetized cats. *Science, 123,* 331–332.

Heron, W. (1957) Perception as a function of retinal locus and attention. *Amer. J. Psychol., 70,* 38–48.

Hershenson, M., & Haber, R. N. (1965) The role of meaning in the perception of briefly exposed words. *Canad. J. Psychol., 19,* 42–46.

Hess, E. H. (1965) Attitude and pupil size. *Scientific Amer., 212* (April), 46–54.

Hick, W. E. (1952) On the rate of gain of information. *Quart. J. exp. Psychol., 4,* 11–26.

Hilgard, E. R. (1962) Impulsive versus realistic thinking: An examination of the distinction between primary and secondary process in thought. *Psychol. Bull., 59,* 477–488.

Hintzman, D. L. (1965) Classification and aural coding in short-term memory. *Psychonom. Sci., 3,* 161–162.

Hirsh, I. J. (1950) The relation between localization and intelligibility. *J. acoust. Soc. Amer., 22,* 196–200.

Hirsh, I. J. (1959) Auditory perception of temporal order. *J. acoust. Soc. Amer., 31,* 759–767.

Hochberg, J., & Berko, M. J. (1965) "Phenomenal displacement" in delayed auditory feedback: I. Disparate interaural intensities. *Psychonom. Sci., 2,* 389.

Höffding, H. (1891) *Outlines of psychology.* New York: Macmillan.

Holt, R. R. (1964) Imagery: The return of the ostracized. *Amer. Psychologist, 19,* 254–264.

Horowitz, M. J. (1967) Visual imagery and cognitive organization. *Amer. J. Psychiat., 123,* 938–946.

Horrocks, J. E. (1964) *Assessment of behavior.* Columbus, Ohio: Charles E. Merrill.

Howarth, C. I., & Ellis, K. (1961) The relative intelligibility threshold for one's own name compared with other names. *Quart. J. exp. Psychol., 13,* 236–239.

Howes, D. H. (1957) On the relation between intelligibility and frequency of occurrence of English words. *J. acoust. Soc. Amer., 29,* 296–305.

Howes, D. H., & Solomon, R. L. (1951) Visual duration threshold as a function of word-probability. *J. exp. Psychol., 41,* 401–410.

Hubel, D. H. (1963) The visual cortex of the brain. *Scientific Amer., 209,* 54–62.

Hubel, D. H., & Wiesel, T. N. (1959) Receptive fields of single neurones in the cat's striate cortex. *J. Physiol., 148,* 574–591.

Hubel, D. H., & Wiesel, T. N. (1962) Receptive fields, binocular interaction, and functional architecture in the cat's visual cortex. *J. Physiol., 160,* 106–154.

Hugelin, A., Dumont, S., & Paillas, N. (1960) Formation reticulaire et transmission des informations auditives au niveau de l'oreille moyenne et des voies acoustiques centrales. *EEG clin. Neurophysiol., 12,* 797–818.

Huggins, A. W. F. (1963) Distortion of the temporal pattern of speech: Interruption and alternation. Unpublished doctoral dissertation, Harvard Univer.

Huggins, A. W. F. (1964) Distortion of the temporal pattern of speech: Interruption and alternation. *J. acoust. Soc. Amer., 36,* 1055–1064.

Hull, C. L. (1952) *A behavior system.* New Haven, Conn.: Yale Univer. Press.

Humphrey, G. (1951) *Thinking.* New York: Wiley.

Hunter, I. M. L. (1957) *Memory: Facts and fallacies.* Baltimore: Penguin.

Hunter, I. M. L. (1962) An exceptional talent for calculative thinking. *Brit. J. Psychol., 53,* 243–258.

Hunter, W. S., & Sigler, M. (1940) The span of visual discrimination as a function of time and intensity of stimulation. *J. exp. Psychol., 26,* 160–179.

Huxley, A. (1959) *The doors of perception* and *Heaven and hell.* (Published in one volume.) Harmundsworth, Middlesex: Penguin.

Jackson, C. W., & Kelly, E. L. (1962) Influence of suggestion and subjects' prior knowledge in research on sensory deprivation. *Science, 135,* 211–212.

Jaensch, E. R. (1930) *Eidetic imagery and typological methods of investigation.* New York: Harcourt, Brace & World.

Jakobson, R., Fant, G. G. M., & Halle, M. (1961) *Preliminaries to speech analy-*

*sis: The distinctive features and their correlates.* Cambridge, Mass.: M. I. T. Press.

Jakobson, R., & Halle, M. (1956) *Fundamentals of language.* 's-Gravenhage: Mouton.

James, W. (1890) *The principles of psychology.* New York: Dover. (Reprinted 1950).

Johnson, H., & Eriksen, C. W. (1961) Pre-conscious perception: A re-examination of the Poetzl phenomenon. *J. abnorm. soc. Psychol., 62,* 497–503.

Johnson, R. C., Thomson, C. W., & Frincke, G. (1960) Word values, word frequency, and visual duration thresholds. *Psychol. Rev. 67,* 332–342.

Julesz, B., & Guttman, N. (1963) Auditory memory. *J. acoust. Soc. Amer., 35,* 1895. (Abstract)

Kahneman, D. (1964) Temporal effects in the perception of form and light. Paper presented at the Sympos. on Models for the Percept. of Speech and Visual Form, Cambridge, Mass.

Kahneman, D. (1965a) Temporal summation in an acuity task at different energy levels—a study of the determinants of summation. *Vision Res., 4,* 557–566.

Kahneman, D. (1965b) Exposure duration and effective figure-ground contrast. *Quart. J. exp. Psychol., 17,* 308–314.

Kahneman, D., & Norman, J. (1964) The time-intensity relation in visual perception as a function of observer's task. *J. exp. Psychol., 68,* 215–220.

Kaplan, I. T., & Carvellas, T. (1965) Scanning for multiple targets. *Percept. mot. Skills, 21,* 239–243.

Kaplan, I. T., Carvellas, T., & Metlay, W. (1966) Visual search and immediate memory. *J. exp. Psychol., 71,* 488–493.

Katona, G. (1940) *Organizing and memorizing.* New York: Columbia Univer. Press.

Kaufman, E. L., Lord, M. W., Reese, T. W., & Volkmann, J. (1949) The discrimination of visual number. *Amer. J. Psychol., 62,* 498–525.

Kay, H., & Poulton, E. C. (1951) Anticipation in memorizing. *Brit. J. Psychol., 42,* 34–41.

Kempler, B., & Wiener, M. (1963) Personality and perception in the threshold paradigm. *Psychol. Rev., 70,* 349–356.

Kempler, B., & Wiener, M. (1964) Personality-perception: Characteristic response to available part-cues. *J. Pers., 32,* 57–74.

Kimble, G. A. (1961) *Hilgard and Marquis' conditioning and learning.* New York: Appleton-Century-Crofts.

Klein, G. S., Spence, D. O., Holt, R. R., & Gourevitch, S. (1958) Cognition without awareness: Subliminal influences upon conscious thought. *J. abnorm. soc. Psychol., 57,* 255–266.

Klemmer, E. T. (1964) Does recoding from binary to octal improve the perception of binary patterns? *J. exp. Psychol., 67,* 19–21.

Klüver, H. (1931) The eidetic child. In C. Murchison (Ed.), *A handbook of child psychology.* Worcester, Mass.: Clark Univer. Press.

Klüver, H. (1942) Mechanisms of hallucinations. In Q. McNemar and M. A. Merrill (Eds.), *Studies in personality.* New York: McGraw-Hill.

Klüver, H. (1965) Neurobiology of normal and abnormal perception. In P. H.

Hoch and J. Zubin (Eds.), *Psychopathology of perception.* New York: Grune & Stratton.

Koffka, K. (1935) *Principles of Gestalt psychology.* New York: Harcourt, Brace & World.

Köhler, W. (1924) *Die physischen Gestalten in Ruhe und im stationären Zustand.* Erlangen: Philosophische Akademie.

Köhler, W. (1940) *Dynamics in psychology.* New York: Liveright.

Kolers, P. A. (1957) Subliminal stimulation in problem solving. *Amer. J. Psychol., 70,* 437–441.

Kolers, P. A. (1962) Intensity and contour effects in visual masking. *Vision Res., 2,* 277–294.

Kolers, P. A. (1964a) The illusion of movement. *Scientific Amer., 211* (Oct.), 98–106.

Kolers, P. A. (1964b) Apparent movement of a Necker cube. *Amer. J. Psychol., 77,* 220–230.

Kolers, P. A., Eden, M., & Boyer, A. (1964) Reading as a perceptual skill. *M. I. T., Res. Lab. of Electronics, Quart. Prog. Rep., 74* (July), 214–217.

Kolers, P. A., & Rosner, B. S. (1960) On visual masking (metacontrast): Dichoptic observation. *Amer. J. Psychol., 73,* 2–21.

Kris, E. (1950) On preconscious mental processes. *Psychoanal. Quart., 19,* 540–560.

Kubie, L. S. (1943) The use of induced hypnagogic reveries in the recovery of repressed amnesic data. *Bull. Menninger Clin., 7,* 172–182.

Lacey, O. W., Levinger, N., & Adamson, J. F. (1953) Foreknowledge as a factor affecting perceptual defense and alertness. *J. exp. Psychol., 45,* 169–174.

Ladefoged, P. (1959) The perception of speech. In *The mechanisation of thought processes.* London: H. M. Stationery Office.

Ladefoged, P., & Broadbent, D. E. (1960) Perception of sequence in auditory events. *Quart. J. exp. Psychol., 12,* 162–170.

Landauer, T. K. (1962) Rate of implicit speech. *Percept. mot. Skills, 15,* 646.

Lane, H. (1965) The motor theory of speech perception: A critical review. *Psychol. Rev., 72,* 275–309.

Lashley, K. S. (1942) The problem of cerebral organization in vision. *Biol. Sympos., 7,* 301–322.

Lashley, K. S. (1950) In search of the engram. *Proc. Soc. Exp. Biol., 4,* 454–482. Reprinted in F. A. Beach, D. O. Hebb, C. T. Morgan, & H. W. Nissen (Eds.), *The neuropsychology of Lashley.* New York: McGraw-Hill, 1960.

Lashley, K. S. (1951) The problem of serial order in behavior. In L. A. Jeffress (Ed.), *Cerebral mechanisms in behavior: The Hixon symposium.* New York: Wiley.

Lashley, K. S. (1954) Dynamic processes in perception. In E. D. Adrian, F. Bremer, and H. H. Jasper (Eds.), *Brain mechanisms and consciousness.* Springfield, Ill.: Charles C Thomas.

Lawrence, D. H., & Coles, G. R. (1954) Accuracy of recognition with alternatives before and after the stimulus. *J. exp. Psychol., 47,* 208–214.

Lawrence, D. H., & LaBerge, D. L. (1956) Relationship between recognition accuracy and order of reporting stimulus dimensions. *J. exp. Psychol., 51,* 12–18.

Lazarus, R. S., & McCleary, R. A. (1951) Autonomic discrimination without awareness: A study of subception. *Psychol. Rev., 58,* 113–122.

Leeper, R. (1935) A study of a neglected portion of the field of learning—the development of sensory organization. *J. genet. Psychol., 46,* 41–75.

Lenneberg, E. H. (1962) Understanding language without ability to speak: A case report. *J. abnorm. soc. Psychol., 65,* 419–425.

Lenneberg, E. H. (1964a) A biological perspective of language. In E. H. Lenneberg (Ed.), *New directions in the study of language.* Cambridge, Mass.: M. I. T. Press.

Lenneberg, E. H. (1964b) The capacity for language acquisition. In J. A. Fodor and J. J. Katz (Eds.), *The structure of language: Readings in the philosophy of language.* Englewood Cliffs, N. J.: Prentice-Hall.

Leonard, J. A. (1959) Tactual choice reactions, 1. *Quart. J. exp. Psychol., 11,* 76–83.

Leonard, J. A. (1961) Choice reaction time experiments and information theory. In C. Cherry (Ed.), *Information theory: Proceedings of the Fourth London Symposium.* London: Butterworth.

Lettvin, J. Y., Maturana, H. R., McCulloch, W. S., & Pitts, W. H. (1959) What the frog's eye tells the frog's brain. *Proc. Inst. radio Engr., 47,* 1940–1951.

Liberman, A. M. (1957) Some results of research on speech perception. *J. acoust. Soc. Amer., 29,* 117–123.

Liberman, A. M., Harris, K. S., Hoffman, H. S., & Griffith, B. C. (1957) The discrimination of speech sounds within and across phoneme boundaries. *J. exp. Psychol., 54,* 358–368.

Licklider, J. C. R. (1952) On the process of speech perception. *J. acoust. Soc. Amer., 24,* 590–594.

Licklider, J. C. R. (1951) Basic correlates of the auditory stimulus. In S. S. Stevens (Eds.), *Handbook of experimental psychology.* New York: Wiley.

Lindgren, N. (1965a) Machine recognition of human language. Part I: Automatic speech recognition. *I. E. E. E. Spectrum, 2* (March), 114–136.

Lindgren, N. (1965b) Machine recognition of human language. Part II: Theoretical models of speech perception and language. *I. E. E. E. Spectrum, 2* (April), 45–59.

Lindgren, N. (1965c) Machine recognition of human language. Part III: Cursive script recognition. *I. E. E. E. Spectrum, 2* (May) 105–116.

Long, E. R., Henneman, R. H., & Garvey, W. D. (1960) An experimental analysis of set: The role of sense modality. *Amer. J. Psychol. 73,* 563–567.

Long, E. R., Reid, L. S., & Henneman, R. H. (1960) An experimental analysis of set: Variables influencing the identification of ambiguous visual stimulus objects. *Amer. J. Psychol., 73,* 553–562.

Luce, R. D., Bush, R. R., & Galanter, E. (Eds.) (1963) *Handbook of mathematical psychology.* New York: Wiley.

McGeoch, J. A. (1942) *The psychology of human learning.* New York: Longmans.

McGinnies, E. (1949) Emotionality and perceptual defense. *Psychol. Rev., 56,* 244–251.

McGinnies, E., Comer, P. B., & Lacy, J. (1952) Visual recognition thresholds as a function of word length and word frequency. *J. exp. Psychol., 44,* 65–69.

McGuigan, F. J. (1966) Covert oral behavior and auditory hallucinations. *Psychophysiology, 3,* 73–80.

McKellar, P. (1957) *Imagination and thinking.* New York: Basic Books.

McKinney, J. P. (1963) Disappearance of luminous designs. *Science, 140,* 403–404.

McKinney, J. P. (1966) Verbal meaning and perceptual stability. *Canad. J. Psychol., 20,* 237–242.

Mackworth, J. F. (1962) The visual image and the memory trace. *Canad. J. Psychol., 16,* 55–59.

Mackworth, J. F. (1963a) The duration of the visual image. *Canad. J. Psychol., 17,* 62–81.

Mackworth, J. F. (1963b) The relation between the visual image and post-perceptual immediate memory. *J. verb. Learn. verb. Behav., 2,* 75–85.

Mackworth, J. F. (1964) Interference and decay in very short-term memory. *J. verb. Learn. verb. Behav., 3,* 300–308.

Mackworth, J. F. (1965) Presentation rate, repetition, and organization in auditory short-term memory. *Canad. J. Psychol., 19,* 304–315.

McNeill, D. (1963) The origin of associations within the same grammatical class. *J. verb. Learn. verb. Behav., 2,* 250–262.

Mahl, G. F., Rothenberg, A., Delgado, J. N. R., & Hamlin, H. (1964) Psychological response in the human to intra-cerebral electrical stimulation. *Psychosom. Med., 26,* 337–368.

Malitz, S., Wilkens, B., & Esecover, H. (1962) A comparison of drug-induced hallucinations with those seen in spontaneously occurring psychoses. In L. J. West (Ed.), *Hallucinations.* New York: Grune & Stratton.

Mandes, E., & Ghent, L. (1963) The effect of stimulus orientation on the recognition of geometric forms in adults. *Amer. Psychologist, 18,* 425. (Abstract)

Marks, L., & Miller, G. A. (1964) The role of semantic and syntactic constraints in the memorization of English sentences. *J. verb. Learn. verb. Behav., 3,* 1–5.

Marshall, G. R. (1965) Sequential probability, pronounceability, content-and-function words: Their relationship to response acquisition. *Amer. Psychologist, 20,* 555. (Abstract)

Martin, E., & Roberts, K. H. (1966) Grammatical factors in sentence retention. *J. verb. Learn. verb. Behav., 5,* 211–218.

Maslow, A. H. (1957) Two kinds of cognition and their integration. *Gen. Semantics Bull., 20,* 17–22.

Mathews, A., & Wertheimer, M. (1958) A "pure" measure of perceptual defense uncontaminated by response suppression. *J. abnorm. soc. Psychol., 57,* 373–376.

Mayzner, M. S., Abrevaya, E. L., Frey, R. E., Kaufman, H. G., & Schoenberg, K. M. (1964) Short-term memory in vision: A partial replication of the Averbach and Coriell study. *Psychonom. Sci., 1,* 225–226.

Meenes, M., & Morton, M. A. (1936) Characteristics of the eidetic phenomenon. *J. gen. Psychol., 14,* 370–391.

Mehler, J. (1963) Some effects of grammatical transformation on the recall of English sentences. *J. verb. Learn. verb. Behav., 2,* 346–351.

Mehler, J., & Miller, G. A. (1964) Retroactive interference in the recall of simple sentences. *Brit. J. Psychol., 55,* 295–301.

Melton, A. W. (1963) Implication of short-term memory for a general theory of memory. *J. verb. Learn. verb. Behav., 2,* 1–21.

Mermelstein, P., & Eden, M. (1964) Experiments on computer recognition of connected handwritten words. *Inform. & Control, 7,* 250–270.

Metzger, W. (1953) *Gesetze des Sehens.* Frankfurt-am-Main: Waldemar Kramer.

Mewhort, D. J. K. (1966) Sequential redundancy and letter spacing as determinants of tachistoscopic recognition. *Canad. J. Psychol., 20,* 435–444.

Miller, G. A. (1953) What is information measurement? *Amer. Psychologist, 8,* 3–11.

Miller, G. A. (1956a) The magical number seven, plus or minus two: Some limits on our capacity for processing information. *Psychol. Rev., 63,* 81–97.

Miller, G. A. (1956b) Human memory and the storage of information. *I. R. E. Trans. information Theory, IT-2,* 129–137.

Miller, G. A. (1962a) Some psychological studies of grammar. *Amer. Psychologist, 17,* 748–762.

Miller, G. A. (1962b) Decision units in the perception of speech. *I. R. E. Trans. information Theory, IT-8,* 81–83.

Miller, G. A. (1965) Some preliminaries to psycholinguistics. *Amer. Psychologist, 20,* 15–20.

Miller, G. A., Bruner, J. S., & Postman, L. (1954) Familiarity of letter sequences and tachistoscopic identification. *J. gen. Psychol., 50,* 129–139.

Miller, G. A., & Chomsky, N. (1963) Finitary models of language users. In R. D. Luce, R. R. Bush, and E. Galanter (Eds.), *Handbook of mathematical psychology.* New York: Wiley.

Miller, G. A., Galanter, E., & Pribram, K. H. (1960) *Plans and the structure of behavior.* New York: Holt, Rinehart and Winston.

Miller, G. A., Heise, G. A., & Lichten, W. (1951) The intelligibility of speech as a function of the context of the test materials. *J. exp. Psychol., 41,* 329–335.

Miller, G. A., & Isard, S. (1963) Some perceptual consequences of linguistic rules. *J. verb. Learn. verb. Behav., 2,* 217–228.

Miller, G. A., & Nicely, P. E. (1955) An analysis of perceptual confusions among some English consonants. *J. acoust. Soc. Amer., 27,* 338–352.

Miller, G. A., & Selfridge, J. A. (1950) Verbal context and the recall of meaningful material. *Amer. J. Psychol., 63,* 176–185.

Milner, P. M. (1957) The cell-assembly: Mark II. *Psychol. Rev., 64,* 242–252.

Minard, J. G. (1965) Response-bias interpretation of "perceptual defense." *Psychol. Rev., 72,* 74–88.

Minsky, M. (1961) Steps toward artificial intelligence. *Proc. Inst. radio Engr., 49,* 8–30.

Minsky, M., & Selfridge, O. G. (1961) Learning in random nets. In C. Cherry (Ed.), *Information theory: Proceedings of the Fourth London Symposium.* London: Butterworth.

Mishkin, M., & Forgays, D. G. (1952) Word recognition as a function of retinal locus. *J. exp. Psychol., 43,* 43–48.

Mooney, C. M. (1958) Recognition of novel visual configurations with and without eye movements. *J. exp. Psychol., 56,* 133–138.

Mooney, C. M. (1959) Recognition of symmetrical and non-symmetrical inkblots with and without eye movements. *Canad. J. Psychol., 13,* 11–19.

Moray, N. (1959) Attention in dichotic listening: Affective cues and the influence of instructions. *Quart. J. exp. Psychol., 11,* 56–60.

Moray, N. (1960) Broadbent's filter theory: Postulate H and the problem of switching time. *Quart. J. exp. Psychol., 12,* 214–220.

Morin, R. E., Konick, A., Troxell, N., & McPherson, S. (1965) Information and reaction time for "naming" responses. *J. exp. Psychol., 70,* 309–314.

Mowbray, G. H., & Rhoades, M. V. (1959) On the reduction of choice reaction times with practice. *Quart J. exp. Psychol., 11,* 16–23.

Murdock, B. B. (1961) The retention of individual items. *J. exp. Psychol., 62,* 618–625.

Neisser, U. (1954) An experimental distinction between perceptual process and verbal response. *J. exp. Psychol., 47,* 399–402.

Neisser, U. (1962) Cultural and cognitive discontinuity. In T. E. Gladwin and W. Sturtevant (Eds.), *Anthropology and human behavior.* Washington, D. C.: Anthropological Society of Washington.

Neisser, U. (1963a) The multiplicity of thought. *Brit. J. Psychol., 54,* 1–14.

Neisser, U. (1963b) Decision-time without reaction-time: Experiments in visual scanning. *Amer. J. Psychol., 76,* 376–385.

Neisser, U. (1963c) The imitation of man by machine. *Science, 139,* 193–197.

Neisser, U. (1964a) Visual search. *Scientific Amer., 210* (June), 94–102.

Neisser, U. (1964b) Experiments in visual search and their theoretical implications. Paper presented at Psychonom. Soc., Niagara Falls, Ontario.

Neisser, U., & Beller, H. K. (1965) Searching through word lists. *Brit. J. Psychol., 56,* 349–358.

Neisser, U., & Lazar, R. (1964) Searching for novel targets. *Percept. mot. Skills, 19,* 427–432.

Neisser, U., Novick, R., & Lazar, R. (1963) Searching for ten targets simultaneously. *Percept. mot. Skills, 17,* 955–961.

Neisser, U., & Stoper, A. (1965) Redirecting the search process. *Brit. J. Psychol., 56,* 359–368.

Neisser, U., & Weene, P. (1960) A note on human recognition of hand-printed characters. *Inform. & Control, 3,* 191–196.

Newbigging, P. L. (1961a) The perceptual redintegration of frequent and infrequent words. *Canad. J. Psychol., 15,* 123–132.

Newbigging, P. L. (1961b) The perceptual redintegration of words which differ in connotative meaning. *Canad. J. Psychol., 15,* 133–142.

Newell, A., Shaw, J. C., & Simon, H. A. (1958) Elements of a theory of human problem solving. *Psychol. Rev., 65,* 151–166.

Newell, A., Shaw, J. C., & Simon, H. A. (1962) The processes of creative thinking. In H. E. Gruber, G. Terrell, and M. Wertheimer (Eds.), *Contemporary approaches to creative thinking.* New York: Atherton Press.

Newell, A., & Simon, H. A. (1963) GPS, a program that simulates human thought. In E. A. Feigenbaum and J. Feldman (Eds.), *Computers and thought.* New York: McGraw-Hill.

Nickerson, R. S., & Feehrer, C. E. (1964) Stimulus categorization and response time. *Percept. mot. Skills, 18,* 785–793.

Norman, D. A., & Wickelgren, W. A. (1965) Short-term recognition memory for single digits and pairs of digits. *J. exp. Psychol., 70,* 479–489.

Orne, M. T. (1951) The mechanisms of hypnotic age regression: An experimental study. *J. abnorm. soc. Psychol., 46,* 213–225.

Orne, M. T. (1959) The nature of hypnosis: Artifact and essence. *J. abnorm. soc. Psychol., 58,* 277–299.

Orne, M. T. (1962a) On the social psychology of the psychological experiment: With particular reference to demand characteristics and their implications. *Amer. Psychologist, 17,* 776–783.

Orne, M. T. (1962b) Hypnotically induced hallucinations. In L. J. West (Ed.), *Hallucinations.* New York: Grune & Stratton.

Orne, M. T., & O'Connell, D. N. (1961) Review of Reiff and Scheerer's *Memory and hypnotic age regression. Contemp. Psychol., 6,* 70–72.

Orne, M. T., & Scheibe, K. E. (1964) The contribution of nondeprivation factors in the production of sensory deprivation effects: The psychology of the "panic button." *J. abnorm. soc. Psychol., 68,* 3–12.

Osgood, C. E. (1953) *Method and theory in experimental psychology.* New York: Oxford Univer. Press.

Oswald, I. (1962a) *Sleeping and waking: Physiology and psychology.* Amsterdam: Elsevier.

Oswald, I. (1962b) Induction of illusory and hallucinatory voices with considerations of behavior therapy. *J. ment. Sci., 108,* 196–212.

Oswald, I., Taylor, A. M., & Treisman, M. (1960) Discrimination responses to stimulation during human sleep. *Brain, 83,* 440–453.

Paul, I. H. (1959) Studies in remembering. *Psychol. Issues, 1,* No. 2, 1–152.

Penfield, W. (1952) Memory mechanisms. *A.M.A. Arch. Neurol. Psychiat., 67,* 178–191.

Penfield, W. (1954) The permanent record of the stream of consciousness. *Proc. 14th Int. Congr. Psychol.,* Montreal Neurological Inst., Rep. No. 486.

Penfield, W. (1958) Some mechanisms of consciousness discovered during electrical stimulation of the brain. *Proc. Nat. Acad. Sci., 44,* 51–66.

Penfield, W., & Roberts, L. (1959) *Speech and brain mechanisms.* Princeton, N. J.: Princeton Univer. Press.

Peterson, L. R. (1963) *Immediate memory: Data and theory.* In C. N. Cofer and B. S. Musgrave (Eds.), *Verbal behavior and learning: Problems and processes.* New York: McGraw-Hill.

Peterson, L. R., & Kroener, S. (1964) Dichotic stimulation and retention. *J. exp. Psychol., 68,* 125–130.

Peterson, L. R., & Peterson, M. J. (1959) Short-term retention of individual verbal items. *J. exp. Psychol., 58,* 193–198.

Pfungst, O. (1911) *Clever Hans: The horse of Mr. Von Osten.* New York: Holt, Rinehart and Winston, 1965.

Pick, A. P. (1965) Improvement of visual and tactual form discrimination. *J. exp. Psychol., 69,* 331–339.

Pierce, J. (1963a) Some sources of artifact in studies of the tachistoscopic perception of words. *J. exp. Psychol., 66,* 363–370.

Pierce, J. (1963b) Determinants of threshold for form. *Psychol. Bull., 60,* 391–407.

Pierce, J. R., & Karlin, J. E. (1957) Reading rates and the information rate of a human channel. *Bell Syst. tech. J., 36,* 497–516.

Pillsbury, W. B. (1897) A study in apperception. *Amer. J. Psychol., 8,* 315–393.

Pine, F. (1960) Incidental stimulation: A study of preconscious transformations. *J. abnorm. soc. Psychol., 60,* 68–75.

Pine, F. (1961) Incidental versus focal presentation of drive related stimuli. *J. abnorm. soc. Psychol., 62,* 482–490.

Pitts, W., & McCulloch, W. S. (1947) How we know universals: The perception of auditory and visual forms. *Bull. math. Biophysics, 9,* 127–147.

Pollack, I. (1959) Message uncertainty and message reception. *J. acoust. Soc. Amer., 31,* 1500–1508.

Pollack, I., & Johnson, L. B. (1965) Memory-span with efficient coding procedures. *Amer. J. Psychol., 78,* 609–614.

Pollack, I., Johnson, L. B., & Knaff, P. R. (1959) Running memory span. *J. exp. Psychol., 57,* 137–146.

Posner, M. I. (1963) Immediate memory in sequential tasks. *Psychol. Bull., 60,* 333–349.

Posner, M. I. (1964a) Information reduction in the analysis of sequential tasks. *Psychol. Rev., 71,* 491–504.

Posner, M. I. (1964b) Rate of presentation and order of recall in immediate memory. *Brit. J. Psychol., 55,* 303–306.

Posner, M. I. (1966) Components of skilled performance. *Science, 152,* 1712–1718.

Postman, L. (1954) Learned principles of organization in memory. *Psychol. Monogr., 68,* No. 374.

Postman, L. (1964) Short-term memory and incidental learning. In A. W. Melton (Ed.), *Categories of human learning.* New York: Academic Press.

Postman, L., & Addis-Castro, G. (1957) Psychophysical methods in the study of word recognition. *Science, 125,* 193–194.

Postman, L., Bronson, W. C., & Gropper, G. L. (1953) Is there a mechanism of perceptual defense? *J. abnorm. soc. Psychol., 48,* 215–224.

Postman, L., & Bruner, J. S. (1949) Multiplicity of set as a determinant of perceptual selectivity. *J. exp. Psychol., 39,* 369–377.

Postman, L., Bruner, J. S., & McGinnies, E. (1948) Personal values as selective factors in perception. *J. abnorm. soc. Psychol., 43,* 142–154.

Postman, L., & Conger, B. (1954) Verbal habits and the visual recognition of words. *Science, 119,* 671–673.

Potter, R. K., Kopp, G. A., & Green, H. C. (1947) *Visible speech.* New York: Van Nostrand.

Pötzl, O. (1917) The relationship between experimentally induced dream images and indirect vision. *Psychol. Issues,* 1960, *2,* No. 3, 41–120.

Prentice, W. C. H. (1954) Visual recognition of verbally labelled figures. *Amer. J. Psychol., 67,* 315–320.

Pritchard, R. M. (1961) Stabilized images on the retina. *Scientific Amer., 204* (June), 72–78.

Pritchard, R. M., Heron, W., & Hebb, D. O. (1960) Visual perception approached by the method of stabilized images. *Canad. J. Psychol., 14,* 67–77.

Quastler, H. (1955) *Information theory in psychology*. New York: Free Press.

Raab, D. H. (1963) Backward masking. *Psychol. Bull., 60,* 118–129.

Rapaport, D. (Ed.) (1951a) *Organization and pathology of thought.* New York: Columbia Univer. Press.

Rapaport, D. (1951b) Toward a theory of thinking. In D. Rapaport (Ed.), *Organization and pathology of thought.* New York: Columbia Univer. Press.

Rapaport, D. (1957) Cognitive structure. In *Contemporary approaches to cognition: A symposium held at the University of Colorado.* Cambridge, Mass.: Harvard Univer. Press.

Rechtschaffen, A., & Foulkes, D. (1965) The effect of visual stimuli on dream content. *Percept. mot. Skills, 20,* 1149–1160.

Reid, L. S., Henneman, R. H., & Long, E. R. (1960) An experimental analysis of set: The effect of categorical restriction. *Amer. J. Psychol., 73,* 568–572.

Reiff, R., & Scheerer, M. (1959) *Memory and hypnotic age regression.* New York: International Universities Press.

Reitman, W. R. (1964) Heuristic decision procedures, open constraints, and the structure of ill-defined problems. In M. W. Shelly & G. L. Bryan (Eds.), *Human judgments and optimality.* New York: Wiley.

Reitman, W. R. (1965) *Cognition and thought: An information-processing approach.* New York: Wiley.

Riley, D. A. (1962) Memory for form. In L. Postman (Ed.), *Psychology in the making.* New York: Knopf.

Rock, I. (1956) The orientation of forms on the retina and in the environment. *Amer. J. Psychol., 69,* 513–528.

Rock, I. (1962) A neglected aspect of the problem of recall: The Hoeffding function. In J. Scher (Ed.), *Theories of the mind.* New York: Free Press.

Rock, I., & Ceraso, J. (1964) Toward a cognitive theory of associative learning. In C. Scheerer (Ed.), *Cognition: Theory, research, promise.* New York: Harper & Row.

Rock, I., & Ebenholtz, S. (1962) Stroboscopic movement based on change of phenomenal rather than retinal location. *Amer. J. Psychol., 75,* 193–207.

Rock, I., & Englestein, P. (1959) A study of memory for visual form. *Amer. J. Psychol., 72,* 221–229.

Rock, I., & Heimer, W. (1957) The effect of retinal and phenomenal orientation on the perception of form. *Amer. J. Psychol., 70,* 493–511.

Rock, I., Tauber, E. S., & Heller, D. P. (1965) Perception of stroboscopic movement: Evidence for its innate basis. *Science, 147,* 1050–1052.

Roffwarg, H. P., Dement, W. C., Muzio, J. N., & Fisher, C. (1962) Dream imagery: Relation to rapid eye movements of sleep. *Arch. gen. Psychiat., 7,* 235–258.

Rosenblatt, F. (1958) The perceptron: A probabilistic model for information storage and organization in the brain. *Psychol. Rev., 65,* 386–408.

Rosenthal, R. (1963) On the social psychology of the psychological experiment: The experimenter's hypothesis as unintended determinant of experimental results. *Amer. Scientist, 51,* 268–283.

Rosenthal, R. (1965) Clever Hans: A case study of scientific method. In O. Pfungst, *Clever Hans: The horse of Mr. Von Osten.* New York: Holt, Rinehart and Winston.

Rosenzweig, M. R., and Postman, L. (1958) Frequency of usage in the perception of words. *Science, 127,* 263–266.

Rycenga, J. A., & Schwartz, J. (Eds.) (1963) *Perspectives on language.* New York: Ronald.

Saltzman, I. J., & Garner, W. R. (1948) Reaction-time as a measure of span of attention. *J. Psychol., 25,* 227–241.

Saltzman, S. S., & Machover, S. (1952) An inquiry into eidetic imagery with particular reference to visual hallucinations. *Amer. J. Psychiat., 108,* 740–748.

Sanders, A. F. (1961) Rehearsal and recall in immediate memory. *Ergonomics, 4,* 25–34.

Savin, H. B. (1963) Word-frequency effect and errors in the perception of speech. *J. acoust. Soc. Amer., 35,* 200–206.

Savin, H. B., & Perchonock, E. (1965) Grammatical structure and the immediate recall of English sentences. *J. verb. Learn. verb. Behav., 4,* 348–353.

Schachtel, E. G. (1947) On memory and childhood amnesia. *Psychiatry, 10,* 1–26.

Schachtel, E. G. (1959) *Metamorphosis.* New York: Basic Books.

Schaefer, T., & Bernick, N. (1965) Sensory deprivation and its effect on perception. In P. H. Hoch & J. Zubin (Eds.), *Psychopathology of perception.* New York: Grune & Stratton.

Schiller, P. H., & Smith, M. C. (1965) A comparison of forward and backward masking. *Psychonom. Sci., 3,* 77–78.

Schiller, P. H., & Smith, M. C. (1966) Detection in metacontrast. *J. exp. Psychol., 71,* 32–39.

Schubert, E. D., & Parker, C. D. (1955) Addition to Cherry's findings on switching speech between the two ears. *J. acoust. Soc. Amer., 27,* 792–794.

Selfridge, O. G. (1955) Pattern recognition and modern computers. *Proc. West. Joint Computer Conf.,* Los Angeles, Calif.

Selfridge, O. G. (1956) Pattern recognition and learning. *Methodos, 8,* 163–176.

Selfridge, O. G. (1959) Pandemonium: A paradigm for learning. In *The mechanisation of thought processes.* London: H. M. Stationery Office.

Selfridge, O. G., & Neisser, U. (1960) Pattern recognition by machine. *Scientific Amer., 203* (Aug.), 60–68.

Shannon, C. E. (1948) A mathematical theory of communication. *Bell Syst. tech. J., 27,* 379–423, 623–656.

Sheehan, P. W. (1966) Functional similarity of imaging to perceiving: Individual differences in vividness of imagery. *Percept. mot. Skills,* 23, 1011–1033.

Shepard, R. N. (1967) Recognition memory for words, sentences, and pictures. *J. verb. Learn. verb. Behav., 6,* 156–163.

Shepherd, R. D. (1964) Classification time and class complexity in inspection tasks. *Occup. Psychol., 38,* 87–97.

Shevrin, H., & Luborsky, L. (1961) The rebus technique: A method for studying primary process transformations of briefly exposed pictures. *J. nerv. ment. Dis., 133,* 479–488.

Shor, R. E. (1959) Hypnosis and the concept of the generalized reality-orientation. *Amer. J. Psychother., 13,* 582–602.

Siipola, E. M., & Hayden, S. D. (1965) Influencing eidetic imagery among the retarded. *Percept. mot. Skills, 21,* 275–286.

Silberer, H. (1951) Report of a method of eliciting and observing certain symbolic hallucination-phenomena. In D. Rapaport (Ed.), *Organization and pathology of thought.* New York: Columbia Univer. Press.

Simon, H. A., & Feigenbaum, E. A. (1964) An information processing theory of some effects of similarity, familiarization, and meaningfulness in verbal learning. *J. verb. Learn. verb. Behav., 3,* 385–396.

Singer, G., & Sheehan, P. W. (1965) The effect of demand characteristics on the figural after-effect with real and image inducing figures. *Amer. J. Psychol., 78,* 96–101.

Skinner, B. F. (1936) The verbal summator and a method for the study of latent speech. *J. Psychol., 2,* 71–107.

Skinner, B. F. (1963) Behaviorism at fifty. *Science, 140,* 951–958.

Smith, G. J. W. (1957) Visual perception: An event over time. *Psychol. Rev., 64,* 306–313.

Smith, G. J. W., & Henriksson, M. (1955) The effect on an established percept of a perceptual process beyond awareness. *Acta psychologica, 11,* 346–355.

Smith, G. J. W., Spence, D. P., & Klein, G. S. (1959) Subliminal effects of verbal stimuli. *J. abnorm. soc. Psychol., 59,* 167–177.

Solley, C. M., & Murphy, G. M. (1960) *The development of the perceptual world.* New York: Basic Books.

Solomon, R. L., & Howes, D. H. (1951) Word-probability, personal values, and visual duration thresholds. *Psychol. Rev., 58,* 256–270.

Solomon, R. L., & Postman, L. (1952) Frequency of usage as a determinant of recognition thresholds for words. *J. exp. Psychol., 43,* 195–201.

Spence, D. P. (1961) The multiple effects of subliminal stimuli. *J. Pers., 29,* 40–53.

Spence, D. P., & Holland, B. (1962) The restricting effects of awareness: A paradox and an explanation. *J. abnorm. soc. Psychol., 64,* 163–174.

Sperling, G. (1960a) The information available in brief visual presentations. *Psychol. Monogr., 74,* No. 11.

Sperling, G. (1960b) Negative after-image without prior positive image. *Science, 131,* 1613–1614.

Sperling, G. (1963) A model for visual memory tasks. *Hum. Factors, 5,* 19–31.

Sperling, G. (1967) Successive approximations to a model for short-term memory. *Acta psychologica, 27,* 285–292.

Spielberger, C. D., & DeNike, L. D. (1966) Descriptive behaviorism versus cognitive theory in verbal operant conditioning. *Psychol. Rev., 73,* 306–326.

Spieth, W., Curtis, J. F., & Webster, J. C. (1954) Responding to one of two simultaneous messages. *J. acoust. Soc. Amer., 26,* 391–396.

Sternberg, S. (1963) Retrieval from recent memory: Some reaction-time experiments and a search theory. Paper presented to Psychonom. Soc., Bryn Mawr, Pa.

Sternberg, S. (1966) High-speed scanning in human memory. *Science, 153,* 652–654.

Sternberg, S. (1967) Two operations in character-recognition: Some evidence from reaction-time measurements. *Percept. & Psychophy., 2,* 45–53.

Stetson, R. H. (1905) A motor theory of rhythm and discrete succession. *Psychol. Rev., 12,* 250–270, 293–350.

Stevens, K. N. (1960) Toward a model for speech recognition. *J. acoust. Soc. Amer., 32,* 47–55.

Stoper, A. (1967) Vision during the pursuit movement. Unpublished doctoral dissertation, Brandeis University.

Stroud, J. (1955) The fine structure of psychological time. In H. Quastler (Ed.), *Information theory in psychology.* New York: Free Press.

Sutherland, N. S. (1957) Visual discrimination of shape by octopus. *Brit. J. Psychol., 48,* 55–70.

Sutherland, N. S. (1959) Stimulus analyzing mechanisms. In *The mechanisation of thought processes.* London: H. M. Stationery Office.

Sutherland, N. S. (1963a) Cat's ability to discriminate oblique rectangles. *Science, 139,* 209–210.

Sutherland, N. S. (1963b) Shape discrimination and receptive fields. *Nature, 197,* 118–122.

Swets, J. A. (Ed.) (1964) *Signal detection and recognition by human observers.* New York: Wiley.

Tart, C. T. (1964) A comparison of suggested dreams occurring in hypnosis and sleep. *Int. J. clin. exp. Hypnosis, 12,* 263–289.

Tart, C. T. (1965a) The hypnotic dream: Methodological problems and a review of the literature. *Psychol. Bull., 63,* 87–99.

Tart, C. T. (1965b) Toward the experimental control of dreaming: A review of the literature. *Psychol. Bull., 64,* 81–91.

Tauber, E. S., & Koffler, S. (1966) Optomotor response in human infants to apparent motion: Evidence of innateness. *Science, 152,* 382–383.

Taylor, M. M., & Henning, G. B. (1963) Verbal transformations and an effect of instructional bias on perception. *Canad. J. Psychol., 17,* 210–223.

Thorndike, E. L. (1931) *Human learning.* New York: Appleton-Century-Crofts.

Thorndike, E. L., & Lorge, I. (1944) *The teacher's word book of 30,000 words.* New York: Teacher's College.

Tinbergen, N. (1951) *The study of instinct.* Oxford: Oxford Univer. Press.

Titchener, E. B. (1915) *A beginner's psychology.* New York: Macmillan.

Tolman, E. C. (1948) Cognitive maps in rats and men. *Psychol. Rev., 55,* 189–208.

Treisman, A. M. (1960) Contextual cues in selective listening. *Quart. J. exp. Psychol., 12,* 242–248.

Treisman, A. M. (1964a) Monitoring and storage of irrelevant messages in selective attention. *J. verb. Learn. verb. Behav., 3,* 449–459.

Treisman, A. M. (1964b) Selective attention in man. *Brit. med. Bull., 20,* 12–16.

Treisman, A. M. (1964c) The effect of irrelevant material on the efficiency of selective listening. *Amer. J. Psychol., 77,* 533–546.

Treisman, A. M. (1965) The effects of redundancy and familiarity on translating and repeating back a foreign and a native language. *Brit. J. Psychol., 56,* 369–379.

Tulving, E. (1962) Subjective organization in free recall of "unrelated" words. *Psychol. Rev., 69,* 344–354.

Tulving, E., & Gold, C. (1963) Stimulus information and contextual information as determinants of tachistoscopic recognition of words. *J. exp. Psychol., 66,* 319–327.

Tulving, E., & Patkau, J. E. (1962) Concurrent effects of contextual constraint and word frequency on immediate recall and learning of verbal material. *Canad. J. Psychol., 16,* 83–95.

Uhr, L. (1963) "Pattern recognition" computers as models for form perception. *Psychol. Bull., 60,* 40–73.

Uhr, L., & Vossler, C. (1961) Recognition of speech by a computer program that was written to simulate a model for human visual pattern recognition. *J. acoust. Soc. Amer., 33,* 1426.

Uhr, L., Vossler, C., & Uleman, J. (1962) Pattern recognition over distortions, by human subjects and by a computer simulation of a model for human form perception. *J. exp. Psychol., 63,* 227–234.

Underwood, B. J. (1964) The representativeness of rote verbal learning. In A. W. Melton (Ed.), *Categories of human learning.* New York: Academic Press.

Wallach, H., & Austin, P. A. (1954) Recognition and the localization of visual traces. *Amer. J. Psychol., 67,* 338–340.

Wallach, H., & Averbach, E. (1955) On memory modalities. *Amer. J. Psychol., 68,* 250–257.

Wallach, H., & O'Connell, D. N. (1953) The kinetic depth effect. *J. exp. Psychol., 45,* 205–207.

Waly, P., & Cook, S. W. (1966) Attitude as a determinant of learning and memory: A failure to confirm. *J. Pers. soc. Psychol., 4,* 280–288.

Warren, R. M. (1961a) Illusory changes of distinct speech upon repetition: The verbal transformation effect. *Brit. J. Psychol., 52,* 249–258.

Warren, R. M. (1961b) Illusory changes in repeated words: Differences between young adults and the aged. *Amer. J. Psychol., 74,* 506–516.

Warren, R. M., & Gregory, R. L. (1958) An auditory analogue of the visual reversible figure. *Amer. J. Psychol., 71,* 612–613.

Watson, J. B. (1913) Psychology as the behaviorist views it. *Psychol. Rev., 20,* 158–177.

Waugh, N. C. (1960) Serial position and the memory-span. *Amer. J. Psychol., 73,* 68–79.

Waugh, N. C., & Norman, D. A. (1965) Primary memory. *Psychol. Rev., 72,* 89–104.

Weisstein, N., & Haber, R. N. (1965) A U-shaped backward masking function in vision. *Psychonom. Sci., 2,* 75–76.

Werner, H. (1935) Studies on contour: I. Qualitative analyses. *Amer. J. Psychol., 47,* 40–64.

Werner, H. (1948) *Comparative psychology of mental development.* Chicago: Follett.

Werner, H., & Kaplan, E. (1950) Development of word meaning through verbal context: An experimental study. *J. Psychol., 29,* 251–257.

Wertheimer, M. (1912) Experimentelle Studien über das Sehen von Bewegung. *Z. Psychol., 61,* 161–265.

Whipple, G. M. (1914) *Manual of mental and physical tests. Part I: Simpler processes.* Baltimore: Warwick & York.

Wickelgren, W. A. (1964) Size of rehearsal groups in short-term memory. *J. exp. Psychol., 68,* 413–419.

Wickelgren, W. A. (1965a) Acoustic similarity and retroactive interference in short-term memory. *J. verb. Learn. verb. Behav., 4,* 53–62.

Wickelgren, W. A. (1965b) Distinctive features and errors in short-term memory for English vowels. *J. acoust. Soc. Amer., 38,* 583–588.

Wickelgren, W. A. (1965c) Short-term memory for phonemically similar lists. *Amer. J. Psychol., 78,* 567–574.

Wickelgren, W. A. (1965d) Acoustic similarity and intrusion errors in short-term memory. *J. exp. Psychol., 70,* 102–108.

Wickelgren, W. A. (1965e) Short-term recognition memory for normal and whispered letters. *Nature, 206,* 851–852.

Wickelgren, W. A. (1965f) Short-term memory for repeated and non-repeated items. *Quart. J. exp. Psychol., 17,* 14–25.

Wickelgren, W. A. (1966a) Phonemic similarity and interference in short-term memory for single letters. *J. exp. Psychol., 71,* 396–404.

Wickelgren, W. A. (1966b) Distinctive features and errors in short-term memory for English consonants. *J. acoust. Soc. Amer., 39,* 388–398.

Wickelgren, W. A. (1966c) Short-term recognition memory for single letters and phonemic similarity of retroactive interference. *Quart. J. exp. Psychol., 18,* 55–62.

Wiener, N. (1948) *Cybernetics.* New York: Wiley.

Witkin, H. A., & Lewis, H. B. (1965) The relation of experimentally induced pre-sleep experiences to dreams: A report on method and preliminary findings. *J. Amer. psychoanal. Ass., 13,* 819–849.

Woodworth, R. S. (1938) *Experimental psychology.* New York: Holt, Rinehart and Winston.

Woodworth, R. S., & Schlosberg, H. (1954) *Experimental psychology.* New York: Holt, Rinehart and Winston.

Worthington, A. G., & Dixon, N. F. (1964) Changes in guessing habits as a function of subliminal stimulation. *Acta psychologica, 22,* 338–347.

Wyatt, D. F., and Campbell, D. T. (1951) On the lability of stereotype or hypothesis. *J. abnorm. soc. Psychol., 46,* 496–500.

Yngve, V. H. (1960) A model and an hypothesis for language structure. *Proc. Amer. phil. Soc., 104,* 444–466.

Yngve, V. H. (1962) Computer programs for translation. *Scientific Amer., 206* (June), 68–87.

Yntema, D. B., & Trask, F. P. (1963) Recall as a search process. *J. verb. Learn. verb. Behav., 2,* 65–74.

Yntema, D. B., Wozencraft, F. T., & Klem, L. (1964) Immediate recall of digits presented at very high speeds. Paper presented to Psychonom. Soc., Niagara Falls, Ontario.

Zangwill, O. L. (1956) A note on immediate memory. *Quart. J. exp. Psychol., 8,* 140–143.

# Illustration Credits

| *Figure* | *Page* | |
|---|---|---|
| 1 | 18 | From G. Sperling, The information available in brief visual presentations. *Psychol. Monogr., 74,* No. 11, 1960. P. 11, Fig. 8. |
| 2 | 19 | From E. Averbach & A. S. Coriell, Short-term memory in vision. *Bell Syst. tech. J., 40,* p. 309–328, 1961. Figs. 1, 2. |
| 3 | 21 | From J. F. Mackworth, The duration of the visual image. *Canad. J. Psychol., 17,* 62–81, 1963. P. 64, Fig. 1. |
| 4 | 25 | From Naomi Weisstein and Ralph Norman Haber, A U-shaped backward masking function in vision. *Psychonom. Sci., 2,* 75–76, 1965. P. 75, Fig. 1. |
| 5 | 28 | From G. J. W. Smith & M. Henriksson. The effect on an established percept of a perceptual process beyond awareness. *Acta Psychologica, 11,* 346–355, 1955. P. 347, Fig. 1. |
| 6 | 29 | From G. Guthrie & M. Wiener, Subliminal perception or perception of a partial cue with pictorial stimuli. *J. Pers. soc. Psychol., 3,* 619–628, 1966. P. 620, Fig. 1. |
| 7 | 31 | From M. Eagle, The effects of subliminal stimuli of aggressive content upon conscious cognition. *J. Pers., 27,* 578–600, 1959. Pp. 582, 583, 584, Figs. 1, 2, 3. Also in G. Guthrie & M. Wiener, Subliminal perception or perception of partial cue with pictorial stimuli. *J. Pers. soc. Psychol., 3,* 619–628, 1966. P. 624, Fig. 3. |
| 8 | 34 | From G. Sperling. A model for visual memory tasks. *Hum. Factors, 5,* 19–31, 1963, P. 25, Fig. 4. |
| 9 | 47 | From O. G. Selfridge, Pattern recognition and modern computers. *Proc. West. Joint Computer Conf.,* Los Angeles, California, 1955. P. 92, Fig. 3. |
| 12 | 52 | From H. Wallach & P. A. Austin, Recognition and localization of visual traces. *Amer. J. Psychol., 67,* 338–340, 1954. P. 338, Fig. 1. |
| 14 | 56 | From E. J. Gibson, J. J. Gibson, A. D. Pick, & H. Osser, A development study of the discrimination of letter-like forms. *J. comp. physiol. Psychol., 55,* 897–906, 1962. P. 898, Fig. 1. |
| 15 | 60 | From R. Leeper, A study of a neglected portion of the field of learning—the development of sensory organization, *J. genet. Psychol., 46,* 41–75, 1935. P. 50, Fig. 2. |
| 16 | 61 | From B. R. Bugelski & D. A. Alampay, The role of frequency in developing perceptual sets. *Canad. J. Psychol., 15,* 205–211, 1961. P. 206, Fig. 1. |

| *Figure* | *Page* | |
|---|---|---|
| 17 | 63 | From Pattern recognition by machine by O. G. Selfridge & U. Neisser. Copyright © 1960 by Scientific American, Inc. All rights reserved. August, p. 61. |
| 18, 19, 20 | 68, 69, 70 | From Visual search by U. Neisser. Copyright © 1964 by Scientific American, Inc. All rights reserved. June, pp. 96–97. |
| 22 | 75 | From O. G. Selfridge, Pandemonium: A paradigm for learning. In the Teddington Symposium, *The mechanization of thought processes,* 1959. P. 517, Fig. 3. The Director, National Physical Laboratory, Teddington, England. |
| 23 | 80 | From Stabilized images on the retina by R. M. Pritchard. Copyright © 1961 by Scientific American, Inc. All rights reserved. June, p. 75. |
| 24 | 81 | From McKinney, J. P., Verbal meaning and perceptual stability. *Canad. J. Psychol., 20,* 237–242, 1966. P. 239, Figs. 1–9. |
| 25 | 84 | From E. J. Gibson, Learning to read. *Science, 148,* 1066–1072, May 1965. Copyright 1965 by the American Association for the Advancement of Science. Fig. 3. |
| 26 | 90 | Figure 26 reproduced from Fig. 36. *Rubin's Ambiguous Figures* (1915) in *Sensation and perception in the history of experimental psychology* by Edwin G. Boring. D. Appleton-Century Company, New York, 1942. |
| 27 | 91 | From C. E. Osgood, *Method and theory in experimental psychology,* New York, Oxford, 1953. P. 235, Fig. 89. |
| 28 | 91 | From S. E. Asch, A problem in the theory of associations. *Psychol. Beitrage, 6,* 553–563, 1962. P. 555, portions of Fig. 1. |
| 29a | 142 | From E. G. Boring, A new ambiguous figure. *Amer. J. Psychol., 42,* 444–445, 1930. Fig. 1. |
| 29b, 29c | 142 | The author is obliged to Irvin Rock for making these figures available for this book. |
| 32 | 175 | From H. Fletcher, *Speech and hearing,* Princeton, Van Nostrand, 1929 ed. |
| 33 | 177 | From R. K. Potter, G. A. Kopp, & H. C. Green, *Visible speech,* Princeton, Van Nostrand, 1947. P. 314, Fig. 13. Also from *Visible speech* by R. K. Potter, G. A. Kopp, & H. C. Green, Dover Publications, Inc., New York, 1966. Reprinted through permission of the publishers. |
| 34 | 181 | Reprinted from Preliminaries to speech analysis, by R. Jakobson, C. G. M. Fant, & M. Halle, *Tech. Rep. No. 13, Acoustics Laboratory, M. I. T.,* by permission of the M. I. T. Press, Cambridge, Massachusetts. P. 43. Table printed in the Netherlands in R. Jakobson & M. Halle, *Fundamentals of Language,* 's-Gravenhage, Mouton, 1956. |
| 35 | 183 | From A. M. Liberman, K. S. Harris, H. S. Hoffman, & B. C. Griffith, The discrimination of speech sounds within and across phoneme boundaries. *J. exp. Psychol., 54,* 358–368, 1957. P. 359, Fig. 1. |
| 37 | 191 | Taken by permission from A. M. Liberman, Some results of research on speech perception. *J. acoust. Soc. Amer., 29,* 117–123, 1957. P. 121, Fig. 3. |
| 38 | 203 | Taken by permission from I. Pollack, Message uncertainty and message reception. *J. acoust. Soc. Amer., 31,* 1500–1508, 1959. P. 1505, Fig. 9. |
| 39 | 204 | From C. W. Eriksen & H. J. Johnson, Storage and decay char- |

| *Figure* | *Page* | |
|---|---|---|
| | | acteristics of non-attended auditory stimuli. *J. exp. Psychol., 68,* 28–36, 1964. P. 32, Fig. 1. |
| 40 | 209 | From Treisman, A. M. (1964) *Br. med. Bull. 20,* 12, Fig. 1. |
| 41 | 229 | From *Verbal behavior and learning: Problems and processes,* edited by C. N. Cofer and B. S. Musgrave. Copyright © 1963 by McGraw-Hill Book Company. Used by permission. P. 392, Fig. 9-2. |
| 46 | 271 | From J. Mehler, Some effects of grammatical transformation on the recall of English sentences, *J. verb. Learn. verb. Behav., 2,* 346–351, 1963. P. 348, Fig. 2. |

# Name Index

Adamson, J. F., 128
Addis-Castro, G., 109, 125
Alampay, D. A., 60–61
Alpern, M., 24, 27
Antrobus, John S., 153
Antrobus, Judith S., 153
Arbib, M. A., 63, 78, 82
Arnheim, R., 53, 55
Asch, S. E., 90–91, 291
Austin, G. A., 49, 96
Austin, P. A., 52–53, 58
Averbach, E., 16, 17, 19, 24–25, 33, 42, 301
Azuma, H., 132

Barber, T. X., 147, 169
Bartlett, F. C., 10, 95, 139, 156, 170, 275, 279, 282, 284, 287–289, 292–293, 296, 302
Békésy, G. v., 178
Beller, H. K., 68, 108, 135
Benussi, V., 91
Berger, R. J., 160
Bergson, H., 94, 190–191
Berko, M. J., 206
Bernick, N., 152
Bernstein, I. H., 134
Bernstein, L., 55, 57
Bertini, M., 152, 159–160
Bever, T. G., 187–188, 196, 256, 267
Biederman, I., 28, 35
Bishop, C. H., 113
Bleuler, E., 297
Boring, E. G., 142, 206, 234
Bousfield, W. A., 288
Boyer, A., 54–55
Braine, M. D. S., 266–267
Brentano, F., 94
Bricker, P. D., 129, 131
Broadbent, D. E., 175, 177, 184–185, 187, 205–206, 208–211, 214, 226, 235, 238–242
Bronson, W. C., 128
Brown, J., 224, 235–238, 240
Brown, J. S., 83, 95
Brown, R., 179
Brown, W. P., 126, 128
Bruner, J. S., 20, 47, 49, 59, 76–77, 88, 96, 110–112, 118, 123, 125–126, 132–133, 193, 227, 287, 289
Brunswik, E., 74
Bryden, M. P., 37–40, 57
Bugelski, B. R., 60–61
Buschke, H., 232, 294
Bush, R. R., 248

Camp, D. S., 38
Campbell, D. T., 125–126
Carmichael, L. C., 139
Carroll, L., 261, 263
Carterette, E. C., 207, 212
Carvellas, T., 66–67, 99
Ceraso, J., 10, 90, 283, 294
Chapanis, A., 129, 131
Cherry, E. C., 185, 187, 206–208
Chomsky, N., 244, 246–248, 250, 252–253, 259, 261, 268–269
Clark, W. H., 44–45
Clifton, C., 269
Cobb, J. C., 214
Cofer, C. N., 265
Cohen, J. A., 266
Coles, G. R., 41, 202
Collins, J. F., 24–25
Comer, P. B., 109
Conger, B., 113
Conrad, R., 222–224, 227, 235
Cook, S. W., 289
Cooper, F. S., 184
Coriell, A. S., 16–17, 19, 33
Crannell, C. W., 220
Crovitz, H. F., 38
Curtis, J. F., 207

Davies, W., 38
Davis, D. R., 98
Deese, J., 289

Delgado, J. N. R., 169
Dement, W. C., 151–152
Denes, P. B., 195
DeNike, L. D., 93
Dennis, W., 281
Deutsch, D., 210
Deutsch, J. A., 210, 211
Diamond, R. M., 291
Dixon, N. F., 133–134
Dittborn, J., 197
Doob, L. W., 149–150, 155
Doyle, W., 76
Draguns, J. A., 22
Dulany, D. E., 131
Dumont, S., 216
Duncker, K., 254

Eagle, M., 30–31
Ebenholtz, S. M., 144, 231
Eden, M., 54–55, 101–102, 193
Egan, J. P., 207, 212
Ellis, K., 211
Engler, J., 118
Englestein, P., 98
Epstein, W., 141, 263–265
Erickson, M. H., 164, 170
Eriksen, C. W., 17, 23–25, 92, 131–134, 162, 203–205, 216, 242
Esecover, H., 164
Evans, F. J., 214
Evey, R. J., 65

Fant, G. G. M., 181
Feehrer, C. E., 66
Fehrer, E., 26, 28, 34–35, 39, 101
Feigenbaum, E. A., 72–74
Feinberg, I., 165
Feldman, J., 151
Finkelstein, S., 155
Fisher, C., 151, 161
Fisher, S., 169
Flavell, J. H., 22, 291
Fletcher, H., 175
Fodor, J. A., 187–188, 196, 248, 256, 267
Foote, W. E., 109, 117–118, 122–123
Forgays, D. G., 37
Foulkes, D., 151–152, 160
Fozard, J. L., 98
Fraisse, P., 205, 234
Francis, W. N., 261
Freeman, J. T., 118, 128
Freud, S., 4, 29, 146, 154, 160, 281, 294, 297–299, 302–303
Fries, C. C., 112
Frincke, G., 126–128, 132
Frohlich, F. W., 27

Fuhrer, M. J., 134
Furst, B., 288

Galanter, E., 233, 247–248, 252, 294
Galton, 145
Ganz, L., 147
Garner, W. R., 7, 43, 135
Garrett, M., 187–188, 196, 256
Garvey, W. D., 41
Gerard, F. O., 32
Ghent, L., 55–57
Gibson, E. J., 50, 55–57, 83–85, 96, 112–115, 117, 123, 182
Gibson, J. J., 55–56, 83, 115, 139–140
Gilbert, L. C., 27
Glanzer, M., 44–45, 264–265
Gleason, H. A., 179–180
Glucksberg, S., 17, 266
Gold, C., 116
Goldiamond, I., 119–120
Goodnow, J. J., 49, 96
Gottschaldt, K., 261
Gough, P. B., 272
Gould, L. N., 192
Gourevitch, S., 30
Granit, R., 295
Gray, J. A., 241
Gregory, M., 210, 241
Gregory, R. L., 197
Griffith, B. C., 183
Gropper, G. L., 128
Gross, J., 151
Gustafson, L. A., 214
Guthrie, G., 28–30
Guttman, N., 201, 205
Gyr, J. W., 83, 95

Haber, R. B., 148–150, 155
Haber, R. N., 22, 24–26, 39–40, 59, 121–122, 124–125, 148–150, 155
Hall, C. S., 158
Halle, M., 84, 101, 180–183, 192–194, 252
Hamlin, H., 169
Hammond, M., 112–114, 123
Harcum, E. R., 38, 125
Harris, C. S., 39–40, 59
Harris, K. S., 183
Harris, Z., 268
Hartline, H. K., 82
Haselrud, G. M., 126
Havens, L. L., 109, 117–118, 122–123, 165
Hawkins, W. F., 119–120
Hay, J., 291
Hayden, S. D., 150, 155
Head, H., 288

Hebb, D. O., 37, 47, 51, 57, 78–80, 83, 86–89, 94, 96, 103, 142–144, 153, 211–212, 242, 246
Heimer W., 53–54, 57, 90
Heise, G. A., 195, 261
Held, R., 178
Heller, D. P., 144
Hellyer, S., 228–229
Henneman, R. H., 41, 118
Henning, G. B., 197
Henriksson, M., 28
Hernández-Peón, R., 216
Heron, W., 37–38, 79
Hershenson, M., 22, 124–125
Hess, E. H., 59
Hick, W. E., 66
Hicks, R. B., 132
Hilgard, E. R., 154
Hille, B. A., 222
Hintzman, D. L., 224
Hirsh, I. J., 179, 184
Hobbes, T., 281
Hochberg, J., 206
Hockett, C., 112
Höffding, H., 47, 50, 54, 62, 65, 78, 190
Hoffman, H. S., 183
Hoffman, M., 23
Hogan, H. P., 139
Holland, B., 134
Holt, R. R., 30, 149–150, 152
Horowitz, M. J., 169
Horrocks, J. E., 219
Howarth, C. I., 211
Howes, D. H., 116, 189
Hubel, D. H., 82–83
Hugelin, A., 216
Huggins, A. W. F., 185–187, 206
Hull, A. J., 224
Hull, C. L., 200
Hull, W., 111
Hume, D., 281, 284
Humphrey, G., 192, 197
Hunter, I. M. L., 155–156
Hunter, W. S., 42
Huxley, A., 156, 163–164

Isard, S., 275

Jackson, C. W., 152
Jaensch, E. R., 147
Jakobson, R., 84, 180–183, 192
James, W., 94, 200, 225, 282, 284
Johnson, H., 162
Johnson, H. J., 203–205, 216
Johnson, L. B., 44–45, 221, 234
Johnson, R. C., 126–128, 132
Jouvet, M., 216
Judd, B., 98
Julesz, B., 201, 205

Kahneman, D., 22–23, 27
Kaplan, E., 266
Kaplan, I. T., 66–67, 99
Karlin, J. E., 43, 67, 108
Katona, G., 44
Katz, J. J., 248
Kaufman, E. L., 42
Kay, H., 223
Kelly, E. L., 152
Kempler, B., 117, 119
Kimble, G. A., 283
Klein, G. S., 28, 30
Klem, L., 200, 222, 233, 236
Klemmer, E. T., 44–45
Klüver, H., 147, 150, 164
Knaff, P. R., 234
Koffka, K., 3, 96, 246, 269–270, 294
Koffler, S., 144
Köhler, W., 50, 52, 89, 246
Kolers, P. A., 24, 27, 32, 54–55, 144, 151
Konick, A., 67
Kris, E., 303
Kroener, S., 205
Kubie, L. S., 160
Külpe, O., 39

LaBerge, D. L., 40
Lacey, O. W., 128
Lacy, J., 109
Ladefoged, P., 184, 187
Landauer, T. K., 43
Lane, H., 191
Lappin, J. S., 23
Lashley, K. S., 62, 139, 233, 245, 287–288
Lawrence, D. H., 40–41, 202
Lazar, R., 68, 70
Lazarus, R. S., 129–132
Leeper, R., 60–61, 141–142
Lenneberg, E. H., 192, 247
Leonard, J. A., 67
Lettvin, J. Y., 82–83
Levinger, N., 128
Lewis, H. B., 152, 159
Liberman, A. M., 183, 191–193
Lichten, W., 195, 261
Licklider, J. C. R., 179, 189–190
Lindgren, N., 101, 181–182
Locke, J., 281, 284
Long, E. R., 41, 118
Lord, M. W., 42

Lorge, I., 116
Luborsky, L., 161
Luce, R. D., 248

McCleary, R. A., 129–132
McCulloch, W. S., 63, 82
McGeoch, J. A., 264–265
McGinnies, E., 109, 126, 129, 132–133
McGuigan, F. J., 192
Machover, S., 155
McKellar, P., 152
McKinney, J. P., 79–81
Mackworth, J. F., 20–21, 33, 222
McMahon, L., 272
McNeill, D., 266
McPherson, S., 67
Mahl, G. F., 169
Malitz, S., 164–165
Mandes, E., 57
Marks, L., 275
Marshall, G. R., 265
Martin, E., 273
Maslow, A. H., 303
Mathews, A., 120
Maturana, H. R., 82
Mayzner, M. S., 17
Meenes, M., 155
Mehler, J., 270–273
Melton, A. W., 242
Merkel, J., 66–67, 101
Mermelstein, P., 101
Metlay, W., 66–67, 99
Metzger, W., 254
Mewhort, D. J. K., 123
Mill, J., 281, 283, 288
Miller, G. A., 7, 42, 110–112, 118, 123, 184, 187, 195–196, 201, 220–221, 225–227, 233–234, 243, 247–248, 250–253, 259, 261, 263–265, 270–273, 275, 294
Milner, P. M., 78
Minard, J. A., 120, 127, 128
Minsky, M., 58, 77–78, 87–88
Minturn, A. L., 59, 88, 124
Mishkin, M., 37
Mooney, C. M., 98
Moray, N., 209–210, 213, 215, 241
Morin, R. E., 76, 101
Morton, M. A., 155
Mowbray, G. H., 67, 101
Mozart, W. A., 197
Murdock, B. B., 228–229, 237–238
Murphy, G. M., 88, 193
Muzio, J. N., 151
Nachmias, J., 22
Necker, L. A., 144, 269
Neisser, U., 9, 46, 50, 63–64, 66, 68–70, 76, 100, 108, 118–119, 135, 290, 298
Newbigging, P. L., 117, 128
Newell, A., 8–9, 146, 296
Nicely, P. E., 184, 225
Nickerson, R. S., 66
Norman, D. A., 200, 223, 232, 238
Norman, J., 22
Novick, R., 68, 70

Occam, 295
O'Connell, D. N., 140, 169, 214
Odom, P., 269
Orne, M. T., 30, 80, 139, 152, 166, 169, 214
Osgood, C. E., 91, 283
Osser, H., 55–56, 83–84, 112–114, 123
Oswald, I., 150–152, 157, 197, 210, 213

Paillas, N., 216
Parker, C. D., 186–187
Parrish, J. M., 220
Patkau, J. E., 227
Paul, I. H., 289
Penfield, W., 167–169, 200–201
Perchonock, E., 272, 275
Peterson, L. R., 200, 205, 228–230, 237, 264
Peterson, M. J., 228–229, 237, 264
Pfungst, O., 31
Piaget, J., 287, 291
Pick, A. P., 55–56, 83–84, 112–114, 123
Pierce, J., 118–119, 122, 125
Pierce, J. R., 43, 67, 108
Pillsbury, W. B., 108–109, 115, 120, 196
Pine, F., 93, 215–216
Pitts, W., 63, 82
Pollack, I., 44–45, 202–203, 205, 221, 234
Posner, M. I., 7, 222–223
Postman, L., 109–113, 116–118, 123, 125, 128, 132–133, 229, 232, 289
Potter, M. C., 125–126
Potter, R. K., 176–177
Pötzl, O., 161–162
Poulton, E. C., 223
Prentice, W. C. H., 139
Pribram, K. H., 233, 247, 252, 294
Pritchard, R. M., 79–80

Quastler, H., 7

Raab, D. H., 24, 26, 28, 34, 39, 101
Rapaport, D., 154, 158–159, 287, 290
Rechtschaffen, A., 160
Reese, T. W., 42
Reid, L. S., 41, 118

Reiff, R., 169
Reitman, W., 9, 58, 296, 299–300
Rhoades, M. V., 67, 101
Riley, D. A., 269, 283
Roberts, K. H., 273
Roberts, L., 167
Rock, I., 10, 50, 52–55, 57, 98, 141, 144, 283, 294
Roffwarg, H. P., 151
Rosenblatt, F., 78
Rosenthal, R., 31
Rosenzweig, M. R., 109
Rosner, B. S., 27
Rothenberg, A., 169
Rubin, E., 90
Rycenga, J. A., 253

Saltzman, I. J., 43
Saltzman, S. S., 155
Sanders, A. F., 223
Savin, H. B., 116–117, 189, 264, 272, 275
Schachtel, E. G., 88, 284, 287, 290
Schaefer, T., 152
Scheerer, M., 169
Scheibe, K. E., 152
Scherrer, H., 216
Schiff, W., 84, 113
Schiffman, H. R., 38
Schiller, P. H., 27, 35
Schlosberg, H., 38, 43
Schubert, E. D., 186–187
Schumann, F., 107
Schwartz, J., 253
Selfridge, J. A. 263, 265
Selfridge, O. G., 47, 50–51, 63, 71, 74–78, 82–84, 87, 96, 103, 190, 298
Shaw, J. C., 8–9, 146
Sheehan, P. W., 147, 156
Shepard, R. N., 98
Shepherd, R. D., 66
Shevrin, H., 161
Shor, R. E., 214, 286–287, 290
Sigler, M., 42
Siipola, E. M., 150, 155
Silberer, H., 157
Simon, H. A., 8–9, 72, 74, 146, 296
Singer, G., 147
Singer, J. L., 153
Skinner, B. F., 5, 197, 246
Smith, E., 26
Smith, G., 22, 28, 30, 32
Smith, J., 84, 113
Smith, M., 27, 35
Smith, S. L., 221, 226
Solley, C. M., 88, 193
Solomon, R. L., 116–118
Spence, D. P., 28–30, 134
Sperling, G., 16–21, 23, 33–39, 41–42, 135, 224, 301
Spielberger, C. D., 93
Spieth, W., 207
Steffy, R. A., 17, 23
Sternberg, S., 66–67, 99–100
Stetson, R. H., 206
Stevens, K. N., 193–195, 252
Stevens, S. S., 121
Stoper, A., 68, 108, 140
Stroud, J., 23, 185
Sutherland, N. S., 47, 51, 76–77, 83, 98, 103, 190
Swets, J. A., 202

Tart, C. T., 158–160
Tauber, E. S., 144
Taylor, A. M., 210
Taylor, M. M., 197
Taylor, W. K., 185, 187
Thomson, C. W., 126–128, 132
Thorndike, E. L., 116, 264, 291
Thwing, E. J., 207, 212
Tinbergen, N., 59
Titchener, E. B., 108, 212, 284
Tolman, E. C., 287, 292
Trask, F. P., 241, 293–294
Treisman, A. M., 207, 209–216, 218, 225
Treisman, M., 210
Troxell, N., 67
Tulving, E., 116, 227, 288

Uhr, L., 50, 77–78, 176
Uleman, J., 77
Underwood, B. J., 232

Vogel, G., 152
Volkmann, J., 42
Vossler, C., 77, 176

Wallach, H., 52–53, 58, 140, 301
Walter, A. A., 139
Waly, P., 289
Warren, R. M., 197
Watson, J. B., 5
Waugh, N. C., 200, 223, 234, 238
Webster, J. C., 207
Wechsler, D., 219
Wedderburn, A. A. I., 241
Weene, P., 46, 64
Weisstein, N., 24–26
Weksel, W., 267
Werner, H., 24, 26–27, 96, 266
Wertheimer, Max, 144, 246

Wertheimer, Michael, 120
Whipple, G. M., 41
Wickelgren, W. A., 223–225, 228–232, 236, 238–239, 265
Wiener, M., 28–30, 117, 119
Wiener, N., 64
Wiesel, T. N., 82–83
Wilkens, B., 164
Willey, R., 83, 95
Witkin, H. A., 152, 159
Woodworth, R. S., 17, 35, 38, 43, 107, 109, 145, 155–157
Worthington, A. G., 134
Wozencraft, F. T., 200, 222, 233, 236
Wulf, F., 269
Wyatt, D. F., 125–126

Yngve, V. H., 273, 275
Yntema, D. B., 98, 200, 222, 233, 236, 241, 293–294

Zangwill, O. L., 275
Zimmerman, C., 118
Zivian, A., 83, 95

# Subject Index


Act psychology, 94
Active verbal memory, 219–242
  for sentences, 259, 263, 264, 272
  in reading, 135–136
  in shadowing experiments, 207, 213
  recoding from iconic memory into, 36, 39–45, 138
  vs. echoic memory, 200, 218
Afterimage, 139, 141, 146–148
Ambiguous figures, 52, 81, 90, 141–142, 144, 245, 269
Ambiguous sentences, 245–246, 256–257, 268–279
Analog processes, vs. categorial, 49
  in preattentive control, 92
Analysis-by-synthesis, 9
  and directed thinking, 302
  in active verbal memory, 224–225, 228, 235
  in rapid reading, 136
  in selective listening, 212–218
  of handwriting, 101–102
  of rhythm, 206, 235
  of sentences, 252, 259, 262, 264
  of speech, 189–190, 193–198, 199, 228, 235, 244, 252
Analyzers, 76; *see also* Feature extraction
Apparent movement, 28, 143–144
Approximations to English, 110–112, 123, 210, 263–265
Argus, 299–300
Artificial intelligence, *see* Computer models of cognition
Association theory, and EPAM, 74
  and pattern recognition, 50
  of active verbal memory, 225, 228–232, 233–234, 236–239, 241
  of language, 246, 253, 263–264
  of long-term memory, 281–284, 289, 291, 293–294
  *see also* Word-association
Attention, and cochlear electrical activity, 216
  and eye movements, 38
  as auditory synthesis, 199, 212–215, 262
Attention—*Continued*
  focal, 86–91, 94, 96, 103–104, 286, 300–302
  in active verbal memory, 225–226
  in negative hallucinations, 166–167
  in selective listening, 205–218
  in visual word-recognition, 106, 115, 123–125
  lapses of, 298
  switching between ears, 185, 206, 241
Auditory memory, 226, 241, 243, 267, 301; *see also* Active verbal memory, Echoic memory
Autochthonous forces, 89, 246
Automatisms, 101

Backward masking, 22–35, 133
Behaviorism, 5, 10, 47, 246, 282–283, 293–295
Belongingness, 264, 291
Bits, *see* Information measurement
Boustrephedon, 54

Categorial processes, in perception and concept attainment, 95–96
  vs. analog, 49
Categories, well-defined vs. ill-defined, 58–61
Cathexis, 281
Cell-assemblies, 37, 78, 83, 86, 143, 211–212
Character recognition, automatic, 47, 62–65, 74–77, 87–88, 101–102
Children, cognitive processes in, 11
  acquisition of language, 247, 266, 291
  auditory localization, 178
  focal attention, 88
  motor activity, as related to, 95
  pattern recognition, 83–85
  physiognomic perception, 96
  spatial orientation, 54–57, 292
Chunks, 187, 218, 220–221, 226, 228–229, 232

Clever Hans, 31
Closed-class morphemes, 260
Clustering, 281, 288
Cocktail-party phenomenon, 178, 206, 212, 214
Cognitive map, 292; *see also* Cognitive structure
Cognitive psychology, defined, 4, 10, 208
Cognitive structure, 286–292; *see also* Executive processes, Linguistic structure, Rhythm
Cognitive units, 114–115; *see also* Chunks, Immediate constituents, Figure-ground, Segmentation
Computer models of cognition, as analogies, 6, 8–9
  criticized, 9, 87–88, 296, 299–300
  for executive processes, 295–296
  for pattern recognition, 74–78, 87–89, 101–102, 176
  for speech recognition, 182, 193–195
  *see also* Argus, EPAM, General Problem Solver, Pandemonium, Perceptron
Concept attainment, 10, 96, 284
Conditioning, 129–130, 253, 282–283
Consolidation, 296
Constancy, perceptual, 58
Constituent structure, *see* Immediate constituents, Phrase structure
Constructive processes, 10
  and time requirements, 16; *see also* Readout rates
  in active verbal memory, 224–225, 235, 239–240
  in auditory attention, 212–218
  in focal attention, 89, 94–97, 103
  in grammatical sentences, 259, 261–262
  in memory and thought, 170, 279–305
  in speech perception, 189, 192, 196–197
  *see also* Analysis-by-synthesis, Figural synthesis
Content words, 260
Context, in analysis-by-synthesis, 102, 195–196, 213
  in recall, 263
  in speech perception, 195–196, 201, 209–211, 213, 261
  in visual recognition, 47, 116
  *see also* Approximations to English, Linguistic structure
Creativity, 244, 297, 303

Decay, of active verbal memory, 223–224, 226, 230, 235–242
  of echoic memory, 201–205, 226
  of iconic memory, 17–22
Decay—*Continued*
  of long-term memory, 295
  of rhythm, 205, 240
Deep structure, 267–275
Demand characteristics, in dream experiments, 159–162
  in imagery experiments, 147, 159–160
  in perceptual defense experiments, 128
  in perceptual fragmentation experiments, 80–81
  in sensory deprivation experiments, 152
  in shadowing experiments, 187
  in subliminal perception experiments, 30–32, 133–134, 161–162
  in visual search experiments, 72
  in visual word-recognition experiments, 115
  in word-association experiments, 128, 289
Depth perception, 140
Detection theory, 202–203, 211
Developmental psychology, *see* Children, cognitive processes in
Distinctive features, of printed letters, 84–85
  of rhythm, 205
  of speech, 180–184, 200, 225
Dreaming, as hallucinatory, 120, 145–146, 150–152
  eye movements in, 39, 151
  in hypnosis, 158–159
  incorporation of stimuli into, 159–162, 197, 214
  primary process in, 297–298, 301
  symbolic transformation in, 154, 157–160
  *see also* Sleep
Drugs, effect of on cognition, 96, 149–150, 162–165
Duplexity theory of memory, 240–242
Dynamic psychology, and cognitive psychology, 4–5, 305
  defined, 4–5

Ear, mechanisms of, 173–179
Echoic memory, duration of, 201–205, 207, 236
  during sleep, 214
  in selective listening, 207, 213
  in speech perception, 200–201, 266–267
  vs. active verbal memory, 200, 207, 218, 219–223, 225–226, 239
  vs. iconic memory, 200
Eidetic imagery, 39, 145–150, 155–156
Eidola, 3, 5
EPAM, 72–74, 190, 299

Enactive representation, 20
Erasure, in tachistoscopic displays, 33–35, 42
Executive processes, 9, 292–296, 299, 302–303
Expectancy, 301–303; *see also* Context, Set
Experimenter, as source of cues, 31–32, 134, 162, 216
Eye movements, analogous to implicit speech, 192, 217
  and stopped image, 79–80
  and visual snapshots, 139–145
  frequency of, 27, 139, 142
  in attention, 38, 92, 103
  in dreams, 151
  in imagery, 147–148, 152–154, 167, 217
  in reading, 27, 37, 54, 139
  in scanning, 65, 67

Feature extraction, 9
  attentive and preattentive, 89–92
  in speech perception, 190–198
  in visual pattern recognition, 51–52, 71–85, 86, 100–101, 103
  in visual word-recognition, 114
  *see also* Distinctive features
Figural aftereffects, 147
Figural synthesis, defined, 94–97, 302
  in dreams, 145–146, 150–151, 162
  in familiarity recognition, 97–99
  in hallucinations, 145–146, 150–151, 162–169
  in imagery, 145–157, 162–169
  in motion perception, 143–144
  in search and reaction-time experiments, 99–101
  in visual snapshot integration, 140–145
  in visual word-recognition, 114–115, 118–126, 136
  physiological mechanism of, 169
  *see also* Analysis-by-synthesis
Figure-ground, 90, 94, 102
Filter theory, 175, 205, 208–210, 214, 216–217, 241
Filter-amplitude theory, 210–212, 214, 216
Focal attention, *see* Attention
Forgetting, *see* Decay, Repression, Retroactive inhibition, Proactive inhibition
Form constants, 164–165
Fragment theories, 115–118, 126, 129–133, 189
Fugue states, 290
Function words, 259–260, 262, 265–266

General Problem Solver, 296
Generalized reality-orientation, 286–287
Generative grammar, 248–253, 258–259, 268–269
Gestalt psychology, analogous to structural linguistics, 245–247, 253–255, 261, 269–270
  apparent movement studies, 144
  isomorphism, concept of, 113, 192
  memory, 282–283, 294, 300
  pattern recognition, 47, 50–51, 61, 65
  perceptual organization, 89–91
  rhythmic phenomena, 234
Gestaltqualität, 234
Grammar, *see* Generative grammar, Linguistic structure, Transformational grammar
Grouping, in active verbal memory, 221–223, 225, 232–235, 241, 262–263

Hallucination, as figural synthesis, 95, 99, 103, 280
  auditory, 192, 196–197
  drug-induced, 150, 162–165
  hypnotic, 147, 166–167
  in sensory deprivation, 152
  negative, 166–167, 303
  schizophrenic, 150, 164–165, 192, 196–197
  vs. perception, 120, 145–146, 150–151, 259
Hierarchical organization, in analysis-by-synthesis of speech, 193
  in computer programs, 75, 295–296
  in Pandemonium, 75
  in preattentive processes, 89
  in rhythm, 233-234
  in sentences, 253–259, 266
  in visual field, 253–255
Higher mental processes, 10–11, 279–305
Höffding step, 47, 50, 62, 65, 78, 190
Holistic, *see* Wholistic
Homunculus, 279, 293, 295, 304
Hypermnesia, 167–170
Hypnagogic imagery, 151–152, 157–160, 168
Hypnosis, 147, 158–159, 166–167, 169, 289–290

Iconic memory, 15–45
  analogous to primary process, 300–302, 304
  and perception, 41, 121–122
  in pattern recognition, 49, 89, 92, 94, 102
  in visual word-recognition, 106–107, 123, 125
  vs. echoic memory, 200

Iconic memory—*Continued*
vs. other forms of visual memory, 138–141
Ill-defined categories, 58–61, 76, 78, 103, 190
Imagery, and brain stimulation, 167–169
auditory, 192, 196
in thinking, 157–158
visual, 138, 145–160, 280, 282, 301
*see also* Afterimages, Dreaming, Eye movements, Eidetic imagery, Hallucination, Hypnagogic imagery
Immediate constituents, 188, 255–256
Infantile amnesia, 290
Information measurement, 7, 66, 111–112, 123, 135, 208, 220
Inner speech, and inward attention, 214–215
and thinking, 215
in active verbal memory, 221, 242
in auditory hallucinations, 192, 197
in tachistoscopic experiments, 36, 42–44
rate of, 42–43, 236–237
*see also* Analysis-by-synthesis, Recoding, Rehearsal
Isomorphism, 113, 192

Learning without awareness, 93, 215–216, 242
Linguistic structure, 143, 188, 196, 228, 235, 243–276
Localization, auditory, 178–179, 207

Markov grammars, 252–253, 263–264
Masking, auditory, 178–179
visual, *see* Backward masking
Memory, 169–170, 279–292; *see also* Active verbal memory, Decay, Echoic memory, Iconic memory, Hypermnesia, Memory trace, Repression, Verbal memory, Visual memory
Memory span, *see* Span of immediate memory, Running span
Memory trace, 50, 54, 111, 170, 236, 246, 281–286, 299, 302–303
Metacontrast, *see* Backward masking
Missing span, 232, 294
Moment, psychological, *see* Quantum of psychological time
Morphemes, 260
Motion perception, 28, 92, 140, 143–144, 302
Motor skills, 292–293, 302–303
Motor theory of speech perception, 191–194, 197, 217–218, 224
Multiple thought processes, 296–304; *see also* Parallel processing

Naive realism, 16, 122, 188, 285
Nativism, 246–247, 261, 287
Neural net theories, 77–78, 83
Newsclip reading, 70–71

Octal number system, 44, 221, 226
Order, cognitive structures representing, 290–291
perception of, 184, 231
recall of, 223, 227, 231, 236, 240
*see also* Word order
Orientation of forms, 51, 53–57, 62–64, 82–83

Paleontology, as analogous to cognition, 94, 97, 103, 114, 115–116, 285–286, 293
Pandemonium, 74–78, 84, 87, 96, 190, 195, 298–299
Parallel processing, 9, 35, 65, 74
in computers, 65; *see also* Pandemonium, Argus
in newsclip reading, 71
in preattentive processing, 89, 102–103
in reaction-time experiments, 35, 67–68, 99, 101
in selective listening, 213
in speech perception, 190
in thinking, 296–304
in visual search, 71–72, 100
limitations of, 86–87, 94, 100–101, 297
vs. sequential processing, 65–72, 86–91, 99–101, 296–299
Parts of speech, 265–266
Pattern recognition, 46–85, 130
and focal attention, 86–89, 94, 102–103
by machine, 75–78, 87–89, 101–102, 176
in speech perception, 190; *see also* Speech perception
Perception, as construction, 94–97, 280
and iconic memory, 41, 121–122
as model for thinking, 300–304
as stage of cognition, 4
learned vs. unlearned, 246
movement, in relation to, 95
vs. categorization, 49
vs. hallucination, 120, 145–146, 150–151, 259
vs. response, 41, 117–124
*see also* Constancy, Depth perception, Figure-ground, Localization, Motion perception, Order, Orientation of forms, Size perception, Speech perception
Perceptron, 78
Perceptual defense, 105, 126–129, 130, 134, 303

Perceptual learning, 96, 115, 138, 141–143, 261
Phi phenomenon, *see* Apparent movement
Phonemes, 112–113, 179–184, 187–195, 201, 224–225, 247
Photographic memory, 55, 162
Phrase-marker, 255; *see also* Phrase structure
Phrase structure, 188, 247, 252–267, 268–269, 273–275
Physiognomic perception, 96–97, 103
Preattentive processes, and physiognomic perception, 96–97
  and primary process, 93, 300–304
  defined, 89–91, 102–103, 286
  during sleep, 213–214
  in everyday life, 91–93
  in negative hallucinations, 167
  in speech perception, 194–195, 199, 213–216
  in visual search and reaction-time studies, 100–101
  lack permanent effects, 93, 215–216
  not subliminal, 93, 303
Primary memory, 200
Primary process, in imagery, 154, 157, 160–161
  in perception, 15, 29, 93, 215, 303
  in thinking, 281, 294, 297–304
Primitive unity, 79, 87, 89
Proactive inhibition, 224, 236, 238, 295
Problems, well-defined vs. ill-defined, 58
Problem-solving, 10, 280, 284, 288, 292–294, 299–300, 302
Proximal stimuli, 3, 173
Psychoanalytic theory, 4, 10, 146, 159, 281, 283, 297–299; *see also* Primary process

Quantum of psychological time, 23–24, 184–185

Rate of presentation, in memory-span experiments, 42, 221–223, 230, 234, 236–238, 241
Reaction time, 34–35, 39, 43, 66–67, 99–101, 187
Reading, eye movements in, 27, 37–38, 54, 139, 143
  features used in, 101, 105–118, 135–136, 181–182
  for meaning, 101, 134–137, 143
  newsclip, 70
  reaction times in, 67–68, 101
  transformed text, 54
  whole-word method of instruction, 15
  *see also* Readout rates, Visual search
Readout rates, 27, 33, 42–43, 45, 103, 107–108, 135
Reality testing, 150–152, 166, 286–287
Reappearance hypothesis, 280–284, 300, 302
Recoding, in active verbal memory, 220–226, 228, 230, 236; *see also* Rehearsal
  in long-term memory, 139, 301; *see also* Cognitive structure
  of grammatical transformations, 273
  of tachistoscopically presented material, 20, 36–45, 103, 107, 138, 219–220, 301; *see also* Readout rates
Recognition, of familiarity, 97–99, 168, 170
  of visually presented words, 105–137
  in memory experiments, 97–99, 139, 225, 232
  tachistoscopic, 15–45
  *see also* Character recognition, Pattern recognition, Speech perception, Speech recognition
Recursive processes, 296
Redundancy, 111, 123, 135, 235
Rehearsal, 36, 218, 221, 223–226, 230, 233–242, 243
Repression, 169, 303
Reproduction, of visual figures, 138–139
Response bias, 118–124
Retroactive inhibition, 224, 236, 295
Rhythm, and echoic memory, 205
  and phrase structure, 256, 262–266
  in active verbal memory, 221–223, 236, 232–235, 238, 240, 242, 243, 275, 282
  in rote learning, 294
  in speech perception, 185, 262
  mechanism of attention, 217
  motor theory of, 206, 217–218
  of poetry, 265
Running span, 234, 237

Scanning, in pattern recognition, 64–65, 103
  of images, 148, 153
  of tachistoscopic displays, 37–38
  *see also* Visual search
Schemata, 8, 286–293
Search, *see* Visual search
Secondary process, 154, 297, 302–304
Segmentation, in active verbal memory, 207, 218, 226; *see also* Chunks
  in rhythm, 205
  of speech, 182–189, 194–196, 200–201; *see also* Phrase structure
  visual, 87–90, 94, 103, 103
Selective listening, 206–218
Sensory deprivation, 152
Sentence frame, 260–261, 263–266

Sequential processing, in computers, *see* EPAM, Argus
in reaction-time experiments, 66–67, 99–100
in speech perception, 190
in thinking, 296–297, 300
in visual search, 71–72
vs. parallel processing, 65–72, 86–91, 99–101, 296–299
vs. serial processing, 72
Serial position phenomena, 222–223, 227, 231, 233–234, 236, 291
Serial processing, 72, 103, 301, 304
Set, and ambiguous figures, 59–61, 141–142
and focal attention, 88
as coding variable, 37, 39–41, 103
for ill-defined categories, 59–61
in auditory attention, 209–210, 213
in problem-solving, 289–290
in speech perception, 195–196
in visual word-recognition, 115–119, 123, 127
*see also* Context
Shadowing, 185–186, 206–218
Short-term memory, *see* Active verbal memory, Echoic memory
Signal detection, *see* Detection theory
Simultaneous translation, 218
Size, perception of, 57–58
Sleep, stages of, 58, 151–152
suggestion during, 214
vigilance during, 210–211, 214
*see also* Dreaming
Slot theory, 226–232, 234, 241
Space, cognitive structure of, 291–292; *see also* Constancy, Localization, Orientation of forms, Size
Span of apprehension, 41–43, 103, 106; *see also* Word-apprehension effect
Span of immediate memory, 42, 219–242, 259, 263–264
Specious present, 200
Spectrogram, 176–179, 182–183, 188, 190–191
Spectrum, 174–175
Speech perception, 102, 173–198, 200–201, 211–213, 219, 259–261
Speech recognition, automatic, 182, 193–195
Spelling patterns, 110–115, 123, 183
Stabilized retinal image, *see* Stopped-image experiments
Stereotypes, 49, 139, 284
Stimulus analyzing mechanisms, *see* Feature extraction
Stimulus equivalence, 47, 49, 86, 130
Stimulus trace, 200; *see also* Echoic memory, Iconic memory
Stopped-image experiments, 79–81
Subception, 105, 129–134, 136; *see also* Subliminal perception
Subitizing, 42–43
Subliminal perception, 15, 28–35, 93, 105, 129–134, 136, 161–162, 303; *see also* Perceptual defense
Surface structure, 253–257, 263, 267–269; *see also* Phrase structure
Symbolism, 20, 157–160, 162, 297, 302

Template-matching, in pattern recognition, 50–51, 61–66, 68, 70, 83–84
in speech perception, 190
in visual word-recognition, 110–111, 113–114
Temporal quantum, *see* Quantum of psychological time
Temporal summation, 21–23
Thinking, 10, 136, 214–215, 280–281, 292–305
Time, cognitive structure of, 290–291; *see also* Rhythm
Transfer, 53; *see also* Cognitive structure, Proactive inhibition, Retroactive inhibition
Transformational grammar, 252–253, 258, 267–275
Transposition, *see* Order

Universals, vs. particulars, 47; *see also* Template matching
Utilization hypothesis, 284–286, 296, 302

Verbal memory, 263–265, 270–275, 301; *see also* Active verbal memory
Verbal transformation effect, 197
Visual acuity, 22
Visual memory, 138–170; *see also* Iconic memory
Visual search, 65–72, 74, 99–100, 108, 135, 143, 213
Visual snapshots, 139–146, 148, 151
Visual synthesis, *see* Figural synthesis

Well-defined categories, 58
Wholistic processes, in active verbal memory, 231–235
in motion perception, 144

Wholistic processes—*Continued*
  in understanding sentences, 244–245, 253–255
  in visual word recognition, 106, 114, 122–126
  preattentive, 89–92, 103, 300–301
  *see also* Cognitive structure, Figure-ground, Rhythm

Word-apprehension effect, 106–110
Word-association, 32, 127–128, 133–134, 161, 266, 289, 291, 297–299
Word-frequency effect, 116–119, 122–123, 127, 189
Word order, 244–245, 265–266, 291
Word-shape, 109